T0302294

# A History of Cold War Industrialisation

'The book aims to open up and provide a new interpretation to the black box of the East-West trade during the Cold War by using the Finnish shipbuilding industry as a case study. By means of examining procedures and practices provided by archival sources, the author attempts to explain how a small peripheral country like Finland could develop into a noteworthy shipbuilding country and industrialise fairly quickly in the postwar period. The author's approach is both innovative and illuminating for readers who are not yet experts in the East-West trade.'

**Timo Myllyntaus**, *Turku School of Economics, Finland*

'An ambitious, elegant, and enjoyable analysis of how an industry and a small state successfully navigate through the muddy waters of the Cold War.'

**Maiju Wuokko**, *University of Turku, Finland*

This monograph explores the economic consequences of the Cold War, a polarised world order which politicised technology and shaped industrial development. It provides a detailed archival-based history of the Finnish shipbuilding industry (1952–1996), which flourished, thanks to the special relationship between Finland and the Soviet Union. Overall, it shows how a small country, Finland, gained power during the Cold War through international economic and technological cooperation. The work places Finland in a firmly international context and assesses the state–industry relationship from five different angles: technopolitics, trade infrastructure, techno-scientific cooperation, industrial reorganisation, and state aid. It presents a novel way to analyse industrialisation as an interaction between institutional stabilisation and fluctuation within a techno-economic system. In so doing, it makes empirical, theoretical, and methodological contributions to the history of industrial change. *A History of Cold War Industrialisation* will be of interest to advanced students and scholars in economic history, maritime history, Cold War history, and international political economy.

**Saara Matala** is Post-doctoral Fellow in the Chalmers University of Technology, Sweden.

**Perspectives in Economic and Social History**
Series Editors: *Andrew August and Jari Eloranta*

For more information about this series, please visit www.routledge.com/series/PESH

# A History of Cold War Industrialisation

Finnish Shipbuilding between
East and West

**Saara Matala**

Routledge
Taylor & Francis Group

LONDON AND NEW YORK

First published 2021
by Routledge
2 Park Square, Milton Park, Abingdon, Oxon OX14 4RN

and by Routledge
605 Third Avenue, New York, NY 10158

*Routledge is an imprint of the Taylor & Francis Group, an informa business*

*British Library Cataloguing-in-Publication Data*
A catalogue record for this book is available from the British Library

*Library of Congress Cataloging-in-Publication Data*
A catalog record has been requested for this book

ISBN: 9780367482497 (hbk)
ISBN: 9781032033341 (pbk)
ISBN: 9781003038825 (ebk)

Typeset in Bembo
by codeMantra

# Contents

**8   Conclusions**                                                          202

# Figures

# Tables

# Abbreviations

| | |
|---|---|
| AWES | Association of West European Shipbuilders |
| CMEA | Council for Mutual Economic Assistance (also SEV/ COMECON) |
| CSCE | Conference on Security and Cooperation in Europe (Euroopan Turvallisuus ja yhteistyökonferenssi, ETYK) |
| DWT | Deadweight tonnage (a measure of how much a ship can carry) |
| CoCom | Coordinating Committee for Multilateral Export Controls |
| EES | European Economic Space (Euroopan talousalue, ETA) |
| EEC | European Economic Community |
| EFTA | European Free Trade Association |
| FCMA | Ystävyys-, yhteistyö ja avunantosopimus YYA (The Agreement of Friendship, Cooperation, and Mutual Assistance between Finland and the Soviet Union) |
| GATT | General Agreement on Tariffs and Trade |
| GT | Gross tonnage (a measure of volume of all of a ship's enclosed spaces) |
| GRT | Gross register tonnage (a measure of ship's internal volume) |
| IAEA | International Atomic Energy Agency |
| MVES | USSR Ministry of Foreign Economic Relations |
| OECD | Organisation for Economic Cooperation and Development |
| OEEC | Organisation for European Economic Co-operation |
| SHP | Shaft horse power (the engine power delivered to the propeller shaft) |
| SVL | Suomen Vientiluotto Oy—Finlands Exportkredit Ab (Finnish Export Credit Ltd) |
| VEB | USSR Bank for Foreign Economic Relations |
| VTL | Vientitakuulaitos (the Finnish Board of Export Guarantees) |
| VTK | Valtion takuukeskus (Finnish Centre for Export Financing, founded in a merger of VTL and SVL 1989) |

# 1 Introduction

## History of Cold War industrialisation

In the dead of the winter in December 1988, two ships from two worlds were moored to the building dock in Helsinki. The first one to be completed was a nuclear icebreaker *Vaygach*. She had just returned from the test run and was soon to steam off eastwards to join the Soviet nuclear fleet of Arctic icebreakers. The other was a luxury cruise ship *Fantasy*, ordered by a Miami-based Carnival Cruise Lines. She was waiting for to be fitted with extravagantly furnished nightclubs, gambling salons, and sun decks before taking off on its journey westwards to entertain American tourists. The Cold War as the confrontation between the two opposite world views—capitalist market economy and centrally coordinated socialist planning—could not be better contrasted in the hulls of those two vessels. That an American enterprise and a Soviet state organisation became customers for the same shipyard in a non-allied country did not fit well with the overall picture of the polarised world.

This book charts the development of the Finnish shipbuilding industry from the post-war years to the turn of the 1990s. It is a story of industrial transformation from a marginal producer of simple tonnage into internationally competitive industrial branch, capable for constructing powerful icebreaking machines for the Arctic and shiny holiday resorts for the Caribbean. It is also a story about a small agrarian country in the European periphery developing into an exporter of knowledge-intensive technology while balancing in the zone of neutrality between the Cold War divide. The underlining historical question is, how decisive the connection between the Cold War political framework and the Finnish shipbuilding was in shaping the industrial transformation.

The history of European shipbuilding in the 20th century was a history of economic globalisation. Until the 1960s, Western European shipbuilders constructed most of the merchant tonnage that carried people, raw materials, and products that enabled the increasingly international supply chains, economic interconnections, and trade exchange. Building movable products, shipyards were also in the front line facing the negative side effects of the international competition and industrial relocation to the Far East. In 1950, Western Europe constructed over 80% of new merchant tonnage but in 1990 barely

15%. The gravity of the global shipbuilding moved from Western Europe to Asian industrialising countries that took advantage of lower production costs, active governmental support, and economies of scale. Only a fraction of knowledge-intensive special ship production remained in Europe.[1]

The European shipyard crisis became the prime example of industrial relocation to Asia. It captured country-specific differences in how national governments and internationalising businesses tried to lay the course towards globalisation. The Finnish shipbuilding industry was a peculiar case *par excellence* in the way it created a unique national trajectory in the development of shipbuilding structure and scale.

The difference was particularly striking in comparison with the neighbour Sweden. After the war, the Finnish shipbuilding industry was a latecomer in European development while the modernisation of the Swedish shipbuilding industry had taken off in the interwar period and the shipyards had invested heavily in modern production facilities. In the post-war decade, Sweden built up to 10% of the global merchant tonnage, but Finland was barely in the margins of the international shipbuilding statistics. In the 1960s, Sweden took advantage of economies of scale and built large crude oil carriers to the booming tanker market, but the Finnish shipyards focused on relatively short series and special-purpose vessels including relatively advanced icebreakers and passenger ships. In the 1970s, the oil crisis triggered a worldwide recession in shipbuilding, and together with global overcapacity in shipbuilding, low demand, and fierce price competition, it forced European governments to introduce extensive rescue programs and close down shipyards. The major shipyards in Sweden were nationalised in 1977 and gradually rationalised close to non-existence. Finland, instead of following the European shipbuilders to the downturn, expanded its production capacity until the 1980s and claimed promptly that it was able to do that without state subsidies. In 1988, when *Vaygach* and *Fantasy* were under construction in Finland, only the shadows of empty shipyards reminded of the past success in Sweden.

The Finnish shipbuilding industry, in sum, took off later, expanded faster, concentrated on knowledge-intensive production earlier, and downscaled later than the European counterparts.[2] The Finnish shipyards were scaled down towards the end of the Cold War but not completely relocated to the Far East. The Finnish maritime cluster today is built on the two pillars that were left behind as the material and intellectual heritage of the Cold War era: icebreakers and passenger ships.

The overarching thesis of *A Cold War History of Industrialisation* is that the history of the modern Finnish shipbuilding industry unfolded as it did not only *during* the period we know as the Cold War but also *because* of it. As such, this study is strongly anchored in the historiography of Cold War technology and business, which is concerned with how the Cold War political framework pushed the development of trade and industry into new trajectories.[3]

The Cold War was a period characterised by geopolitical and ideological confrontation between the socialist East and the capitalist West. The perception of the ideological zero-sum game between two mutually exclusive models of modernity created a prolonged state of national emergency that underlined the national security as the ultimate priority in all political decision-making. It politicised technology and industrial development which were seen as instrumental in the competition for military statecraft and ideological superiority.

Questions concerning the politicisation of technology and interaction between state and industry are at the core of the Cold War history of technology and business.[4]

Through studies on strategic Big Science projects in the leading countries, we now know that technologies, companies, and academic disciplines that contributed to the state-level agenda on security and superiority often enjoyed generous funding, political patronage, and large project contracts which, in turn, shaped to which technologies, disciplines, and applications the scientists, engineers, and companies focused on. The Cold War historiography has also scrutinised the military-industrial clusters and their close relationship with governmental decision-making over national security. Over decades of close cooperation, participants adopted coincident values and perceptions to such an extent that coercive manipulation and active lobbying became unnecessary; everyone was already convinced that they were acting in the public interests rather than their own.[5] Scholars have also shown the diversity and complexity of the mechanisms through which the political agenda shaped techno-scientific projects and pointed out cases where scientists managed to utilise it to advance their interests in academic research. Yet, by large, the politicisation of technology in the Cold War is understood in terms of national security and strategic applications.[6]

Finland, like most countries in the world, was not a superpower. The Finnish shipbuilding industry was not a part of military-industrial cluster. Small, neutral countries resided on the same globe with the superpowers and were in many ways exposed to and involved in the zero-sum game, but the world looked different from their point of view.[7] Therefore, the Cold War as a framework of decision-making at the Finnish shipyards did not mean the same as it did in the foreign offices in Washington D.C. and Moscow.

The historical context for Cold War industrial transformation is the same, but the Cold War in a small neutral country and civilian industry is a different framework of explanation.

State concerns over national security in a small non-allied country and civilian shipbuilding industry manifested themselves more often through cooperation and compromises than conflicts. Decisions over foreign relations were seldom only strategic in nature but related to civilian economic matters. Industrialisation provided the nation with export revenues and industrial occupations that translated into increasing living standards. Economic growth promised a steadily increasing standard of living and served both as a source of legitimisation for the prevailing social order and as an antidote against rebellion.[8] Finally, outstanding technological artefacts like giant ships supported national ideas of self-sufficiency, modernity, and prowess in the international comparisons.[9]

Unlike in the most famous technological consequences of the Cold War, such as satellites and space rockets, nuclear missiles, and submarines, the Cold War politics in the Finnish shipbuilding history was less striking and more mundane. It was mostly embedded in diplomatic liturgies, complex organisation charts, occasionally curious trade arrangements, and legions of engineers in grey suits sitting around negotiation tables talking about steel and money.

Domestic and international observers agreed on the prime explanatory factor for the special trajectory of the Finnish shipbuilding industry during the Cold War—the Soviet Union. The position of Finland next to the socialist superpower created simultaneously political necessities and economic possibilities to establish an extensive trade partnership that benefitted the Finnish shipyards through extensive demand and profitable prices. Throughout the Cold War, V/O Sudoimport, the Soviet Foreign Trade Organisation for ship import, was the biggest customer for the Finnish shipyards. After the Cold War, the prosperity of the Finnish Cold War shipbuilding industry has been a key argument that Finland not only survived but prospered as well.[10]

This book grew out of the observation that despite the broad understanding of that Finland's geopolitical position in the Cold War had a decisive impact on the development of shipbuilding, there is significantly less scientifically rigorous analysis on primary sources about how the Cold War politics actually turned into concrete investment plans, ship contracts, and R&D projects.

The non-military influence of a powerful external force over the internal development of a sovereign country is not an idle, abstract question but constitutes a central part of how we understand the long-term effects of the Cold War on industrial development and the agency of a small country.

The two ships, *Vaygach* and *Fantasy*, moored next to each other at the Helsinki Shipyard, already hinted that critical for the development of the Finnish shipbuilding industry was not its location next to the Soviet Union but its position *in between* the two blocs. The Finnish Cold War shipbuilding industry was not an object of the Cold War power game nor its result, but it took shape in the cross-currents of the international development and cemented the influence in its structures. In that way, it captured the material and economic consequences of the Cold War in a small, unallied country and civilian industry.

## Steel, money, and political power: outlining the research approach

Large shipyards provide excellent point of departure for explorations of state–industry relationship in the Cold War Finland. The shipbuilding industry occupied a position in multiple nation-level political considerations of security, welfare, and technological prowess, but was not dominated by any single definition. Merchant shipbuilding in the second half of the 20th century took form in the cross-currents between national and international; the shipyards were critical for local industrial communities and salient for domestic economy, but they competed in increasingly global markets. Shipbuilding was an art of both steel and money, operating for commercial interests but dependent on state regulation and institutional environment. To survive in business, shipyards had to provide technological solutions for customer's various needs and wishes with an acceptable price tag while remaining solvent.

The position of the shipbuilding industry in the troubled waters between hard technology and financing, and between private entrepreneurship and state support, shaped my research approach and located it between history of technology and business.

My understanding of ships as technological products and shipyards as technological sites is strongly influenced by the fundamental idea of the social construction of technology: Technology does not develop along predetermined trajectories but comes into being as a part of human activities. At the same time, technological artefacts, processes, and knowledge provide new possibilities and restrictions for individuals, nations, and interest groups. Governments—10–20 men and women with suitcases—cannot accomplish much just by themselves but need technology and industries to create employment, welfare, and security. In myriad ways, technology shapes and is shaped by its material qualities and social context.

Shipyards were complex problem-solving entities consisting of heterogeneous tangible, intangible, human, and non-human components. Their main function was to build and sell ships, but they also had other political, social, and economic functions during the Cold War.

As such, my approach to shipbuilding draws heavily on the research tradition of large technological systems (LTS).[11] Thomas Hughes originally introduced the LTS concept in his study of electricity networks to examine how different national contexts grow different technological systems.[12] Later, Hughes developed the system approach in his studies on large, complex projects that were typical for the Cold War era.[13]

In the process of research and writing of this book, my prime theoretical starting point was, however, the notion that a system of technological development alone does not constitute the necessary conditions for a viable industry. A profit-driven civilian technology industry would not exist without an economic dimension. No shipyard built ships just because they could. No ship was built without a customer and financing. Besides the technical facilities, the shipyards needed education and knowledge production to be able to build and develop competitive vessels; contacts and communication with customers and access to the negotiation tables; classification and insurance societies to decrease risks; financing organisations; credit and guarantee granting bodies to fuel the business and many others.

I chose to approach the Finnish shipbuilding industry as it was a techno-economic system, instead of just a technological one, to underline the equal weight of technological and economic factors in industrial transformation.[14]

The most important limitation in this study is the exclusion of labour market relations. The shipbuilding industry is primarily represented by company managers and shipbuilding engineers in leading positions. Shipbuilding was a labour-intensive industry, and the shipyard workers were often politically active and ready to use strikes to influence state politics. The political role of shipyard workers in the Cold War Finland is an enormously important and multifaceted topic that could not possibly fit within the frames of this study. In addition, it is a topic in the Finnish shipbuilding history that has been relatively well addressed by labour historians and social scientists in their studies.[15]

The position at the crossroad between history of technology and business had an impact on how I conceived industrial change in the analysis. The LTS approach fits most conveniently with the analysis of the creation, building, and stabilisation of certain locally embedded LTSs: the kind of use for which Thomas Hughes originally created the system concept.[16] When the system matures, Hughes argues that it gathers momentum from several sources such as specialised skill and knowledge, special-purpose machinery, physical structures, and organisational bureaucracies.[17] System momentum resists changes and establishes systemic rigidities that may eventually appear as deterministic path dependencies. Gradually, a mature system becomes increasingly independent from its environmental factors.[18]

This kind of a forward-moving development towards a steady system juxtaposed with the business-historical understanding of industrial longevity. Corporations, if they are lucky, grow, expand, and control their supply chains to gain stability, but because their existence depends on selling goods externally, they are never able to become self-reliant systems independent from external jolts. Business longevity is a perpetual struggle to change and adapt to new circumstances rather than a linear opportunity to mature.[19]

The dynamics between institutional stabilisation and industrial transformation brings us to the question of systemic change and disintegration. LTS scholars have argued that while political and technical struggles characterise the early phases of system building, the mature system gathers momentum, becomes more independent from its environment, and eventually may turn seemingly apolitical.[20] The hypothesis that inspired this project's research focus on the end rather than the beginning of the Cold War era was that the system disintegration reawakened the dormant political tensions in the system. In that sense, the transformation processes that shaped the end of the Cold War shipbuilding system, instead of those that constructed its beginning, provided a way of reconsidering the politics embedded in the mature system as well. The difficult challenges at the end of the Cold War, rather than the lucrative opportunities at its beginning, compelled the actors to formulate their strategies within a more restricted framework to explicitly re-evaluate their priorities and future expectations. This methodological detour comes useful in the Finnish context, where public discourses were strongly shaped by the geopolitical realities of the Cold War, as discussed in the next section.

## Sources of Cold War industrialisation

### *Finlandisation and national myths*

Historians study the fragments that have been left behind by the past activities aiming to reconstruct a bridge over the old and the new. But the picture the historical sources represents is never clear. The language the historical actors use, the arguments they make, the self-evident details they do not mention all belong to the world that no longer exists. As this book studies the Finnish shipbuilding industry intermingling with the Finnish geopolitical situation in the Cold War on the one hand, and the Finnish industrial and societal modernisation on the other hand, it is necessary to devote some space to discuss how this history presents itself in the primary sources and retrospective accounts.

In 1950, J. K. Paasikivi, President of Finland, contemplated how the Cold War geopolitics restricted public discourses in Finland:

> It seems that people do not understand at all, what this all is about. Here the folk should understand the things without anyone speaking about them clearly. Because we have issues, related to the communists and Russia that cannot be spoken out loud but that should be understood without words.[21]

What had concerned the president in the 1950s was later articulated by a middle-ranking civil servant when he recalled his job at the Ministry of Foreign Affairs:

> The task of routine speech writing was mainly about articulating the same content with different words all over again. You had to use beautiful worlds until you felt sick [...] The meaning of words was in the impression they created. With the careful wordings we communicated [to the Soviets] that we are peaceful and not dangerous.[22]

The president and the civil servant observed essentially the same thing: Finland's geopolitical position affecting the language and giving all public documents a specific flavour. In research, this flavour is called as *finlandisation*. The concept refers to the process of a sovereign state accommodating itself to a superpower's interest in a way that biased communication about Soviet-related issues.[23] This was described in 1977 by Walter Laquer in his article about the Soviet influence in Finland's internal affairs.

> [A]ccording to Kekkonen's line, it [was] also imperative that Finnish political leaders, parties, the media, and individual citizens all behave "responsibly"; otherwise they will endanger the very survival of the country. To act "responsibly" means to refrain from doing anything the

> Russians may not like, and this involves not only self-censorship but also the need to anticipate Soviet wishes, and even a willingness to accept a Soviet veto if self-censorship breaks down.[24]

In short, finlandisation in Cold War publications appears as a systematic practice to avoid topics that could irritate the Soviet Union and to deliberately sugar-coat articles on the Soviet Union for opportunistic reasons.[25] A watershed in the Finnish finlandisation discussion was Timo Vihavainen's book 'Kansakunta rähmällään'[26] (1991) that strongly criticised the Finnish public culture especially during the 1970s and made the phenomenon a conversation topic.[27]

To clarify the difference between contemporary and retrospective sources, I adopted the practice of including the publication year in all literature footnotes. Contemporary literature is a wide group of books and studies connected only by the fact that they were published before the disintegration of the Soviet Union in 1991. Although this border is artificial, it is methodologically useful to separate books written without knowing the end result of the Soviet experiment.

A great deal of the contemporary literature consists of economic reporting and analysis of the mechanisms of the Finnish–Soviet trade. When they are descriptive rather than interpretative, many of these studies provide relatively unproblematic information on the trade system and mechanisms. Other contemporary accounts, however, are heavily corrupted by the political liturgy that was typical for Finnish–Soviet affairs. These texts are better sources on the politics and discourses of trade than the trade itself.[28]

Another aspect to keep in mind when writing about the Finnish shipbuilding industry in the second half of the 20th century is that the shipbuilding industry played one of the leading roles in the transformation of Finland from an agrarian country into a modern industrial country. While ships like *Fantasy* materialised the story of development that the Finns were unanimously proud of—the rapid progress from domestic boats and barges into the builder of floating dreams to the international market—ships like *Vaygach* remind the Finns of the painfully woven strand in the fabric of national understanding—the Soviet influence on the Finnish internal development.

The historiography of Finnish shipbuilding is mainly written in Finnish for the Finnish audience, and it has been formed in the cross-currents of the national efforts of making sense of the past. To start a study about the Cold War effect on Finnish industrialisation, we need to identify what we actually know and distinguish it from what we only assume.

Academic research, oral history, common discourses, and memoirs intermingle in narratives that constitute the essence of the national folklore of Finnish–Soviet Cold War affairs. They provide testimonies that the politically supported, bilateral Finnish–Soviet trade system made Finnish shipbuilding during the Cold War predictable, profitable, and stable.[29] The array of stories repeats how the prices were lucrative, the Soviet demand for ships was endless, the bilateral system secured high-volume demand, the political support from President Kekkonen was invaluable, and vodka was abundant. On the other hand, the supply of technologically advanced vessels made Finland a critical resource for the Soviet Union while making the Finnish shipyards dependent on the Soviet trade.[30]

Despite the great interest in shipbuilding heritage, scholarly rigorous historical studies are rare. Most Finnish shipbuilding companies have preferred a readable book instead of scientific study 'with the dusty taste of archival records', as the historical review of the state-owned company Valmet stated in the late 1980s.[31] Viljo Lundelin described his book on Laivateollisuus Shipyard history 'not as a historical study but a historical memoir'.[32] Wärtsilä appointed not a historian but a poet to write its history in 1984.[33] Of the Finnish shipbuilding companies, only Rauma-Repola and Hollming contracted a trained historian to conduct archival research.[34] Apart from Mikko Uola's monograph on Rauma-Repola in 1996, shipyard histories are mainly derivatives of existing literature, magazines, and oral history sources.

Outside the field of shipyard and company histories, Finnish maritime history is wide, academically rigorous and often focused on the pre-Second World War time. Aaro Sahari's doctoral thesis on the relationship between state and shipbuilding industry provides the first completed evaluation of the interwar shipbuilding in Finland.[35] *Innovation and Specialisation* by Kalle Id and Bruce Peter is one of the few overviews of the Finnish modern shipbuilding history written in English and focuses on the design of icebreakers and passenger ships.[36]

Academic historians never hold a monopoly over how people remember the past. The non-scholarly literature and the vivid oral history tradition constitute a significant part of a living history culture. The problem arises only if these stories are never critically evaluated but they keep contributing to the national echo chamber of established narratives.

I treat the commonly shared narratives concerning the Finnish–Soviet ship trade during the Cold War as 'myths'. Myths are not necessarily false but culturally charged stories that communities tell themselves to give meanings to their past.[37] Methodologically, understanding established narratives to be widely shared but rarely validated myths implies the need to systematically practice source criticism on all prior literature on the Finnish–Soviet ship trade. Instead of a solid foundation of undisputed factual knowledge on which to build the empirical analysis, this literature provides hypotheses that require critical evaluation.

### Archival sources

The availability of new source material has driven historiographic progress in Cold War research.[38] Yet, it is not only the declassification process that propels historical research but also new methodological approaches and the re-evaluation of collections that are already available. I examine the Cold

War through public and private archives which both come with their own restrictions, challenges, and opportunities.

Industrial archives are seldom comprehensive, systematically organised collections readily available to satisfy the needs of historical inquiry. The multiple mergers and amalgamations that occurred in the Finnish shipbuilding industry throughout the 1990s and early 2000s have further contributed to the fragmentation of Finnish shipbuilding archives. Many collections have been destroyed on purpose or by accident. The main Finnish industrial archives hold the collections of the four largest shipbuilding companies in Finland. The existing collections of the privately owned Wärtsilä, the state-owned Valmet, as well as their amalgamation of Wärtsilä Marine (1987–1989) are all stored in the Central Archives for Finnish Business records, ELKA, located in Mikkeli. The archiving practices in both companies have been inconsistent and primarily reliant on some active individuals. For instance, while the negotiations on Wärtsilä's Soviet trade department with the Soviets have been carefully documented and stored, the same collection has hardly any material at all concerning commercial negotiations with Western or domestic customers. The archives of the West Coast shipbuilding operations, the Rauma-Repola and Hollming Shipyards, are currently stored at the UPM central archives in Valkeakoski. Compared to the South Coast shipbuilders Wärtsilä and Valmet, these archives are quite extensive.

The overall fragmentation of the industrial archival collections has contributed to the historiography in which the secondary sources, such as professional magazines, newspapers, and biographies, have often outgrown the primary sources in importance. Not having complete archival collections is a challenge shared by most historical projects. It necessitates careful consideration of whether the shortcomings of the industrial collections are systematically biased in a way that might lead to an inaccurate overemphasis on certain aspects.

Governmental organisations have systematic practices for filing documents. As a result of the strong role of the Soviet trade as a part of the Finnish foreign affairs, the main public collections related to ship exports to the Soviet Union are located in the archive of the Ministry of Foreign Affairs in Helsinki. The Ministry of Trade and Industry, which collections are stored in the Finnish National Archive, remained secondary in shipbuilding policy until the late 1980s.

The Cold War emphasised the role of the highest level of the political hierarchy also in trade and industrial politics. The personal archives of President Kekkonen are located in Orimattila. President Koivisto's collection is stored in the National Archive. Both presidential collections are, to an extent not exactly known, selected and organised by the presidents themselves. These collections contain private correspondence and other documentations concerning shipbuilding indicating that the affairs of the Finnish shipbuilding industry had a distinctive position in Finnish political considerations. Especially so when compared to the textile industry, another labour-intensive branch that also depended on the Soviet trade.

The US archives complement the domestic collections by providing a Western mirror on which the political and economic aspects of the Finnish shipbuilding industry can be reflected. Methodologically, to extract useful results from the vast collections in the US national archival system, I chose to focus my examination on two key aspects. First, because the Cold War presidents had a distinctive role in export promotion, I examined the declassified material from Finnish state visits to the United States in the US presidential archives. This enabled me to evaluate the relative position of shipbuilding in relation to other export branches. Second, I focused on Arctic maritime technology, especially icebreakers, in the US Coast Guard archival collections. Representing a narrow technological niche in which the Finnish shipbuilding industry had a relative competitive advantage, the icebreaker discussions stood out from the background noise and functioned as a methodological lens for the American attitude towards Finland and the Finnish technology.

For research-economic reasons, it was not possible for me to visit Russian archives. Instead, I chose to focus on the Finnish point of view. This put me in the same position as the historical Finnish actors, trying to interpret the incomplete and sometimes conflicting information about Soviet intentions. Nevertheless, the study of the politics of the Finnish–Soviet ship trade from the perspective of Soviet archives is a natural and intriguing topic for future research.

### Scale and structure of the Cold War shipbuilding

I have combined qualitative analysis of archival documents with statistical data of industrial development. The most comprehensive data set of global shipbuilding is Lloyd's Register for Shipping (LRS).[39] The LRS annual summaries include merchant ships over 100 tonnes or more, with their own propulsion. Thus, they exclude barges, small tonnage, and governmental special purpose vessels, which on occasion made up a considerable proportion of the Finnish shipbuilding production.

To complete the LRS tables, I have created a separate data collection of ships built in Finland 1952–2016 based on lists collected by shipyards and shipbuilding organisations. No single source of information was complete; some sources included the names of the ships but not their volume, some other sources listed ships using various units such as dead weight tonnages, gross tonnages (GTs), compensated gross tonnages (CGT), horse power (HP), shaft horse power (SHP), megawatts, or even kilograms. Whenever possible, I have cross-referenced the list of ships using the information from shipyards and other available lists of ships built.[40] While there is still room to develop the database, it presents the scale, structure, and geographical distribution at the degree of precision that is sufficient for this study.

Finnish Cold War shipbuilding had three markets with distinct trade and financing practices, customers, and production structure. To analyse the geographical division of trade, I classified the ships in my database into three categories based on the destination. 'Eastern trade' consists of ships sold to European socialist countries, which barring a few exceptions primarily meant the Soviet Union.[41] 'Domestic trade' refers to the ships sold to Finnish shipowners. 'Other' is the category for ships sold to all other countries. Even though Finland sold some vessels to non-European socialist countries such as China,[42] this category mainly refers to Western trade.

Figure 1.1 presents the difference between these two data sets. In 1952–1960, the exclusions of barges and governmental vessels from the LRS statistics are the two most important factors in widening the difference between the two sources. Between 1958 and 1960, the Finnish shipyards completed altogether 135 different barges. Another difference between the two data sets is that the LRS data present the ships' launches, and the other database presents the ships completed. Several months might pass between the launch and the completion of a ship.

Both LRS statistics and my own data set measure the ships built by GT.[43] It is widely used in maritime statistics and the only unit applicable for a reasonable long and comparable time-series. GT is a measure of the internal volume and not the value of the ship. It does not reflect the materials or machinery needed or the man-hours required to build the ship.[44] Comparisons based on ship volumes are particularly biased between large tanker shipbuilders, such as Sweden or Japan, and Finland, where the shipyards built rather small but design-intensive vessels.[45] Here, too, the accurate volume of the shipbuilding in any given year is of secondary importance in this study as long as the middle-term and long-term trend it presents is right. The industrial and political decision-makers responded to the changes in the production curve or to the expectations of the future development and not to the absolute number of tonnages completed in a given year.

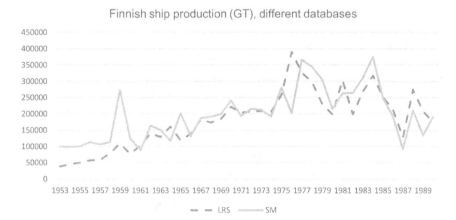

*Figure 1.1* Shipbuilding volumes in Finland, 1950–1990. Data: LRS and author from
    various sources.

The number of shipyard workers is another significant measurement describing the industrial development but like the shipbuilding volumes, it comes with limitations. International statistics typically follow the International Standard Industrial Classification (ISIC). Finland had its own Standard Industrial Classification (*Toimialaluokitus*, SIC) for national uses that corresponded roughly to the ISIC from 1968 to 1988. In the early 1950s, the Central Statistical Office of Finland classified the workforces of both ship and boat building in the same category as 'industrial and handicraft production'. As large-scale industrial manufacturing differs from boat building to a significant degree, this category provides only approximate information about the post-war development of shipyard industry. From 1956 onwards, the official statistical yearbooks separated the building and repairing of steel ships into their own category (SIC 3812, from 1973 onwards SIC 3841). After 1988, shipbuilding was no longer a category of its own in the official industrial statistics.[46] Due to changes in industrial standards, statistical practices, and differences in how to count outsourced production, it was not possible to collect time-series of shipyard employment over 40 years. Instead, I had to rely on varying statistical tables on shipbuilding employment drafted by industrial interest groups or governmental committees. Here, too, important is the trend and scale of employment and not the accurate number of the workers. For source critical reasons, it is still important to keep in mind that these tables were often produced to make an argument about domestic policy discussions.

## Navigational chart of the study

*A Cold War History of Industrialisation* explores the dynamic triangle of technology, economy, and politics by approaching the Finnish shipbuilding industry from five different perspectives: technopolitics in state-level relations, bilateral Finnish–Soviet institutions, scientific-technical and industrial cooperation, industrial reorganisation, and state-aid and financing. Each approach is like a spotlight that illuminates something while leaving many other processes in the shadows. Together, these five spotlights aim to light up the main characteristics of the research object.

The exploration of the Cold War shipbuilding starts with an introduction to the geopolitical and industrial history that laid the foundation for the further development. Several features that characterised the Finnish Cold War shipbuilding stemmed from the 19th century. These include the export orientation, the trade with Russia, and low vertical integration between shipowners and shipbuilders but strong social ties between state and industry. Chapter 2 discusses the historical foundation of Finnish shipyards and serves as an introduction to the Finnish geopolitical and economic circumstances before the mid-20th century.

The gravity of the empirical research lies in Chapters 3 to 7, each of which focuses on certain aspects of Finnish shipbuilding industry in the course of the Cold War. Instead of one chronologically proceeding narrative, the study is structured into five parallel narratives to compromise between the messy complexity of multi-layer historical processes and focused storylines following isolated factors. The aim is to simplify the analysis of interrelated but not synchronised developmental processes and to make the main political, technological, and financial sides of shipbuilding to fit in one book. The minutia of the Finnish-Soviet bilateral payments, for example, had a very different dynamics and actors than the presidential meetings between Finland and the United States. In addition, because one aim of this locally concentrated research project is to provide starting points for later internationally comparative studies, the thematically organised structure serves the selective readers when helping to find the aspects that resonate with their interests. I have tried to keep repetition minimal, especially when it comes to more general discussion of industrial development, but historical processes are naturally overlapping and messy.

Perhaps most notably, in these five empirical descriptions of the Finnish Cold War shipbuilding, the Soviet Union will collapse five times, and every time, it is a surprise for the actors. That we know what the historical actors did not know invites us to consider carefully the information the decision-makers had at the time.

The first spotlight will be turned on the role of ships in Finland's relations with foreign nations. By definition, 'technopolitics' refers to 'the strategic practice of designing or using technology to constitute, to embody or to enact political goals'.[47] The chapter focuses on the state–industry interaction and the role of influential politicians in relation to certain ship projects that emerged as objects in the Finnish foreign relations: The entrance of the Finnish shipbuilding industry in the Soviet polar icebreakers; the icebreaker diplomacy between Finland and the United States that employed Finnish icebreakers as diplomatic tools to discuss Finnish–American relations without damaging Finland's policy of neutrality; the Finnish–Soviet nuclear icebreaker project that was moulded by a private company to enact state-level goals of peaceful coexistence; and Finnish–American controversy over deep-sea submersibles that captured Finland's position as being simultaneously insider and outsider of the Western technology embargo CoCom.

None of the ships in this chapter was a naval ship, at least not officially, but the state leaders used them as objects to articulate meanings over national security and national prestige in international affairs.

Chapter 4 scrutinises the bilateral clearing trade and payment institutions in the Finnish–Soviet relations and the impact of the bilateral trade in the development of the Finnish shipyards. By so doing, it turns the focus from the high politics to the role of allegedly apolitical trade institutions and trade administration in industrial transformation.

The bilateral clearing trade and payment system coordinated roughly one fifth of the Finnish foreign trade between 1952 and 1990. The high-volume and long-lasting bilateral trade system was the most striking institutional difference between the ship trade with the Soviet Union and the trade with capitalist countries. The Finnish shipbuilding industry did not only adapt to the dualism between multilateral and bilateral trading but embraced it. The chapter shows how the bilateral framework of trade became the single most important factor in the expansion of the Finnish shipbuilding until the 1980s, and on the other hand, how the real and alleged benefits of the clearing trade and payment system to the Finnish shipbuilding became the single most important reason for the trade administration to maintain the bilateral trade infrastructure.

Chapter 5 focuses on the Finnish–Soviet technological, scientific, and industrial cooperation in shipbuilding that went beyond conventional commercial exchange. Leaving the high politics and trade administration behind, this chapter concentrates on the motives and rationales of the shipbuilding companies to participate in border-crossing scientific, technical, and industrial cooperation.

The inter-governmental institutions of scientific-technical and industrial cooperation in the Finnish–Soviet relations originated from the Soviet interests in using transnational cooperation as a tool to create economic dependencies and to get access to Western technology through Finland. The chapter shows, however, how the Finnish shipbuilding companies applied and repurposed these institutions to enact their own business goals. In particular, the bilateral techno-scientific cooperation became influential in the development of expertise in Arctic maritime technology in Finland—a country without Arctic waters.

Chapter 6 turns the attention to the relationship between Finnish shipbuilding companies on the one hand and the relationship between the industrial companies and the state on the other hand. The main part of this chapter examines the state-industry negotiations over shipyard crisis and its impact on the scale and structure of the Finnish shipbuilding industry. Until the late 1970s, the industrial development had been a shared goal of the government and the companies because the industrial expansion provided employment for the growing urban population. From 1977 onwards, the state and shipbuilding industry renegotiated over their relationships in a situation in which industrial development meant downscaling and rationalisation rather than contribution to full employment.

Another central theme in this chapter is the dismantling of the consensus culture. The formal and informal cooperative practices between the industrial leaders had coordinated the competition within the Finnish shipbuilding industry, which effectively froze the market shares of the companies for over 20 years. In the 1980s, the shipbuilding companies tried to find new ways to coordinate the competition through mergers and acquisitions in a situation in which the overall volume of ship orders decreased. During the decade from 1982 to 1992, the Finnish shipbuilding capacity decreased to half, and half of the industry was sold abroad.

Finally, Chapter 7 examines the role of state-aid and financing in the period that was generally characterised by increasing economic liberalisation and European integration. It concentrates on the state-level decision-making about Finnish domestic and Western trade and industrial policy. In the period of the Cold War, different state interventions, interest subsidies, and direct state-aid schemes established as an integral part of international shipbuilding competition and their use exploded after the 1970s crisis. Finland differentiated itself in the Western European comparisons by claiming promptly that the Finnish shipyards did not receive nor wish for state-aid.

The chapter discusses how and to what extent the Finnish Cold War shipbuilding industry truly was free from state subsidies. It shows that even though the state-aid for shipbuilding was generally lower and came in different forms than in most rival countries, the Finnish shipyards too received significant financial support from the government. The chapter also describes how Finland gradually adjusted its shipbuilding policy to European standards in the course of the European integration process. The shipyard financing forced the state and the industry to reconsider their stand in relation to national competitiveness and national welfare. The policy change took place not as a grand statement but through *ad hoc* decisions that were often specific, exceptional, and made in haste.

## Notes

1 Lloyd's Register for Shipping, *Shipbuilding Returns*; Poulsen et al., "Global Shifts in Marine Manufacturing, 1950–2010," 2012; Stråth, *The Politics of De-industrialisation*, 1987; Todd, *Industrial Dislocation*, 1991; *Shipbuilding and Ship Repair Workers Around the World: Case Studies 1950–2010*, eds. Varela et al., 2017; Johnman & Murphy, *British Shipbuilding and the State since 1918*, 2002; Slaven, *British Shipbuilding 1500–2010*, 2013; Cho & Porter, "Changing Global Industry Leadership: The Case of Shipbuilding," 1986, 541–567; Lorenz, *Economic Decline in Britain*, 1991.

2 There were, of course, national differences in Europe. Notably, Denmark was able to delay the downfall for a decade thanks to technical specialisation and vertical integration. Poulsen & Sornn-Friese, "Downfall Delayed," 2011.

3 For a versatile edited volume presenting the state-of-the-art, see *Science and Technology in the Global Cold War*, eds. Oreskes & Krige, 2014.

4 For introduction to the diverse and large field, see MacKenzie, *Inventing Accuracy*, 1990; Gavin, *Nuclear Statecraft*, 2012; Hecht, *The Radiance of France*, 2009; Abbate, *Inventing the Internet*, 2000; Leslie, *The Cold War and American Science*, 1993; McLauchlan & Gregory, "Last of the Dinosaurs?" 1995; Galison, "The Many Faces of Big Science," 1992; Reynolds, "Science, Technology, and the Cold War," 2010.

5 Adams, *The Politics of Defense Contracting*, 1982, 25; Lundin & Stenlås, "Technology, State Initiative and National Myths in Cold War Sweden," 2010, 13; 16–19.

6 See Oreskes, "Science in the Origins of the Cold War," 2014; Siddiqi, "Fighting Each Other," 2014; Schmid, "Defining (Scientific) Direction," 2014; Asner, "The Linear Model, the U.S. Department of Defence, and the Golden Age of Industrial Research," 2004.

7 Particularly, the post-Cold War economic, social, and cultural historians using transnational and micro-history perspectives have demonstrated how an isolated analysis of the polarised high politics may not provide an accurate picture of the Cold War in different national contexts. Autio-Sarasmo & Miklossy, "The

Cold War from a New Perspective," 2010; Mikkonen & Koivunen, "Beyond the Divide," 2015.

8 Lundin & Stenlås, "Technology, State Initiative and National Myths in Cold War Sweden," 2010; Kansikas, "Room to Maneoevre?" 2010, 193–209; Schmid, "Nuclear Colonisation?" 2011, 125–154.

9 Fridlund, "De nationalistiska systemen," 1998; Fritzsche, *A Nation of Fliers*, 1992; Edwards & Hecht, "History and the Technopolitics of Identity," 2010; Gagliardone, "A Country in Order," 2014; Gärdebo, *Environing Technology*, 2019; Paju, *Ilmarisen Suomi*, 2008.

10 Studies indicating the relationship between the Soviet trade and Finnish shipbuilding development include, among others, Id & Peter, *Innovation and Specialisation*, 2017, 5, 19; Teräs, "From War Reparations to Luxury Cruise Liners," 2017, 214; Hanhimäki, "Self-Restraint as Containment," 1995; Viita, *Kapitalismin ja sosialismin puristuksessa*, 2006, 132–137. Rainio-Niemi has analysed the legacy of the Cold War neutrality policy in post-Cold War discussions. See Rainio-Niemi, "Cold War Neutrality in Europe. Lessons to Be Learned?" 2017; Examples of post-Cold War uses of the "Finlandisation" concept, see Inboden, "Is Finland Rejecting "Finlandisation," 2014; Gilley, "Not so Dire Straits: How the Finlandisation of Taiwan Benefits US Security," 2010, 44.

11 Social Construction of Technology (SCOT). Pinch & Bijker, "The Social Construction of Facts and Artifacts," 2009.

12 Hughes, *Networks of Power*, 1983. See also: Hughes, "The Evolution of Large Technological Systems," 2012; Summerton, "Stora tekniska system – en introduktion till forskningsfältet," 1998, 19–44.

13 Hughes, *Rescuing Prometheus*, 1998.

14 My understanding of 'techno-economic system' is in harmony with the similar concepts that align technology with economy. Most notably, the neo-Schumpeterian economist Carlota Perez has used the concept of techno-economic paradigm to analyse the impact of technological change in socio-economic development. See Perez, *Technological Revolutions and Financial Capital*, 2002. Claes-Fredrik Helgesson has also used 'techno-economic system' in his study on Swedish telecommunications to emphasise the interwoven nature of technological, economic, and social elements. In comparison with my approach, Helgesson leans more towards the Actor Network Theory (ANT) than to the LTS. Helgesson, *Making a Natural Monopoly*, 1999, 34. See also Callon, "Techno-Economic Networks and Irreversibility," 1990.

15 Aho, "Creators of Ships and Welfare: Shipbuilders' Experiences in the 1960s-1980s," 2018; Teräs, "From War Reparations to Luxury Cruise Liners," 2017.

16 On shipbuilding systems, see Olsson, *Technology Carriers*, 2000; Olsson, "Offshore som livboj. Varvkrisen och försöken till omorientering, 1974–1985," 1998; Sahari, *Valtio ja suurteollisuuden synty*, 2018.

17 Hughes, "Technological Momentum," 2009, 146.

18 Hughes, "The Evolution of Large Technological Systems," 2012, 64–73.

19 Van Rooij, "Sisyphus in Business," 2015, 204; Napolitano et al., "In Search of an Integrated Framework of Business Longevity," 2015; McGovern, "Why Do Successful Companies Fail?" 2007. On longevity discussion, see Riviezzo et al., "Who Wants to Live Forever," 2015; Capasso et al., "Standing the Test of Time: Does Firm Performance Improve with Age?" 2015; Eriksson & Stanfors, "A Winning Strategy? The Employment of Women and Firm Longevity During Industrialisation," 2015.

20 Blomkvist & Kaijser, "Introduktion – De osynliga systemen," 1998; Hughes, "Technological Momentum," 2009, 145.

21 J. K. Paasikivi's diaries, published in 1985–1986. *J.K. Paasikiven päiväkirjat 2: 1944–1956*, 1986, 241.

18    *Introduction*

22  Holopainen, *Orpo Piru*, 2007, 110–111.
23  According to Johanna Rainio-Niemi, the term was coined by former Austrian Foreign Minister Karl Gruben and presented as a cautionary example for Austria to avoid. Rainio-Niemi, *The Ideological Cold War*, 2014, 55; Professor Richard Loewenthal's analysis of West-Berlin has also been presented as the origin of the concept. Klinge, "Ecce Finnia Tridentem! – Tässä Suomi valtikkasi!," 2001; Vihavainen, *Kansakunta rähmällään*, 1991, 18.
24  Laquer, "Europe: The Specter of Finlandization," 1977, 38.
25  Vihavainen, *Kansakunta rähmällään*, 1991; Quester, "Finlandisation as a Problem or an Opportunity?" 1990; Peterssen, "Scandinavia and the 'Finlandisation' of Soviet Security," 1991; Berndtson, "Finlandization: Paradoxes of External and Internal Dynamics," 1991; Forsberg & Pesu, "The 'Finlandisation' of Finland," 2016.
26  Roughly meaning "The nation on its knees" but with a Finnish wording bearing more pejorative connotations.
27  Vihavainen, *Kansakunta rähmällään*, 1991.
28  *Kauppa ja kansojen etu*, 1987; Gorbačev, *Sotrudničestvo SSSR I Finlândii V Oblasti Sudostroeniâ: Suomalais-neuvostoliittolainen yhteistyö laivanrakennuksen alalla*, 1990; Keskinen, *Idänkauppa: 1944–1987*, 1987; *Finnish-Soviet Economic Relations*, 1983.
29  Sutela, "The Folklore of Finland's Eastern Trade," 2007.
30  Including but not restricted to: Rantanen, "The Development of the System of Bilateral Agreements between Finland and the Soviet Union," 1983, 46; Ihamuotila, "Cooperation from the Company Point of View," 1983, 113; Häikiö, *Sturm und Drang*, 2001, 49; Sutela, "Finnish Trade with USSR: Why Was It Different?" 2005, 7–8; Piskulov, *Näin teimme idänkauppaa*, 2009; Fjodorov, *NKP:n Suomen osastolla 1954–1989*, 2001; Derjabin, *Omalla nimellä*, 1997.
31  Björklund, *Valmet*, 1990.
32  Lundelin, *Laivanrakentajana vuosina 1945–1988*, 1998, 9.
33  Haavikko, *Wärtsilä 1834–1984*, 1984.
34  Uola, "*Meidän isä on töissä telakalla*," 1996. Uola's other shipyard book on Hollming shipbuilding relies to a great extent on the same archival sources but lacks consistent footnotes. *Uola, Hollming 1945–2000*, 2001. The historical reviews also include the following: *Sandvikens Skeppsdocka genom hundra år*, ed. Christoffer Ericsson, 1965 (unpublished); von Knorring, *Aurajoen veistämöt ja telakat*, 1995; Eerola, *Kun rauta kelluu*, 2017; For an English overview, Id & Peter, *Specialization and Innovation*, 2017.
35  Sahari, *Valtio ja suurteollisuuden synty*, 2018.
36  Id & Peter, *Innovation and Specialisation*, 2017.
37  William H. McNeill originally formulated the concept of 'national myths' to analyse the relationship between collective identity and collective action. Per Lundin and Niklas Stenlås have applied the concept to analyse national narratives in Sweden during the Cold War arguing that the myths of 'modernity' and 'neutrality' shaped large technological systems as they were widely used to justify political priorities, mobilise resources and investments. Lunding & Stenlås, "Technology, State and National Myths in Cold War Sweden," 2010, 4–9.
38  In 1997, J. L. Gaddis titled his book "We now know" referring to post-Cold War historians who were to start new era of critical re-evaluation of the Cold War narratives using the known outcome and new, recently declassified governmental archival collections as their guidance. Gaddis, *We Now Know: Rethinking Cold War History*, 1997. Also: Westad, "The Cold War and the International History of the Twentieth Century," 2010.
39  Lloyd's Register, *Shipbuilding Returns*, 1900–1990. Digitalised by Aaro Sahari at Lloyd's Information Centre, London. Data set created by Sahari and Matala.

40 Meriteollisuus Ry archive, UPM archive; published lists of ships completed in *Navigator 1955–1990* and in Uola, *Meidän isä oli töissä telakalla*, 1996; Haavikko, *Wärtsilä 1834–1984*, 1984.
41 Socialist countries, excluding China.
42 Finnish post-war ship export to China remained statistically irrelevant even though it occasionally was, as Jensen-Eriksen has presented, politically complicated. Jensen-Eriksen, "Lost at Sea," 2013.
43 International Maritime Organisation replaced the Gross register tonnages (Grt) as the main standard by Gross tonnages (Gt) in 1969. International Convention on Tonnage Measurement of Ships, adoption June 23, 1969, into force July 19, 1982. http://www.imo.org/en/About/Conventions/ListOfConventions/Pages/International-Convention-on-Tonnage-Measurement-of-Ships.aspx. Retrieved 28.11.2017.
44 Maritime historian Yrjö Kaukiainen has extensively discussed the problems in the use of gross tonnages in studies of historical maritime activities and has argued for the use of Deadweight tonnages (DWT) which refer to the ship's carrying capacity. Kaukiainen, "Tons and Tonnages: Ship Measurement and Shipping Statistics," 1995. However, as argued above, as DWT data being seldom available, GTs remained the only viable option.
45 In 1970s, the OECD created a Compensated Gross tonnage standard system which aimed to provide more informative measures to describe shipbuilding activities. The CGT system consists of certain estimated coefficients that indicate the average amount of work required to build a tonnage of a certain type of ship. Directorate for Science, Technology and Industry. Council Working Party on Shipbuilding. *Compensated Gross Ton (CGT) System*, 2007. Available: http://www.oecd.org/industry/ind/37655301.pdf. Retrieved 28.11.2017.
46 Standard industrial classification, *Toimialaluokitus määritelmineen*, 1988, Central Statistical Office of Finland, Handbooks 4, 1988; *International Standard Industrial Classification of All Economic Activities*, 1968.
47 Hecht, *The Radiance of France*, 1998, 15.

# 2 Before the Cold War shipbuilding

Next to a busy traffic junction in central Helsinki stands a massive monument to the first post-war President of Finland, J. K. Paasikivi (1870–1956). The monument itself is abstract and ambiguous, but onto the granite base, the artist has carved a citation that became a guideline in Finland's post-war politics: *All vishets begynnelse är att erkänna fakta*—the beginning of all wisdom is the acknowledgement of the facts. It was clear to everyone living in the Cold War Finland that in that context 'wisdom' meant survival outside military conflicts and 'the facts' translated as the Soviet Union.

Finland's foreign relations during the Cold War were framed by geopolitical preconditions that enclosed much of the development of the shipbuilding industry. This chapter provides an introduction to Finland and Finnish shipbuilding industry from the period of autonomy, when Finland was part of the Russian Empire, until the completion of war reparations to the Soviet Union in 1952, that marked the final milestone in the transition from the Second World War to the Cold War.

## Seafaring in the borderland before the Second World War

The history of Finland as a Northern periphery that slowly integrated into the international economy and Western European cultural community is in a very concrete way carried forward by ships. Geopolitically, the area of Finland has been a borderland between east and west. While the south-west part of the mainland belonged to the Kingdom of Sweden since the 13th century, the eastern border was subject to frequent changes as a result of power struggles with Novgorod and later Russia. Under the Swedish influence, the population adopted Western culture, institutions, and identity, the elite also the Swedish language. In 1809, Tsar Alexander I annexed most of the Finnish-speaking parts of Sweden into the Russian Empire after a war against Sweden. As an autonomous Grand Duchy in the 19th century, Finland was able to establish institutions and practices for self-governance as well as to create a national identity separated from its neighbouring nations Russia and Sweden. Finland declared independence in the aftermath of the Russian revolutions in 1917.[1]

Geographically, the population and economic activities of Finland have been concentrated on the headland surrounded by the Baltic Sea on two sides. The Gulf of Bothnia in the west and Gulf of Finland in the south prevent direct land connection to Western Europe giving reasons for Finns to depict their land as an island. Because all the Finnish ports by the Baltic Sea froze over during a normal winter forming an insurmountable barrier for wooden-hull sailing ships, the island metaphor has been predominantly understood in terms of isolation. Yet, as maritime historian Yrjö Kaukiainen has underlined, the sea has enabled connections as much it has separated by waterborne transportation for goods and people.[2]

In the early modern period, shipping routes to Western Europe and beyond were already established as a modest-sized but critical component of the livelihood on the shores of Finland. Ships brought in salt and grain and exported natural products. First fur and timber, then tar, later butter and processed wood products such paper. Alongside urban shipowners, peasant shipping constituted a significant sideline of the Finnish seafaring often navigating in the grey area of law, spreading foreign influence, goods, and connections to the coastal countryside. In the 17th century, the Ostrobothnia region on the West Coast developed into a locally important centre of shipbuilding. The region took advantage of systematic technology transfer and its position as a well-connected but relatively low-cost backyard of Stockholm with easy access to raw materials. Occasionally, in the 18th century, the Ostrobothnian shipbuilders produced vessels beyond domestic needs evolving into a notable export branch.[3]

The Finnish international shipping in the era of wood and sails reached its apogee after the mid-19th century. At the time, large ocean-going sailing ships still had a competitive advantage over steamships when carrying bulk cargo for intercontinental routes. After 1875, however, the development of Finnish merchant tonnage lagged behind international development due to increasing competition, persistent decline in freight rates, and the late adoption of new technology.[4]

The transition from wood to metal hulls in shipbuilding started in the late 18th-century Britain in tow of the development of machine building, railways, and bridge construction technologies and fuelled by the shortage of timber.[5] Gradually after a slow start, the iron and steel structures overcame the traditional wood, because they enabled stronger hulls, larger ships, and more cargo. What appeared as a logical step forward from the point of view of a shipowner often marked a discontinuance from the point of view of a shipbuilder. The traditional Finnish ship constructors continued building small-sized wooden vessels for the Baltic or coastal traffic until the First World War, but the short-distance shipping generated seldom enough capital to upgrade to state-of-the-art steamships. At the shipyards, long traditions of forming and hewing wood did not translate well into rolling, bending, and riveting metal plates. Metal ship manufacturing required investments in machinery, lifters, and raw material that were capital-intensive and inaccessible for most small-scale ship constructors.[6] Moreover, the wooden shipbuilding was unable to compete against the cheap and good-quality second-hand tonnage that came available when the leading Western European seafaring nations updated their fleet from sails to steam.

Instead of the well-established wooden ship constructors, urban bridge and railway builders were typical first movers in metal shipbuilding. Steamship building started to develop slowly as a side branch of general machine shops into a modestly sized industry on the Finnish South-west Coast towards the end of the 19th century.[7] The traditions of wooden shipbuilding in Finland declined.[8]

The maritime business is all about making connections. Shipyards build technology to make those connections possible. The development of the Finnish shipbuilding industry before the First World War was linked to international technological and economic development and it shared most of the general trends with other European maritime countries. Yet, as we are exploring the historical background of the Finnish Cold War shipbuilding, it is worth pointing out the aspects that enlighten some of the national characteristics typical for the later development.

As a part of the Finnish nation-building during the era of autonomy, economic nationalism expressed itself in the development of increasingly liberal trade policy. In the export-oriented country far away from European markets, national welfare considerations placed the priority on cost-efficient transportation over the employment of the domestic shipbuilding industry. The most expensive ships of the Grand Duchy were icebreakers. Breaking the winter isolation, the state-icebreakers became instrumental in transforming Finland from the Western part of Russia into the Northern part of Europe both logistically and symbolically. Yet, even those ships of national importance were ordered from abroad: the icebreaker *Murtaja* (1889) from Sweden and the icebreakers *Sampo* (1898) and *Tarmo* (1907) from the United Kingdom. The difference in experience, quality, and price was too large that even the dedicated Finnish nationalists opted for foreign shipyards.[9]

In the international context, Finnish shipbuilding was marginal. Before the First World War, the United Kingdom was the unquestioned leader of the world shipbuilding. Prime movers in the application of both steam and steel, the British shipbuilders were renowned for cost-efficient production, advanced design of different types, and reliable delivery in a way that the other shipbuilding nations only tried to follow.[10]

Despite its critical logistical function, seafaring and shipbuilding remained rather marginal also in the Finnish national identity especially in comparison with such characteristic European maritime countries like the United Kingdom or Norway. Instead of the geography and merchant shipping, the establishment of modern steel shipyards in the Grand Duchy of Finland was fuelled by geopolitics and Russian strategic considerations.

Peter the Great had founded St. Petersburg in the mouth of River Neva in 1703. After that, the safety of the metropolis dominated Russian interests in the Finnish territory. Russian Navy relied on technology transfer in its modernisation efforts, and Finnish engineers and shipyards took part in this transnational project. The most important Finnish shipyards in the 19th century Eastern trade were Hietalahti Shipyard,[11] a relatively modern dry-dock in Helsinki founded in 1865, and the two shipbuilding companies in Turku on the banks of the river Aura, Ab Crichton and Ab Vulcan, which were later merged into one company, Crichton-Vulcan in 1924.[12] Located near the imperial naval bases in Turku and Helsinki, these shipyards sold up to three-fourth of their ships for the Russian Navy. They became, in essence, part of the Russian military-technological defence system of St. Petersburg.[13]

During the autonomy, the quasi-domestic Eastern trade evolved into an art of its own. The high share of just one buyer came with business opportunities as well as high risks. Despite Finland being part of the Russian Empire, there was a tariff border between the autonomous Grand Duchy and the imperial mainland. The strategic needs of the Russian Navy for Western technology and shipbuilding capacity mixed with the nationalist policy and economic protectionism. The trade policy was fickle and unpredictable. In the 1880s, Russia imposed customs duty to protect its shipyards against Finnish competition. At the turn of the year 1900, the orders for non-Russian shipyards stopped altogether. The restrictions were replaced by a sudden peak in demand after the disaster of the Russo-Japanese War (1904–1905), but the tariffs were soon raised again. The one lesson that the Finnish businessmen learned from this period of ship trade was that successful business with Russians required personal connections, flexibility, and readiness for technical adaptations.[14]

The First World War boosted demand for new military and merchant tonnage and sparked shipyards to expand their construction capacity. After the war, surfeit of ships and decreasing prices turned the trend downwards. After the immediate post-war peak in demand 1918–1922, the merchant shipbuilding in Finland collapsed close to non-existence. By the same token, the Finnish shipyards lost their Eastern market. The Finnish Civil War in 1918 had ended with the defeat of the socialist Reds and the relationship with the Bolshevik government remained distant, even hostile, during the 1920s.[15]

In the inter-war period, the United Kingdom maintained its leading position thanks to its horizontally integrated industrial clusters but also new shipbuilding nations rose their heads pursuing different strategies.[16] In Japan, where economic nationalism and a systematic state-led strategy of technology transfer had started to fuel rapid industrialisation, large shipyards were often forerunners in the development of related engineering branches.[17] In Europe, most of the innovative activities and technological development took place in cooperation between shipbuilders and shipowners.[18]

Finland lacked any significant horizontal or vertical integration that facilitated the expansion of merchant shipbuilding in countries such as Norway and Denmark.[19] When the Finnish merchant fleet switched finally from sails and wooded hulls to steam and steel during the inter-war period, the shipowners preferred rather old second-hand ships or state-subsidised new tonnage of foreign origin instead of placing newbuilding orders for domestic shipyards. The salaries and safety regulations in Finnish shipping followed behind Western Europe. Finland was characteristically a low-cost country where old and labour-intensive tonnage could still find a competitive edge. Quite succinctly, Kaukiainen has described the modernisation of the Finnish merchant tonnage as 'poor man's version of the revolution'.[20]

Finnish shipbuilding industry survived the interwar period thanks to two interrelated governmental decisions that were largely motivated by national security concerns and fear of the Soviet Union[21]: the decision to launch a large programme to build a navy for the newly independent country and the decision to prefer Finnish shipyards in these governmental procurements. The material results of the inter-war coastal defence program included a class of two coastal defence ships, *Ilmarinen* and *Väinämöinen*, submarines *Vetehinen* (1930), *Vesihiisi* (1930), *Iku-turso* (1931), *Vesikko* (1933), and the smaller *Saukko* (1930), and a multipurpose icebreaker *Sisu* (1939). Maritime historian Aaro Sahari has underlined the long-lasting immaterial results of this naval programme. The programme created networks for technology transfer from Sweden and Germany and established connections between the Finnish state and private industry.[22]

The Finnish state had two naval docks in Helsinki –Suomenlinna,[23] and Katajanokka– but they were used to little else than to repair naval ships. All the advanced naval vessels were constructed at the private-owned shipyards in Turku and Helsinki.[24] To ensure that the technical expertise and financial resources were enough to satisfy the needs of the sophisticated naval ships, Hietalahti and Crichton-Vulcan shipyards were acquired by a single manufacturing company, Kone-ja Siltarakennus, and later merged with a rapidly expanding conglomerate Wärtsilä in the mid-1930s.[25] This re-organisation of the Finnish metal industries made Wärtsilä the unquestioned leader among the Finnish shipbuilders in terms of production capacity and competence and Wärtsilä's director, Wilhelm Wahlforss (1891–1969), an influential actor in the Finnish industrial landscape.[26]

Crichton-Vulcan and Hietalahti shipyards renewed their position as the main actors in the Finnish Eastern trade when Finland established economic relation with the Soviet Union in 1931. Despite the general mistrust between the socialist Soviet Union and the democratic Finland, this inter-war ship trade was built on the foundation of the experiences and language skills from the era of autonomy.[27]

Together with the naval programme, this early Soviet trade helped the shipyards to develop and maintain skills that propelled them forward in the prewar upswing and helped them to get orders from domestic shipping companies as well. The role of the Soviet trade as a springboard should not be overestimated, though. The upturn at the Finnish shipyards in 1935–1939 was parallel to the international development. When the economy was booming, demand for new tonnage increased, supply of second-hand tonnage decreased, and shipowners had to place orders for less experienced shipyards as well.[28]

When the Second World War broke out in 1939, the Finnish shipbuilding industry was small, but it had a presence in state-level considerations; it had established close connections to the Finnish government, and it had maintained some contacts with the Soviet Union. The most advanced shipyards, Crichton-Vulcan and Hietalahti, were able to meet the technical requirements of relatively demanding state orders but the generally poor cost-competitiveness did not motivate Finnish shipowners to build strong vertical integration on the domestic ground.

## From war to peaceful coexistence between Finland and the Soviet Union, 1944–1948

In August 1938, Soviet Foreign Minister Vyacheslav Molotov and German Foreign Minister Joachim von Ribbentrop signed a pact of non-aggression. In secret, they completed the agreement by dividing the Europe between the USSR and Germany. According to the protocol, Finland belonged to the Soviet sphere of influence together with the Baltic states and parts of Poland.[29] Unlike the other Eastern European small countries, it managed to resist Soviet invasion in the defensive Winter War 1939–1940. This was followed by the Continuance War 1941–1944 alongside Germany as the only available ally. The Moscow Armistice in September 1944 ended hostilities between Finland and the Soviet Union but started yet another war in Northern Finland to expel German troops from the Finnish territory.

The wars were harsh and the peace not easy. According to the terms of the peace treaty, Finland lost its access to the Arctic Sea, territories in south-east Finland were annexed to the Soviet Union. Among the other things, the peace treaty imposed heavy war reparations on Finland and forced it to lease a military base in Porkkala which was located close to Finland's capital region.

Afterwards, the post-war years from the Moscow armistice in 1944 to the ratification of the Paris Peace Treaty in 1947 were coined as 'the years of danger'. The Soviet-controlled Allied Control Commission stayed in Helsinki to observe Finnish compliance with the terms of the armistice. The overall atmosphere was characterised by uncertainty about the Soviet goals in Finland. Underneath the strategic overtone of this period, it also became formative in the establishment of the Finnish–Soviet economic relations.

The wars left Finland devastated and drew its economy and society close to the limits. Yet, the society and democratic institutions were not broken down. Finland was not occupied by the Red army. The Soviet Union demonstrated its power over Finland demanding war-responsibility trials based on *ex post facto* legislation that offended the popular sense of justice but generally became not guilty of excess. The relatively low number of civilian casualties and the fact of being spared from the terror caused by the presence of a foreign army, created a feasible, if not ideal, foundation for the peaceful coexistence with the Soviet Union.

To understand the transition from the wartime hostilities to the Cold War cooperation, it is important to locate Finland in its post-war geopolitical context. When signing the ceasefire with Finland in the fall of 1944, Stalin and other Soviet leaders were still busy with the race to Berlin and the post-war power balance in Central Europe. While the Finnish fierce resistance against the Red army had demonstrated the expenses and difficulties of occupation, the military force of the small, lonely, and war-torn country posed no immediate threat against the Soviet military power. More likely was that other countries would use the Finnish territory to attack Leningrad. The post-war Finland was, in sum, in the sphere of Soviet interest with no escape, but aside from the centre of Stalin's attention. The Finnish sovereignty next to the expansive socialist superpower was fragile, but it had more leverage than many other small countries in the buffer zone the Soviet Union wanted between itself and Germany.[30]

The minimum strategic objective of the Soviet Union in Finland was to establish a loyal government in Helsinki to guarantee the safety of Leningrad. The maximum target would have been a communist government to usher Finland into the way of people's republics but, as Tatiana Androsova and Kimmo Rentola have argued, it appeared not as a fundamental precondition.[31] The Finnish communists failed to seize power by themselves, and Moscow did not care to help them. As an opposite, Moscow discouraged Finnish communists from striking if that disturbed too much the production it found useful.[32]

One of the main architects of the Soviet post-war policy in Finland was the chair of the Allied Control Commission Andrey Zhdanov. Zhdanov recognised the Finnish fear of military occupation as a practical political tool to gain leverage but made plans to use merely economic methods to enact the strategic goals.[33] According to Androsova, Zhdanov drafted systematic plans to use war reparations and trade to reconstruct Finnish industry in a way that would make it an extension to the socialist planning, to decrease the Western influence in Finland, and to increase economic dependency on the Soviet market.[34] The war still going on, the Soviet Union put a high price on the Finnish industrial capacity that had remained substantially intact in comparison with the demolished facilities in Eastern Europe.[35] A stable buffer zone next to the Soviet border and reliable industrial production counted more than the communist revolution in Helsinki.

The minimal target of the Finnish government was to maintain sovereignty and to facilitate the reconstruction of the society. The maximum target was to catch up with the Western European standards of living, but the trade and industrial policies were subordinated to the preservation of national security.

These minimum and maximum targets framed the formation of the Finnish–Soviet Cold War relations in the post-war years: The first concern in Finland was to stay out of military conflict, while the Soviet Union had the loyalty and stability of Finland as its priorities. Yet, both countries were devastated and yearned for economic and technical development and the considerations of national security were closely interlinked with industrial and technological interests. That the countries signed the first post-war trade protocol already in February 1945 demonstrated the urgency of economic matters notwithstanding its rather limited extend. Finland bartered Soviet grain and sugar for prefabricated wooden houses and battleship repairs.[36]

The Soviet strategic interests to use Finnish trade and industry to enact its security goals shaped also the institutional foundation of the Finnish–Soviet

Cold War relations. In 1947, Finland and the Soviet Union signed the Treaty of Commerce in which the countries granted each other the status of most favoured nation (MFN) in foreign trade.[37] The MFN status alone created a distinctive position for Finland in terms of the Soviet foreign trade and vice versa. Throughout the Cold War, however, a more frequently cited foundation for the Finnish–Soviet trade relationship was the security pact—the Agreement of Friendship, Cooperation, and Mutual Assistance (*Ystävyys, Yhteistyö-ja Avunantosopimus*, commonly known as the YYA treaty, hereafter FCMA), which Finland and the Soviet Union signed the following year 1948.

The FCMA treaty obligated Finland to resist any military aggression on the part of Germany or countries allied with Germany threatening Finland or the Soviet Union through the territory of Finland, assisted by the Soviet army if needed. Rather paradoxically, as Johanna Rainio-Niemi has underlined, this declaration of the Cold War 'friendship' became the cornerstone in the Finnish policy of non-alliance while simultaneously making Finland *de facto* part of the Soviet security system in a time of crisis.[38] The two meanings of the Cold War friendship—Finnish aspiration to remain neutral and the Soviet desire for security—co-existed in the Finnish–Soviet affairs until the disintegration of the Soviet Union.

The two postwar presidents Juho Kusti Paasikivi (in office 1946–1956) and Urho Kekkonen (1956–1982) built their policy on the premises that the Finnish and Soviet versions of the friendship could co-exist only in a time of peace and made it a priority to avoid provoking the Soviet Union into retaliation and building trust between the countries.[39]

The FCMA also articulated the economic dimension of the Finnish–Soviet relations as the contracting parties gave their assurances that they will act 'in a spirit of cooperation and friendship towards the further development and consolidation of economic and cultural relations between Finland and the Soviet Union'.[40] President Paasikivi saw commercial exchange with the Soviet Union as a source of positive interaction between the two countries. However, he advised against increasing the Soviet share of the Finnish foreign trade to prevent the Soviet Union from using Finnish dependency on the Soviet market as an instrument in economic warfare.[41]

His successor, President Kekkonen of the Agrarian League, occupied a central role in Finnish–Soviet affairs already before his terms in office when he served in government in several positions. The bilateral trade with the Soviet Union became a political instrument used both by Kekkonen and the Soviet leadership—the former to strengthen his hold within the Finnish political system and the latter to achieve their political goals in Finland.

Finland's Cold War foreign trade policy was built on the foundation of these dualistic geopolitical considerations. To avoid inflaming tensions, Finland opted out of the Marshall plan and Bretton Woods conference that outlined the post-war reconstruction and international economic order, but it was able to join the General Agreements of Tariffs and Trade (GATT) in 1950 and to receive loans from the United States.[42] Despite expressing deep distrust in Finnish Western connections, it was not of Soviet interest to close off them altogether.

No one knew exactly where the limits of political restrictions and economic opportunities were located. The Finnish foreign trade policy became characterised as continuous explorations of its room to manoeuvre.[43]

It was obvious to all that trade and technology diplomacy had become the continuation of the war, just by other means. Yet, economic warfare was different from military warfare. It created reciprocal dependencies and provided more leverage for Finland in relation to the Soviet Union. In January 1953, President Paasikivi recorded in his diary how he had heard the Soviet diplomat Viktor Lebedev saying to the Minister Törngren: 'trade politics is a part of regular politics. If it goes well, it shows that the Finnish–Soviet relations are as they should be'.[44]

This dualism of strategic and economic interests presented itself already during the negotiations for war reparations that is on focus in the next section.

## War reparations and industrial restructuring, 1944–1952

On September 19, representatives of the Finnish government signed the armistice agreement in Moscow. The 11th article obliged Finland to pay war reparations worth of USD300 million[45] to compensate for the wartime damage to the Soviet Union:

> 11. Losses caused by Finland to the Soviet Union by military operations and the occupation of Soviet territory will be indemnified by Finland to the Soviet Union to the amount of three hundred million dollars payable over six years in commodities (timber products, paper, cellulose, seagoing and river craft, sundry machinery).[46]

Unexpectedly, the Soviet negotiators placed most of the reparation burden on metal manufacturing—ships, locomotives, and cables. The reparation demand was clearly inconsistent with the Finnish industrial and foreign trade structure. Metal manufacturing, which had covered less than 15% of the manufacturing output in 1943, comprised over 60% of the reparations. Approximately one-third of the total value consisted of ships and necessitated shipbuilding capacity that far exceeded the Finnish existing shipyards.[47]

The war reparation production (1944–1952) constituted a massive project with a single purpose to organise domestic—public and private—resources to fulfil the Soviet demands and thereby survive the national crisis. From the point of view of industrialisation, the Soviet dictate created an unprecedented demand shock in the postwar Finnish shipbuilding as well as on Finland's industrial policy. That shaped the industrial structure and, in many respect, served as a prologue to the Cold War ship trade with the Soviet Union.

The actual impact of the war reparations on the shipbuilding industry is a controversial topic. The financial, industrial, and human resources needed for the war reparation production were away from the domestic reconstruction, and as such, its effect on the Finnish economy could be nothing but negative. On average, the war reparations represented 5% of the Finnish GDP for 1944–1952. The government budget covered both the direct costs of the war reparation products as well as the capital-intensive investments that the companies were required to make to be able to produce the required products.[48]

However, the war reparation production also boosted Finnish industrialisation and accelerated the transformation of the predominantly agrarian country into an industrial country. Economist Matti Mitrunen's dissertation presents a quantitative study on the long-term effects of the war reparations. Mitrunen points out that in the conditions where capital was a scarce resource, the governmentally subsidised financing for investments was a competitive advantage for those sectors and companies who participated in the war reparation production. In the long run, the war reparations constituted an exogenous factor in the Finnish industrial policy that facilitated the re-allocation of workforce from the traditionally dominant forestry and agricultural sectors to new, relatively skill-intensive, higher-paid, and more productive industrial and service sectors.[49]

Contemporary commentators[50] had a tendency to highlight the positive aspects and present the war reparations as the starting point for the modern Finnish shipbuilding, and the post-Cold War writers have often repeated the storyline.[51] The *New York Times* reported in 1949 how Finland 'defeated in the war, emerged from otherwise disastrous consequences with at least one gain – a working shipbuilding industry. [...] Starting from scratch, the Finns have in less than three years created a shipbuilding industry commanding respect...'.[52] The small Finland turning the military defeat into an engineering feat was undeniably an inspirational story. It had historical drama and moral lessons that resonated in the post-war atmosphere.

A columnist of *Herald Journal* in 1965 served another illustrative example as he described his conversation with a Finnish icebreaker salesman: 'You see, we didn't even want to be in the icebreaker business', said this real or imaginary salesman according to the column:

> but we had to get into it because Russia demanded a huge payment, in icebreakers – among other items – for the damage we did to Russia during the Finnish-Russian war [...] The Soviet Union is our biggest, nearest neighbour. If it says we damaged it, I guess we did. Anyway, by the time we finished paying off Russia in icebreakers, we were stuck with a huge icebreaker industry.[53]

What makes these stories of the Finnish high-technology shipbuilding industry rising from the ashes of the war so fascinating is not their correspondence with the facts. The current understanding among the Finnish economic historians is that the war reparations to the Soviet Union did not start the Finnish shipbuilding industry. Post-Cold War economic historians have pointed out the upward trend preceding the Second World War or focused the attention on the technical development afterwards and argued that the reparations only boosted the development that was going on in any way.[54] Specifically, Finland built no new icebreakers as a part of war reparations even though two old steam icebreakers *Voima* (1924) and *Jääkarhu* (1926) and a rather small harbour icebreaker *Turso* (1944) were included in the deliveries.

Yet, the national myth of the war reparations effect on the Finnish shipbuilding is not completely deceptive either. The quantifiable data on the war reparation deliveries show an unquestionable stimulus to post-war shipbuilding. The war reparations put the national sovereignty at risk in the time of peace and forced the government to launch an unprecedentedly large industrial policy project that transformed the industrial structure through state orders, technical support, and subsidies.

Figure 2.1 shows the expansion of the Finnish shipbuilding industry during the war reparations. In 1952, when the last war reparation delivery was sent cross the border, the Finnish shipbuilding industry totalled 16 shipyards, seven

*Figure 2.1* Finnish shipyard locations after the war reparation 1952. Data and picture credit to Aaro Sahari, *Valtio ja suurteollisuuden synty*, 2018. Used with permission.

of which were new in business.[55] The completed fleet consisted of total 583 new-built vessels and ranged from wood-composite barges, tugboats, and trawlers to general cargo ships and an anti-magnetic research vessel. Overall, the war reparation production was characterised with relatively simple technology and relatively long series. The series of wood-composite barges consisted of 205 vessels, while the series of trawlers (65 vessels), schooners (91 ships), and tugboats for lakes and sea (50 and 30 ships) were also sizable. In addition to the newbuildings, a considerable share of the Finnish merchant fleet, altogether 105 vessels, was expropriated from their owners and delivered to the Soviet Union as a part of the reparations.[56]

Wärtsilä, which owned Hietalahti Shipyard in Helsinki and Crichton-Vulcan in Turku, outperformed the other Finnish shipyards in all sectors. It represented the organisations that had been responsible for building the most advanced governmental ships in the inter-war period including the submarines and the icebreaker *Sisu*, and it had also built ships for the Soviet Union in the 1930s. This experience made it always the first choice for metal ships. Wärtsilä had quite accurate understanding of its cost structure, and it was able to pick out the types of vessels that were less risky and yielded most profits.[57]

The state-owned Valmet (Valtion Metallitehtaat 1946–1951) represented a strict contrast to Wärtsilä. It had been established out of the merger of state-owned factories to facilitate the transition from war economy to post-war reconstruction. The state-owned shipyards in Helsinki and Turku had been used mainly for repairs and had limited experience in ship construction or design. As a state-owned company, Valmet was forced to accept orders that Wärtsilä or other private companies declined as too risky or loss-making.[58] After the war reparations, it failed to receive profitable orders from outside the Soviet Union, and in 1954/1955, the company board of directors was already considering closing its loss-making shipyards.[59]

The closure plan was not executed. Valmet continued to build ships because it had a national function besides the technical one. The state-owned shipyards provided a counterweight to the private companies and were under the influence of political patronage. In the Finnish–Soviet negotiations on war reparations and trade, Valmet became 'the governmental safety valve' as Sahari has succinctly described the rather ungrateful position of the state-owned shipyards.[60]

In addition to the pre-war dry docks in Helsinki and Turku by the Gulf of Finland, the West Coast had become another important centre of shipbuilding during the war reparation deliveries. The privately owned Rauma-Repola had started to build a dry dock to Rauma during the war and later established its position as the second largest shipbuilding company in the Cold War Finland.[61]

As shown in Table 2.1, the war reparations included a high number of wooden and glued laminated vessels. The wooden hulls, steam engines, and even sails stood out in the post-war context in which the world shipbuilding

Table 2.1 War reparation production in shipbuilding industry.

| War reparation position | Vessel type | Spec | Initial delivery quota | Vessels eventually delivered | Shipyards |
|---|---|---|---|---|---|
| 165 | Sea going tug | 800 hp | 30 | 30 | WT |
| 166 | Sea going tug | 600 hp | 20 | 20 | WH |
| 167 | Ice-strengthened sea going tug | 500 hp | 3 | 3 | RuoR |
| 168 | Inshore tug with Cort-tunnel | 2 × 250 hp | 9 | 9 | AAW, E-GL |
|  | Inshore tug with Cort-tunnel | 400 hp | 27 | 27 | WT, VMTH, R-RR |
| 169 | Sea going pram | 3,000 T | 30 | 30 | WH, VMTP |
| 170 | Inshore pram | 2,000 T | 25 | 25 | WT |
| 171 | Motor ship, cargo, Germanischer Lloyd spec. | 3,000 T | 3 | 3 | – |
| 172 | Motor ship, cargo, Morskoy Registr spec. | 3,000 T | 5 | 0 | WT |
| 173 | Steamship, cargo, Morskoy Registr spec. | 3,200 T | 0 | 7 | WT |
| 174 | Steamship, cargo, Germanischer Lloyd spec. | 3,200 T | 2 | 2 | WH |
| 175 | Steamship, cargo | 2,000 T | 2 | 2 | VMTH |
| 176 | Ocean going trawler | 800 hp | 10 | 10 | VLP, R-RR, TTP, RKP, UTKU, VMTP, HoR, LTP |
|  | Inshore pram, wood-steel composite | 1,000 T | 200 | 205 | LTP, HoR, AEP, VLP |
| 177 | Schooner, wood/wood composite hull | 300 T | 90 | 90 | LTP, HoR, AEP, VLP |
|  | Research schooner, antimagnetic construction | 300 T | 0 | 1 | AH (WH) |
| 178 | Floating dock for long vessels |  | 2 | 2 |  |
|  | Floating dock for short vessels |  | 2 | 2 |  |
| 204 | Inshore tug | 150 hp | 0 | 50 | VMTP, AAW |
| C.3.2.47/131 | Trawler |  | 0 | 65 | HoR, UTKU, RKP, AVH, R-RR, LTP |
| Total |  |  | 460 | 583 | Builders in descending order of vessels delivered |

Data from Sahari, *Valtio ja suurteollisuuden synty*, 2018. Used with permission.

was moving beyond the paradigmatic shift towards steel hulls and combustion engines. Advanced shipbuilders like Wärtsilä did not want to get involved in these 'wooden ship monsters' (*puulaivamörkö*) as Wahlforss pejoratively called them. According to Sahari, these old types demonstrated not the Soviet technical backwardness but the aim of the Soviet Union to maximise the tonnage it could get out from Finland. The Soviet negotiators estimated it easier to re-start wooden shipbuilding in a country with no remarkable tradition in steel or marine engine production than to expand the limited steel shipbuilding.[62]

The companies that took upon themselves to build the wooden and wood-composite vessels were new in shipbuilding with the exception of Uusikaupunki Shipyard that had previously specialised in ship repairs. Due to the scale of the project, the starting point was to introduce modern methods of serial production, rationalisation, and prefabrication to the traditional craft of wooden shipbuilding. For example, Laivateollisuus Oy (LATE) shipyard, which was founded in 1945 in Pansio, Turku, focused on building wooden schooners in efficient series. The most famous of its vessels was the anti-magnetic research vessel *Zarya* (1952), which earned a nickname 'Gold schooner' (*Kultakuunari*) because of its high costs. Less famous, yet more long-lasting, result of the war reparation production at LATE shipyard was the expertise of glued laminated timber that was developed to address the shortage of high-quality timber.[63]

Hollming, another shipbuilding company in Rauma, was an interesting exception in the general mode of industrialisation. It entered into modern shipbuilding business while preserving continuance of shipbuilding traditions that stemmed from peasant shipping and shipbuilding. Hollming relocated artisans with experience of wooden ships from territories that had been annexed to the Soviet Union to construct the war reparation schooners. Realising the poor prospects of wooden shipbuilding after the war reparations, Hollming re-educated most of its artisans during the war reparation production preparing them to switch from timber and hammer to metal sheets and welding torch.[64]

Overall, the war reparations facilitated rationalisation and modernisation of shipbuilding processes rather than state-of-the-art innovations in maritime technology. Due to the inter-war submarine project, Wärtsilä possessed already experience in welding, but now also other shipyards adopted it between 1946 and 1949. The relatively rapid transition from riveting to welding was accelerated by the pressures coming from the Soviet side, and paradoxically, the lack of skilled shipbuilders. When shipyards had to educate their workers in any case, they opted to invest in the future of welding instead of maintaining the technology of the past, riveting.[65]

The war reparations dominated the Finnish shipbuilding in 1944–1952. The secured orders and pricing practices during the war reparation production did not, mostly, spur for cost-efficiency, technological innovations, or investments in market research and customer relations. The newly founded or expanded shipyards were able to survive the competition only if they proved capable to adjust their production to the circumstances after the war reparation.

In addition to the calculable effect on the industrial structure, the extensive war reparation project had a recognisable impact on the practices between the state and the industry.

The Soviet demands for war reparations made the efficient and reliable ship production a matter of national security for which the state took primary responsibility in close collaboration with the private industry. It added a new urgency to domestic industrialisation placing the economic rationality and technical efficiency over everything else. As such, the project predicated a transfer of power from the state to the technocratic groups of private industrialists.[66]

The state organisation coordinating the war reparations project, Soteva, was subordinated to the Ministry of Trade and Industry. Its board of directors, which had the main responsibility of the operations, was manned with representatives from industry and business. Soteva negotiated with the Soviet representatives on the type and number of items, represented the buyer of the vessels towards the shipyards, and bid for contracts with the Finnish companies. Instead of exclusive groups of experts, the state preferred established, stable structures, and long-term planning that would later facilitate industrialisation in a coordinated fashion in cooperation between industrial and state actors.[67]

To conclude, the war reparations did not start the Finnish shipbuilding, but they had a long-standing effect on the industrial structure and the Finnish national style of administration. It also ushered in the bilateral trade with the Soviet Union.

To that end, Prime Minister Kekkonen gave a speech on radio to mark the end of the war reparation project in September 1952:

> As the age of the war reparations no comes to the end, it would be most useless and unwise to complain about how hard it was, feeling pity for ourselves. Even though the war reparations was a quite heavy burden for our country, it has had many positive outcomes to our future economy. The war reparation production has developed to a great degree those sectors in our economy that have previously been neglected. In particular, the shipbuilding industry […]. On the final day of the war reparations, we need to look also and foremost to the future. We have to secure the employment in the industry built on the foundation of the war reparations. This will be best done by maintaining close and confidential trade relationship with the Soviet Union, that knows our products and trusts in our capacity to deliver. If we can manage our Soviet trade well, the eight lean years will be followed by eight years of abundance.[68]

This narrative transmutation of the war reparations from the Soviet diktat into Finnish industrial feat was historically inaccurate but therapeutic for the national understanding: an economic victory in defence after the defeat in the military battle. As such, it laid a foundation for the peaceful co-existence that contrived to build a bridge between the wartime hostilities and the mutually beneficial Finnish–Soviet relations.

## The foundations for the Cold War shipbuilding

On November 27, 1954, a red flag with sickle and hammer flew alongside the blue-white cross over Helsinki Hietalahti Shipyard. It was a day of celebration for Wärtsilä Corporation. Not only it launched its largest export product thus far, the icebreaker *Kapitan Voronin*, but sent its sistership, *Kapitan Belousov*, to a test voyage while also laying the keel for the third ship of the class, *Kapitan Melehov*. These three vessels presented the state-of-the-art Baltic icebreakers with their 10,500-horsepower diesel-electric engines and two bow propellers. Yet, the international press was more interested in the prestigious guests than the technical finesse. The buyer of all three icebreakers was the Soviet Union. The wife of the Soviet Ambassador in Helsinki acted as the godmother of the icebreaker, and the naming ceremony was witnessed by a high-ranking delegation led by the Minister of Foreign Trade, Anastas Mikoyan. During the following pleasure cruise, the Soviet ministers had an opportunity to enjoy refreshments and socialise with the Finnish political and economic elite, including Prime Minister Urho Kekkonen and other representatives of the Finnish government, business, and Bank of Finland.

Only ten years had passed after the Moscow armistice. That decade had been decisive as a transition from the war to the Cold War in Europe in general and in the Finnish shipbuilding industry in specific. The Finnish shipbuilding industry had got inextricably interwoven into the Finnish–Soviet relations with complex political and economic ties. Before making progress to the Cold War shipbuilding, I will use this as an opportunity to conclude the main elements that composed the point of departure for the later development.

As indicated earlier, the national security constituted the first priority for Stalin and other Soviet leaders, but their targets in Finland remained relatively unspecified and took shape in the broader international context. Kimmo Rentola has described the Soviet perception of Finland during the formative period from the Peace Treaty 1947 to the first Berlin crisis 1956 as a 'land of possibilities': first, a possible People's Republic, then a possible enemy, later a possible ally. When Stalin accepted the Finnish government without communists in 1950, it marked a turning point towards a stable relationship. When the Cold War slowly froze the geopolitical set-up in Europe, the FCMA treaty fulfilled the minimum strategic needs, and the Finnish governments proved to be accommodating to Soviet interests, 'Finland, hitherto for Moscow a bottle of vodka half empty, was suddenly seen as half full'.[69]

The shipbuilding industry was one main component in the cocktail. The Soviet Union did not, in purely technical terms, need Finnish ships. Yet, as the structure of the war reparations had indicated, it did need ships. The Finnish government needed to affirm to the Soviet leaders that they were committed to the FCMA treaty. The Finnish shipyard managers, who had invested in new production facilities, needed future prospects. Under these circumstances, state-level bilateral trade negotiations became political instrument on both sides of the border to address questions of national security and welfare.

Between 1946 and 1950, the extent and structure of the trade exchange between Finland and the Soviet Union was coordinated at the state-level by yearly agreements, first with narrow barter agreements and then slightly more elaborated USD-based clearing accounts. Chapter 4 will discuss the mechanisms of bilateral trade in detail. In short, the clearing trade referred to a system, whereby the aggregate value of exports was used to settle the costs of the imports to minimise the need to transfer money across the national border.[70] The main benefit of the post-war economy was that the clearing system allowed foreign trade without foreign currencies. In comparison with multilateral trade, the main drawback with bilateral agreements was inflexibility that hampered adjustments according to changing needs.

The Finnish trade negotiators tried to balance between security and welfare; politics and trade. What would appear today as a system of rigidity and state control, came out as a promise for stability, predictability, and escape from financial restrictions in the post-war circumstances. According to Androsova, it was the Finnish side that first took the initiative to extend the original year-long trade agreement to longer protocols. The first five-year agreement for the period of 1951–1955 blueprinted a framework in which the Soviet Union exported to Finland necessary commodities, grain, fertilisers, and fuels while Finland paid back by exporting ships, machinery, and prefabricated wooden houses. The five-year cycles fit seamlessly with the Soviet economic planning schedule. Additionally, it supported the Soviet underlining objective to push the industrialisation in Finland towards the direction that would increase its economic dependency on the Soviet trade.[71]

The bilateral trade became an arena to exercise the state-level friendship that was not completely fake but always rooted in geopolitical realities. Prime Minister Kekkonen reported with details his travel to Moscow to sign the first five-year trade agreement in June 1950. The memorandum describes conversations with Soviet leaders and cites Stalin, who promised more orders to the Finnish shipbuilding industry if it proved to be a reliable supplier. Yet, much of the 25-page long report concerns not with trade but the Soviet hospitality, toasts raised for the Finnish–Soviet relations, and friendly jokes about Finnish cultural stereotypes.[72]

The bilateral trade system made shipbuilding a state-level matter, and state-level relations were often also personal. Only in these conditions, trade negotiations between such odd bedfellows like Finland and the Soviet Union could end with cigars, brandy, and a movie night in Stalin's personal theatre. This intermingling of strategic needs and economic opportunities was also clear for the *New York Times* reporter, who analysed the Soviet economic warfare in Finland in 1953: 'This is a free country where you may safely say about Malenkov what you want – though you usually don't'.[73]

In the international comparisons, Finland was still a marginal shipbuilder. In 1953, when Lloyd's Register added Finland to its statistical country reports, the Finnish merchant ship production in gross tonnage totalled 0.8% of the world's total, while neighbouring Sweden built over 9.5%.[74] The development of the global maritime industries was rapid at the time, fuelled by increasing demand for larger vessels and facilitated by new production technologies, such as welding and the use of prefabricated sections. Standardisation, automation, and economies of scale as well as the evolution of new ship types—larger and larger oil carriers and later container ships—revolutionised cargo handling, decreased transportation costs, facilitated worldwide economic transactions, and increased the global demand for new ships. Finland was not near the frontline of this development. The Finnish shipyards were important to the Soviet Union not because of their technological superiority but because the Cold War context made them a convenient compromise in political, economic, and technical terms.

An external factor that leveraged Finnish competitiveness in the Soviet market was the Coordinating Committee for Multilateral Export Controls (CoCom). NATO countries established it as an economic extension of the military cooperation 1949–1950 with the aim to control the flow of strategic technological assets to communist countries.[75] The European neutral countries officially remained outside the embargo but were gradually incorporated into the export control system. Sweden and Austria agreed to follow CoCom regulations while keeping this cooperation in secret to protect their non-aligned status.[76] Finland avoided all signs of formal cooperation but maintained *de facto* state control over technologies exported to socialist countries. The Finnish requirements for export licences in the Soviet trade were justified by the need to balance the bilateral trade, but the system satisfied the minimum strategic needs of the Americans.[77]

In the early phase of the Cold War, the CoCom restrictions boosted rather than restricted the Finnish competitiveness in the Soviet markets by reducing the number of Western competitors.[78] While Finland would not even dream of exporting weapons to the Soviet Union, dual-use technologies were more open to interpretations. Particularly controversial was the Finnish exports of non-military but potentially strategic equipment such as cables, fast cargo ships, and icebreakers.[79]

Finland's standard answer to the Western observers complaining about too large ship export to the Soviet Union, as well as to the Soviet negotiators complaining of too small number of ships, was that in Finland, the government had no legal ways to dictate private companies. That was a convenient lie. The wartime and the post-war situation had established circumstances where the state actors had a habit and means to interfere in business if that was of national interest. For example in 1952, the Finnish Ministry of Foreign

Affairs decreed that a Finnish shipping company, the Finland South American Line, should cancel its order for a large ice-strengthened diesel-driven cargo liner that Crichton-Vulcan had already launched so that the shipyard could sell the vessel to the Soviet Union instead. This cargo ship, *Arkangelsk*, became eventually the first of a series of 22 similar vessels and world-famous in 1962–1963 when it carried nuclear warheads between the Soviet Union and Cuba.[80] Like *Arkangelsk*, also the Finnish Cold War trade policy operated in the grey areas between war and peace.

The United States and its Western allies were not pleased with the Finnish shipyards exporting to the Soviet Union.[81] Even when the ships themselves were made for purely commercial use, the ship import contributed to the Soviet military production through saving shipbuilding capacity for naval vessels.[82] Yet, the US was also aware of the serious harm to the Finnish economy caused by Western sanctions that would eventually put the Finnish social stability and democratic development at risk. That was not in accord with the US National Security Council policy 'to avoid any steps which would threaten the delicate balance of Finnish–Soviet relations and call forth drastic Soviet measures inimical to Finnish independence'.[83]

The US intelligence further estimated that similar concern over the Finnish neutrality in the buffer zone between east and west limited also the Soviet willingness to exploit extensive economic pressure on Finland:

> The USSR probably realizes that any more direct economic pressure on Finland, which the Finns deem inimical to Finnish national interest, is likely to result in a net political loss for the USSR and the Finnish Communist Party. It would serve not only to revive to its fullest extent the bitterness felt by most non-Communist Finns towards the USSR but also to ruin the much advertised Soviet picture of friendly coexistence between the Communist giant and its small capitalist neighbor.[84]

In addition to the geopolitical aspects in the Finnish–Soviet economic relations, it is also important to locate the post-war Finnish shipbuilding in its broader domestic and international context.

First, the post-war expansion of the Finnish shipbuilding industry was part of an overall social transformation from a backward agrarian country into a modern industrial country. The rate at which Finland caught up with Western Europe was particularly high from the post-war years until the 1970s oil crisis. The industrial production surpassed agricultural production in the post-war years and held its share of the Finnish GDP steadily between 30% and 40%.[85]

After the war, the countryside could no longer offer a livelihood to the growing population. In January 1945, J. K. Paasikivi, Prime Minister at that time, commented on Finnish national urgencies in his diary '[w]e undoubtedly need more, and *many* more fields, but no more agrarian workers. We need *industry* and *industrial workers* more'.[86] Ten years later, Industrial Advisory

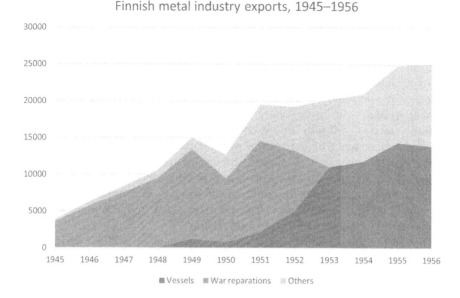

*Figure 2.2* Exports of Finnish metal industry products 1945–1956 (m. FIM). Data: Suomen Metalliteollisuusliitto, *Vuosikirja 1956*, 36.

Board articulated same priorities in its report to the Finnish government: 'the aim has to be to create such occupations in which the productivity of labour is so high that it will provide sufficient income and living standards'. These new jobs were to be found in industrial production.[87]

Industrialisation was a national project on which Finland's future as a modern and independent state depended. As a committee report in 1950 articulated, 'in the era of technology, the level of engineering industry corresponds directly to the level of culture and welfare of the nation'.[88]

The forestry-based exports of paper and pulp remained the single most important sector of the Finnish economy, but industrial design and metal engineering evolved into an alternative way to construct an internationally distinct national image as a modern sovereign country.[89] Whereas the automatisation of forestry was about to decrease the labour input, the modern metal engineering industry was still based on a labour-intensive production. While the large paper and pulp factories had to be located near the raw material sources, the metal manufacturing was concentrated on the densely populated areas of Southern Finland.[90]

The increasing number of urban shipyard workers was interconnected to the questions of national security and welfare. The labour at the shipyards was well-organised and eager to react to both organisational and political changes. Especially, Wärtsilä Turku Shipyard had an active role in determining the development of Finnish labour relations.[91] As director Wahlforss reminded President Paasikivi in 1955, the full employment at the shipyards contributed to social stability: 'Metal workers are *intelligentsia* among the workers. They did the revolution in Russia in 1917 and they are always the first'. Russian trade was, as Wahlforss underlined, of critical importance in providing employment and therefore also stability at the shipyards.[92]

In its original wartime plans, the Soviet Union had high hopes that the growing industrial working class in Finland would understand its historical role as a revolutionary force, but it overestimated the lure of communism among workers who had recently returned from the war and now enjoyed monthly salary.[93] Finnish and Western accounts estimated that the urban unemployment was a bigger risk for social stability than the growing group of politically active, but employed, shipyard workers. While Western observers were worried that the post-war economic decline would push the Finnish working class towards communism, Moscow feared that a prolonged recession would support conservative politicians and strengthen anti-Soviet undercurrents among the Finnish political elite.[94]

Due to the interlinked national security and national welfare considerations in the Finnish–Soviet trade, the high share of ships was simultaneously an economic asset and political risk (Figure 2.2). According to an unofficial rule of thumb, the Soviet share of the Finnish foreign trade should not exceed one-fifth to avoid economic dependency.[95]

As the foreign trade statistics below illustrate (Figure 2.3), the vast majority of the Finnish foreign trade was conducted with Western countries, especially the United Kingdom, Sweden, and West Germany. The trade with the Soviet Union alone did not translate the Finnish shipbuilding into a potential instrument in Cold War diplomacy. The risk lay with the trade structure. In the course of the 1950s, approximately one-third of the Finnish exports to the Soviet Union consisted of ships. The rapid post-war expansion of the Finnish Cold War shipbuilding from 1951 to 1955 took place at the time when Finnish shipyards were kept employed almost entirely by Soviet orders and seemingly unable to get contracts from elsewhere.

The cluster effect of the Soviet ship trade spread beyond the shipyards when Finnish companies launched domestic production of machinery and components that had previously been imported from Western countries. In part, this was motivated by the requirement for high domestic content in the goods sold to the Soviet Union: only one-fourth of an exported ship could be of foreign origin.

The main engines constituted a critical bottleneck that was frequently addressed in the Finnish–Soviet negotiations. Although marine engines were available in the Western market, the Finnish shipyard needed special permission from the Bank of Finland to make the large foreign currency procurements.[96] The Crichton-Vulcan shipyard in Turku had previously produced diesel engines in its machine shop based on foreign licences. In the 1950s, Wärtsilä increased the engine production and concentrated it on Wärtsilä Vaasa factory while gradually switching from foreign licences to own design over the course of the 1960s.[97]

Finnish imports by Country of Origin (%), 1945–1992

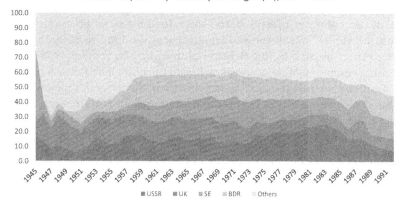

Finnish exports by country of destination (%), 1944–1992

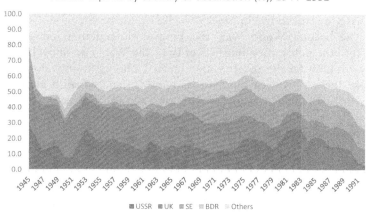

*Figure 2.3*  Finnish export and import trade with the Soviet Union, the United Kingdom, Sweden (SE), and West Germany (BDR). Imports by countries of
origin, exports by countries of destination, shares of total imports and
exports. Data: Finnish Custom.

At the same time, this development from Western imports to Finnish
production resonated with the Soviet post-war plans to decrease Western
connections in Finland. One argument for the Soviets to support Finnish
domestic machine building was that it would make it more difficult for
Finland to decline the Soviet orders using the Western trade restrictions as
an excuse.[98] Even Stalin took upon himself to propose the establishment of
domestic steel industry in Finland: 'How can you protect your country without steel production? [...] Foreign steel is cold/blunt steel'.[99]

To sum up, the Soviet merchant marines did not need the Finnish
shipbuilding industry to produce merchant tonnage in large quantities. With

the exception of the very beginning of the Cold War, it could buy those vessels from elsewhere at cheaper price. Instead, the Finnish shipyards became important in producing tailor-made vessels that were too strategic for CoCom countries to export, too specialised for serial production at the largest shipyards, but not too military to harm the Finnish neutrality. This setting brings us back to the Helsinki Shipyard in November 1954 and the launching ceremony of the icebreaker *Kapitan Voronin*. The Finnish ministers and businessmen rubbing shoulders with their Soviet colleagues were not unaware of the potential of economic warfare included in the high share of Soviet trade. Yet, their smiles were hardly completely fake. Director Wahlforss would have even a broader smile on his face when Mikoyan confirmed a new order for a larger polar icebreaker after the same visit.

After the celebration at the shipyard, Mikoyan had an audience with President Paasikivi during which he expressed his hope that the trade would be only a beginning for closer cooperation. Paasikivi replied by citing Stalin: 'Finland and the Soviet Union can nothing to their geographical location. [The geopolitical facts] have to be acknowledged and accepted and our nations have to learn to live in peace'.[100]

After the Second World War, the Finnish shipbuilding industry was moored into the politics and business of the Cold War. The ships the Finnish shipyards built for the Soviet Union created a bridge from war to peace, they broke the ice between capitalist businessmen and socialists customers, and they carried Finland towards an industrial and urban society. Chapter 3 examines the technopolitics of shipbuilding when it made itself an actor in the international relations.

## Notes

1 For a comprehensive introduction to the history of Finland, Jussila et al., *From Grand Duchy to Modern State*, 1999.
2 Kaukiainen, *A History of Finnish Shipping*, 1993; Kaukiainen, *Ulos Maailmaan! Suomalaisen merenkulun historia*, 2008, 9–10.
3 Kaukiainen, *Ulos maailmaan!*, 2008, 60–66; 76–77; 106; 116; 158; 172–177.
4 Kaukiainen, *A History of Finnish shipping*, 1993, 77–85; 97–110; Kaukiainen, "The Transition from Sail to Steam in Finnish Shipping, 1850–1914," 2004.
5 Ferreiro, *Bridging the Seas*, 2019, 78–92.
6 Ferreiro, *Bridging the Seas*, 2019, 80.
7 Myllylä, "Konepajat ennen itsenäisyyden aikaa," 1994, 20–35; Meronen, "Shipbuilding and Engineering Workshops in Turku 1800–1880," 2018, 28–73; Kaukiainen, *Ulos Maailmaan!*, 2008, 158.
8 Kaukiainen, *Ulos maailmaan!*, 2008, 289–295.
9 Matala & Sahari, *Small Nation, Big Ships*, 2017, 225; 226–227.
10 Slaven, *British Shipbuilding 1500–2010*, 2013, 46–47.
11 The shipyard had several names including Hietalahden laivatelakka, Sandvikens Skeppsdocka. Later, it became Wärtsilä Helsinki Shipyard. In 2018, it is known as the Arctec Helsinki Shipyard. In this thesis, when referring to the events after

the Second World War, the shipyard is referred as Wärtsilä Helsinki Shipyard or simply as Helsinki Shipyard. The other shipyards located in Helsinki in Katajanokka, Suomenlinna, and Vuosaari are referred by those names.

12 von Knorring, *Aurajoen veistämöt ja telakat*, 1995, 43–51.
13 Myllylä, "Venäjän laivatilaukset," 1994; Sahari, *Valtio ja suurteollisuuden synty*, 2018, 56–57.
14 Sahari, *Valtio ja suurteollisuuden synty*, 2018, 57–58; 61–62; 65.
15 Kaukiainen, *Ulos maailmaan!* 2008, 358–358; Sahari, *Valtio ja suurteollisuuden synty*, 2018, 54; 66–67; 72–73.
16 Johnman & Murphy, *Scott Lithgow: Deja vu All Over Again!* 2005.
17 Fukasaku, *Technology and Industrial Growth in Pre-war Japan*, 1992; Davies, *Japanese Shipping and Shipbuilding in the Twentieth Century*, 2009, 101.
18 Olsson, "Big business in Sweden," 1995, 310–338; Johansen, "International søfart mellen verdenskrisen og 1960'ernes højkonjunktur," 2016, 267–291.
19 Andersen, "Producing Producers: Shippers, Shipyards and the Cooperative Infrastructure of the Norwegian Maritime Complex since 1850," 1997; Christensen, "Skibsbygning og værftsanlæg – utviklingen af et tankskibsværft," 2016.
20 Kaukiainen, *Ulos maailmaan!* 2008, 363–371.
21 Sahari, "Saving the Finnish Shipbuilding Industry," 2018, 77–80; 136; Sahari, *Valtio ja suurteollisuuden synty*, 2018, 90–94; 123–126; 130.
22 Technology transfer from Germany to Finland was particularly important in the development of the diesel-electric submarines. This was interwoven with a camouflaged German operation that used Finland as a base for R&D activities to bypass restrictions against submarines set by the Versailles treaty. Forsén et al., *Saksan ja Suomen salainen sukellusveneyhteistyö*, 1999. The Swedish diesel-electric icebreaker Ymer served as an example for the Finnish icebreaker builders in the design of Sisu. Sahari, *Valtio ja suurteollisuuden synty*, 2018, 151–152.
23 The fortress island in the Helsinki archipelago, known as Sveaborg in Swedish, and as Viaborg until 1918.
24 Björklund, *Valmet*, 1990, 13–16.
25 von Knorring, *Aurajoen veistämöt ja telakat*, 1995, 106–107.
26 For historical reviews on pre-Second World War shipbuilding in Hietalahti and Turku, see *Osakeyhtiö Hietalahden sulkutelakka ja konepaja*, 1935; Haavikko, *Wärtsilä 1934–1984*, 1984; von Knorring, *Aurajoen veistämöt ja telakat*, 1995; Id & Peter, *Innovation and Specialisation*, 2017, 11–17.
27 von Knorring, *Aurajoen veistämöt ja telakat*, 1995, 106–107.
28 Sahari, *Valtio ja suurteollisuuden synty*, 2018, 72–73.
29 Treaty of Non-Aggression between Germany and the Union of Soviet Socialist Republics, August 23, 1939.
30 Judt, *Postwar. A History of Europe Since 1945*, 2010, 118–121.
31 Rentola, "From Half-Adversary to Half-Ally," 2000, 75–102; Androsova, "Economic Interest in Soviet Post-war Policy on Finland," 2011, 33–48; Androsova, "Kauppapolitiikka Suomen ja Neuvostoliiton suhteissa vuoden 1944 jälkeen," 2002, 152–158; Androsova, "Economic Interests in Soviet-Finnish relations," 2007.
32 Rentola, *Niin kylmää että polttaa*, 1997; Rentola, "Great Britain and the Soviet Threat in Finland," 2012, 171–184.
33 Androsova, "Economic Interest in Soviet Post-war Policy in Finland," 2011, 33–34.
34 Andorosova, "Kauppapolitiikka Suomen ja Neuvostoliiton suhteissa," 2002, 155.
35 Andorosova, "Kauppapolitiikka Suomen ja Neuvostoliiton suhteissa," 2002, 153–155.
36 Laurila, *Finnish-Soviet Clearing Trade and Payment System*, 1995, 60.

37  The Treaty of Commerce between the Republic of Finland and the Union of Soviet Socialistic Republics, SopS 13/1948; Laurila, *Finnish-Soviet Clearing Trade and Payment System*, 1995, 60; Hjerppe, "Finland's Foreign Trade and Trade Policy in the 20th Century," 1993, 69.

38  Rainio-Niemi, "Cold War Neutrality in Europe," 2017, 21. On Finland as a part of the Soviet security system, Kansikas, "Dismantling the Soviet Security System," 2017.

39  Hentilä, "Living Next Door to the Bear," 1998, 130; Kähönen, "Veteen piirretty viiva," 2002, 163; Jakobson, *Finland in the New Europe*, 1998. On policy of neutrality: Rainio-Niemi, *The Ideological Cold War*, 2014; Hanhimäki, "Non-aligned to What?" 2016, 31–46.

40  Agreement on Friendship, Cooperation and Mutual Assistance (FCMA), SopS 17/1948.

41  25.3.1954 in *J. K. Paasikiven Päiväkirjat 1944–1956* II, 1986.

42  Majander, "The Limits of Sovereignty, Finland and the Question of the Marshall Plan in 1947," 1994, 306–326; McKenzie, "GATT and the Cold War," 2008.

43  Aunesluoma, *Vapaakaupan tiellä*, 2011, 82.

44  15.1.1953 in J. K. Paasikivi's diaries. *J.K. Paasikiven Päiväkirjat 1944–1956* II, 1986, 324.

45  In 1938 prices, equivalent USD5.45 billion in 2019.

46  Armistice Agreement between the Union of Soviet Socialist Republics and the United Kingdom of Great Britain and Northern Ireland, on the one hand, and Finland on the other, 1944.

47  Sahari, *Valtio ja Suurteollisuuden synty*, 2018; Aunesluoma, *Vapaakaupan tiellä*, 2011, 95–98; 110–111; Mitrunen, "Essays on the Political Economy of Development," 2019, 14–15.

48  Heikkinen, "Sotakorvaukset ja Suomen kansantalous," 2014, 103–106; Harki, *Sotakorvausten Aika*, 1971, 341.

49  Mitrunen, "Essays on the Political Economy of Development," 2019, 22.

50  Horn, "Varustamoelinkeino ja telakkateollisuus – kaksi elinkeinoa, yhteiset edut," 1970, 24; 28; *Kauppa ja kansojen etu*, 1987, 27.

51  Sipilä, "Laivasarjoista erikoisaluksiin," 1994, 67; Sipilä, "Sotakorvausalukset ja uudistuvat telakat," 1994, 66; Eerola, *Kun rauta kelluu*, 2017, 32–33; Uola, *Hollming 1945-2000*, 2001, 29–31; Harki, *Sotakorvausten aika*, 1972, 342; Viita, *Kapitalismin ja sosialismin puristuksessa*, 2006, 132.

52  "Finland Expands her Shipbuilding while Paying reparations to Russia", *The New York Times*, 7.5.1949.

53  Don Maclean, "Need a Finnish icebreaker?" *Herald Journal* 3.9.1965.

54  Fellman, "Suomen sotakorvaukset ja metalliteollisuus," 1996, 429; Jensen-Eriksen, "Telakkateollisuus ja kylmä sota," 2014, 212–247; 97–98; Hjerppe, "Finland's Foreign Trade and Trade Policy in the Twentieth Century," 1993, 68.

55  The first complete re-evaluation on the war reparations and the Finnish shipbuilding based on archival research, Sahari, *Valtio ja suurteollisuuden synty*, 2018.

56  Sahari, *Valtio ja suurteollisuuden synty*, 2018, 206.

57  Sahari, *Valtio ja suurteollisuuden synty*, 2018, 165; 167; 196; 284.

58  Harki, *Sotakorvausten aika*, 1971, 124; 146–149.

59  Björklund, *Valmet*, 1990, 154–155.

60  Sahari, *Valtio ja suurteollisuuden synty*, 2018, 284; 307; 315.

61  Uola, *Meidän isä on töissä telakalla*, 1996, 72–73.

62  Sahari, *Valtio ja suurteollisuuden synty*, 2018, 199; 289.

63  On the founding of LATE, see Lundelin, *Laivanrakentajana vuosina 1945–1988*, 1998, 14–27.

Before the Cold War shipbuilding 45

64 Wahlqvist, *Sydämellä rakennetut seililaivat*, 2011, 50–51; Uola, *Hollming 1945–2000*, 2001.
65 Teräs, "From War Reparations to Luxury Cruise Liners," 2017, 200–205; Sahari, *Valtio ja suurteollisuuden synty*, 2018, 258; Harki, *Sotakorvausten aika*, 1971, 129; 133.
66 Michelsen, "Sotakorvaukset: Suuren teollisen projektin anatomia," 2014, 195–200; See also Hughes, *Rescuing Prometheus*, 1998, 6–9.
67 Sahari, *Valtio ja suurteollisuuden synty*, 2018.
68 Kekkonen, Speech on the radio, 19.9.1952. http://www.doria.fi/handle/10024/7487.
69 Rentola, "From Half-Adversary to Half-Ally," 2000, 75; 77–78; Rentola, *Niin kylmää että polttaa*, 1997.
70 Laurila, *Finnish-Soviet Clearing Trade and Payment System*, 1995, 17.
71 Androsova, "Kauppapolitiikka Suomen ja Neuvostoliiton suhteissa," 2002, 155; 157.
72 Prime Minister Kekkonen's trip to Moscow, June 1950, f. 22/1, UKA.
73 Clausen, *New York Times*, November 15, 1953.
74 Lloyd's Register, *Shipbuilding Returns*. Merchant ships launched 1953, over 100 tons and more.
75 Jensen-Eriksen, "CoCom and Neutrality," 2010; Autio-Sarasmo, "Technological Modernisation in the Soviet Union and Post-Soviet Russia," 2016, 80.
76 Hanson, "The Soviet Union's Acquisition of Western Technology after Stalin," 2010, 19; Jensen-Eriksen, "CoCom and Neutrality," 2010, 51.
77 Jensen-Eriksen, "CoCom and Neutrality," 2010, 50; 54.
78 Jensen-Eriksen, "CoCom and Neutrality," 2010, 59.
79 Jensen-Eriksen, "CoCom and Neutrality," 2010, 49–50; Jensen-Eriksen, "Telakkateollisuus ja kylmä sota," 2014, 214; Uola, *Meidän isä on töissä telakalla*, 1996, 255–256.
80 Id & Peter, *Innovation and Specialisation*, 2017, 29–30; Jensen-Eriksen, "Telakkateollisuus ja kylmä sota," 2014, 212.
81 Jensen-Eriksen, "CoCom and Neutrality," 2010, 53.
82 CIA/RR PR-60, Western European shipbuilding for the Soviet bloc, 1954. CIA Electronic Reading Room. https://www.cia.gov/readingroom.
83 PM No. 414, Progress Report by the Under Secretary of State (Smith) on the Implementation of NSC 121S/S–NSC files, lot 63 D 351, NSC 121 Series. https://history.state.gov/.
84 CIA/RR IM 59-2, Recent trends in Finnish-Soviet trade, 1959. CIA Electronic Reading Room. https://www.cia.gov/readingroom.
85 Hjerppe & Jalava, "Economic Growth and Structural Change," 2006, 33–64.
86 Italics original. 10.1.1945 in *J. K. Paasikiven Päiväkirja II*, 1944–1956.
87 *Teollisuusneuvottelukunnan mietintö* [Industrial Advisory Board committee report], 1959, 13.
88 Committee report on developing metal industry and maintaining full-employment, 1951, f. 21/81, UKA.
89 Matala & Sahari, "Small Nation, Big Ships," 2017; Myllyntaus, "Design in Building an Industrial Identity," 2010.
90 Industrial Advisory Board committee report 1959, 67–68.
91 Teräs, "From War Reparations to Luxury Cruise Liners," 2017, 196; 208.
92 *J. K. Paasikiven Päiväkirjat II: 1944–1956*, 1986, 919–929.
93 Androsova, "Kauppapolitiikka Suomen ja Neuvostoliiton suhteissa," 2002, 157.
94 Kähönen, "Veteen piirretty viiva," 2002, 161.
95 Androsova, "Kauppapolitiikka Suomen ja Neuvostoliiton suhteissa," 2002, 157–158.

96 Meeting between Consul General G. Palmroth and Soviet commercial representative Sosunov 28.7.1952; Export to the Soviet Union 30.7.1952; Telegram
   200/199 from Palmroth to Ministry of Foreign affairs (Formin) 18.9.1952; Telegram from Palmroth to Formin 3.9.1952; Telegram 152 25.8.1952 from Ingman
   to Formin 26.8.1952; Message from Palmroth to Formin 22.8.1952; Message
   from Palmroth to Formin 21.8.1952; Meeting on 3.9.1952; f. 106, 58 B1, UMA.
97 Haavikko, *Wärtsilä 1934–1984*, 1984, 104–107.
98 Androsova, "Kauppapolitiikka Suomen ja Neuvostoliiton suhteissa," 2002, 158.
99 Prime Minister Kekkonen's trip to Moscow, June 1950, f. 22/1, UKA.
100 *J. K. Paasikiven Päiväkirjat II: 1944–1956*, 867–869.

# 3 Technology diplomacy

## Civilian ships carrying political weight and state leaders

The Finnish Industrial Advisory Board concluded in 1959 that in trade and business 'the decisions should usually be made by company managers [without state intervention]'. However, the report added that 'there are certain occasions when we have to give, besides the commercial factors, a decisive role to general points of views and the Finnish economy as a whole'.[1] The committee report did not elaborate what the 'certain occasions' might be, but in the Finnish Cold War vocabulary, the unspecified general factors usually meant geopolitical considerations, namely the Soviet Union.

The separation between the state politics and the allegedly apolitical business was an essential performance in the Finnish Cold War foreign affairs. It maintained a façade of neutrality, while the industrial affairs got intermingled with the politics of East-West technology transfer. At the same time, the high political actors got deliberately and proudly involved in the shipbuilding business. In a small country, close personal networks within the elite facilitated informal communications and consensus-oriented practices. The strong vertical connections had their roots in the historical co-evolution of the state institutions and big business in Finland, and they had been further reinforced during the war economy and war reparations.[2]

This chapter starts our journey to the Finnish shipbuilding with four cases on ship projects that became objects of foreign relations: the successful entrance to the Soviet arctic icebreaker business, the unsuccessful efforts to sell icebreakers to the United States, the controversy over deep-sea submersible vessels, and the Finnish–Soviet nuclear icebreaker project that was utmost successful until it was no more. In addition to the mechanisms of the political mediation, we need to understand its reasons: the rationales for the high-ranking politicians for personal engagement in export promotion; the impetus for a private shipyard to provide vessels to be used as political instruments.

Icebreakers and deep-sea submersibles are oddities in global ship production. In the Cold War East-West trade, nuclear technology, submarines, and icebreakers were subject to increased scrutiny, which was closely interwoven with questions of national security and prestige. Cases of unique products like these provide both methodological risks and rewards. Technological exceptionalism made the projects more strategic, more valuable, and more controversial than the bulk of the Finnish shipbuilding. The exceptionalism made them appear on the desks of state leaders, and it made them instruments in state-level strategic considerations as well as in personal political aspirations.

All the ships in this chapter were non-military. At most, they navigated the passage of dual-use technologies between strategic and civilian technologies. Exactly the characteristic of being fuzzy political objects make them appropriate points of departure to study the nuances of the Cold War technopolitics. Unlike the illustrious Cold War ships such as the Soviet deathly nuclear submarines and the US gigantic aircraft carriers, these Finnish projects were not overshadowed by their military capacities. Instead, they carried a diverse mixture of Cold War technopolitics, the state needs for national security, national prestige, and national welfare. As such, they demonstrate the Cold War technopolitics of civilian ships in a small neutral country as it was complex, controversial, strongly related to personal relations, and sometimes a bit ridiculous.

### Entrance to the Soviet Arctic: building business relations on ice, 1952–1975

Images of President Kekkonen sitting and singing with foreign political leaders, drinking vodka, and selling Finnish icebreakers are part of the popular imaginary of the Finnish–Soviet ship business. The picture is not without historical justifications. There is no irony in the occasions when Kekkonen has been titled as the 'Master of the Eastern trade'.[3] Yet, the active role of the leading politicians in Finnish Cold War ship trade opens up questions on the practices, scale, and rationales of the personal engagement of high political figures. Without scrutiny, the entertaining hero stories remain shallow caricatures.

This section examines the use of political networks through the specialisation of Wärtsilä Helsinki Shipyard in Arctic maritime technology. Big, public, and powerful as the icebreakers were, they were objects of personal and political ambitions. During the war reparations, Finland had built the types of ships the Soviet Union needed the most and trusted the Finnish shipyards to deliver. After the socialist countries had rebuilt their shipyard capacity and Western embargo on technology trade had relaxed, the Soviet Union was able to satisfy its need for standard tonnage elsewhere and concentrate orders for certain special purpose vessels on the Finnish yards.

In effect, Finnish shipyards became an extension to the socialist division of labour. Technological competence, experience, and business relations determined what kind of a niche a Finnish shipyard could occupy in the Soviet economic planning. Wärtsilä Helsinki Shipyard wanted to be an icebreaker builder.

Inspiration for Wärtsilä's ice-oriented strategy had come from domestic demand. Winter navigation was an imperative in a country where national welfare and economic sovereignty relied on the seaborne exports of paper and pulp to Western markets but where all ports and critical sea routes froze over in winter. The most powerful ships of the Finnish pre-war icebreaker fleet had been ceded to the Soviet Union as a part of war reparations. The remaining old steam icebreakers had been built in the 19th century and were able to provide little more than moral support for the modern cargo ships.[4]

In this context, the first post-war state icebreaker was as important and big milestone as it possibly could be in the small country. The state-icebreaker project mustered the best available expertise and experience in icebreaker design and construction, and brought it to Wärtsilä Helsinki Shipyard. *Voima* ('Force') was a game changer when it was completed in 1954. It was the biggest and most powerful of the Baltic icebreakers with its diesel-electric power transmission for 10,500 shp and symmetric four-propeller configuration that improved the manoeuvrability and efficiency when the icebreaker proceeded through the brash ice.[5]

Successful design and construct of such a vessel required special knowledge and expertise that was significantly different from the open-water navigation. To maintain an extensive design bureau not directly employed in production, and to support its specialisation in the marginal niche of naval architecture, the Baltic Sea market was too limited. The Soviet Arctic, instead, seemed to provide endless opportunities.[6]

When *Voima* was still under construction at the shipyard, Wärtsilä started its efforts to include similar icebreakers to the Soviet ship orders from Finland. Wilhelm Wahlforss (1891–1969), director of Wärtsilä, presented the Voima project to his contacts in Moscow, but without much success. The Soviet administration was not interested in the rather small icebreaker and was sceptical about the endurance of the bow-propellers in the heavy ice conditions in the Soviet Arctic. Instead of buying expensive, sophisticated, and strategically important vessels from a Finnish yard, which most important technical reference was still uncompleted, they would have preferred building tailor-made polar icebreakers domestically.[7]

Director Wahlforss, described as Finland's 'biggest capitalist and a true friend of the Soviet Union,' had experience of working with both the Finnish and Soviet states.[8] He understood the value of personal contacts when trying the entrance into the new niche market without pre-existing customer relations or completed prototypes. Urho Kekkonen, who was Prime Minister at the time, provided that kind of a connection.

Personally, Wahlforss disliked Kekkonen and did not hesitate to speak against his growing dominance over Finnish–Soviet relations. Yet, the mutual interests in icebreakers created a working relationship between the two headstrong directors. With Kekkonen's assistance, Wahlfross managed to arrange a high-ranking Soviet representative to visit the Wärtsilä ship dock and to push Wärtsilä's icebreaker design forward in the Soviet state planning administration. Kekkonen, on his behalf, was running for president and needed all the political and monetary support he could get from the industrial elite.[9]

While the details of the interaction were not documented, the material results of this lobby campaign were concrete. Wärtsilä managed to contract for the first Voima-class icebreaker with the Soviet Union and did that even before the completion of *Voima*. The construction of the first Soviet icebreaker started in 1952, but Aaro Sahari has estimated that the contracts were confirmed even before the intergovernmental trade negotiations had started in 1951.[10]

The contracts for altogether three Baltic icebreakers opened the route to proceed in the Soviet markets by providing tangible proofs of technological competence and creating personal contacts with the Soviet foreign trade circles. When the Soviet statesman Anastas Mikoyan came to Finland in 1954 to participate in the launching ceremony of the *Kapitan Belousov*, it gave Wahlforss a change to start negotiations for larger arctic icebreakers.[11] The contracts for the two first polar icebreakers, *Moskva* and *Leningrad*, were confirmed in 1956. Eventually, the Moskva class came to consist of five polar icebreakers almost twice as strong as *Voima* with 22,000 shp and design suitable for breaking the thick polar ice.

As expensive and impressive orders, icebreakers evolved into the showcases of the Finnish–Soviet trade, which was noted in the Western newspapers. Icebreakers depicted the national significance of shipbuilding in terms of employment and prestige better than the hundreds of barges and tugs that were also sold to the Soviet Union. They stood visually out in the townscape; their names were recognisable for the public. In 1966, *Moskva* even received the highest civilian decoration in the USSR, Order of Lenin, for her service on the Northern Sea Route.

Because of their visible role as flagships of the Finnish–Soviet trade, icebreakers became instruments not only to project good business relations but also to demonstrate dissatisfaction during diplomatic crises. In 1958, the 'Night Frost Crisis' sparked off when the USSR protested against a particular formation of a Finnish government by freezing the ongoing trade negotiations.[12] President Kekkonen anticipated in his diary that the Soviet Union would underline its message by cancelling the participation of Anastas Mikoyan to the ceremonial delivery of Wärtsilä's icebreaker.[13] The statesman's visit to a shipyard had no direct economic nor technological impact but freezing out ship trade was a strong diplomatic signal that everyone involved understood.[14]

On another instance in 1961, Kekkonen conjectured that Kremlin might cancel a contract for an ongoing icebreaker project and send Wärtsilä's representatives home from Moscow to display its support for Kekkonen in the upcoming presidential elections against a liberal-minded anti-Kekkonen campaign in which Wahlforss had an active role.[15]

Despite the successful cooperation in the early 1950s, the relationship between Kekkonen and Wahlforss remained cold. Wahlforss retired from Wärtsilä's operational management in 1961 at the age of 70 even though he controlled Wärtsilä's Soviet trade until his death in 1969. Wahlforss had a desire for Wärtsilä's shipbuilding director, Christian Landtman (1922–2019), to take over his position as the director of Wärtsilä corporate group. Landtman was a principled shipbuilder who had clearly found his calling at the technical side of the business. He gave Wahlforss credit for his competence in business while also expressed frustration about his faults in engineering. To compromise with Wahlforss regarding his career, Landtman suggested that Wärtsilä would nominate a director whose greatest expertise was not technical but political networking.

The proposal was inspired by Wärtsilä's state-owned competitor Valmet, which had recruited its director Olavi Mattila from the Foreign Trade Department (*Kauppapoliittinen osasto, KPO*) of the Ministry of Foreign Affairs in 1965. Besides being Kekkonen's old associate from his youthful career as a national-level athlete, he had held several ministerial positions. Mattila felt at home in the rarefied of Soviet trade.

To match Valmet's choice, Tankmar Horn (1924–2018) was an ideal candidate for Wärtsilä. Horn held a Master's degree in economics and business and had a successful career in the Ministry of Foreign Affairs. As a former diplomat and director of the Foreign Trade Department, he had unproblematic and close networks with the Finnish foreign policy administration and President Kekkonen. He did not hesitate to use his connections for the company's benefit.[16] Horn became Wärtsilä's deputy director in 1969, and a year later, Wärtsilä's director. 'Horn brought a new dimension to Wärtsilä', Landtman noted in his memoirs, 'he repaired our relations with the Finnish state'.[17]

An example illustrates the practices of this new relationship. In the early spring of 1970, director Horn wrote a letter to President Kekkonen describing how Helsinki Shipyard had been negotiating with the Soviets on an order of three 36,000 shp polar icebreakers over four years unable to close the deal. Technical specifications had been completed in 1968, but now the Soviets were making excuses for not returning to price negotiations. The polar icebreakers were a priority for the company. They were central to the company's technical specialisation strategy, and they also had lucrative profit margins that could be used to compensate for the company's effort to establish a position in the Western passenger ship competition. Before filling the order book with secondary orders or lowering the final offer, Horn asked President Kekkonen to find about the cards the Soviets had in their hand:

> It would be valuable to know if the Soviets are procrastinating for tactical reasons or if there are other factors hampering the negotiations. For example, would it be possible that the Soviet Union is seriously planning to pull out its offer and build these heavy-duty icebreakers domestically?[18]

Two weeks later, the overwhelmed Horn sent another letter to the president expressing his gratitude for assistance. On April 29, Wärtsilä Helsinki Shipyard confirmed the order of three polar icebreakers, namely *Yermak* (1974), *Admiral Makarov* (1975), and *Krasin* (1976). The scale of the project was impressive. The Wärtsilä-Sulzer main engines together with auxiliary engines provided

146,760 hp for the three icebreakers in total granting them the status of the strongest non-nuclear icebreaker class in the world. The contract price of 350M FIM made it the biggest single export contract in Finland at the time.[19]

The Finnish Cold War shipbuilding history is rich in similar episodes of private companies using the president or ministers as icebreakers to break through political barriers in the Soviet trade. Based on archival collections, this kind of export promotion through personal correspondence was relatively frequent from the late 1960s to the late 1970s when the position of Kekkonen as the leader of Finnish–Soviet relations reached its zenith.[20]

The orders the Finnish shipyards got from the Soviet organisations did not originate from abstract, faceless market forces of demand and supply but from the priorities of the Soviet central plans. The Soviet Union was a hierarchical planning economy with the political leaders on the top of the pyramid of power. High-ranking officials had means to influence in the economic plans and the structure of foreign trade. They had human faces. Like in any other country, Soviet Union had no resources to contract for all the technologies it needed or wanted but foreign procurements were decided based on prioritising different needs and wants. Personal relations up to the Soviet political circles provided one way to shape those priorities by adding political arguments to the commercial and technical ones.

The personal connections gave the private ship projects political impetus they needed to proceed in the Soviet planning economy; the exceptional icebreaking ships provided high-ranking politicians an opportunity to promote their career. When Wärtsilä Helsinki Shipyard commissioned its next-generation icebreaker in 1975, no one was surprised to learn that the ship was named *Urho* after Kekkonen.[21]

## Icebreaker diplomacy: friendship, delivered, 1965–1976

The icebreaker *Urho* was completed at Helsinki Shipyard in 1975. Like the icebreaker *Voima* 20 years earlier, she became the flagship of the Finnish icebreaker fleet and a showcase of Finnish technological prowess. *Urho* was the most powerful and most efficient Baltic icebreaker with 16.2 MW propulsion power, a heeling pump mechanism preventing the vessel from getting stuck in ice, a refined hull-structure cultivated through model-scale trials, and a bridge with 360-degree visibility.[22] For other technopolitical purposes, the icebreaker was also equipped with a comfortable cabinet that could accommodate high-class social gatherings. In the middle of the Cold War, the two Urhos of Finland, President and icebreaker, were ready to promote Finland in international relations.

As a democratic market economy, Finland was culturally and socially inclined to lean towards the Western world but the economic relations between Finland and the United States remained limited compared to the Finnish–Soviet trade. While Finland exported over 15% of its foreign trade to the Soviet Union, Finnish exports to the United States never exceeded 5% during the Cold War.[23] Despite the strategic location of Finland in the democratic buffer zone next to the Soviet Union, the Finnish–American relations remained rather abstract and distant.

Wärtsilä had launched marketing efforts in the United States in the mid-1960s. From the Finnish point of view, there was a natural demand for strong icebreakers in the US Great Lakes and polar regions. Yet, selling a foreign ship to a US federal organisation was an ambitious, close to unrealistic, plan not least because of American protectionist attitude and legislation. At the state level, the possibility of selling icebreakers was discussed between the Finnish Minister for Foreign Affairs Ahti Karjalainen and his American colleague Dean Rusk in 1966 but only because 'there were no other bigger open political and economic issues'.[24]

Wärtsilä decided to try an alternative route to the American waters and formed a consortium with American steel and manufacturing companies. The consortium proposed the US government to replace the old USCG icebreakers with four 'best possible' icebreakers. Two first icebreakers would be built in Helsinki, two latter in the United States under Finnish supervision so that the total share of American work would be within the provision of the Buy American Act.[25]

Wärtsilä sought assistance from the diplomatic circles. Finnish Ambassador Olavi Munkki got actively involved in the project. He created connections for the company in Washington and participated in the negotiations with the Coast Guard, congressmen, and representatives from the Department of State and Department of Transportation. He also scheduled his communication with the American political elite so that it was coincidental with the press release of Wärtsilä's contract for the 36,000 hp icebreaker to the USSR. By so doing, the Finns tried to underline the weakness of the American Wind-class icebreakers, which had engine power of only 10,000 hp, and to spark competitive spirit in comparison to the Soviet fleet.[26]

The technical argument for the cooperation project was that it would enable the USCG to get more advanced vessels faster and cheaper than what would be possible when building them domestically starting from scratch. The proposed project was essentially about technology transfer from Finland to the United States. Technological assistance from a peripheric Finland to the United States, which had used to be the centre of technological development, was a delicate question.[27] Without high-level political support, the project failed to gain the necessary momentum to proceed.

In 1975, Helsinki hosted the historical Conference on Security and Cooperation in Europe (CSCE, *Euroopan Turvallisuus ja yhteistyökonferenssi*, ETYK). The meeting seated the leaders of the divided world around the same table, brought human rights onto the international agenda, and little Finland under the spotlight of the international press. President of the United States Gerald Ford was among the most prestigious visitors to Helsinki. During his visit, Kekkonen invited him and the members of his entourage to enjoy refreshments onboard the brand-new icebreaker *Urho*.

President Ford was neither innocent nor ignorant of the underlying technopolitical implications when he accepted the invitation. From the early spring of 1975, the US State Department had sought a way to discreetly strengthen Finland's economic independence and liberal–democratic orientation without hampering its position on the neutral ground between East and West. The cocktail party on an icebreaker had been a brainchild of the US Ambassador Mark Austad who had arrived in Helsinki only a couple of months before in March 1975. He had immediately recognised the Finnish icebreakers as technological artefacts that could be used to address both the US diplomatic aims in Finland and domestic regional policy in the Great Lakes.[28]

On May 2, the Ambassador wrote to President Ford and proposed that Finnish icebreakers could be used as technopolitical tools to help the United States to solve two problems at once: '[The Finns] desperately need economic encouragement. We desperately need icebreakers. More important than the economics is the ability to give them financial strength and less economic dependence upon the Soviet Union'.[29]

The US Department of State recommended the US Coast Guard to purchase one or more icebreakers from Finland. The rationale was to signal 'to Kekkonen, his government and the Finnish people that the US not only understands Finland's present difficulties, but is willing to do something concrete to alleviate them'. Through this, the State Department sough to provide 'a strong psychological boost to those forces in Finland who are striking against some odds to maintain the Western orientation of Finnish foreign trade'. At the same time, the icebreaker trade would decrease 'Finnish criticism of the imbalance in the US–Finnish bilateral trade'.[30] All these technological and political interests were at stake when the American delegation arrived in Helsinki and President Ford—as *Seaway*, a Great Lakes navigation magazine put it—'went shopping for an icebreaker'.[31]

The discussion continued the next year when President Kekkonen travelled to Washington. At his meeting with the US Secretary of Transportation William T. Coleman, Kekkonen opened the discussion by explaining that his state visit to the United States had two primary purposes. One was to contribute his salutations to the US bicentennial celebration. The other one was to address certain economic questions, namely the possibility of selling a Finnish icebreaker to the USCG.[32]

Indeed, when the President of Finland met the American leader at the height of the Cold War, they spoke about icebreakers and not in the metaphorical sense. The Finnish press concentrated its reporting on Kekkonen's role as the 'super-salesman' of Finnish icebreakers. The journalists applauded when they learned that as a result of Kekkonen's conversation with Ford, Secretary of State Henry Kissinger had picked up a phone to call the Secretary of Transportation Coleman to underline that the Finnish icebreakers were a political priority. Thanks to this conversation, Austad announced to the Finnish daily newspaper *Helsingin Sanomat*, Wärtsilä could now make an offer for four 2,500 shp icebreakers for the USCG.[33]

So overwhelming was the national ecstasy in Finland at the possibility to deliver an icebreaker to the country of technological supremacy that it took a while before the press noticed that a 2,500 shp icebreaker was not a huge Urho-class icebreaker but rather a small harbour tug.[34] What was also left unnoticed by the Finns was that President Ford had made no promises of buying icebreakers but only offered an opportunity to bid. His foreign policy advisers had recommended him to provide moral support for the Finnish–American trade but otherwise stay in the background. This was necessary to avoid getting involved in the domestic debates that would inevitably follow the foreign acquisition of governmental ships.[35]

The public competition for the small harbour tugs was not what Wärtsilä Helsinki Shipyard had hoped to achieve when pushing the icebreakers to the diplomatic agenda. Building such small-sized harbour vessels was sub-optimal if not totally unfeasible in its production facilities. From Wärtsilä's point of view, these vessels were not even real icebreakers, as Wärtsilä's ship-building director stated in a condescending tone. They were boats that 'any boat-building shop' was able to put together.[36]

Meanwhile in Washington, the diplomatic rationale was not enough to override the domestic opposition against foreign technological purchases. In contrast, the USCG officials appeared rather irritated by the political intervention in their acquisition plans that seemed to question their prevailing competence in icebreaking.[37] Wärtsilä made a bid, but it was easy to the USCG to reject as too expensive in comparison to American alternatives. Wärtsilä never sold an icebreaker, big or small, to the United States.

Despite all these and coming efforts, the diplomatic rationale in the White House was not enough to override the domestic opposition against foreign technological purchases. This did not mean that the efforts of the Finnish–American governments to promote Finnish icebreakers had been in vain. The US government managed to show its support to Finland without endangering the Cold War balance of power. As Austad concluded in his letter to the Special Advisor to President, Brent Scowcroft, the attention the United States had devoted to Finland had increased Finnish leverage in relation to the Soviet Union: 'There is no question in my mind, the more attention we pay to them, the more respect they get from the east'.[38]

President Kekkonen strengthened his position in Finland. Wärtsilä gained international visibility as a builder of sophisticated vessels. Even for the lower-ranking Finnish politicians across the political spectrum, the icebreakers provided possibilities to demonstrate their service for the people and the country. A young social democrat Paavo Lipponen took upon himself to remind the State Department in 1977 that Finnish icebreakers were among the best in the world.[39] Minister of Foreign Affairs Paavo Väyrynen from the Agrarian League underlined in his letter to the Secretary of Treasury the principles of free trade and market specialisation when proposing an icebreaker trade.[40] When the Prime Minister Kalevi Sorsa visited Washington in 1978, he, too, spoke for icebreakers.[41] Esko Rekola, then Minister of Foreign Affairs, expressed his strong interest in bringing Finnish icebreakers to the Great Lakes in 1980.[42]

Icebreakers in intergovernmental relations had become an instrument for breaking the ice and opening up new connections between countries without unnecessarily heating up the Cold War into hostiles.

## Submersible War: technopolitics of state-industry demarcation, 1986–1987

In the spring of 1986, President Mauno Koivisto received a book from the American Ambassador to Finland, Rockwell Schnabel. The book was Tom Clancy's novel *Hunt for the Red October* about the US-Soviet submarine war. The plot circles around the innovative silent propulsion system that hid the Soviet submarines from the American audio detection system and was about to escalate into a full-scale nuclear war. Despite the semi-official publisher, the US Naval Institute Press, the book was entirely fictional. It was meant, however, to convince President Koivisto about the dramatic consequences if Finland allowed Finnish companies to export strategic technology to the Soviet Union. According to Koivisto's memoirs, Ambassador Schnabel had accentuated his message by implying American power over Finnish industry: '[D]ozen license applications submitted by Finnish importers were frozen in the United States and would remain frozen until the Rauma-Repola question had been resolved. I [Koivisto] pretended not to hear the threat'.[43]

The reading recommendations Ambassador Schnabel gave to President Koivisto were part of the controversies over two Finnish-built submersibles *Mir*-1 and *Mir*-2. It was among the most severe conflicts in the Finnish–American Cold War relations and captured the tensions within the alleged compartmentalisation of politics and business in the Finnish East-West technology transfer.[44]

Chapter 2 described how Finland stayed outside CoCom to protect its neutrality policy and relations with the USSR. To secure the vital technology transfer from Western industrial countries, however, Finland had to convince the US authorities that it still complied with the CoCom restrictions while officially staying outside the embargo. This was achieved by two measures: first, by the export licence system in the Soviet trade. Officially the export licence system was a technical measure to control the balance of the bilateral trade, but it was accepted by the US authorities as a guarantee that the Finnish government had means to bloc strategic technology flow to the socialist countries. Second, the US export control authorities created micro-level connections between low-ranking officials and businessmen to monitor Finnish re-exports to the Soviet Union. Most Finnish companies were willing to cooperate with the US authorities by providing information and allowing inspections to safeguard their technology imports from the CoCom countries. Although the Finnish government exonerated all state authorities from the CoCom cooperation, these informal contacts increased trust in the US export control authorities that Finland and Finnish companies did what they could to prevent re-export of strategic technologies to the Soviet Union.[45]

After the freezing start of the Cold War in the early 1950s, the CoCom restrictions on dual-use technologies were partly relieved. The Finnish ship-building companies navigated most of the Cold War without remarkable difficulties caused by the Western embargo until the Red army marched to Afghanistan in 1979, Ronald Reagan took office in 1981, and the détente in East-West technology transfer ended. In 1984–1985, the CoCom countries agreed on the new list of embargoed technologies and on a common policy on their contacts with non-CoCom countries with the aim to prevent neutral countries from becoming loopholes in the embargo.[46]

The two previous sections in this chapter have focused on the role of high-ranking politicians in export promotion presided over Urho Kekkonen. His retirement in 1982 after 25 years in office marked a change, if not in the content of the Finnish–Soviet relations then at least in the practices of state–industry interaction.[47] Kekkonen had enjoyed casual interaction with foreign political leaders and members of the industrial tycoons to the extent that the images of the Finnish–Soviet trade sometimes resembled an obscure catalogue of outdoor activities: Kekkonen hunting, fishing, and skiing with the members of Finnish and Soviet political and economic elite. The next president, social democrat Mauno Koivisto (1923–2017), was criticised for being passive particularly by those Finnish businessmen, who had admired Kekkonen's authoritarian style using political influence to override bureau-cratic constraints.[48]

Koivisto was one of the few Finnish politicians who had actual work ex-perience at a ship dock, but otherwise he remained something of an enigma to the shipbuilding leaders.[49] He was a sociologist by education and econo-mist by work experience. Compared to Kekkonen, Koivisto appeared as a pragmatic technocrat with a formal and distant relationship with the Finnish business elite.[50]

Rauma-Repola's project, which rose to the presidential level during Koivis-to's first term in office, had started in the early 1980s as a combination of two oceanographic projects for the Soviet Academy of Science: a diving sphere and a surface research vessel for test mining of manganese nodules. At first, only the submersible project appeared as extraordinary even though it was not the first deep-sea research vessel the Soviet Union had acquired from the West. In the 1970s, Canadian and Swiss companies had delivered submersibles that had capability of diving down to 2,000 metres. Not only had Rauma-Repola promised for the Academy of Science to exceed the previous depth record but to triple it by constructing a submersible with the capability to operate in 6,000-metre-deep water. Yet, as the company underlined in its report to the Finnish Ministry of Foreign Affairs, they 'had no reason to connect the deep-sea technology and these two projects with anything military'.[51]

According to the informal practice to keep the Americans informed about high-technology transfer, the company had contacted the American Embassy in Helsinki in the spring of 1984. During the following months, the company representatives had provided the U.S. authorities at the Embassy detailed technical information concerning the projects and answered questions, even the ones the company regarded as 'commercially intrusive'.[52]

American officials raised no objections at this point, which was later explained by their strong disbelief that the Finnish shipbuilding company would be able to complete the demanding project. Rauma-Repola took the absence of any negative reaction as a sign of approval and signed the contract on May 17, 1985.[53]

Most of the submersible projects, including the production design and testing, was based on Finnish engineering and manufacturing, even though the contract documents also included a description of several components that were planned to be purchased from CoCom countries (Table 3.1). The company expected some difficulties related to the re-export of technological components acquired from NATO countries. While the responsibility for acquiring re-exporting licences for these subcontracted items was on Rauma-Repola, the agreement recognised the possibility that the embargo would prevent the purchases of certain specified items and should be replaced with Finnish or Soviet production.[54]

The heavy reliance on Finnish technology explains in part both the Finnish optimism about the submersibles that would navigate through the Western embargo without difficulties and the American scepticism that the project would ever come close to completion.

The sceptical attitude towards the Finnish competence was based on the in-experience of the company with submarines in general and the unprecedented choice of material in specific. A deep-sea diving sphere needs to be extremely strong to endure the high pressure of the water and its specific weight has to equal the weight of the water it displaces to enable the submersible to dive and surface by filling and emptying its ballistic tanks.[55] All other known deep-sea submersibles had been welded from titanium plates to obtain high weight-strength ration but Rauma-Repola was planning to use cast steel—an untested choice of technology for extremely harsh conditions.

Rauma-Repola had acquired a Finnish machine work company Lokomo in 1970. Since then, it had invested heavily in the high-strength steel foundry technologies needed in the development of off-shore technology. In 1982, Lokomo had purchased the world's first vacuum oxygen decarburisation converter (VODC) that could be used to process high-quality maraging steel, low-carbon iron alloy with additions of cobalt, nickel, chrome, and titanium, that was extraordinary hard.[56] The problem with cast steel was that it always contained small air bubbles that decreased the strength. Instead of welding the diving sphere using steel plates, Lokomo casted the sphere in two parts in a way that left the strongest possible steel on the outer edge of the hemispheres and processed away the porous material from inside.

In early 1986, two years after Rauma-Repola had first contacted the American intelligence and nine months after signing the trade contract, the

*Table 3.1* The equipment specified in the contract for two deep-sea submersibles, which were planned to be bought from the third countries, enclosed to the trade contract May 17, 1985, dated October 30, 1984. f. 542C, Rauma-Repola, UPMA

| Spec. item | Description | Possible supplying country |
|---|---|---|
| 4.1 | Electrical penetrators | United States, France, Denmark |
| 4.2 | Hydrazine tanks | France |
| 4.4 | Fairing | Sweden, Belgium |
| 4.5 | String | Norway |
|  | Buoyancy material | Belgium, United States |
|  | Electric motor | United Kingdom, FRG |
|  | Gear | United Kingdom, FRG (Finland?) |
|  | Autolocking device | United Kingdom, FRG (Finland?) |
| 5.1 | High pressure pump | FRG |
|  | Valves | FRG |
|  | Electric motors | FRG, United Kingdom |
|  | Sensors | United States, FRG |
| 5.3 | Syntactic foam | Belgium |
|  | Patterns | Belgium |
|  | Moulds | Belgium |
| 6 | Life support | FRG |
| 7 | Power package | France |
| 8.1 | Electric motors | FRG, United Kingdom |
|  | Hydraulic motors | FRG |
| 8.2 | Control unit of electric motors | FRG, United Kingdom, United States |
| 8.3 | Batteries | United States, (Finland?) |
|  | Hydraulic system | FRG |
| 8.4 | Power distribution | United States, United Kingdom, FRG, Norway, Denmark |
| 9.1a | Underwater telephones, up and down transducers and power amplifier | Canada |
| 9.1b | VHF FM radios | United Kingdom, United States, Japan |
| 9.1c | Gyro compasses | United States |
| 9.1d | Sonar systems with transponder, interrogator device, and a set of transponders | United States |
| 9.1e | Positioning systems | Canada |
|  | Directional hydrophones | Canada |
|  | Pinger receivers | Canada |
|  | Precision profiling systems | Canada |
| 9.1f | Doppler speed measuring systems | France |
| 9.1g | Outboard emergency transmitters | Canada |
|  | Low frequency emergency pingers | Canada |
| 9.1h | Submersible transmitters | United States |
|  | Submersible flashers | United States, Canada |

*(Continued)*

| Spec. item | Description | Possible supplying country |
|---|---|---|
| 10.1 | Manipulators | United States, United Kingdom, (Finland?) |
| 10.2 | Exterior lights | United Kingdom, FRG |
| 10.3b | Colour TV-cameras with pan and tilt unit and zoom lens | United States |
| 10.3c | Sear water sampling system | United States |
| 10.3e | Instrument suit | United States, Sweden 11.1 |
| 11.1 | Spares | Acc. to the supplier |
| 11.2 | Tools | Acc. to the supplier |
| 11.3 | Battery chargers | United States, (Finland?) |
| 11.4 | Fuelling equipment of hydrazine tanks | France |
| 11.5 | Rescue operation equipment | The supplier is being looked for |

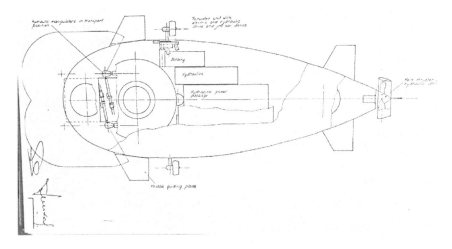

*Figure 3.1* A draft of Rauma-Repola's deep-sea submersible project. Source: Rauma-Repola's collection, UPMA.

US authorities raised objections against the submersibles and—even more unexpectedly—against the surface nodule ship that had not previously been of interest during the conversations between Rauma-Repola and American representatives.[57] In January 1986, the US Ambassador to Helsinki Keith Nyborg invited himself to a meeting with the highest ranking civil servant in the Ministry of Foreign Affairs, State secretary Åke Wihtol, and 'strongly urged' Finland to find ways to prevent the production and delivery of the test mining nodule ship. The reason was that it could be used to inspect and harm 'the sensitive equipment which the US and its allies have located onto the bottom of the sea [...] part of which are directly related to the military deterrence between the superpowers'. Indeed, the US diplomats underlined, if the Soviet Union got the ship, it would put the world peace in danger. Nyborg admitted that the Finnish company had been in contact with the US representatives, but the technical information had not reached the right people. Now, when the US government was aware of the project, it was prepared to use all possible measures to prevent the delivery.[58]

Later in the spring, US representatives specified that the technology in question was related to the US submarine surveillance system (The Sound Surveillance System, SOSUS)—the same system that was central in *The Hunt for Red October*.[59] According to the US officials, the oceanographic instruments and the test-mining equipment the Soviet Academy of Science had ordered were economically unfeasible, which proved that the primary use would be strategic.[60] Indeed, as the Department of State, Department of Defence, and the US Embassy in Helsinki stated in concert, Rauma-Repola's project was not only about to destroy the Finnish neutrality policy and the US-Finnish relationship but it was also about to hamper the nuclear deterrence and risk the balance of power.[61]

As the chief official in the Ministry of Foreign Affairs, Wihtol's answers to these serious accusations were monotonous and directly from the Finnish neutrality playbook: The Finnish legislation gave the government and state administration no right to interfere in the legal business of a private company.[62] When the administrative channels denied assistance, the US authorities brought the issue to the highest political level. In May 1986, the vice-president of the United States George Bush wrote to President Koivisto. Referring to Koivisto's 'strong personal commitment to peace and stability', Bush appealed him to stop the project.[63]

Koivisto replied by invoking to the Finnish tradition of neutrality and the separation of private commerce and state politics:

> [O]ur immediate concern must be Finland's own security, which among other things requires that Finland maintains its role and position as a neutral country, reliable and true to its international commitments, open for cooperation and exchange with all countries. I am sure that contract clauses regarding for example the non-transfer of sensitive technologies originating in any foreign country are scrupulously respected by all those concerned in Finland. At the same time, it is evident that our government cannot restrain Finnish firms in their trade with products of high technology which have been created in our own country. [...] It is legally not possible for the Finnish Government to interfere with its [Rauma-Repola's] plans regarding manufacture and sales of its own products. When Rauma-Repola informed me the first time about the matter I noted that if the Finnish Government had any competence on this question, which it does not have, the government should in my opinion encourage the company to act in accordance with good business practice and fulfil its contracts. [64]

This channel of private correspondence directly with Koivisto and not his office protected the Finnish state from not getting officially involved. Yet, the line between state and business was thin and fuzzy. As Ambassador

Schnabel had threatened in his meeting with Koivisto in 1986, the United States was prepared to punish Finnish industry as a whole by denying export licences for technology, thereby leaving Finnish companies on the wrong side of the Iron Curtain.[65] In his response to Bush, Koivisto warned about an international scandal that would risk the US self-image as the leader of the free trade and world: 'Finland has sometimes been held up as a warning through talk of "Finlandisation": now there seems to be an attempt to show that those who are small should also be humble'.[66]

The language so strong was far from the cool diplomatic composure that usually covered the undercurrent tensions in foreign relations. American authorities were seemingly frustrated by the Finnish reluctance to recognise the gravity of the issue.[67] Finnish diplomats expressed irritation when implying how their American colleagues did not understand Finland's position but only tried to please their bosses by playing hard.[68] Koivisto especially was annoyed by Ambassador Schnabel who was appointed as Ambassador from the business life without diplomatic experience.[69] Rauma-Repola's engineers hardly covered their contempt for the American officials who lacked technological training and 'whose reactions were over-the-top and suspicions exaggerated, even ridiculous'.[70] Above all these struggles, there was an overarching concern that the case would leak to public. It could risk the Finnish neutrality policy and precipitate tensions between the superpowers.[71]

The Finnish submersible case did have many elements in common with the *Hunt of Red October*: Strategic secrets in the deep sea, superpower confrontation, conflicted international relations where politics and money got interwoven. But here comes the difference between the bestseller novel and Cold War technology politics: Most of the actors in the real life preferred a compromise to a conflict. Finnish state and the company had only to lose in an open conflict against the US. For the United States, Finland was too insignificant to risk at provoking the Soviet Union.

The Finnish Ministry of Foreign Affairs arbitrated negotiations between the US authorities and Rauma-Repola that finally settled the dispute. According to the terms of the 'mutual understanding', Rauma-Repola agreed to restrain from selling any nodule mining ships to the Warsaw Pact countries and no further submersibles after the two deep-sea mining spheres it had already contracted for. The technical capacity of these submersibles was to be downgraded, and the delivery delayed as much as possible. In exchange, the US authorities promised to facilitate Rauma-Repola's business relationship with CoCom countries.[72]

Instead of a formal agreement, the mutual understanding was reached through informal correspondence between American and Finnish officials. To fade out the state involvement in the settlement, Wihtol replaced the references to 'Finnish government' to 'Finnish authorities' on the final draft.[73]

The choice of words did not change the fact that the US authorities accepted the correspondence as a confirmation that the Finnish government was committed to restricting strategic technologies from entering the socialist bloc. By the same token, Finland renewed the Import Certificate and Delivery Verification system in a way that better responded to the CoCom's requirements.[74] In return, the Finnish companies were granted the same privileged treatment in the American export licence system as CoCom countries, the so-called '5(k) status' as a reference to Section 5(k) of the Export Administration Act of 1985.[75]

As an illustrative example of the Finnish balancing on the tightrope of neutrality, Finland's 5(k) status sparked off a minor diplomatic incident. President Koivisto considered withdrawing from the list of privileged countries in anticipation of negative reactions from Finland's neighbours: From the Soviet Union because Finland was on the list, and from Sweden because it was not on the list: 'The absence of Sweden would raise questions about what Finland had done to please the Americans more than the Swedes'.[76]

Afterwards, Rauma-Repola tried to compensate the lost projects by selling midget submarines and nodule mining vessels to the United States but without success.[77] The two submersibles Rauma-Repola sold to the Soviet Academy of Science, *Mir-1* and *Mir-2*, remained the only material outcomes of the conflict. Historian Mikko Uola concluded in his study on Rauma-Repola that the submersible project was financially 'very good', and it managed to cover all the R&D costs. This estimation is however difficult to be put in perspective with the absence of references.[78]

Nevertheless, the political storm that erupted around the submersibles and test-mining ship set light on the position of Finnish shipbuilding in the technological Cold War and the alleged separation between the Finnish government and private business. The Cold War straitjacket forced the small country to be pragmatic in its international relations, but innovative ship projects provided the nation also an appropriate way not to be humble.

## Non-radiant nuclear ships: technopolitical radiance fading out, 1978–1989

In 1977, the personnel magazine of Wärtsilä Shipyards, *Wärtsilä*, published a special issue in celebration of the 60th anniversary of Finnish independence and the Russian Revolution. Finnish Foreign Minister Paavo Väyrynen, chair of the Finnish–Soviet Intergovernmental Economic Commission Ahti Karjalainen, and the Soviet commercial representative in Helsinki M.V. Gubanov all contributed to the issue by praising Wärtsilä's open-minded and unprejudiced activity in developing the relationship between Finland and the Soviet Union.[79] In 1978, another special issue commemorated the 30th anniversary of the Finnish–Soviet Treaty of Friendship, Cooperation, and Mutual Assistance. While not directly stating that Wärtsilä's ship trade was thanks to the security pact, the issue underlined that during the term of the treaty, Wärtsilä had delivered a ship per month to the Soviet Union.[80]

Those special issues with their high-ranking contributors stood out from the overall journalistic content of the personnel magazine that otherwise concentrated on internal news and recreational activities. The company understood the value of making itself an actor in the friendship between the states, even if it was mainly rhetorical.

The same year 1977, Wärtsilä opened negotiations for the biggest Finnish–Soviet cooperation project in shipbuilding that would manifest the technological consequences of the peaceful coexistence. This last section of the chapter examines the transformation of technopolitical priorities towards the end of the Cold War through the discussion on nuclear icebreakers.

The origin of Wärtsilä's nuclear icebreaker project dated back to the postwar nuclear-enthusiasm. In 1958, the young technical director of Wärtsilä Helsinki Shipyard, Christian Landtman, had been struck by news of the first nuclear surface vessel, the Soviet nuclear icebreaker *Lenin*. Compared to the 22,000 shp diesel-powered icebreaker *Moskva*, which used 110 tons of diesel daily and required monthly refuelling, the reactors of the *Lenin* were able to produce almost twice as much power for a non-stop, year-long journey. The long operational range and the lightness of fuel advocated in favour of nuclear reactors. The ice-strengthened hulls made polar icebreakers suitable to accommodate nuclear power plants on board.[81] Indeed, nuclear propulsion and polar icebreaking appeared as a match made in heaven.

The Helsinki Shipyard set up a project to design a 50,000-shp nuclear icebreaker and presented this tentative project idea to their contact person in Morflot, the USSR Ministry of Merchant Marines, in Moscow in 1961.[82] Despite some interest at the Soviet side, Wärtsilä failed to reach a deal. After *Lenin*, the Soviet Union announced its new 'Arktika'-class polar icebreakers with an astonishing 70,000 shp.[83] When the Soviet technology strategy focused on domestic development, there were no technopolitical reasons to order those imposing nuclear flagships from abroad.

Rather paradoxically, the Helsinki Shipyard brought the old nuclear icebreaker project to the negotiation table in 1977 when the nuclear enthusiasm had already turned to increasing criticism in Western countries. The peaceful applications of atom energy had failed to meet the expectations. Project after project proved that nuclear propulsion was more expensive and too risky in merchant shipping.[84] Wärtsilä's nuclear icebreaker project was essentially the same as earlier, but now the technopolitical needs of the Finnish–Soviet relationship were different. In the new situation, the re-introduced project became an appropriate remedy for new problems.

The structure of the Finnish–Soviet trade had remained asymmetric throughout the Cold War. Finland exported technology and imported raw materials. In the 1970s, the Soviet organisations started to prioritise the import of knowledge over the import of machinery, and the export of refined goods over the export of raw materials.[85] The technology export had not only economic value to the Soviet foreign trade negotiators, but the machines should also demonstrated the technological prowess of socialism. These aspirations had a few immediate effects on the Finnish–Soviet trade structure, but they made innovative cooperation projects politically invaluable.[86]

Aims to cultivate the political relationship and balance the bilateral trade exchange motivated governmentally pushed parade projects, such as the procurements of a nuclear power plant and electric locomotives from the Soviet

Union.[87] Yet, any pathologically alert Western observer noticed that these major public projects compromised the separation of politics and business in the Finnish–Soviet affairs. The state leaders promoting projects that increased economic dependency on the Soviet Union demonstrated the embarrassing level of Soviet influence in Finland. The government-driven Finnish–Soviet cooperation projects to buy Soviet goodwill, then, came with a price and risked the Finnish neutrality.

In the ship negotiations, Soviet delegations were particularly eager to include in the counter-purchases related to ship contracts the main diesel engines which were easily the single most valuable part of a ship. Most of the Finnish managers were equally eager to reject these suggestions because the Soviet diesels would compete against their own engine production. Neither the Soviet Union nor the Finnish government could force private enterprises to buy components they did not want, but to maintain their good reputation in the Soviet foreign trade, they had to give the Soviets something in response.[88]

Within the context of these underlying trends, Wärtsilä proposed the nuclear icebreaker project to the Finnish–Soviet Scientific and Technical Committee as a potential cooperation project in the spring of 1977. The project provided a convenient way to express willingness to cooperate while escaping Soviet suggestions for replacing Finnish diesel engines with Soviet machinery.[89]

According to the proposal, the Helsinki Shipyard would take the principal responsibility for designing and building a nuclear icebreaker, but the nuclear reactors would be built and installed in the Soviet Union.

The combination of the Finnish icebreaker expertise and the Soviet nuclear technology had genuine technical justifications as well as definite financial rationales. Wärtsilä had never planned to develop its own reactor technology. Outfitting an icebreaker with Soviet reactors was hardly a sacrifice but a creative response to the Soviet demands.

At this stage, the efforts focused on persuading high-up political decision-makers in the Soviet Union.[90] In December 1978, President Kekkonen returned from his state visit to the Soviet Union with the piece of information that Morflot would like to include two nuclear-powered icebreakers in the next five-year protocol of bilateral trade (1981–1985).[91] Director Tankmar Horn received further confirmation for the order in 1980, when he joined Kekkonen on his state visit to the Soviet Union. The official cooperation agreement on the Finnish–Soviet nuclear icebreaker project in November 1980 was a clear breakthrough in the decades-long process.

As Horn described afterwards in his overwhelmingly grateful letter to the President:

> Nationally important economic and commercial issues were agreed at a high hierarchical level that guarantees that their completion will take place as scheduled. It was encouraging to witness how Mr President's

determined, far-reaching decades of work on relations with the Soviet leadership is still bearing fruits [...]. The task given to Wärtsilä of developing a nuclear icebreaker together with Soviet organisations is one tangible result of Mr President's visit to the Soviet Union.[92]

The trip to Moscow was the last one for the aging President Kekkonen. At that point, however, the technopolitical value propelled the nuclear icebreaker project forward without presidential impetus. In 1982, Wärtsilä organised a big celebration in Moscow to commemorate the 50th anniversary of its ship trade with the Soviet Union. In his speech, the Deputy Minister of Foreign Trade Aleksei Manzhulo presented Wärtsilä and the nuclear icebreaker project as the prime example of the fruitful Finnish–Soviet cooperation between Finnish corporations and Soviet customers.[93]

For the Soviet negotiators, the highest possible proportion of Soviet technology in the nuclear icebreaker was imperative. In addition to the nuclear reactors, the Soviet Union wanted to deliver special low-temperature steel developed originally for its submarines as well as turbines and propellers. These components and materials together raised the Soviet share of the project up to 13%, which was enough to reframe the old Finnish nuclear icebreaker project as a Finnish–Soviet cooperation project (Figure 3.2).

A technically pivotal alteration to differentiate the cooperation project from the Soviet nuclear icebreakers was to specify it as a shallow-draft nuclear icebreaker.[94] The giant Arktika-class icebreakers of the Soviet nuclear fleet were strong and powerful enough to penetrate anywhere in the Arctic except

*Figure 3.2* The three propellers of *Taymyr* were made in the Soviet Union with Japanese Toshiba machine tools that should not have been in the Soviet Union according to the CoCom regulations, as recalled by the Finnish shipbuilding engineers (Niini 16.4.2014; Saarikangas 5.2.2014). Photo: Aker Arctic Inc.

for the shallow coastal waters due to their deep draft.[95] The year-round shipping of minerals and hydrocarbons by the Yenisei River and on the Kara Sea required strong icebreakers able to operate at a depth of less than 9 metres.[96] Wärtsilä had experience in the design of an icebreaker that could break thick ice and could almost navigate 'morning dew', as demonstrated in concurrent river icebreaker projects (Figure 3.3).[97]

Finally, in the festive week of the October Revolution in 1984, the Soviet buyer finally agreed to sign the order for two shallow-draft nuclear icebreakers.[98] A quarter-century after the initiation of the Finnish nuclear icebreaker project, it succeeded in aligning with all the major political, technological, and commercial interests.

In 1988, Finnish and Soviet leaders manifested their Cold War bond by commemorating the 40th anniversary of the Finnish–Soviet Treaty on Friendship, Cooperation, and Mutual Assistance. The Finnish private shipbuilding industry participated in the celebrations when the first Finnish-made nuclear icebreaker was ceremoniously named *Taymyr* after an old imperial Russian icebreaking steamer and the northernmost part of the Eurasian mainland.

When *Taymyr* steamed to the Soviet Union, Wärtsilä Marine (Wärtsilä's newly organised subsidiary for shipbuilding operations) was in severe financial troubles and in dire need of new profitable orders. Wärtsilä had longstanding networks in Moscow but now shrinking resources, loosening up of political coordination, and increasing number of Western competitors began to hamper the Finnish–Soviet ship business in a new way.[99]

*Figure 3.3 Kapitan Evdokimov* (1983) had a draught of only 2.5 metres, and it demonstrated Wärtsilä's capability of designing shallow-draft icebreakers. Wärtsilä Helsinki Shipyard built eight ships of this class to operate in the Siberian rivers. Photo: Aker Arctic Inc.

*Figure 3.4* The first Finnish-built nuclear icebreaker, *Taymyr,* under construction. In Finland, the ship was powered by temporary steam boilers on the helicopter deck. The nuclear reactors were later installed in Leningrad. Photo: Aker Arctic Inc.

In the tight economic situation, the shipyard needed a project that would be too tempting for the Soviet buyer to reject or to bargain down, or too easy for Western competitors to win. The political, economic, and technical exceptionalism expressed in the nuclear twins *Taymyr* and *Vaygach* seemed to make nuclear icebreakers suitable lifeboats for the struggling shipyard. Politically, this high-technology cooperation was just what the Soviets had kept requesting for. In economic terms, the profitability of the Taymyr-class contrasted starkly with the shipyard's other projects. A strategic service ship without a clear market price was a flexible object in political negotiations. It promised a wider profit margin and opened a possibility to override economic restrictions in the Soviet Union.[100] Moreover, it had no Western competitors. Wärtsilä's Soviet trade representative Lars Jakobsson discussed ship financing with Soviet officials in 1988, and noted in his memorandum that without bilateral trade, the Soviet Union would always find better credit schemes from other Western countries: 'as a result only the exceptional vessels such the 3rd *Taymyr* will be ordered from Finland'.[101]

Pekka Laine, the newly appointed CEO of Wärtsilä Marine, quickly realised the persuasive power of nuclear exceptionalism. As his company was falling deeper into a liquidity crisis, Laine translated the nuclear icebreaker project from beneficial to its business strategy into imperative for its survival.[102] Discussion of the continuance of the Finnish–Soviet nuclear icebreaker cooperation started in 1987. The prime alternative was a third Taymyr-class icebreaker. The 'new generation *Taymyr*' or 'T3' would replace the previous ones during their maintenance breaks and involve even more cross-border collaboration.[103]

The vast number of visits and the extensive list of persons involved in the negotiations indicated the great significance of this nuclear icebreaker proposal. In December 1987 alone, Wärtsilä's negotiators had audiences with every Soviet organisation that were in any way involved in ship imports from the end-user organisation Morflot to the Kremlin.[104] Several informants confirmed to the Finns that the Soviet Northern Fleet was truly in need of a third shallow-draft nuclear icebreaker to replace *Taymyr* and *Vaygach* during their temporary shutdowns, and it would be ordered in the near future.[105]

However, further discussions with the Soviets had also brought to light more contested points of view. The reorganisation of the Soviet economy had diminished the power of central coordination and made Morflot financially more independent from the government. Expected to be self-sufficient, Morflot had to evaluate new ship purchases within a restricted economic framework.[106]

As they had done previously in deadlock situations, Wärtsilä and its shipbuilding subsidiary tried to push the project forward through political channels. CEO Laine requested assistance from the Finnish Minister of Trade and Industry Ilkka Suominen, who invited the Soviet Shipbuilding Minister Volmer to discuss the Finnish–Soviet cooperation in shipbuilding.[107] Expectations were positive. In November 1988, the Soviet Deputy Minister of Shipbuilding articulated that the 'T3' was '95-percent guaranteed'.[108] Later, the Helsinki Shipyard honoured Minister Suominen by appointing him as the godfather for *Vaygach*.[109]

The Finnish confidence turned into disappointment at the beginning of 1989 when Gosplan reallocated a large sum of the national shipbuilding budget from Morflot to the Ministry of Fisheries.[110] Having to operate within strict budget limits now, Morflot decided to prioritise SA-15-type (short for Sub-Arctic 15,000 dwt) Arctic icebreaking freighters over the nuclear icebreaker. Those freighters were able to tackle ice a metre thick and had proved their functionality as icebreaking vessels during the severe winters in the early 1980s, but they provided a few advantages for the company in price negotiations.[111] The technical complexity and nuclear exceptionalism that had made the nuclear icebreaker project a political priority were now an unaffordable luxury for the end-user organisation that could get three icebreaking cargo ships at the price of one *Taymyr*.[112]

Months passed without anyone confirming whether the nuclear icebreaker project was to continue. In January 1989, the Soviet civil servants had repeated unanimously that they had neither power nor resources to order a nuclear ship from Finland. In February, a high-up political official had assured that these rumours were simply untrue.[113]

Directors Laine and Horn put their hope in the only remaining level of the Soviet hierarchy, General Secretary Mikhail Gorbachev, who was coming for an official state visit in October 1989. Gorbachev was expected to be able, and according to some sources also willing, to bypass the normal protocols and economic restrictions, and to confirm the order of the third nuclear icebreaker (Figure 3.5).[114]

25. 10. 1989

Kari, copyright © 1989 by arrangement with Helsingin Sanomat

*Figure 3.5* General Secretary Gorbachev (on the left) visited President Koivisto (on the right) in October 1989. As the cartoonist Kari Suomalainen noted, the visit coincided with increasing economic problems at Wärtsilä's Shipyards. The picture implies that the expensive technology projects were no longer a priority for the Soviet leadership but consumer goods. Published HS. 25.10.1989. Photo: Visavuori Museum, used with permission by Kari Suomalaisen perikunta.

Indeed, the late autumn of 1989 became globally memorable. Politically, the Finnish–Soviet affairs were perhaps as relaxed as they had ever been during the Cold War, but the bilateral trade had no longer a meaning as a mirror of this political relationship.[115] Wärtsilä Marine, the biggest Finnish shipyard company, went bankrupt. A while later, the Soviet Union collapsed. The T3 project was forgotten.

Nuclear icebreakers were still politically and technologically exceptional objects. The company had successfully mustered all the diplomatic support it could get and many high politicians appeared to like the project. At the end of the Cold War, however, the nuclear icebreakers just were no longer appropriate instruments of technopolitics in the Finnish–Soviet relationship. In the turbulence of Soviet *perestroika*, there was neither need nor resources in Moscow for a hero project of the peaceful coexistence. Mundane fishing ships and freighters overran the flashy nuclear flagships.

The framework in which the Finnish icebreakers had gained its political meanings broke apart. The long and unsuccessful negotiations over the third *Taymyr* demonstrated how the arguments that had led to such a rewarding agreement in 1984 had lost their argumentative power in only five years.

## Conclusion

Finnish presidents, particularly Urho Kekkonen, with his bold head and heavy eyeglasses, were central figures in the Finnish foreign affairs and

Cold War shipbuilding. Kekkonen's active involvement in trade promotion helped to break through some bureaucratic red tape in a handful of cases and granted him a position as the paramount gatekeeper, guarantor, and mediator in Finnish–Soviet trade. The interwoven politics and business in the personal state-industry networks should not be ignored but to be put in perspective.

The Cold War characterised the Finnish shipbuilding as a fusion of politics and business. The Finnish circles of governmental and economic elites were small and clustered. The state–corporate relationship became easily a matter of personal relations. The turbulent relationship between Wahlforss and Kekkonen in the 1950s and 1960s, the dynamic and respectful relationship between Horn and Kekkonen in the 1970s, and the distant relationship between Horn and Koivisto in the 1980s all had their influence in how the corporation chose to advance its stakes in state-level affairs.

Industrial actors employed their contacts in diplomatic circles to promote their projects directly to the highest possible level of political decision-making. The state leaders accepted requests for assistance because the shipyards provided them with diplomatic tools to enact their political goals or promote their personal careers. The Finnish governments needed to assure the Soviet leaders that Finland was committed to the FCMA treaty. When navigating the uncharted waters in the zone of neutrality, the big ship contracts were something tangible. They provided material objects to reflect the abstract rhetoric of 'friendship' and 'cooperation'.

By the 1970s, the Finnish shipbuilding industry was so closely interwoven with Finland's national security and national prestige that taking it into account at state-level diplomatic negotiations was no longer just about advocating for private business but about advocating for Finland. From the point of view of foreign affairs, the border between the techno-economic shipbuilding system and the state was unclear: blurred political and economic interests and close personal connections made the separation of power fuzzy and virtually impossible.

Simultaneously, the alleged separation of political and economic decision-making became an important performance that supported Finland's policy of neutrality and even-handed approach to both superpowers. It provided an opportunity for Kekkonen to market Finnish icebreakers in the United States as a seemingly innocent but politically powerful tool, and it provided an essential backbone for Koivisto to resist American requests to interfere in private business.

I wanted to open the empirical part of this book with the chapter focusing on the role of personal networks because these connections between state and industrial actors constituted a characteristic part of how business information and political messages were transmitted. Human faces also make the complex interactive processes between state and industry easier to understand. But here comes the disclaimer: while recognising certain individuals whose personality or personal ambitions had a distinctive impact on Finnish shipbuilding and trade, their role should not be overestimated.

In the following chapters, I continue the discussion on the interconnections between politics and business in the Finnish Cold War shipbuilding but shift the focus from the high political limelight to the institutions of the Finnish–Soviet bilateral trade. Instead of a specific decision or certain decision-makers, I will concentrate on the trajectories that had determined the agenda and alternatives.

## Notes

1 *Teollisuusneuvottelukunnan mietintö* [Industrial Advisory Board committee report], 1959, 154.
2 Ojala & Karonen, "Business: Rooted in Social Capital over the Centuries," 2006.
3 Seppänen, *Idänkaupan isäntä*, 2011; Keränen, *Moskovan tiellä*, 1990; Koulumies, *Kohtalona Kostamus*, 2012, 56.
4 Kaukiainen & Leino-Kaukiainen, *Navigare necesse est*, 1992, 226; Matala, "Läpi kylmän sodan ja jään," 2015, 8.
5 Sahari, *Valtio ja suurteollisuuden synty*, 2018, 337–338; Matala & Sahari, "Small Nation, Big Ships," 2017.
6 Landtman, *Minnen från mina år vid Wärtsilä*, 2011, 52.
7 Landtman, *Minnen från mina år vid Wärtsilä*, 2011, 62; Mattson, *Suomen idänkauppaneuvottelut 1950–1965*, 1998, 38; Zilliacus, *Wilhelm Wahlforss*, 1984, 283–295; Sahari, *Valtio ja suurteollisuuden synty*, 2018, 337.
8 Landtman, *Minnen från mina år vid Wärtsilä*, 2011, 62.
9 Especially in this early stage, this type of cooperation between industrial companies and political actors probably included also monetary donations to the parties, the election campaigns, or the Finnish-Soviet Friendship Society (*Suomi-Neuvostoliitto Seura*, SNS). See also Landtman, *Minnen från mina år vid Wärtsilä*, 62; Zilliacus, *Wilhelm Wahlforss*, 1984, 300–301; 303–305; Suomi, *Urho Kekkonen: 1950–1956*, 1990, 320; Jensen-Eriksen, *Läpimurto*, 2007, 274; Rentola, *Niin kylmää että polttaa*, 1997, 310–311. Majander, *Paasikivi, Kekkonen ja avaruuskoira*, 2010, 224–227.
10 *Finnish-Soviet Agreement on Trade Exchange*, 1956–1960, 3279, SPA; Sahari, *Valtio ja suurteollisuuden synty*, 2018, 227.
11 Rentola, *Niin kylmää että polttaa*, 1997, 350.
12 CIA/RR IM 59-2, Recent trends in Finnish-Soviet trade, 1959. CIA Electronic Reading Room.
13 *Urho Kekkosen päiväkirjat* 1, 1958–1962, 2001. See also Zilliacus, *Wilhelm Wahlforss*, 1984, 305–307; *Urho Kekkosen päiväkirjat* 1, 1958–1962, 8.6.1961, 423; Majander, *Paasikivi, Kekkonen ja avaruuskoira*, 2010, 224–227.
14 Kähönen, *The Soviet Union, Finland and the Cold War*, 2006, 129–130; 133–138; Rentola, *Niin kylmää että polttaa*, 1997, 451, 488–502; Kuisma, *Kylmä sota, kuuma öljy*, 261–268; Aunesluoma, *Vapaakaupan tiellä*, 113–114; 120–123; Paavonen, "Special Arrangements for the Soviet Trade," 2005, 153; Jensen-Eriksen, "The First Wave of the Soviet Oil Offensive," 2007, 349.
15 *Urho Kekkosen päiväkirjat* 1, 1958–1962, 8.6.1961, 423; Majander, *Paasikivi, Kekkonen ja avaruuskoira*, 2010, 224–227.
16 As demonstrated in his correspondence with President Kekkonen: T. Horn to U. Kekkonen 23.2.1970, 22/11; T. Horn to U. Kekkonen 15.3.1977, 1/94 H-J 1977; see also f. Visit to United States 3.8.1976–4.8.1976, 22/23; U. Kekkonen to T. Horn 18.10.1987 and T. Horn to U. Kekkonen 2.2.1976, 1976 H-J 1/87;

T. Horn to U. Kekkonen 29.11.1977, and T. Horn to U. Kekkonen 23.12.1976, 1/94 H-J 1977, UKA.

17 Landtman, *Minnen från mina år vid Wärtsilä*, 2011, 144–146; Id & Peter, *Innovation and Specialisation*, 2017, 53.

18 T. Horn to U. Kekkonen 23.2.1970, f. 22/11, UKA.

19 "Jäänmurtajien suurtilaus," *Navigator* 5/1970.

20 T. Horn to U. Kekkonen 23.2.1970, folder Matkat Neuvostoliittoon 68–71 22/11; T. Horn to U. Kekkonen 15.3.1977 in Kirjeenvaihto 1/94 H-J 1977; see also folder "Vierailu Yhdysvaltoihin 3.8.1976–4.8.1976," 22/23; U. Kekkonen to T. Horn 18.10.1987 and T. Horn to U. Kekkonen 2.2.1976, in Kirjeenvaihto 1976 H-J 1/87; T. Horn to U. Kekkonen 29.11.1977 and T. Horn to U. Kekkonen 23.12.1976, in Kirjeenvaihto 1/94 H-J 1977, O. Mattila to Kekkonen 6.9.1978, 22/40,UKA. Examples from other industries: Koulumies, *Kohtalona Kostamus*, 2012, 56; Viita, *Kapitalismin ja sosialismin puristuksessa*, 2006, 53–57.

21 Matala & Sahari, "Small Nation, Big Ships," 2017, 15–17.

22 *Urho* had a sister-ship in Finland, the *Sisu* (1976), and three in Sweden, where it was known as "Atle-class": *Atle* (1974), *Frej* (1975), and *Ymer* (1977).

23 Statistical Yearbooks, Statistics of Finland.

24 Meeting between Rusk and Karjalainen, 1.6.1966, Vuosikirja 1966, UKA.

25 Establishment of a consortium 22.4.1969; On the Icebreaker Joint Venture, 23.4.1969, WW 20, NA.

26 Ambassador Olavi Munkki to director Christian Landtman 10.4.1969; Landtman to Munkki 22.4.1969, WW 20, NA.

27 Munkki to Landtman, 10.4.1969, WW 20, NA.

28 DoS to Lieutenant General Brent Scowcroft, on the call on President Ford by Ambassador to Finland Mark Austad, 25.2.1975; Secretary Kissinger on letters to the President from Ambassador Austad, 6.6.1975, NSA Finland, box 7, GFA.

29 Ambassador Austad to President Ford, 2.5.1975, NSA, country files Finland 1973, box 7, Gerald Ford Archive (GFA).

30 DOS George S. Springsteen, State Department to White House to Brent Scowcroft. 13.12.1975, Covering letter from T. Horn to Kekkonen 18.10.1976, f. 1/87, UKA.

31 *Seaway Review* 5:3 (1975).

32 Meeting between Kekkonen, Sorsa, Coleman, Austad, 4.8.1976, NSA Finland, box 7, GFA.

33 "Jäänmurtajat esillä UKK:n vierailulla," HS 1.8.1976; "USA:n ulkoministeriö jäänmurtajakaupan taa," HS 5.8.1976; "Murtajakauppa liikahti," *Turun Sanomat*, 6.8.1976; "Jäänmurtajia ja kromia," *Kansan uutiset*, 7.8.1976.

34 "Murtajakaupat USA:an ohi suun. Wärtsilältä tarjoukset satamahinaajista," HS 7.8.1987; *Turun sanomat*, 15.9.1976.

35 From Special Assistant to the President Brent Scowcroft to President Ford 3711 on Kekkonen visit—Finnish interest in selling icebreakers; from Clift to Scowcroft 21.7.1976 on Kekkonen visit and icebreakers, Presidential Briefing material for VIP visits, Box 22, 8/3-4/76 Finland, GFA.

36 "USA:n laivakaupat: Korkea hinta vienee tilauksen Wärtsilältä," HS 17.9.1976.

37 USCG statements in Hearings before the Subcommittee on Coast Guard and Navigation of the Committee on Merchant Marine and Fisheries House of Representatives, 95th Congress, 29.3.1977–30.3.1977.

38 Austad to Scowcroft 16.9.1976, NSA Finland, box 7, GFA.

39 Meeting with Paavo Lipponen, Finnish SDP, 6.5.1977, Country file Europe 1/77-12/78, container 22, Brzezinski Material, NSA 6, JCA.

40 Paavo Väyrynen to W.M. Blumenthal 29.8.1977; Sec. Treasury W.M. Blumenthal to DoT Brock Adams, 29.9.1977, box 201, USCGA.

41 "Sorsa Washingtonissa: Lentoreitit ja murtajat esillä keskusteluissa," *Suomenmaa* 4.11.1978.
42 PM Secretary of Commerce 16.5.1980, f. 5/19/80, container 162, JCA.
43 Koivisto, *Witness to History*, 1997, 86.
44 Jensen-Eriksen, "The Northern Front in the Technological Cold War," 2019: 166–173; Uola, *Meidän isä on töissä telakalla*, 1996, 450.
45 Jensen-Eriksen, "CoCom and Neutrality," 2010, 54.
46 Jensen-Eriksen, "The Northern Front in the Technological Cold War," 2019, 155, 160.
47 Wuokko, "Layers of Disunity," 2013, 621; For a detailed analysis on the business elite as a political agent, see Wuokko, *Markkinatalouden etujoukot*, 2016.
48 Juri Piskulov and Esa Seppänen even use a concept of "Kekkosenergy," to coin the role of the president who was all the time in control and facilitated the Finnish-Soviet relations. Piskulov, *Näin teimme idänkauppaa*, 2011, 271; Seppänen, *Idänkaupan isäntä*, 2011, 268–277; Suomi, *Epävarmuuden vuodet*, 2006, 101.
49 Koivisto's PhD in sociology examined labour relations in Turku harbour. Before his studies, he had worked at Laivateollisuus shipyard for a short period.
50 Wuokko, *Markkinatalouden etujoukot*, 2016, 181–182, 193; Tiihonen, *The Ministry of Finance*, 2012, 172.
51 Rauma-Repola's Deep Sea Research Vessel, Nodule Test Mining Ship, 4.6.1986, f.1, Vientivalvonta 1986–1987, UMA.
52 Rauma-Repola's Deep Sea Research Vessel, Nodule Test Mining Ship, 4.6.1986, f.1, Vientivalvonta 1986–1987, UMA.
53 Contract 77-10/70049-133, 16.5.1985. f. 542C, RR, UPMA.
54 Contract 77-10/70049-133, 16.5.1985; enclosure no. 13, the equipment which were planned to be bought from the third countries, f. 542C, RR, UPMA.
55 Contract 77-10/70049-133 and attachments: (1) Technical specification and enclosed technical specification, 28.6.1983, (2) Design documentation 10.10.1984, f. 542C, RR, UPMA.
56 Contract 77-10/70049-133 and attachments: (1) Technical specification and enclosed technical specification, 28.6.1983, (2) design documentation 10.10.1984, f. 542C, Rauma-Repola, UPMA; Törmä, "Lokomo-100 vuotta konepaja ja teräs-teollisuutta," 2016.
57 Rauma-Repola's Deep Sea Research Vessel, Nodule Test Mining Ship, 4.6.1986, f.1, Vientivalvonta 1986–1987, UMA.
58 US Ambassador Nyborg visit to State Secretary Wihtol, 30.1.1986, f.1 Vientivalvonta 1986–1987, UMA.
59 Assistant Secretary of Defense Richard Perle to Lieutenant General Aimo Pajunen, Ministry of Defense, 10.3.1986, f.1, Vientivalvonta 1986–1987, UMA.
60 Visit of the US delegation 24.3.1986, f. 1, Vientivalvonta 1986–1987, UMA.
61 Meeting with representatives from DoS 24.2.1986; Perle to Pajunen, 10.3.1986; Meeting between Nyborg and Wihtol, 30.1.1986, f. 1, Vientivalvonta 1986–1987, UMA.
62 Finland's answer to the US Embassy in Helsinki, 14.2.1986; Meeting between Nyborg and Wihtol 30.1.1986; Meeting with representatives of DoS 24.2.1986; Ambassador Rockwell Schnabel's visit to Åke Wihtol, 9.4.1986, f. 1, Vientivalvonta 1986–1987, UMA.
63 Vice-President George Bush to President Mauno Koivisto 29.5.1986, Koivisto 33, NA.
64 Koivisto to Bush 8.8.1986, Koivisto 31, NA.
65 Koivisto to Bush 8.8.1986, Koivisto 31, NA; Jensen-Eriksen, "The Northern Front in the Technological Cold War," 2019, 168–169; Tuuri, *Tauno Matomäki: Suvipäivänä Syntynyt*, 2005, 187–188; Jukka-Pekka Kervinen, "CIA tuhosi

Rauma-Repolan parhaan bisneksen, *Tekniikka ja talous*, 5.12.2008; Jari Korkki, "Punaisen lokakuun metsästys. Näin Suomen ja Yhdysvaltain kauppasota ratkaistiin tasan 30 vuotta sitten," Yle Uutiset www.yle.fi/uutiset, 22.7.2017; Kari Kortelainen, "Teknologinen läpimurto, poliittinen mahalasku," *Tekniikan historia* 1 (2003).
66 Koivisto to Bush 8.8.1986, Koivisto 31, NA.
67 Meeting with representatives of DoS 24.2.1986, f.1 Vientivalvonta 1986–1987, UMA.
68 Meeting in DoS 29.7.1986, f.1, Vientivalvonta 1986–1987, UMA.
69 Meeting with Michael Durkee 18.9.1986, f.1, Vientivalvonta 1986–1987, UMA.
70 Meeting in Nuottaniemi 19.3.1986, f. 1, Vientivalvonta 1986–1987, UMA.
71 Schnabel's visit to Wihtol, 9.4.1986, f.1, Vientivalvonta 1986–1987, UMA.
72 Meeting on 17.6.1987, f.10, Vientivalvonta 1986–1987, UMA.
73 Wendt to Wihtol, 17.6.1987, Vientivalvonta 1986–1987, f. 6, UMA.
74 Matomäki to Allan Wendt 1.6.1988; Wendt to Wihtol 17.6.1987, f.6., Vientivalvonta 1986–1987, UMA.
75 Jensen-Eriksen, "The Northern Front in the Technological Cold War," 2019, 161.
76 Presidential Office, notes, 11.11.1988; discussions between Wihtol and Wendt in Washington, 21.11.1988, f. 6, Vientivalvonta 1986–1987, UMA.
77 PM 1060 on Rauma-Repola's submersibles 3.11.1989; Seppo Seppälä to Lauri Korpinen on Advanced Seal Delivery System (ASDV), 26.10.1989; Ilkka Eerola to Jaakko Laajava, 28.9.1989, f. 6, Vientivalvonta 1986–1987, UMA.
78 Uola, *Meidän isä on töissä telakalla*, 1996, 454.
79 *Wärtsilä* personell magazine, special issue 1977.
80 *Wärtsilä* personell magazine 2/78.
81 Landtman, "Technische Gesichtspunkte über modern grosse Eisbrecher," 1961, 167; Josephson, *Red Atom*, 2005, 120.
82 Landtman, *Minnen från mina år vid Wärtsilä*, 2011, 97–98; Interview Landtman 9.9.2014.
83 Christian Landtman, *Icebreaking and Winter Navigation in the Baltic Area with Some Remarks Concerning Winter Navigation on the Great Lakes*, presentation before the Economic Club of Detroit, December 7, 1970, Cobo Hall. Landtman's personal collection; "Neuvostoliitto rakentelee 2 atomijäänmurtajaa", *Navigator* 2/1965.
84 Olsson, *Skall vi bygga atomfartyg*, 1997, 17.
85 Meetings of the Economic Commission 1974–1978, KTM Hsa:12, KA.
86 Androsova, "Economic Interests," 2011, 42–45; Autio-Sarasmo, "Soviet Economic Modernisation," 2006, 107; 110–111; Aunesluoma, *Vapaakaupan tiellä*, 2011, 116.
87 Aunesluoma, *Vapaakaupan tiellä*, 341; Michelsen & Särkikoski, *Suomalainen ydinvoimalaitos*, 2005; Moilanen, "Uusi junankuljetusmetoodi," 2014.
88 Economic Commission, Shipbuilding Divisions meetings 31.8.1976; 8.9.1975; 17.12.1974, KTM [Kauppa ja teollisuusministeriö, hereafter KTM] Hda:10, NA.
89 Horn to Paavo Rantanen 18.9.1979; T. Horn to N.S. Patolitshev, to Guzhenko (Morflot), and to Kovaljov (GKNT) on the Soviet-Finnish cooperation project of new nuclear polar icebreakers 3.11.1978, f. 168, 58 B1, UMA; Meeting of the Economic Commission 22.2.1978; KTM Had:12, NA.
90 Horn to Rantanen 18.9.1979; T. Horn to Patolitshev, to Guzhenko, and to Kovaljov on the Soviet-Finnish cooperation 3.11.1978, f. 168, 58 B1, UMA.
91 Finnish delegation of the Economic Commission, preparatory meeting on the trade agreement 1981–1985, 11.12.1978, f. 166, 58 B1, UMA. Interview with Saarikangas 5.2.2014.
92 Horn to Kekkonen 1.12.1980, f. 1/114 A-H 1980, UKA.

93  *Wärtsilä* personnel magazine 6/82.
94  Aker Arctic reference ships <akerarctic.fi> retrieved 24.5.2016; Veikko Koskivirta in "Taymyr-ydinmurtaja: Atomivoimalla päin ahtojäitä," *Navigator* 4/1988; "First nuclear icebreakers launched at Wärtsilä Marine", *Navigator* 1987 reprinted in English.
95  Bukharin, "Russia's Nuclear Icebreaker Fleet," 2006, 27; "Neuvostoliiton pohjoisten alueiden liikenteellinen käyttöönotto," "Neuvostoliiton pohjoisten alueiden liikenteellinen käyttöönotto" in *Navigator* 4/79; Interview G. Wilkman, 16.1.2014.
96  "Taymyr-ydinmurtaja: Atomivoimalla päin ahtojäitä," *Navigator* 4/1988; "First nuclear icebreakers launched at Wärtsilä Marine", *Navigator* 1987 reprinted in English; Josephson, *Soviet Arctic Conquest*, 188–189; Barrand & Wilson, "The Shipping Crisis in the Soviet Eastern Arctic"; Interview G. Wilkman 16.1.2014.
97  Aker Arctic Ship references. www.akerarctic.fi.
98  Haapavaara, *Iso-Masa*, 2002, 92. Interview Saarikangas 5.2.2014; Interview Hannu Eskelinen and Kari Ketola 26.3.2014 with Aaro Sahari; "Telakkateollisuuskatsaus 1984", *Navigator* 2/85.
99  KPO [Kauppapoliittinen osasto, Department of Trade and Industry in the Finnish Ministry of Foreign Affairs] on the future of the Finnish-Soviet clearing trade, 3.4.1989, Suomi-NL 1.1.1989–30.6.1989, 43.41, UMA; Lainela "Neuvostoliiton ulkomaankauppajärjestelmän uudistus," 1990, 151–152; 156–157.
100 Meeting in MVT 23.12.1987, WM [Wärtsilä Meriteollisuus] 29, ELKA; Gosplan 3.3.1988, WM 30, ELKA.
101 Meeting with Pugin and Litov, 17.3.1988, WM 30, ELKA.
102 PM on the Soviet trade 1991–1995, 27.3.1989, WM 30, ELKA.
103 Jakobsson to Laine 10.11.1987; Meeting in MVT 27.12.1987; Meeting in Gosplan 28.12.1987, WM 29, ELKA.
104 Meeting in MVT 17.12.1987; Meeting in MVT 27.12.87; Meeting in Gosplan 28.12.1987; Meeting in Kremlin 22.12.1987 and on meeting at Wärtsilä's office in Moscow 22.12.1987; WM 29, ELKA.
105 WM's internal memorandum 6.5.1988; Meeting in the Wärtsilä's office in Moscow 28.12.1987 and in Kremlin 22.12.1987; Meeting in Gosplan 3.3.1988, WM 30, ELKA.
106 Meeting in Gosplan 28.12.1987, WM 30; Meeting in the Soviet Ministry of Foreign Economic Relations (MVES) 17.12.1987, WM 29, ELKA; KPO 325 on the role of MID in foreign trade policy, 27.3.1991, f. Suomi-NL 1.1.1991–31.3.1991, 43.41, UMA; KPO on the future of the Finnish-Soviet trade, 3.4.1989, f. Suomi-NL 1.1.1989–30.6.1989, 43.41, UMA.
107 Lunch meeting between Pugin and L. Jakobsson 12.1.1988; Meeting with Pugin on ship financing, 17.3.1988; Laine to Ilkka Suominen 31.5.1988, WM 30, ELKA.
108 Secret memorandum on ship prioritising in the 13th five-year period as evaluated in June 1988, 19.7.1988, WM 30; Zvegintsev, Sudoimport to Laine 20.10.1988; Meeting in Gosplan 24.11.1988, WM 30, ELKA.
109 Suominen to Ju. N. Volmer 29.6.1988; Meeting in MVES 2.2.1989, WM 30, ELKA.
110 Meeting at Helsinki Shipyard 19.2.1989, WM 30, ELKA.
111 Barr, "The Shipping Crisis in the Soviet Eastern Arctic," 1985.
112 L. Jakobsson's phone call with Soviet Inspector Danilov 26.1.1989; Meeting at Helsinki Shipyard 19.2.1989; Meeting with Soviet representatives in the Economic Commission 2.2.1989; Meeting with Komarov and Zvegintsev in Moscow 6.1.1989, WM 30, ELKA.

113 Meeting with the Soviet representatives in the Economic Commission 2.2.1989; Meetings in Sudoimport 3.5.1989; Meeting in Sudoexport 7.6.1989; Meeting in Morflot 27.1.1989; Meeting at WMH 19.2.1989, WM 30, ELKA.
114 Meeting with V. D. Pugin 19.8.1989; WM's memorandum on internal meeting on ongoing projects in the Soviet Union 22.8.1989; PM titled "The Third Taymyr," 19.10.1989, WM 30, ELKA.
115 Matala, "Idänkauppa oli varmaa mutta sitten se loppui," 2012.

# 4 Institutional interface to the Soviet market

## Bilateral trade and Finnish shipbuilding

Finnish shipbuilding industry grew fast after the post-war reconstruction from roughly 38,000 GT launched in 1953 to almost 206,000 GT in 1974. In the international context, there was nothing spectacular about this production growth over fivefold. Volume-wise, Finland followed the global shipbuilding boom that was fuelled by upsurge in seaborne transportation.[1] The boom turned to bust in 1975 after the OPEC-shock in oil market had slumped the demand for crude oil carriers, and other cargo ships followed the tanker market down to a worldwide recession. It was after this watershed when the trajectory of Finnish shipbuilding volume diverged from the international trend. As a contrast to the accelerated de-industrialisation process in the well-established European shipbuilding countries, Finnish companies continued to increase their capacity for over a decade after the first oil shock.[2]

Domestic and foreign observers alike agreed on the overarching explanation for the Finnish exceptionalism: the extensive trade with the socialist countries. As *The New York Times* reported in 1983:

> The doorstep of the Soviet Union is not normally regarded by capitalists as prime investment territory, [but] precisely because of their heavy trade with the Soviet Union, a number of companies here at the gateway to northern Russia scarcely noticed the recent worldwide recession.[3]

The strong position of the Finnish shipbuilding industry in the Soviet Union had emerged in the context of the Cold War divide. The previous chapters have shown how the standing between East and West had made Finland the best political and technological compromise of the Western countries for the Soviet leaders to deal with. The same factor had made the Soviet ship buyers for the Finnish shipyards the most profitable customers to trade with.

This chapter focuses on an administrative aspect of the Finnish–Soviet ship trade that shaped Finland's bargaining position in the Soviet Union and differentiated the Finnish shipyards from most of the Western competitors: the bilateral trade system.

During the first part of the Cold War, Finnish foreign trade adapted to the dualist world order by establishing different institutions for the trade with capitalist and socialist countries. While the conventional system of multi-lateral trade with convertible currencies comprised the vast majority of the Finnish foreign trade in total, the 'Eastern trade', the trade with the Soviet Union and socialist countries, relied on bilateral agreements. On average, one-fifth of the Finnish total foreign trade was conducted through bilateral clearing trade agreements between 1952 and 1990. The duration, scale, and great popularity made the Finnish bilateral trade system with the Soviet Union an exception in market economies.

In the Finnish colloquial use, clearing trade was a synonym to the profitable, stable, and state-supported Eastern trade. Indeed, the clearing trade and payment system may have been the single most important element that contributed to the distinct developmental trajectory of the Finnish shipbuilding industry after the oil crisis. The causation might also be reverse, and the shipbuilding industry may have been the single most important sector that motivated the state actors in the capitalist Finland to maintain the exceptional, rigid, and centrally coordinated trade system that went against the general trend towards liberalisation.

In this chapter, I will shift the focus from the big ships and high political actors to the bank protocols, foreign trade institutions, and civil servants. The first subchapter describes the structure and function of the bilateral trade and payment system, and the rest of the chapter analyses the development and dismantling of the Finnish–Soviet bilateral trade and payment system in relation to the ship trade.

This will bring us to the political agency of the apolitical trade administration. The merely bureaucratic clearing trade and payment infrastructure had no explicit political aims of their own, but they were active actors. The decision the civil servants made and the practices they maintained contributed to the Finnish competitive position in the Soviet market and to the profits the Eastern exports generated to the shipyards. Through that, the trade infrastructure became one mechanism that connected the industrialisation in Finland to the Cold War political considerations.

## Institutional interface to the socialist planning

A clearing trade and payment system consists of a set of intergovernmental arrangements between two or more countries to conduct trade without having to transfer money across the border. At the core of the Finnish–Soviet bilateral clearing trade and payment system there was two bank accounts, one in the Bank of Finland and another in the Soviet Bank for Foreign Economic Relations (VEB), which coordinated the trade exchange to compensate the imports to one country by the returns from exports to the other.

Figure 4.1 presents the overall mechanism of the bilateral exchange of goods and payments. When a Finnish shipyard sold a ship to a Soviet buyer, the company claimed the payment through a commercial bank in Finland. The bank contacted VEB, which, in turn, invoiced the Soviet buyer. The

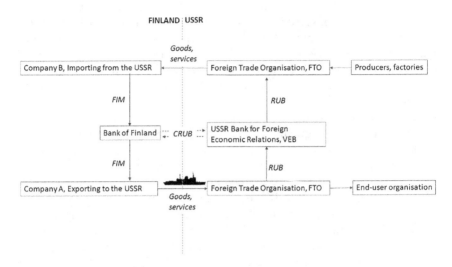

*Figure 4.1* Payments within the Finnish–Soviet clearing system. By the author based on various sources on the Finnish–Soviet trade institutions including: Laurila (1995), 75–86; *Tieteellis-teknisen ja taloudellisen yhteistyön vuorovai-kutus* (1980), parts I, II.

Soviet buyer paid the VEB in roubles. After receiving the payment, the VEB notified the Bank of Finland. After the Bank of Finland received the payment order, it paid the Finnish company using Finnish markka (FIM).

The clearing trade and payment system was a sophisticated version of simple barter arrangements in which, for example, a shipyard selling a fishing ship to a fishery would get fish as payment. The clearing system balanced the aggregate revenues from all sales and capital flows between the two countries and did not require the participating companies to exchange goods directly with each other. However, similar to barter trade, also bi-lateral trade system tied the two countries together because the clearing roubles on the clearing accounts were only valid for purchases within the bilateral framework. Therefore, the balance of the clearing accounts in the Bank of Finland and VEB reflected the difference between the aggregate imports and exports.[4]

Originally, the clearing trade arrangements had their origins in the lack of convertible currencies during the 1930s recession and 1940s war-economies. Until the early 1950s, the Finnish–Soviet bilateral trade system did not stick out as an exception in international comparison when most European countries conducted their foreign trade within the framework of different clearing arrangements. In the post-war decade, however, the International Monetary Fund (IMF), the General Agreement on Tariffs and Trade (GATT), and the Organisation for European Economic Co-operation (OEEC) outlined the return of the non-socialist economies to the multilateral free trade and convertible currencies and campaigned against bilateral agreements that discriminated against third countries.

After the war, Finland followed the other Western countries and committed to the multilateral economic order. It joined the GATT in 1950 and tied the external value of Finnish markka to the USD in 1951. From 1959 onwards, the Finnish markka was in practice a convertible currency.[5] While preferring multilateral agreements and convertible currencies in the Western trade, Finland maintained the bilateral agreements in its trade with socialist countries.

The most compelling argument for the continuance of the clearing trade system was the shortage of foreign capital. In Finland, the financial markets were strongly regulated until 1980s, and foreign currencies were a scarce resource. In the Soviet Union, the possibilities of buying directly from the international markets were restricted by the limited exports and chronical distrust of the West that advocated the policy of keeping capital reserves high and debt low.[6]

At the Finnish shipyards, there were other reasons to stand in favour of the clearing system. They were not affected by the disadvantages of the bilateralism because they received the payments through the Bank of Finland in Finnish markka. The clearing trade and payment system did not tie the Finnish companies in the bilateral framework in the way that would force them to use the revenues for purchases from the Soviet Union. Instead, the bilateral trade system created a stable framework for the shipyards to trade with the Soviets and provided the shipyards with advantageous financing arrangements.

The basic laws of demand and supply explain most of the industrial development in merchant shipbuilding. Normally, a private ship buyer would make the purchasing decision based on a consideration of whether the price of the ship was worth the future revenues and specify the size and type of the vessel according to the business strategy and market expectations. The ship buyer would invite tenders directly from shipyards or use a broker and select the contractor among the competitive yards based on price, terms of delivery, and ship design and specifications.[7]

In the Soviet economic system, there was no such market demand, but the volume and type of new tonnage were determined in the State Planning Committee, Gosplan. The economic plans drafted in Gosplan administrated all production, and adjusted them according to the available resources, estimated domestic output, and prevailing economic policy doctrines. Gosplan created the frames within which ministries and end-user organisations were able to purchase ships from abroad.[8]

Therefore, the principles of demand and supply functioned differently in the Finnish trade with the Soviet Union in comparison with the trade with Western countries. The Soviet demand originated from the priorities of the state planning organisation, and it was framed by the need to balance the value of exports and imports between the two countries. To control the balance, an extra layer of state and industrial organisations was involved to coordinate the trade exchange.

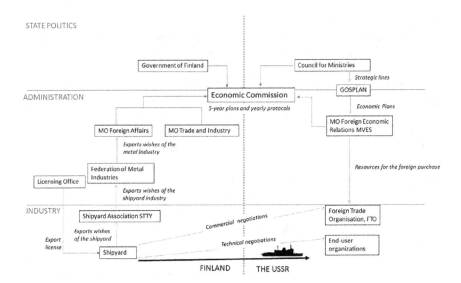

*Figure 4.2* Trade negotiations in the Finnish–Soviet bilateral framework. By the author based on various sources on the Finnish–Soviet trade institutions including Laurila (1995), 59–74; *Tieteellis-teknisen ja taloudellisen yhteistyön vuorovaikutus* (1980), parts I, II.

Figure 4.2 presents the main organisations and their relations when a Finnish shipyard negotiated for a ship contract. When a Finnish shipyard sold a vessel to the Soviet Union, it needed first to contact the customer. Finnish ship seller would negotiate on the technical specifications with the end-user organisation of the ship, such as the Ministry of Merchant Marines (Morflot) or the Ministry of Fisheries. However, those organisations had no rights to conduct foreign trade. Therefore, the shipyard had to negotiate on the contract price and other details with a certain Foreign Trade Organisation (FTO). In the case of ship trade, the most important customer was the Soviet FTO for ship trade V/O Sudoimport that represented the buyer and payer of merchant fleet vessels.[9]

To export a ship to the Soviet Union, the Finnish shipyard needed then to make sure that the contract fit within the bilateral framework of the trade exchange which was determined in intergovernmental negotiations. Every five years between 1951 and 1990, trade delegations from Finland and the USSR confirmed an agreement on exchange of goods and payments that outlined the volume and structure of the trade exchange for the next five-year period. For example, the five-year trade agreement 1956–1960 outlined that Finland would deliver 20 tankers of two sizes, 105 trawlers and other type fishing ships, 15 rescue tugs, 15 tug boats for lakes and rivers, 15 cargo ships, 8 motor ships, up to 300 barges, one 10,500 shp icebreaker, and two 20,000 shp icebreakers with a total value of 3,110 billion roubles.[10]

The five-year agreements were specified in annual protocols, 'Protocols for the exchange of goods' (*Tavaranvaihtopöytäkirja*, TVPK). For example, the protocol for the trade exchange in 1968 enumerated that the Finnish ship quota included one icebreaker of 22,000 shp, one cable vessel, three motor cargo vessels of 12,500 dwt, nine timber cargo vessels of 3,400 dwt, eight ocean-going tankers of 4,600 dwt, three accommodation vessels, four motor cargo vessels for inland waterways of 1,800 dwt, spare parts or ship engines for 500,000 roubles, and ship repairs for the value of a thousand roubles.[11]

In Finland, the Ministry of Foreign Affairs coordinated all exports to the Soviet Union. Specifically, the Foreign Trade Department prepared the international trade agreements, coordinated the work of bilateral economic organisations, and participated in export promotion. The Ministry of Trade and Industry coordinated the imports from the Soviet Union, and it also participated in the preparation of trade treaties, export control, and export credit guarantees.[12] The two ministries collected the lists of export and import plans from the industrial organisations, which had gathered them from their member companies. In shipbuilding, the central organisation was the Federation for Metal Industries in Finland.[13]

From the point of view of foreign trade administration in Finland, the export side was usually unproblematic: Finnish companies were willing to sell, and the Soviet organisations were ready to buy. Roughly half of the Finnish exports consisted of metal manufacturing and machines, ships constituted 15%–30% of the total. The responsibility for the equal size of imports fell on the raw-material supply of two state-companies: the petrochemical refinery Neste and the chemistry and fertiliser company Kemira. To maximise the imports, Finland maintained a *de facto* Soviet monopoly on the Finnish oil imports until the 1990s.[14]

After the Finnish shipyard had completed the technical and commercial negotiations with the Soviet end-user organisation and the relevant FTO, contracted for the ship order, and confirmed that the order was included in the state-level trade agreements, there was still one administrative level it had to pass: all exports and imports to and from the Soviet Union needed a licence from the Finnish Licensing Office.[15] In addition to its unofficial function complying with the CoCom embargo described in the previous chapter, it was an instrument of protectionism. In practice, the Licensing Office allowed less than 20% of foreign content in the products exported through the clearing system. The rationale was to prevent third countries from using the Finnish–Soviet clearing trade as a channel to sell goods to the Soviet Union at the expense of Finnish industry.

The degree of bureaucracy of the bilateral trade and payment system made the Cold War divide between socialist planning economies and capitalist market economies tangible on the Finnish–Soviet border. It underlined the difference between Western trade, where companies aimed for generating profits and were independent from the state, and the socialist planning economy, where production and foreign trade were subordinated to central coordination. In the Finnish–Soviet relationship, the bilateral clearing trade and payment system evolved into an interface that facilitated high-volume trade between the countries with different economic systems.

The Soviet FTO for merchant fleet, Sudoimport, was among the biggest ship buyers in the world, and it bought ships in bulk for the vast empire. From its point of view, the central coordination and five-year agreements of the Finnish–Soviet clearing trade and payment system fit well with the practices of the socialist planning system. On the Finnish side, the shipyards benefitted from the economies of scale of the relatively long series in the centrally coordinated trade system. The five-year planning cycles brought in a degree of predictability that allowed the shipyards to optimise their production to reinforce the counter-cyclical effect of the Soviet trade. Moreover, the high requirement for domestic content in ships prevented extensive purchases and subcontracting from foreign countries and supported domestic industrial clusters.[16]

From the point of view of the Finnish shipyards, the bilateral clearing trade system seemed to safeguard a privileged position for Finland in the Soviet market. Overall, the benefits of the clearing trade system with the Soviet Union exceeded the added bureaucracy that required the shipyards to establish different practices and maintain different FTOs for Eastern and Western trade.

Another reason for the Finnish shipbuilders to like the clearing trade system was related to financing. Modern shipbuilding was a capital-intensive business. Shipyards needed pre-delivery financing to pay for the design, raw materials, and workforce over a construction period of months or years. The ship purchaser needed to find liquidity to cover the price, even though the investment payback period of a merchant vessel was likely to be longer than the period preferred by commercial banks. In the inter-war Europe, state-subsidised credit schemes had entered international shipbuilding first as domestic instruments for competing against British dominance and then to support shipyards after the 1930s recession. In Asia, especially Japan fuelled its ambitious state-led industrialisation by cheap financing for shipyards allowing them to lend their customers up to 70% of contract prices with a reasonable interest rate and generous payback period.[17] In the post-war shipbuilding, the terms of pre-delivery and post-delivery financing had become deal-breakers in the global shipbuilding competition.[18]

As a contrast to the international financing practices in shipbuilding, the Finnish shipyards needed no external financing in their trade with the Soviet Union. The Finnish–Soviet ship contracts typically scheduled the payments for a ship in four parts: 25% when signing the contract, 25% when laying down the keel, 25% when launching the ship, and 25% when the ship was completed. Because the inward cash flows from the pre-payments accumulated faster than the outward cash flows, the pre-payments not only minimised the expenses for external financing. In addition, the pre-payments generated financial profits when the shipyards re-invested the liquid cash reserves.[19]

Moreover, the Finnish shipyards were not required to provide bank guarantees for the pre-payments they received from the Soviet Union. According to international practices, the customer typically asked the supplier for guarantees to ensure that the shipyard will meet its liabilities and complete the ship. In the Finnish–Soviet trade, the Soviet customers trusted the Finnish shipyards to use the pre-payments for the ship contract without these additional securities.

The Finnish shipbuilding companies had Wilhelm Wahlforss' sense of humour to thank for this exceptional sign of trust. According to the Finnish Eastern trade folklore, the Soviet negotiators had inquired after bank guarantees from the Wärtsilä corporation during trade negotiations in 1954, but director Wahlforss had jokingly misinterpreted the question and replied by asking which bank the Soviet Union wanted Wärtsilä to guarantee. The Soviet negotiators, amused by the arrogance of the private entrepreneur from a small country in the face of socialist superpower, eventually agreed that Wärtsilä did not need a bank to guarantee its projects.[20] The authenticity of the narrative details can be questioned, but the actual results are beyond doubt: The Soviet buyers trusted the financial standing and the trustworthiness of the big Finnish conglomerates without extra guarantees.[21]

On the one hand, the Finnish–Soviet bilateral trade system was a mechanical infrastructure for companies to conduct business. On the other hand, it involved a high level of bureaucratic coordination and conjoined governmental actors in economic exchange. This intermingling of politics and business in the Finnish–Soviet affairs got an institutional form in 1967. The Permanent Finnish–Soviet Intergovernmental Commission for Economic Cooperation (*Sosialististen Neuvostotasavaltojen Liiton ja Suomen Tasavallan pysyvä hallitusten välinen taloudellinen yhteistyökomissio*, hereafter in short, the 'Economic Commission') was founded by a presidential decree to advance economic cooperation between the two countries. The Economic Commission received a permanent secretariat in both Helsinki and Moscow, and it convened each autumn for an annual general meeting to study trade-related questions, to develop economic relations, and to discuss other cooperation possibilities.[22]

The Economic Commission created a direct link between the Finnish and the Soviet governments and established a standing forum for Finnish–Soviet economic cooperation. It was not the only bilateral commission that the Soviet Union had with capitalist countries, but it was the first and its chairs hold the highest rank in the Soviet administration.[23] The first Soviet chair was Nikolai Patolichev, a long-time Minister for Foreign trade. The Finnish government, having already nominated a relatively unknown Bank of Finland board member to the task, had to change its candidate to match the rank of the Soviet representation and appointed President Kekkonen's close ally, Minister Ahti Karjalainen (1923–1990).[24] The other members in the Finnish delegation came from ministries, the Bank of Finland, and big industrial enterprises.[25] The representation of the business world in an intergovernmental organ was compatible with the corporatist practices in Finland. It incorporated the industry into the state-level decision-making over Soviet trade, blurred the distinction between business and politics, and helped to cohere the political interests in the Finnish–Soviet relations with technical and economic possibilities.

## Expanding shipyards and dependency on Soviet market, 1952–1974

Economic growth and liberalisation of the international trade fuelled world shipping after the years of war and reconstruction. Economies of scale pushed ship owners to prefer bulk carriers and tanker ships with greater cargo capacity for cost-efficient transportation of commodities. The growth rate accelerated as a result of the closures of the Suez Canal because the alternative route via the Cape of Good Hope both demanded and permitted larger ships.

Figure 4.3 shows how the global shipbuilding followed in the wake of the shipping industry and expanded until the peak in 1975. During the upturn, the maritime business developed through innovations in production, organisations, cargo handling, and naval architecture. The technological development set new standards for shipyards. Cargo ships outgrew the old shipyards, their building berths, and the capacity of cranes and steel-handling facilities. Especially Japan opened larger greenfield sites designed to fulfil the new demand. In 1958, Japan launched the largest ship, SS *Universe Apollo* with 61,100 tons. In 1966, the first Very Large Crude Carrier (VLSS) *Idemitsy Maru* exceeded already 107,957 tons but lost the title for the largest tanker only two years later for the first Ultra Large Crude Carrier (ULCC), *Universe Ireland*, with 149,609 tons in 1968. Of the Northern European shipyards, Sweden and Denmark invested in modern production facilities, concentrating on efficient serial production of large tonnage.[26]

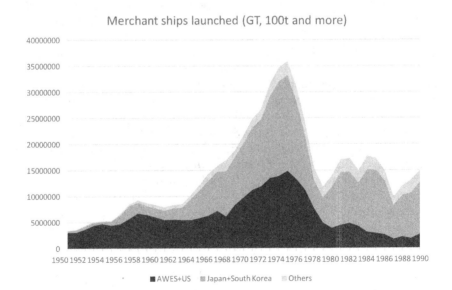

*Figure 4.3* Shipbuilding volume by region. Data: LRS.

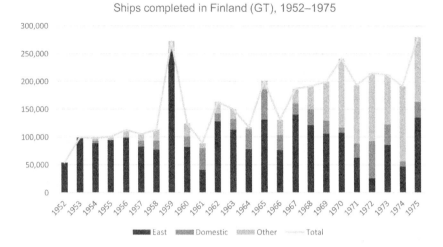

*Figure 4.4* The geographical distribution of the Finnish shiptrade (GT) 1952–1974. Data: Author from various sources.

Lloyd's Register added Finland to its annual country reports in 1953. In comparison to world leaders, Finnish ship production was marginal, but the growth was steady and kept up with the international development. As Figure 4.4 shows, the post-war expansion took place at the time when Finnish shipyards were kept employed almost entirely by the bilateral trade with the Soviet Union.

This dependency of the Finnish shipyards on the bilateral trade with the Soviet Union had both political and economic reasons. The political push to prioritise the Soviet orders above other customers was highest during the Korean War (1950–1953), when the Soviet need for new tonnage was the direst and the Western embargo the most restrictive.[27] In particular, the Soviet negotiators supplemented their commercial arguments with political arm-twisting and put pressure on the Finnish government to get the shipyards to contract for more oil tankers than they had original capacity to deliver.[28]

The economic explanation for the high share of the Soviet orders was the lack of Finnish competitiveness in the international shipbuilding markets. The war reparation production had pushed the Finnish shipyards to expand their capacity but not to streamline their organisations or refine their cost-competitiveness. Fast inflation rate on raw materials and industrial wages, lack of export financing, and the shortage of modern machinery also raised the Finnish production costs over international market prices.[29] Yet, the productivity and competitiveness varied greatly between shipyards, those who were established and experienced steel shipbuilders and those who were founded in a hurry to construct small and simple barges.

The Finnish shipyards started to find domestic and Western customers after the mid-1950s. On the one hand, the political pressure to prioritise Soviet

Origin of ships registered in the Soviet Union (GT), 1948–1975

*Figure 4.5* Country of origin, ships (GT) registered in the Soviet Union 1948–1974. Data: LRS.

orders decreased after the end of the Korean War. The Western embargo on non-military technology—such as oil tankers and fast cargo vessels—loosened and made it easier for the Soviet Union to purchase ships from other countries, as shown in Figure 4.5. On the other hand, the international upturn in shipbuilding forced ship buyers to turn to less competitive and less experienced shipyards like those in Finland. At the same time, domestic economic policy adjustments, including the devaluation of the Finnish markka by 39% in relation to the US dollar in September 1957, improved the Finnish competitiveness.

From the point of view of the Finnish shipbuilding industry, the problem was not the dependency on the Soviet exports as such, but the dependency on exports in general.[30]

The Finnish maritime cluster never developed vertical alliances between ship owners and shipyards that were typical in many other established maritime countries, like Denmark. Throughout the Cold War, shipbuilding in Finland remained export-oriented business, and domestic market remained limited.

In the 1960s, some Finnish shipyards won certain salient contracts that provided them with springboards for further development in the domestic market. For example, the 15,000-dwt tanker *Tervi*, ordered by the oil company Neste from Rauma-Repola in 1961, was such a jump-start. Rauma-Repola had previous experience only in vessels that were a quarter of the size of *Tervi*, but the growing unease about the dependency on Soviet orders motivated it to take the risk. While not being economically rewarding, it proved that Rauma-Repola was a capable builder of advanced merchant vessels and yielded strategic rewards later with further orders (Figure 4.8).[31]

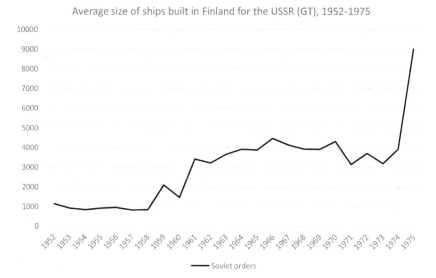

*Figure 4.6* Average size of ships built in Finland for the USSR (GT). Data: Author from various sources.

Domestic orders were critical also for the accumulation of technical competence in the segment of passenger ships. Passenger traffic in the Baltic had been traditionally frequent. After the war, it was fuelled by the Nordic Passport Union (1954), immigration from Finland to Sweden, and price differences between the countries that encouraged both work-related and leisure travelling. In the 1960s, the passengers were more often travelling with their cars that set new requirements for the ferries.

Wärtsilä Helsinki Shipyard completed the first modern Ro-Ro[32] ship for the Finnish-Swedish line, *Skandia*, in 1961. *Skandia* was followed with an array ferries whose size and design developed rapidly. New routes, cheaper tickets, comfortable vessels, and the lure of onboard duty-free shopping attracted new passengers to regular ferry lines and maintained a steady demand for new vessels that could both carry vehicles on wheels and entertain their drivers.[33]

The experience from the domestic passenger ferries contributed to the competitiveness in the cruise ship market that took off after 1967. A breakthrough in this market segment was Wärtsilä's contract for three cruiser ships with the newly founded Norwegian-owned cruise line company, Royal Caribbean.[34] The construction of these sophisticated floating hotels set different requirements for the shipyard structure, organisation, and network of subcontractors, which made them unattractive to big, streamlined mass-production yards. A world-class tanker builder had no competence or interest in interior design.[35] As a contrast to the large, streamlined ship factories, the Finnish shipyards were accustomed to shorter series and flexible production, they had sizable in-house design offices, and their large, multi-branch parent companies could accommodate special production. For example, Wärtsilä had branches for cabin modules and sanitation technology developed in tow of the passenger vessels.

Additional domestic factors that promoted Finnish competitiveness in the Western market in the 1960s included the devaluation of Finnish markka by 31% in 1967 and the moderate income agreement between the Finnish employers' organisations, labour unions, and the government, which controlled the wage increases.[36]

While the technical experience and cluster effects contributed to the Finnish competitiveness in certain special niches of the global shipbuilding market, the concrete dimensions of the shipyards determined the size of vessels for which they could compete. During the third five-year period 1961–1965, the emphasis of the Soviet demand structure changed corresponding to the global trend from small and simple ships and barges towards fewer, but larger vessels (Figure 4.6).[37] In 1969, Valmet estimated that its shipyard in Katajanokka, Helsinki, was wide enough to build only 5% of the vessels in the global shipbuilding markets; in 1975, the share was expected to shrink to 2%.[38] To stay in business, Finland needed new, larger shipyards (Figure 4.9).

First mover was the state-owned conglomerate Valmet. The Valmet board of directors had already decided to downscale the shipbuilding branch in 1963, but this strategy experienced a complete U-turn after the appointment of Olavi Mattila as the new director in 1964. The Soviet ship trade was a priority for him. Under Mattila's command in 1969–1970, Valmet decided to replace its old small shipyard in Helsinki with a new modern production unit on the outskirts of the city in Vuosaari. The Vuosaari Shipyard was to be spacious enough to construct vessels ranging from 20,000 dwt to 100,000 dwt, which the Soviet Union was interested in buying but which did not push the shipyard into the overheated competition for ultra large tankers. President Kekkonen himself opened the construction site in Vuosaari in 1971.[39]

The private shipbuilding companies conducted similar calculations. In 1969, Wärtsilä launched a series of investments that modernised its Helsinki Shipyard and opened a new modern shipyard in Perno, Turku. Like Valmet's Vuosaari Shipyard in Helsinki, Perno's location was outside the city of Turku. There the shipbuilding operations had room to expand in a way that had not been possible at their previous location on the banks of the river Aura inside the city.[40] Once again, President Kekkonen honoured the construction site by his presence, symbolically starting the project by ordering the first blast while a symphony orchestra played *Finlandia* by Jean Sibelius. This all underlined the impression that the Finnish shipbuilding expansion had a secure, state-supported function as the engine of Finnish industrial modernisation (Figure 4.7).[41]

The second largest private shipbuilding company Rauma-Repola chose to expand through acquisition. In 1973, the company bought up all the shares of Uusikaupunki Shipyard, a shipyard with long traditions going back to 1892. The shipyard had previously participated in the Finnish–Soviet trade building carriages of timber, dry cargo vessels, and even some passenger ships

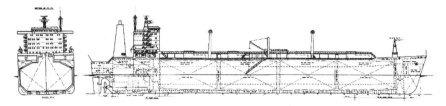

*Figure 4.7* The contract for five ice-going LPG-tankers to a Norwegian shipping company in 1974 determined the Wärtsilä's investment in the new modern shipyard in Perno, Turku. At the opening ceremony, shipbuilding director Christian Landtman reflected on the new standards of shipbuilding by saying that 'even if the new ships were ugly, they are more efficient'. *Wärtsilä* personnel magazine 2/74.

*Figure 4.8* M/S Tervi, the first tanker the state-owned oil refinery Neste purchased from Finland, was a ship of national importance. Its launching ceremony was attended by the state's political and industrial elite. In the photo, the godmother of the ship Sylvi Kekkonen together with her husband, President Urho Kekkonen (behind), celebrating the successful launch in Rauma 1961. They are accompanied by director of Rauma-Repola, Paavo Honkajuuri (left), and bank director Matti Virkkunen (right). Photo: National Board of Antiquities, The Picture Archives of Maritime Museum of Finland.

including the ice-capable cruise ship, the *Lindblad Explorer* 1968–1969. According to historian Mikko Uola, Rauma-Repola was however not interested in its facilities and machines but the workforce. In the 1974–1975 upswing, Rauma-Repola suffered from an acute lack of skilled labour. Uusikaupunki was located conveniently in the proximity of Rauma on the Finnish West Coast and had 900 skilled shipyard workers. Rauma-Repola could use the yard to build smaller vessels, borrow its electricians and plumbers, and take advantage of its ship repair experience.[42]

Rauma-Repola's other extension of maritime technology in the 1970s occurred through serendipity rather than strategic planning. In 1970, the company decided to establish a large new machine workshop in Mäntyluoto, Pori, with good logistical connections on the shore. The original plan was to produce large steel components for pulp mills and nuclear power plants. Because it happened to have a large production hall next to the deep sea just when the oil drilling in the North Sea was booming, Mäntyluoto ended up contracting for drilling drifts and platforms instead. The factory completed its first Pentagone-type oil-drilling platform in 1974 with a French customer.[43]

In the 1970s, the reliance on the Soviet market was already a very different question than it had been in the early 1950s. The Western and domestic markets balanced the dependency on the Soviet Union (Figure 4.11). Depending on the year and the shipyard, the share of the Soviet orders varied between 0% and 100%. While the private-owned Wärtsilä and Rauma-Repola had footholds in certain international market segments, the state-owned Valmet relied on the Soviet orders.

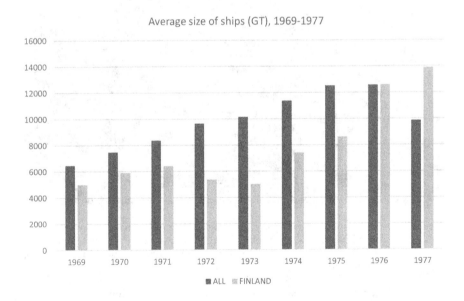

*Figure 4.9* Average size of vessels built globally and in Finland (GT). Data: LRS.

For all Finnish shipbuilding companies, however, the bilateral trade was an important element of stability that hedged risky projects in the other markets. The Soviet five-year trade agreements provided the basic load at the shipyards increasing predictability and facilitating long-term planning. It was clear to all concerned that when a Finnish shipbuilding director in 1973 referred to 'dark clouds raising from the east', he did not mean the Soviet Union but Japan.[44]

The bilateral trade system with the Soviet Union was critical for shipbuilding as a whole. In 1973, Bank of Finland director Mauno Koivisto concluded that clearing payment system and especially the pre-payments were indispensable. Otherwise, Finland could not provide the companies with competitive export credit schemes for the exports of capital goods. Indeed, without the bilateral trade with the Soviet Union, Finland could not afford the high-volume ship trade.[45]

The year 1974 was full of future prospects in Finland: Valmet Vuosaari Shipyard was completed, Mäntyluoto factory delivered its first oil-drilling platform, and Wärtsilä launched the construction of Perno Shipyard in Turku. The same year came to be catastrophic in international shipbuilding. As a result of Yom Kippur War in 1973, Arab petroleum exporting countries decided to use oil embargo and production cuts as a weapon against major industrial countries supporting Israel. The oil market prices skyrocketed, and the demand for crude oil shipping collapsed. In shipbuilding, this first oil crisis initiated a dramatic turn from boom to bust when shipping companies reacted to the depressing economic prospects by delaying and cancelling newbuilding contracts. The tanker market slumped first, dry cargo vessels a while later. The oil shock triggered a prolonged recession in international shipbuilding, accelerated industrial re-location from Western Europe to the Far East, and forced many well-established European shipbuilding countries to reduce their capacity.[46]

Paradoxically the oil crisis, which was a tragedy for most West-European shipbuilders and all oil-importing countries, fuelled positive development at the Finnish shipyards and strengthened the Finnish trust in the bilateral clearing trade.[47] Because oil and energy products dominated the Finnish imports from the USSR, the hike in oil prices increased the value of the Soviet trade and expanded the limits of the bilateral exchange. Like other energy importing countries, the Finnish economy suffered from growing energy expenses. Unlike the others, the Finnish economy was able to pay for the oil imports by increasing its selling to the Soviet Union, automatically and without competition.[48]

In the 1970s, the institutional framework of the Finnish–Soviet bilateral economic relations was completed with new elements that contributed to the Finnish perception of the steady and state-supported upward trend in the Soviet trade. In 1974, Finland's free trade agreement with the European Economic Community (EEC) came into force. Next year, Leonid Brezhnev proposed extending the planning horizon in the Finnish–Soviet relationship beyond the frames of the five-year plans to counterbalance the Western orientation in the Finnish trade.[49] The Long-Term Programme (*Pitkän Ajanjakson Ohjelma* PAO) 1977 outlined that the Finnish–Soviet ship trade was to grow between 13% and 33% in every five-year period until 1990. In the revised PAO in 1981, the trade quotas for bilateral ship exports were further expanded. [50]

While the 1970s demonstrated the straightforward connection between the Finnish–Soviet trade balance and the international oil market, it strengthened the contemporary illusion of the Soviet trade being insulated from global insecurities that would not oscillate as a 'pointer of the barometer of the international situation'.[51] Indeed, the support for the clearing trade and payment system was even stronger among the Finnish trade negotiators than on the Soviet side.[52] In the sixth and seventh five-year plans (1976–1980 and 1981–1995), the clearing trade and payment system was specified as the system of trade only at the special request of the Finnish delegation.[53]

During the first half of the Cold War, the Finnish shipbuilding expanded and adapted to the dualism of the Cold War. It developed practices for different contracting, different financing instruments, and different production structures in the bilateral Eastern trade and multilateral Western trade. There was no accurate answer to the contrafactual question, how the industry would have developed in absence of the bilateral institutions, but it was clear that the central decision-makers in foreign trade administration and industry understood the clearing trade and payment system as critical for the future of the Finnish shipbuilding. The widespread understanding of the bilateral trade being imperative for Finland set the undertone of the Finnish administration when it addressed the increasing problems of the clearing trade and payment system in the 1980s.

## Creating an illusion of stability, 1982–1985

In 1981, the director of the Bank of Finland's Eastern Trade Department Kari Holopainen received an invitation to a recreational fishing trip. The event was organised by Wärtsilä for the Soviet foreign trade delegation before the annual trade protocol negotiation in Helsinki, but bank officials were usually not invited to this type of business networking. The invitation foreshadowed that the shipbuilding industry had encountered problems they hoped the Bank of Finland to solve.[54]

In his memoirs, Holopainen recalled the year 1981 as a turning point in the Finnish–Soviet bilateral trade. The steady expansion had to make way to the growing structural imbalance and instability even though the public image of profitable, predictable, and state-supported trade still prevailed. In the Finnish Eastern trade folklore, the pictures of President Kekkonen catching salmon and telling fishing yarns with Soviet leaders on board luxury yachts and icebreakers had depicted the golden years of the Finnish–Soviet trade in the 1970s. Holopainen's description of civil servants fishing for cod in sleet and slush would capture the spirit of the clearing trade administration in the 1980s.

Balance of the Finnish-Soviet clearing account (SUR), 1971–91

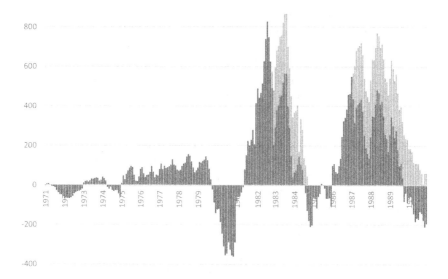

*Figure 4.10* Balance of the Finnish-Soviet clearing account in the Bank of Finland, monthly average in SUR (dark grey) and the auxiliary, interest-bearing account (light grey). In the figure, positive balance means that the Finnish exports to the USSR were more than the imports and vice versa. Data: Bank of Finland.

The oil price had stayed high, but as Figure 4.10 demonstrates, the value of the Soviet imports from Finland grew faster than that of Soviet exports to Finland. The deficit reached a new record in 1981–1982.[55] Alarmingly, as Holopainen noted to the government, the Soviet administration appeared to have lost control over foreign trade and allowed the FTOs to import more than they could afford.[56]

The growing imbalance of the bilateral trade worried the Finnish shipbuilding industry for good reasons. The risk that the Licensing Office would deny export licences until the Soviet clearing account had funds to pay for the purchases loomed large.[57] Metal engineering and ships comprised almost half (46%) of the Finnish total exports in 1982. The valuable ship projects had considerable impact on the balance in a way that was much out of the control of the clearing administration. The prime instrument in controlling the bilateral exchange, the five-year agreements and annual protocols, explicated the volume of goods and services crossing borders but not their values or the schedule of capital flows. In ship trade, the pre-payments spread over several years, and the long contract negotiations often took place outside the five-year trade framework. Referring to the long-term programme, the shipyards trusted that the already signed contracts would be included in the intergovernmental protocols afterwards.[58]

Three governmental organisations were involved in finding the solution for the imbalance problem: Ministry of Foreign Affairs coordinating the exports, Ministry of Trade and Industry taking care of the imports, and the Bank of Finland managing the balance of payments.

Ministry of Foreign Affairs was reluctant to interfere in the ship exports. There were no political rewards available for those who rejected export licences and by so doing endangered thousands of jobs. Åke Wihtol, a high-ranking civil servant in the Ministry of Foreign Affairs, acknowledged to his Soviet colleague in 1982 that withdrawing export licences would stand in a drastic contrast to the 'spirit of the Finnish-Soviet trade'.[59] The Soviet Deputy Minister for Foreign Trade A.N Manzhulov agreed with the Finns that especially 'the metal sector should not be bothered with these problems'.[60]

Instead of strict orders, Minister Esko Rekola politely appealed for the Federation of Metal Industries to collect more accurate and up-to-date information of the planned, negotiated, and confirmed contracts and terms of payments and to keep the Ministry updated of any changes. Besides some uncomfortable feelings among the industrial recipients, the ministerial letter had no consequences.[61]

Ministry of Trade and Industry was being caught in a severe political dilemma as well. Despite the efforts to increase purchases from the Soviet Union, crude oil had remained the only significant import product and the state-owned petrochemical company Neste was already buying almost all its raw materials from the Soviet Union. Finland was not dependent on the import of Soviet oil, but the exports that the imports of the oil enabled.

The limits of Finland's capacity to absorb Soviet oil inspired a curious transit oil trade (*välitysöljy*) which only aim was to artificially increase the value of the Soviet energy imports to Finland. Literally, the transit oil referred to the transfer of oil from third countries via Finland. Neste purchased mostly Libyan oil at the OPEC price and resold it in smaller shipments at current spot-prices. Not only this arrangement brought large shipments of oil that never arrived in the Soviet Union or in Finland to the Finnish–Soviet bilateral exchange of goods. It also indirectly engaged the neutral Finland in the Soviet-Libyan arms trade. Moreover, this arrangement constituted a rare exception in business history as a successful affair that was carried through by buying oil at higher prices and reselling it at lower prices. The Bank of Finland compensated Neste to offset the difference by providing Neste with clearing roubles at discount prices.[62]

Between 1982 and 1984, the value of the transit oil totalled SUR760 million (FIM5.3 billion) costing FIM175 million for the Bank of Finland. Director Holopainen was not unconditionally pleased with these manoeuvres that forced the Bank of Finland to carry increased business risk for political reasons.[63] As a whole, however, the transit oil was better than the alternatives because it enabled continuous exports without having to delay any ship orders.[64]

The Bank of Finland understood the gravity of shipbuilding in the Finnish–Soviet relations but as the account-holder bank, it felt concretely the consequences of the chronic imbalance of the clearing accounts. The Bank of Finland and VEB had previously lubricated the clearing trade by allowing the temporary off-balance of the accounts. When the scale of the deficit expanded unprecedently and seemingly uncontrolled, this administrational flexibility translated into an interest-free credit for a foreign country without means to protect the loan against exchange rate changes or inflation.[65] Under these circumstances, the Bank of Finland took an initiative to control the ship payments in a way that went far beyond its traditional role as a technical account keeper and made it deeply involved in private business contracts.

In the late 1970s, the customary payment schedule in Finnish–Soviet ship trade involving four payments of equal size during the construction period had been temporarily delayed with a 10–25–40–25 distribution of payments but the 25-25-25-25 distribution had been re-established in 1980.[66] In 1981, a Soviet delegation brought up the pre-payments during negotiations for the next five-year agreement 'initially as a joke' as described by the Bank of Finland notes from the meeting: 'the prepayments hampered Finnish monetary policy, facilitated inflation, worsened the position of Finnish workers and made the shipyards beneficiaries of unjust enrichment'.[67]

The representatives of the Bank of Finland promised to forward the message to the bank board of directors but what they did not reveal to the Soviets was that they did not like the extensive pre-payments, either. The front-heavy pre-payment schedule fuelled grey financing markets, accelerated inflation, and pushed the clearing accounts off balance.[68] The bank evaluated that a moderately tail-heavy payment schedule for ship deliveries, such as a distribution of 10-20-20-50, would correspond better to the actual cost-accumulation at the shipyards.[69]

Thus, when the Soviet representatives later, and this time officially, proposed re-scheduling the ship pre-payments in 1983, it was in alignment with the Bank of Finland's monetary policy goals. Instead of the traditional four-times-25% payments, the bank officials agreed that the Finnish shipyards would receive a maximum of 15%–20% of the price during the construction period and the rest at the delivery.[70]

The Finnish shipyards were not pleased with the new payments schedule. They protested loudly to the Finnish ministries about the increasing costs of financing arguing that it would only harm the Soviets through increased prices. In negotiations with the Soviets, though, they had remarkable few arguments for the extensive pre-payments. Instead, they were compelled to accept the delayed payment schedule for not to provoke the Soviets to claim similar post-delivery financing schemes the ship buyers received in other Western countries.[71]

The Bank of Finland civil servants did not find sympathy for the industrial outcry but suspected that the companies exaggerated their financing problems. For monetary policy reasons, Bank of Finland was reluctant to use public funds to compensate the delayed pre-payments for the shipyards in fear that it would increase monetary instability. Observing the trends in international shipbuilding, the central bank also wanted to save the use of state aid for the future:

> It is completely possible that the shipyard industry will turn to the Bank of Finland at the end of this decade hoping for subsidies for Western exports and domestic trade on the grounds of experienced difficulties. To put it simply: Is it reasonable to go to a permanent subsidy policy already now and with these reasons?[72]

As a compromise, therefore, the Bank of Finland board of directors only allowed the shipyards to borrow 40% of their pre-delivery financing from foreign financing markets.[73]

In the early 1980s, the ship trade through the bilateral Finnish–Soviet clearing system required increasing involvement from the trade administration, but the problems were kept out of the public. The Bank of Finland had clear instructions on how its employees should address the clearing imbalance only as a natural implication of the high volume of Finnish-Soviet trade. All details of the special arrangements were treated as bank secrets.[74] Instead, the advantages of the bilateral clearing trade were justified with statistical time-series: clearing-based Finnish–Soviet trade had grown substantially faster compared to Finnish foreign trade in general.[75]

*Figure 4.11* Geographical distribution of the Finnish shipbuilding. Data: Author from various sources.

In 1982, director Holopainen published an article about the Finnish–Soviet trade system in which he vaguely referred to the administrative creativity required to keep the bilateral clearing working by pointing out that 'the development of the trade has been essentially influenced by how the system has been administrated in practice'.[76] By this note, he gently disputed the role of the clearing trade and payment system as the solid foundation for endlessly expanding Finnish–Soviet trade and attributed the trade balance to the administrative practices. That was about as harsh as criticism of the clearing trade and payment system could get in the early 1980s Finland.

## Farewell to the special relationship, 1986–1990

The innovative measures introduced by the Finnish clearing trade administration maintained the illusion of functional and balanced bilateral trade as long as the energy prices remained high. In 1986, the value of the Soviet imports dropped rapidly due to the slump in oil price (Figure 4.12).[77] From 1986 to 1988, the value of the Soviet imports covered only 75% of the Finnish exports to the Soviet Union.[78]

The widening gap between the imports and exports triggered the first serious polemic of the continuation of the Finnish–Soviet clearing system. When the problems became too big to hide from the public, both Finnish and Soviet parties blamed the fluctuations of the oil markets: a factor that was external to the bilateral relations. At the beginning, the discussion on the oil price overshadowed more profound processes that were transforming the political foundation on which the bilateral trade had been constructed.

Mikhail Gorbachev (1931–) had been nominated as the General Secretary of the Communist Party and thus the leader of the Soviet Union in 1985. Succeeding a sequence of elderly men, he represented the possibility for change. He addressed the Soviet economic problems in public and launched

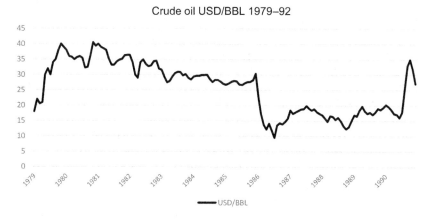

*Figure 4.12* Crude oil Brent price USD/barrel. Data: Bank of Finland.

campaigns to reconstruct Soviet political and economic culture. The Soviet economic reformations, especially the *perestroika* campaign, decentralised decision-making in the foreign trade and increased budget responsibility of the organisations. The old and rigid clearing trade system did not fit well with the Soviet modernisation plans. Finland was exceptional, as President Koivisto reasoned in 1987, 'the only capitalist country having a bilateral trade relationship with them, otherwise [clearing] is just for trade with socialist or developing countries. This is how we, our system, is clearly a disturbing factor in their internal restructuring'.[79]

The managers of the Finnish shipbuilding companies greeted the small steps in the Soviet Union towards a more liberal and open economy with anxiety. After four decades of adaptation to the Cold War dualism of two economic regimes, the Finns were concerned that they might lose the established market position and business connections if the bilateral clearing trade system was dismantled.[80] Living next to the unpredictable socialist superpower had made the Finns to appreciate stability in political and economic relations. The bilateral clearing trade and payment system was one tangible instrument of creating stability that guaranteed that the ship trade would go on in the future as it had used to.[81] Neither President Koivisto nor the Finnish foreign trade politicians wanted to take a leap into the unknown and abandon the bilateral trade.[82]

Shipbuilding companies set up working groups to monitor weak signals of transformation in the socialist bloc and to analyse their effects on the Finnish–Soviet trade. Especially younger-generation engineers and businessmen, who were frequently in Moscow and mingled with lower levels of Soviet administration, brought up the possibility of changes in the Soviet trade. Rauma-Repola's Soviet trade manager, Kari Ketola, suggested at the company strategy meeting in 1986, that it would be 'time to retarget [our trade] a little more towards the west. However, only on the quiet. In public, the efforts towards, and the importance of, the east should be emphasised'.[83] While many were ready to accept some adjustments in the established state of affairs, the documentation reveals no expectations about the bilateral trade partnership being on the brink of a revolutionary change.[84] Change would come but 'not in our lifetime', as estimated in Wärtsilä.[85]

During President Koivisto's visit to Moscow in 1987, the Soviet Union proposed credit-based financing in the ship trade. In international comparison, the request was rather modest. The Soviet Union asked for similar OECD terms of export credits that were widely available in international shipbuilding markets: A loan for 80% of the contract price for eight years at an 8% yearly interest rate.[86] In the light of the Finnish experience of the bilateral trade, however, it meant dismantling one of the most important advantages in the Soviet trade.

The Bank of Finland adopted a strictly negative stand on the export credits in clearing-based ship trade. The official rationale was that the clearing trade system should be based on the bilateral exchange of goods and services and it should be balanced by adjusting the imports and exports: credit arrangements were alien to the principle of bilateralism.[87] This principle resonated well with the rhetoric of mutually beneficial economic cooperation but was technically an excuse.

In the history of the Finnish–Soviet clearing trade, the Soviet Union had provided credit for Finnish project imports. For example in 1966, the Soviet Bank for Foreign Economic Relations VEB had granted a loan of SUR5 million for Valmet to be paid and paid back through the clearing account. Originally, the credit had been a supplier-credit for Valmet to deliver a sack paper factory, but it became linked to the purchase of a floating ship dock.[88]

A more comprehensive reason for the Bank of Finland to resist export credits in the Soviet trade was the fear of losing control. Credit sales would initially allow the Soviets to buy more products than they could afford, but when the interest and amortisations became due, the Finnish export opportunities would diminish. Moreover, the export credits should be financed by capital import from the Western financing markets, which increased national debt and could risk the national credit rating.[89]

Gradually, though, the Bank of Finland shifted its position towards a more conditional 'no'. The principle of clearing trade being cash trade remained, but the central bank became ready to accept export credits in exceptional cases, namely the ship trade. The prime reasons were political, as Holopainen contemplated in 1985: 'Difficulties in contracting [with the Soviets] become easily a "national" question. The "unreasonably" strict policy may provide an unnecessarily easy excuse to impeach the Bank of Finland for the problems [in the bilateral trade]'.[90]

In 1988, the Soviet trade organisations refused to make new orders without getting post-delivery financing. In doing so, they pushed Finnish shipbuilding companies to appeal to Finnish ministries to save the ship export from a collapse, which finally put enough political pressure on the Finnish government to introduce export credits in the Soviet trade.[91]

In the fall of 1988, Finland and the Soviet Union agreed on modifications to the clearing system.[92] The agreement was a curious compromise over increasing flexibility in financing and increasing control over the clearing accounts. The strategic stick was to place a strict ceiling and interest rate for the clearing deficit and to require automatic down-payments in convertible currencies. The tactical carrot was to allow Finnish Export Credit Ltd. and commercial banks to finance the export of ships and other capital goods to the Soviet Union. These export credits were to be based on the OECD terms of export credits—the same that the Finnish shipyards received in Western trade—and they were eligible for public guarantees from the Finnish Board of Export Guarantees.[93]

In the defence of the clearing trade, which had been beneficial for shipbuilding because of the low financing costs, Finland ended up introducing state-supported schemes for export credits. The state guarantees for Soviet exports rose rapidly to 30% of the liabilities of the Finnish Board of Export

Guarantees but posed no imminent problems. The Soviet Union still enjoyed the best class 'A' credit rating in Finland.[94]

In October 1989, when Mikhail Gorbachev visited Finland, the streets of Helsinki were crowded with people greeting the Soviet General Secretary. The governments of the two countries manifested good relations by signing the five-year agreement on bilateral trade exchange for the period 1990–1995.[95]

Only two weeks later, the people of Berlin tore down the wall, manifesting the starting point of the new post-Cold War era. In Finland, though, this brought about no radical alteration in foreign policy.[96] For a small country, even the weak Soviet Union was strong enough to be treated with respect; for Finnish shipbuilders, even a poor superpower was rich enough to buy an icebreaker or two.

In December 1989, the Ministry of Finance analysed the future of shipbuilding in Finland concluding that 'still in this situation we should be prepared to build special-purpose vessels for the Soviet Union'.[97] The Long-Term Programme had been recently revised in 1987. It outlined the future of the trade exchange up to the new millennium.[98]

The management of the bilateral clearing system had never been so difficult for the Finnish foreign trade administration, hampered by the Soviet economic reforms and low oil price. At the same time, the bilateral trade had never been so popular among the Finnish industries. It was clear to all that the Finnish shipyards had been able to cash in on the special trade relationship with pre-payments, longstanding personal connections, long-term planning, and economies of scale.[99] It would seem that the political and industrial actors mistakenly confused the technical trade and payment system with the broader political and economic framework of the Finnish–Soviet relationship that had provided a hospitable environment for industrial growth. It was as if the temporary, state-level five-year agreements had secured continuation; the state-level trade protocols had confirmed company-level contracts; and the bilateralism had promised a steady position for the Finnish industry in the Soviet market.

The world around the Finnish–Soviet bilateral relationship, allegedly isolated from international turmoil, kept transforming. Only two months after the Finnish and Soviet leaders had confirmed the continuance of the clearing trade, the socialist CMEA countries agreed to abolish clearing mechanisms in all trade.[100] This opened up an intense year of Finnish–Soviet negotiations on whether or not the decision involved also Finland. Finnish civil servants put a lot of effort into negotiating a special arrangement that would effectively extend bilateralism, including the possibility to couple the Soviet energy imports with Finnish exports of capital goods and ships. The minimum target was to use the next five-year term as a transition period to cushion the threatening collapse.[101]

The information that the Finns gathered in the following meetings from the Soviets was obscure and inconsistent. In May 1990, the vice-director of

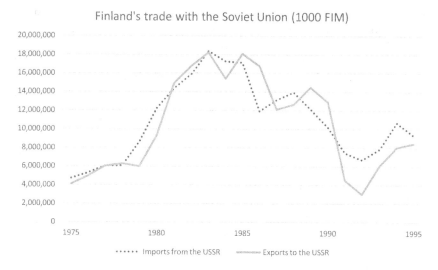

*Figure 4.13* The development of the Finnish trade with the Soviet Union 1975–
1995. Data: Finnish Custom.

Wärtsilä Marine Martin Saarikangas presented as his assessment to the daily
newspaper *Helsingin Sanomat* that the contracts the Finns were negotiating
in Moscow would be covered through clearing.[102] As late as in October
1990, Rauma-Repola's Mäntyluoto factory contracted with Sudoimport for
jack-up platforms.[103]

On December 6, during the celebration of the Finnish Independence Day,
the Soviet Deputy Prime Minister Stephan Sitarjan announced to the Finnish
Ambassador Heikki Talvitie that the Finnish–Soviet clearing accounts would
be terminated by the end of the year.[104] Notwithstanding this somewhat
intimate channel for delivering the message that meant a revolution in the
state-level economic relations, it signalled that the trade with Finland was no
longer of special interest in Moscow.

The Bank of Finland and VEB closed the clearing accounts on the first day
of January 1991.[105] In the spring of 1992, Finland and the Russian Federation
signed a commercial treaty. Instead of bilateralism and special institutions,
this new agreement based trade relations on GATT, multilateralism, and convertible currencies.[106]

The share of the Soviet trade dropped to 4% in 1992 and was estimated to
have caused a total loss of 150,000 jobs.[107] The collapse of the Eastern trade
was coincidental with a severe bank crisis and economic recession. Overall,
the end of the Cold War era in Finland was characterised by unemployment,
bankruptcies, and dramatic changes in industrial structure. Especially, the
Soviet trade experts of older generations, who had been used to the steadily growing bilateral trade and regulated market conditions, were inclined

to place the blame for the downturn to the end of the clearing trade system. Director Tankmar Horn took upon himself to publicly accuse President Koivisto for the decline of Finnish industry: 'It was wrong to break down the clearing system on [Finland's] own initiative'.[108]

The bilateral clearing trade system had contributed to the expansion of the Finnish shipbuilding industry from the 1950s onwards by creating an institutional interface between the market economy and socialist planning, providing predictability and cheap financing, facilitating negotiations for longer series, and engaging state-actors in the maintenance of the economic relations. The disintegration of the clearing trade system in 1990 was not, however, the reason for the collapse of the Finnish–Soviet ship trade. That trend had started before as shown in Figure 4.13. Most of the special features of this partnership, including cheap financing, long-term planning and the foreign policy implications of the economic cooperation, had started to faint away from the late 1970s onwards. As severe as the economic difficulties in the Finnish–Soviet trade were at the turn of the 1990s, they were now merely a Finnish internal problem. The high-volume ship trade was no longer a factor in the Finnish–Soviet peaceful coexistence.

The line of reasoning that implies causality between the termination of the bilateral clearing trade system and the difficulties in Finnish shipbuilding, is widely spread in the popular history culture. From the Finnish point of view, it downplays Finland's active role in supporting the bilateral trade partnership with the Soviet Union and provides an opportunity to outsource the responsibility for the economic problems to the disintegration of the Soviet Union. By so doing, the discourses of the Finnish–Soviet trade served a therapeutic purpose in the post-Cold War Finland.

## Conclusions

The positive development in the Finnish shipbuilding industry after the oil crisis exemplified the Finnish exceptionalism among the Western shipbuilding countries. The interesting question was how the ships, which were built in Finland, came to be built in Finland and not elsewhere: who paid for them, how much, and why? The bilateral clearing trade and payment system is a partial answer to these questions.

From the point of view of the 21st century, it may be difficult to understand the lure of bilateral clearing. As Philip Hanson remarked, '[b]ilateral clearing has all the disadvantages of barter between individuals. It is unlikely that countries will trade efficiently on that basis. Prices will typically be manipulated, or unwanted merchandise accepted, to strike an accounting balance'. He continues by observing that the socialist block traded through clearing because the inconvertibility of the currency left them no choice. Finland, according to Hanson, adopted the clearing trade system because its history and geography provided no alternative than to consent to Soviet dictates.[109]

As this chapter makes clear, the Finnish shipbuilding companies did not merely accept the clearing trade system; they loved it. Bilateral institutions provided an efficient interface to facilitate buying and selling between two different economic systems.

Nevertheless, the clearing trade system did not create trade. It could facilitate it only as long as the prime decision-makers, profit-driven companies in Finland and state-organisations in the pre-*perestroika* Soviet Union, had the will and the funds to engage in the bilateral ship trade. During the first half of the Cold War, the Finnish–Soviet bilateral trade exchange had become a symbol of the peaceful co-existence. The meaning of the bilateral trade as an indicator of the political relationship was further emphasised in the five-year plans, long-term agreements, and other intergovernmental institutions that systematically constructed and reconstructed the picture of stabile, on-going, and state-supported bilateral trade.

This discursive illusion made the Finnish shipbuilding companies slow to realise that the special trade relationship with the Soviet Union was about to end. The volumes and cash payments of clearing trade were too important for the Finnish shipyards, the shipyards were too important for the Finnish–Soviet trade, and the Soviet trade was too important for the Finnish–Soviet political affairs that neither Finnish politicians or industrialists would have dared to risk abandoning the bilateralism. Escaping the Cold War straitjacket was a leap into the unknown. The only certain thing was that landing without the Eastern trade cushion would damage the shipbuilding industry. The Finnish capitalists and the centrally coordinated trade system remained strange bedfellows even after the bilateral system began to be too rigid, expensive, and old-fashioned for the socialist countries.

## Notes

1 Total production (merchant ships launched, over 100 tons) in 1953 5,094,836 GT and 1974 34,624,410 GT. In Finland, respectively, 38,301 GT and 205,905 GT. Lloyd's Register for Shipping.
2 Stråth, *The Politics of De-industrialization*, 1987; Todd, *Industrial Dislocation*, 1991.
3 Barnaby Feder, "Finland's Booming Shipyard: A Profitable link to Soviet," *The New York Times*, 8.8.1983.
4 Laurila, *Finnish-Soviet Clearing Trade*, 1995, 19–24; 75–82; Alho et al., *Neuvostoliiton kauppa Suomen kansantaloudessa*, 1986, 12.
5 Hjerppe, "Finland's Foreign Trade and Trade Policy in the 20th Century," 1993, 69; Kuusterä & Tarkka, *Suomen Pankki 200 vuotta II*, 2012, 225; Hirvensalo, *Suomen ja SNTL:n välinen clearing maksujärjestelmä*, 1979, 13.
6 Hanson, *The Rise and Fall of the Soviet Economy*, 2014, 84.
7 Stopford, *Maritime Economics*, 2009, 208–209.
8 Hanson, *The Rise and Fall of the Soviet Economy*, 2014, 9–15; Sutela, *Trading with the Soviet Union*, 2014, 55.
9 V/O short from *Vsesojuznoe Objedinenie*, All-Soviet group, Sudoimport meaning ship import.

10  Trade Agreement between Finland and the Soviet Union, 1968, f. 45, 3279, SPA.
11  Agreement between Finland and the Soviet Union on trade exchange, 1956–1960, f. 45, 3279, SPA.
12  Salminen, *Ulkomaankaupan erityisesti idänkaupan päätöksenteko valtion keskushallinnossa*, 1978, 143–144.
13  *Suomen Metalliteollisuusyhdistys.* Later, *Teknologiateollisuus Ry*, Technology Industries of Finland.
14  Laurila, *Finnish-Soviet Clearing Trade*, 1995, 70–71; On Finnish economic dependencies and import regulations: Kuisma, *Kylmä sota, kuuma öljy*, 1995, 232–245.
15  In the late 1980s clearing-based export, a permit was required for all deals over FIM2000. If convertible currencies were used, the permit was always required but automatically granted. Laurila, *Finnish-Soviet Clearing Trade*, 1995, 70–71.
16  On the costs and benefits of Finnish–Soviet clearing, see Laurila, *Finnish-Soviet Clearing Trade*, 100–102.
17  Stopford, *Maritime Economics*, 2009, 276.
18  Stråth, *The Politics of De-industrialisation*, 1987, 15–16; Stopford, *Maritime Economics*, 2009, 276.
19  Herranen, *Valtion raha vauhditti*, 2009, 82; 216–217.
20  Landtman, *Mina år vid Wärtsilä*, 2011, 62–63.
21  Bertel Långhjelm to Arvid Helsingius 10.3.1954, Wärtsilä keskushallinto 40, ELKA.
22  Agreement on the founding of the Intergovernmental Finnish-Soviet Economic Commission, SopS 45/1967; Laurila, *Finnish-Soviet Clearing Trade*, 1995, 65–67; Holopainen, "Suomen ja Neuvostoliiton välisen kaupan toimintaperiaatteet ja kaupan kehitys," 1981, 309–310.
23  In 1987, the Finnish Embassy in Moscow concluded that only China, India, and Finland had a vice Prime Minister Vladimir Kamentsev as the chair of the bilateral commission, other countries having to settle for lower-ranking officers. Finnish Embassy in Moscow 149 on clearing countries in the Soviet foreign trade, 9.3.1987, f. "ITÄ-clearingit," SPA.
24  Keskinen, *Idänkauppa: 1944–1987*, 1987, 293.
25  Laurila, *Finnish-Soviet Clearing Trade*, 1995, 65; Salminen, *Tapaustutkimus talouden, politiikan ja hallinnon keskinäisistä kytköksistä*, 1983, 3; 34.
26  Lloyd's Register of Shipping, *Shipbuilding Returns*.
27  Rauma-Repola to Formin 8.10.1952 on four tankers of 4,000 tons to the Soviet Union; Rauma-Repola to Palmroth 14.8.1952; Encrypted message 25.8.1952; Encrypted message 22.8.1952; Minutes from a meeting between Palmroth, Enckell, Loshakov, Sosunov et al., f. 106, 58 B1, UMA.
28  Meeting between Consul general G. Palmroth and Soviet commercial representative Sosunov 28.7.1952; KPO on additional exports to the Soviet Union 30.7.1952; Telegrams from Palmroth to Ministry of Foreign Affairs (Formin), 21.8.1952; 22.8.1952; 26.8.1952; 18.9.1952; 3.9.1952; Telegram 152 from Ingman to Formin 25.8.1952; f. 106, 58 B1, UMA.
29  According to Niklas Dahl, the joint Finnish-American attempt to decrease Finnish dependence on Soviet ship orders by increasing Western trade failed only because of the 30% price difference between Finnish prices and market prices. Dahl, *"Länsikauppakin meille sentään jotakin merkitsee." Johann Nykopp Suomen Washingtonin –lähettiläänä 1951–1958*, 2016, 44–46. Similar argument in Jensen-Eriksen,"CoCom and Neutrality," 2010, 54.
30  Kaukiainen, *Ulos Maailmaan!*,2008, 412–415; 419–420; 426; Ojala & Kaukiainen, "Finnish Shipping – A Nordic Exception?" 2012, 130.

31 Uola, *Meidän isä on töissä telakalla*, 1996, 180–188; Kuisma, *Kylmä sota, kuuma öljy*, 1997, 323–324.

32 Roll on/Roll off, a ship type designed to load wheeled vehicles along ramps on their own wheels without having to use cranes to load and unload the cars on board.

33 Kaukiainen, *Ulos Maailmaan!*, 2008, 432; For an in-depth review of the development of ship design, see Id & Peters, *Innovation and Specialisation*, 2017.

34 Id & Peters, *Innovation and Specialisation*, 2017, 58–62.

35 *Navigator* 10/1970; Id & Peters, *Innovation and Specialisation*, 2017, 60.

36 Tiihonen, *The Ministry of Finance*, 2012, 179–180.

37 Id & Peter, *Innovation and Specialisation*, 31.

38 *Navigator* 12/1971.

39 Björklund, *Valmet*, 1990, 185–186; 306–309; *Navigator* 12/1971.

40 Christian Landtmanin interview in *Wärtsilä* personnel magazine 1/73.

41 *Wärtsilä* personell magazine 2/74.

42 Uola, *Meidän isä on töissä telakalla*, 1996, 342–351.

43 Uola, *Meidän isä on töissä telakalla*, 1996, 376–384.

44 "Pilviä idästä," *Wärtsilä* personell magazine 1/73.

45 Notes 8.3.1973 from a meeting on Eastern trade, Koivisto 119, NA.

46 Todd, *Industrial Dislocation*, 1991, 3–4; Stråth, *The Politics of De-industrialization*, 1987, 4; 83–115.

47 Starck, *Foreign and Domestic Shocks and Fluctuations in the Finnish Economy*, 1990; Honkapohja et al., *Economic Prosperity Recaptured*, 2009, 10–11.

48 SP on Finnish–Soviet trade prospects 30.1.1980, f. 45, SPA; chair of STTY Pentti Helpiö on current issues in shipbuilding industry in the shipbuilding and shipping seminar 28.11.1979, STTY 1, ELKA.

49 SP on Finnish–Soviet PAO, f. 59, 4742, SPA.

50 From SUR1.2 billion in 1976–1980 to 1.6–1.8 billion in 1986–1990. Long-Term Programme on the Development and Intensification of the Economic and Scientific-Technical Cooperation between Finland and the USSR, SopS 54/1977; Holopainen, "Suomen ja Neuvostoliiton välisen kaupan toiminta-periaatteet ja kaupan kehitys," 1981, 308–309.

51 N.N. Inozemtsev, Introduction to *Finnish-Soviet Economic Relations*, 1983. The same argument also used by Minister Jermu Laine in KPO 500 on meeting of Laine and B.I. Aristov in Moscow 19.9.1986, Koivisto 7, NA.

52 Teollisuuden Keskusliitto 68/1976 on PAO 1990 24.8.1976: Metalliteollisuuden keskusliitto on PAO 15.9.1975, f. f59, 4742, SPA; Meeting between Ahti Karjalainen and N.S. Patolitshev 26.1.1976, IV:5, UKA.

53 KPO on the meeting between Arvo Rytkönen and V. M. Ivanon in Moscow 31.8.1978, f. 47, SPA; Kuusterä & Tarkka, *Suomen Pankki 200 vuotta II*, 2012, 475–476.

54 Holopainen, *Orpo piru*, 2007, 130–131.

55 Holopainen, *Orpo piru*, 2007, 134–135.

56 KPO 114 on the payment situation in the Finnish-Soviet trade, 9.2.1982; SP on Finnish-Soviet payments v.198,2 3.2.1982, 4979; KPO 748 on Finnish-Soviet trade protocol 1982, 16.12.1981, 3279, SPA.

57 Working Group for Trade Politics, meeting 27.5.1982, 3279, SPA.

58 KPO 748 on Finnish-Soviet trade protocol 1982, 16.12.1981, 3279, SPA.

59 KPO on the meeting between M. V. Gubanov and Wihtol 29.3.1982, 3279, SPA; KPO 145 on imbalance of Soviet trade and exports in coming years 19.2.1982, Ef 122, 4979, SPA.

60 KTM on the visit of Deputy Minister Manzhulo in Finland, 27.9.1983; KPO 477 on Finnish-Soviet trade 1984; PAO meeting in Helsinki 23.9.1983, f. 50, 4741, SPA.

61  UM21151, Esko Rekola & Åke Wihtol to Metalliteollisuuden Keskusliitto 17.2.1982 on project and ship exports to the Soviet Union, STTY 2, ELKA.
62  KPO 497 on the visit of Deputy Minister Manzhulo in Helsinki, 19.9.1983, f. 50, 4741, SPA.
63  Holopainen to Laine 21.9.1983, f. 50, 4741, SPA.
64  KPO 497 on the visit of Deputy Minister Manzhulo in Helsinki, 19.9.1983, f. 50, 4741; SP on payments for transits oil, 4.1.1984; SP on transit oil to balance the clearing accounts; SP draft on the transit oil affairs, 10.5.1984; Holopainen & Levo, "Arvio Suomen ja Neuvostoliiton välisestä raakaöljyn välityskaupasta," 18.7.1984, f. 12, 2876, SPA.
65  Kuusterä & Tarkka, *Suomen Pankki 200 vuotta II*, 2012, 476.
66  Finnish-Soviet Export Financing Working Group on pre-delivery financing 17.4.1978, f. 127, 4986, SPA.
67  SP, Ilkka Vasara on Finnish-Soviet negotiations 23.6.1981–26.6.1981, 3279, SPA.
68  SP, Vasara on acute issues in the Soviet trade 4.9.1981, 3279, SPA.
69  SP on financing ship and project export to the Soviet Union 21.4.1983, f. 50, 4741, SPA.
70  SP on financing ship and project export to the Soviet Union 21.4.1983, KPO 437 on Finnish-Soviet civil servant meeting in Moscow 29.8.1983–31.8.1983 and Sudoimport's PM on ship payment, 26.8.1983, f. 50, 4741, SPA; Shipyard Committee meeting 1.11.1983, f. 327, UPMA; Meeting between Koivisto and Sorsa 9.1.1987, Koivisto 33, NA.
71  STTY on ship payments in the Finnish-Soviet trade 17.8.1983, STTY pöytäkirjat 1981–1983, ELKA; Shipyard Committee meeting 1.11.1983, f. 327; STTY on payments in Finnish-Soviet trade, f. 327, UPMA; SP on changes in the Finnish-Soviet ship payments 16.6.1983; KPO 497 on the visit of Deputy Minister Manzhulo in Helsinki, 19.9.1983, f. 50, 4741, SPA.
72  SP 1DA24.1 on ship financing in the Soviet trade 1986–1990, Ed 1, 246, SPA.
73  SP 1DA24.1 on ship financing in the Soviet trade 1986–1990; SP on payments in Eastern trade, 16.4.1985, Ed 1, 256, SPA.
74  Instructions for communication concerning the Finnish-Soviet special account, 4.11.1982 and 10.11.1982, f. 50, 4741, SPA.
75  *Kauppapolitiikka* 1–2/84.
76  Holopainen, "Suomen ja Neuvostoliiton välisen kaupan toimintaperiaatteet," 1981, 325.
77  Kuusterä & Tarkka, *Suomen Pankki 200 vuotta II*, 2012, 522.
78  Laurila, *Finnish-Soviet Clearing Trade and Payment System*, 1995, 108–115; Hukkinen, "Suomen vientimenestys Neuvostoliiton markkinoilla," 1990, 270–272; KPO 497 on Finnish-Soviet trade negotiations 9.9.1986, Koivisto 7, NA.
79  UAVK 13.10.1987, Koivisto 34, NA.
80  Jouko Sere on the Kauppalehti symposium, 17.10.1986, f. 542C, Ketola, UPMA; Meeting between Koivisto and Wihtol 13.2.1987, Koivisto 33; UAVK 13.10.1987, Koivisto 34, NA.
81  Interview of Tankmar Horn in *Suomen Kuvalehti* (SK) 5.9.1986; WM memorandum dated on 24.8.1987, f. Telakkateollisuus 1986–1987, 51.4; Ministerial Committee for Economic Policy on the Finnish-Soviet trade, 18.3.1988, f. Suomi-NL 1.1.1988–30.6.1988, 42.1, UMA.
82  TPK 142 on meeting in the presidential palace 11.11.198, f. Talouspolitiikka 1986, Koivisto, NA.
83  Rauma-Repola Strategy meeting 7.2.1986, Ketola 542C, Ketola, UPMA.
84  Rauma-Repola's Soviet trade, 27.6.1988, Ketola 542C; Rauma-Repola's Soviet trade 1986–1990, 29.10.1986, Ketola 642C, UPMA.
85  WM on the perestroika-working group 24.9.1987, WM 29, ELKA.

Institutional interface to Soviet market 109

86 Koivisto, *Kaksi kautta*, II, 1995, 243.
87 KPO 63 on meeting between Minister Suominen and Ambassador Sobolev 28.1.1988, f. Suomi-NL f. 1.1.1988–30.6.1988, 42.2, UMA; Laurila, *Finnish-Soviet Clearing Trade*, 1995, 51; Koivisto, *Kaksi Kautta: 2*, 1995, 243; Meeting between Holopainen and Koivisto, 20.10.1987, Koivisto 34, KA.
88 Olavi Mattila to Kekkonen 9.6.1966, Vuosikirja 1966, UKA; SP on Valmet's rouble loans, 10.11.1972, Ef 1948–1978, 10769, SPA. For other examples of the use of convertible currencies in the Eastern trade, see also SP on credits taken in convertible currencies and used for purchases in non-convertible currency 17.6.1977; SP on Western financing on Eastern trade, 16.9.1977; SP on regulation of credits used to finance imports, 10.1.1979, SPA.
89 SP on credits in the Finnish-Soviet trade 21.3.1985, Ed 1, 256, SPA.
90 Quotation marks original. SP 1DA35.1 on pre-delivery financing of Finnish-Soviet ship trade, 22.10.1985, Ed 1, 256, SPA.
91 KPO 63 on meeting between Suominen and Sobolev 28.1.1988; WM memorandum, dated 24.8.1987, f. "Telakkateollisuus 1986–1987," 51.4, UMA.
92 KPO on meeting in MVES 9.6.1988, f. Suomi-NL 1.1.1988–30.6.1988; KPO 704 on Finnish-Soviet trade 17.8.1988, f. Suomi-NL 1.7.1988–31.10.1988, 43.41, UMA.
93 Meeting of the clearing payment working group 8.8.1988–10.8.1988, Koivisto 11b, NA; Records dated 9.9.1988, f. 56, SPA; *Talouselämä* 33/1988; Laurila, *Finnish-Soviet Clearing Trade*, 1995, 51–52.
94 In January 1990, the Finnish Board of Export Guarantees decreased the Soviet Union's credit rating from the best A class to the second-best B class. The Finnish Board of Export Guarantees on export and investment guarantees for the Soviet Union and Eastern Europe, f. Suomi-NL 1.6.1990–31.10.1990, 43.41, UMA; Herranen, *Valtion raha vauhditti*, 2009, 271.
95 Finnish Embassy in Moscow, trade political report 1.10.1989–1.3.1990, 21.6.1990, f. Suomi-NL 1.6.1990–31.10 1990, 43.41, UMA.
96 Hanhimäki, "Henry Kissinger: Vision or Status Quo?" 2012, 193–203.
97 Shipyard Subsidy Working Group report 1989, VM 27, 1989.
98 *Bank of Finland Bulletin* 11/1989.
99 Laurila, *Finnish-Soviet Clearing Trade*, 1995, 99–106.
100 KPO on clearing system Finnish-Soviet trade 25 9.1.1990, f. Suomi-NL 1.6.1990–31.10.1990, 43.41, UMA.
101 KPO 1029 on discussion on the Finnish-Soviet trade 9.11.1990, f. Suomi-NL 1.6.1990–31.10.1990, 43.41, UMA.
102 "N-liiton laivatilaukset edelleen vailla vahvistusta, kaikki telakat neuvottelevat Moskovassa," HS 26.5.1990.
103 Uola, *Meidän isä on töissä telakalla*, 1996, 425.
104 MOSA 298 from Moscow Embassy to Formin on meeting with Sitarjan 6.12.1990, f. Suomi-NL 1.12.1990–31.12.1990, 43.41, UMA.
105 Records no 1183 on the ending procedures of Finnish-Soviet clearing trade 19.12.1990, f. Suomi-NL 1.12.1990–31.12.1990, 43.41, UMA.
106 Trade Treaty between Finland and the Russian Federation 1992, SopS 63/1992; Treaty between the Governments of Finland and the Russian Federation on Trade and Economic Cooperation, SopS 70/1992.
107 Laurila, *Finnish-Soviet Clearing Trade*, 1995, 58.
108 Tankmar Horn in *Kauppapolitiikka* 4/1993.
109 Hanson, *The Rise and Fall of Soviet Economy*, 2014, 82–83.

# 5 Beyond business as usual

## Techno-scientific and industrial cooperation

The visit of the Soviet statesman Anastas Mikoyan to Finland in November 1954 was an important milestone for the Finnish–Soviet relations. It marked a sea change in the Soviet approach to its non-socialist neighbour after Stalin's death. That the Soviet delegation took upon itself to arrive at the Wärtsilä Helsinki Shipyard to witness the launching of the first icebreakers ordered by the Soviet Union, accentuated also the political gravity of trade and technology transfer in the state-level relations. In the friendly atmosphere after the ceremony, Mikoyan was told even to have proposed a toast to Wärtsilä's director Wilhem Wahlforss, 'progressive capitalist [...] who shall build more and more ships for the Soviet Union'.[1]

The valuable ship contracts on the horizon helped the Finns to keep up with a polite expression when Mikoyan's delegation before its departure proposed in public and without warning joint scientific and technological cooperation that would elevate the commercial interaction to the next level.[2] Cooperation that went beyond economic exchange puzzled the Finnish businessmen. It was one thing to share champagne and toast for harmonic companionship but another thing to share technological information in the spirit of friendship.

When the state leaders signed treaties and established intergovernmental committees in the limelight of international public attention, they established the institutions for transnational interaction. In 1955, the Finnish–Soviet intergovernmental agreement founded a Scientific-Technical Committee that was to have frequent meetings and facilitate the exchange of technological and scientific knowledge and know-how between the countries. Despite the state involvement, it was not the government that realised the cooperation plans in actual projects but independent scholars and mostly private enterprises who were involved in, but not bound by, the governmental gestures towards improving relations.

This chapter examines transnational scientific and technical cooperation in shipbuilding. After the technopolitics in state-level relations in Chapter 3 and the foreign trade administration in Chapter 4, I turn the focus now on the shipyard companies and analyse the industrial motives to engage in cooperation projects with foreign organisations. Most of the chapter deals with the various extensive and sometimes bizarre expressions of the Finnish–Soviet scientific-technical cooperation. These cooperative elements included counter-purchases, scientific and technical cooperation, and joint production, and were often more intensive, more complex, and less profitable than what would be acceptable under normal trade conditions. They interwove Finnish companies in the technopolitical fabric of the socialist technology strategy.

Two overarching themes run through the chapter. The concrete contribution of transnational cooperation projects to the technical specialisation especially in the narrow field of Arctic maritime technology and the active role of the industrial actors in relation to the state-level cooperation institutions adapting to them, adjusting them, and repurposing them to enact their commercial interests.

In the Cold War context, scientific and technical cooperation projects were used by both superpowers to support friendly countries, create new alliances, establish economic dependencies, or to bypass export restrictions. At the state level, the Finnish–Soviet institutions for scientific-technical cooperation had their roots in the same ground. Cooperation with the non-allied Finland had potential to create a loophole in the Iron Curtain for strategic technology transfer. In addition, it served for the Soviet purpose to challenge American hegemony in the academic and scientific fields in Finland by endorsing research exchange and cooperation. At least, the Finnish–Soviet agreement for scientific-technical cooperation promoted the doctrine of peaceful coexistence between capitalist and socialist countries.[3]

The political implications and rationales of the Finnish companies to participate in border-crossing technical cooperation stemmed also from the Cold War context. As such, the scientific-technical cooperation and their results provide one approach to how the Cold War politics shaped the agency and performance of the private industry.

## Re-branding capitalist companies: beginning of the cooperation

The Soviet public proposal for scientific-technical cooperation in 1954 was difficult to decline for the Finnish government, especially because the benefits of the economic cooperation had just been so concretely manifested at the shipyards. The beginning of the Finnish–Soviet scientific-technical cooperation became a demonstration of the Finnish skills in diplomatic acrobatics: Finland approached the Soviet negotiation table seemingly without hesitation but simultaneously took side steps to lure the Soviet attention towards a less dangerous direction to protect national sovereignty and economic privileges.

The rationale behind the Soviet interest in scientific-technical cooperation with the capitalist Finland originated from the Soviet modernisation plans. After Stalin's strive for autarky, during Nikita Khrushchev's era (1953–1964) technology transfer became a key element in the ultimate economic plan to catch up and overtake the West.[4] In this project, scientific-technical cooperation was one way to increase the import of technical know-how and expertise alongside the import of machines and tools.

When the Soviet leaders composed the scientific-technical delegation to Finland, they had hard natural sciences and industrial technologies in their mind. The delegation consisted of representatives of the Ministry of Foreign

Trade, shipbuilding industry, and forestry. Finland, on its behalf, sent to the negotiation linguists, ethnologists, and political representatives, whose expertise was not science but Russian language and trust of President J. K. Paasikivi and Prime Minister Urho Kekkonen. The first Finnish chair of the Scientific-Technical Committee was Kustaa Vilkuna, a close friend of Kekkonen and Professor of Ethnology.

While showing willingness to cooperate, Finland managed to steer the scientific cooperation away from sensitive topics, such as nuclear technology and energy, towards fields with no direct military applications, such as history, linguistics, and veterinary sciences.[5] Another small but profound victory was when the Finnish side managed to replace the Soviet note about 'transfer of technical documents' into 'exchange' of documents and exclude patents and licences from the final agreement. Finnish industrial production, including the marine engines, relied heavily on Western licences. Protecting the intellectual property from the Soviet Union, which had not joined the international patent convention, was critical for the Western relations.[6]

The organisational structure within the Finnish–Soviet scientific and technical cooperation developed similarly to the commercial cooperation; it became bilateral, hierarchical, and symmetrical. It was hierarchical in the way it incorporated all levels from industrial companies to central organisations and ministries to the state-level treaties, and symmetrical as the Finnish institutions came to mirror the organisational structure in the Soviet Union (Figure 5.1).[7]

During the first half of the Cold War, this novel institutional interface to the Soviet planning economy had no major consequences in the Finnish shipbuilding industry. Metal engineering companies had no representatives in the Scientific-Technical Committee and no interest in participation beyond the absolute necessity.[8] Technological cooperation for most part included Soviet delegations visiting Finnish shipyards. The visitors' explicit interests in restricted knowledge sometimes irritated the Finnish hosts, but usually the companies considered these visits as a part of business cooperation and other marketing activities.[9]

Despite the lack of interest in joint R&D projects with the Soviets, the Finnish corporations understood the economic value of political goodwill. To that end, it was rational to invest some amount in non-commercial activities that could lead to profit-generating technology exports. The establishment of the 'Eastern Trade Promotion Committee' illuminates this line of thinking. The central associations for metal and forestry industries founded the committee in the 1950s to coordinate activities related to technology purchases from the Soviet Union. These activities included advertising Soviet products in Finnish magazines and importing a modest number of Soviet cars in Finland. The activities were merely cosmetic. They aimed to conceal the rather colonial trade structure in the Finnish–Soviet trade –the Soviets selling raw materials and buying technology– by giving an impression that the Finnish companies valued Soviet products and that the technology transfer had two directions (Figure 5.2).[10]

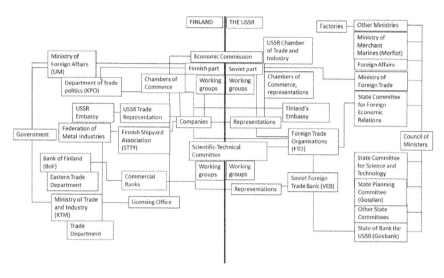

*Figure 5.1* Key organisations involved in Finnish–Soviet economic, scientific, and technical cooperation, adapted from: *Suomi-SNTL tieteellis-teknisen ja taloudellisen yhteistyön vuorovaikutus*, part 2. Helsinki 1980, 54.

*Figure 5.2* Finnish industrial enterprises paid for advertisements for Soviet technological production through the Eastern Trade Promoting Committee, for example in the Reserve Officers' magazine.

## Co-creating Arctic expertise: specialisation in technology with no domestic demand

Previous chapters have touched the technical specialisation at the Finnish shipyards to passenger ships, icebreakers, and offshore technology. What those three niches had in common was the dependency on overseas markets. Creation of competitive advantage on the knowledge of such narrow niches as icebreaking or passenger vessels was possible because the Eastern and Western export markets completed the domestic demand, increased the volumes, and allowed the shipyards to share part of the specialisation costs between multiple ships in series.

What was different in the specialisation in passenger ferries on the one hand, and polar icebreakers and offshore platforms on the other hand, was that the two latter segments necessitated technology development for conditions that did not exist in Finland. Finland had no polar waters to test polar icebreakers and no offshore industry to give feedback from drilling rigs. International techno-scientific cooperation constituted a salient element in the Finnish specialisation strategies in shipbuilding, first in Arctic icebreaking and then in offshore technology.

Despite the generally pivotal role of the Soviet trade in the accumulation of specialised knowledge in ice-going vessels, the project that first prompted scientific-technical breakthroughs in the field was not a Soviet project but American. As mentioned earlier in Chapter 3, Wärtsilä Helsinki Shipyard tried to gain a foothold in the American winter navigation since the 1960s without much success. At that point already, the Finnish shipyard had designed and constructed more heavy icebreakers than any other shipyard in the world and considered itself as the world leader in this self-defined competition.[11]

As a part of the marketing efforts in the US, Wärtsilä's shipbuilding director Christian Landtman wrote a feature about Finnish icebreaker development for the *US Naval Institute Proceedings* in 1969. In the publishing process, the bragging ending of the article, implying that only certain shipyards were capable of building icebreakers, was toned down to formulation that any competent shipyard was able to build an icebreaker. According to Ambassador Olavi Munkki, the semi-official publication did not want to offend the 'local, overly sensitive shipbuilding industry' by implying Finnish superiority in the narrow technical field.[12] This was, however, the exact opposite to the self-understanding of the confident Helsinki Shipyard. The Finnish naval architects did look down on the American competence in icebreaking.

In 1968–1969, the American oil company Exxon launched a project to test the feasibility of oil transit from Alaskan North Slope to the American East Coast with an icebreaking crude oil carrier. Wärtsilä first rejected the invitation to join the risky cooperation project but agreed later reasoning that without Finnish assistance, the inexperienced Esso would certainly fail the project and eventually ruin the reputation of the icebreaker business as a whole.[13s0]

The plan was to re-design and partly repurpose a large oil tanker *Manhattan* into an icebreaking vessel capable of navigating independently through the Northwest passage. *Manhattan* had been the largest ship of the US merchant fleet at the time of its launch in 1962. It had a strong, two-inch-thick steel hull, and it still was a sheer giant with 106,000 DWT. In normal shipping, its strengths had been its weakness, the overbuilt vessel was too sturdy and heavy for economic shipping because its operation costs exceeded the lighter-built vessels. These same features, however, made it appropriate for icebreaking. The reconstruction of the icebreaking bow, which allowed the ship to rise atop of the ice surface and break the ice by bending it down with its weight, was critical for the modification project. The design concept of the bow was based on the research by Roderick White, who had completed his dissertation on the topic in Massachusetts Institute of Technology in 1965. The bow itself was built by Bath Iron Works in Maine.[14] Wärtsilä's task was to conduct a test and research program based on the full-scale experiments and the closer examination of the performance of wooden 1:50 scale models. To that end, the shipyard set up a new ice model testing laboratory in an old bomb shelter in Helsinki with a 50-meter long and 4.8-meter wide basin with saline water.[15]

Model scale testing had emerged in naval architecture already in the 19th century, when the transition from wood and sails to steel and propellers overwrote the centuries-long experience of shipbuilding, and shipyards needed a way to test the performance of their new prototypes before paying for the construction of the full ship.[16] The transition from open-water naval architecture to ice-going vessels denoted a similar paradigmatic shift in the hull–ice interaction. Uncertainty about the performance of new prototypes indicated huge financial risks in full-scale experiments. While towing tanks for open water model testing had become commonplace, ice basin tests were conducted only in the laboratory of the Arctic and Antarctic Research Institute (AARI) in Leningrad. Water in model scale was still water, but to test the hull–ice interaction, the properties of sea ice had to be downscaled as well. Thanks to its Soviet contacts, Wärtsilä was able to learn from the model-ice technology developed in AARI. Based on the Soviet techniques, the model scale ice was created by spraying fresh water on the surface of saline basin water in a way that first created a thin ice layer on the surface of the water which then started to grow downwards.[17]

The Arctic 'Manhattan project' became the largest full-scale experiment in icebreaking and—for the Finnish shipbuilding community—a great deal more momentous than its wartime namesake in nuclear technology. Funded by the American oil money and relying on the technology from the Soviet Union, Wärtsilä got in the possession of the only second ice model testing laboratory in the world. With the data from the full-scale experiments with *Manhattan* and the model-scale experiments in the ice basin in Helsinki, the research engineers could start experimental work calculating the coefficients in model scale that would translate into performance in full scale. Understanding the correspondence between the scale models and full-scale ships opened now a novel opportunity to optimise the bow shape, hull coating, propellers positioning, and other factors affecting the icebreaking performance. In short, with the ice model laboratory, Wärtsilä Icebreaking Model Basin (WIMB), the shipyard was able to examine the existing theories of icebreaking and to apply the knowledge to design bigger, better, and more cost-efficient icebreakers.

In the US, the test voyage of *Manhattan* proved the feasibility of the concept but led to no further consequences because the decision about the Trans-Alaskan pipeline made the sea route uncompetitive. In Helsinki, however, the concrete basin full of carefully frozen model-scale ice, together with some theoretical understanding of how the model scale experiments translated into full-scale solutions, became a striking example of locally and materially embedded competitive advantage that was not easy to relocate or challenge.[18]

## Scientific-technical cooperation: towards the Arctic offshore, 1977–1990

President Kekkonen's visit to Moscow in May 1977 climaxed with a grand ceremony in Kremlin where the state leaders confirmed with their signatures the further development and intensification of the economic, technical, and industrial cooperation between the countries. What was left out of the public limelight was that the Long-Term Programme of the Finnish–Soviet relations until the 1990s (*Pitkän ajanjakson ohjelma*, PAO) expressed only loosely defined political aspirations rather than concrete plans. Furthermore, President Kekkonen was unqualified to signing the state treaty according to the Finnish legal praxis, and the actual document was later signed by Foreign Minister Paavo Väyrynen 'somewhere in the back offices of Kremlin'.[19] But these were only minor details in the big picture which presented the state-level commitment to the Finnish–Soviet scientific-technical future.

The latter term of Leonid Brezhnev (1906–1982, in office 1964–1982) is commemorated as 'the era of stagnation' when the Soviet economy on the whole slowed down, and the 'increasingly creaky men' led the increasingly 'creaky economy'.[20] The ostensibly stagnated surface hid profound changes in the undercurrents that altered the perception of the Finnish shipyards towards joint scientific-technical projects even though the formal institutions of this cooperation had left unchanged.

After 20 years of trying to evade scientific-technical engagements as much as possible, Wärtsilä contacted the Finnish delegation of the Scientific-Technical Committee and proposed a large cooperation project on Arctic technologies. This took place immediately after the New Year holidays in 1976. Three months later, a group of seven Finnish companies submitted a proposal for an extensive scientific and technological project in which Finnish and Soviet corporations and research laboratories would jointly study and develop Arctic maritime technologies.[21] Of the Finnish companies, Wärtsilä,

Rauma-Repola, Valmet, and Navire were shipbuilders and Rautaruukki was a steel manufacturer closely connected to the ship production. Neste was the state-owned oil refinery, which had in 1972 joined an international oil prospecting consortium operating on the North Sea close to Spitsbergen.[22] What joined them together was their shared interest in the Soviet offshore fields in polar regions.

These seven companies were among the biggest Finnish exporters to and importers from the Soviet Union and they had demonstrated their competitiveness in the market. The rationale behind the proactive approach to cooperation that went beyond conventional business transactions was related to the current turbulence in the shipbuilding markets that had made the Finnish companies keen to look for alternative routes to leverage their competitive position in the Soviet Union.

The first environmental jolt was related to the crash in demand for merchant tonnage in the aftermath of the oil crises. Encouraged by the temporary thaw in the international relations, new shipyards showed increasing interest in entering the socialist markets. Even though this hardly hampered the Finnish position in the Soviet shipbuilding, it decreased the price level of standard type vessels (Figure 5.3). The Finnish shipyard managers were on the lookout for new branches of special-purpose vessels that would be strategic or sophisticated enough to eliminate cost competition.

Second, the Finnish companies had recognised the growing economic activity related to the exploitations of hydrocarbon deposits under the ocean floor. Rauma-Repola's Mäntyluoto factory had become an oil platform manufacturer in the early 1970s, swept along with the booming oil explorations in the North Sea. In the late 1970s, other Western shipyards were also seeking

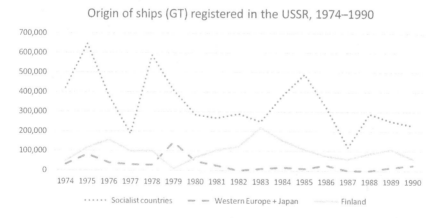

*Figure 5.3* Country of origin of the merchant ships registered in Russia/Soviet Union (GT): Socialist countries including East Germany, Poland, and Yugoslavia (dotted line), Western European countries (Finland excluded) and Japan (dashed line). Data: LRS.

for the entrance to the offshore technology production as an alternative to the depressed shipbuilding market.[23] Wärtsilä and the other Finnish technology companies anticipated the Soviet Union to refocus its oil and gas strategy from West Siberia onto the Barents Sea. After the easily reachable oil wells ran dry, the oil explorations were expected to move into deeper, colder, and harsher areas. While the Soviet oil and gas technology was quite capable in shallow onshore fields, they relied on Western technology for exploring and exploiting hydrocarbons in the demanding Arctic offshore conditions.[24] This would increase demand for ice-strengthened oil platforms and drilling ships, icebreakers, ice-capable supply ships, ice-strengthened tankers, and a wide range of offshore subsystems that could endure the freezing polar temperature, pressure of the polar ice, and the depth of the ocean.

Finland had no domestic Arctic waters nor hydrocarbon resources. The Finnish shipbuilders had experience in building ice-going vessels, but the conditions in the Baltic Sea—pack ice, drift ice, shallow archipelago, low salinity water—were different from the Arctic Sea, where multi-year ice in the saline water formed thick and strong level ice and distance to the nearest harbour could be weeks. Wärtsilä Helsinki Shipyard had successfully participated in the development of vessels for polar conditions including the Soviet Moskva-class and the aforementioned American *Manhattan*. Yet, systematic ice research in the Soviet Far North was hampered by the expenses and strategic sensitivity of the area. Paradoxically, as a representative of the Finnish Ministry of Foreign Affairs noted, Finnish shipbuilders had better understanding of the Canadian Arctic waters than the conditions close by in the Barents Sea.[25]

A further factor that pushed the Finns to make the proactive stance on scientific-technical cooperation in Arctic offshore was, if not quite jealousy of other Western countries, at least a sense of competition against them. The Soviet Union had already initiated projects in oil exploration and pumping with American, French, Canadian, and Japanese companies.[26] That motivated the Finnish industry to do what it could to maintain its position as one of the leading experts in Arctic shipbuilding and Soviet business relations.

Thus, the Finnish companies were primarily in search of business opportunities when they proposed a Finnish–Soviet scientific-technical cooperation on Arctic technology in the spring of 1976.[27] They had recognised a growing market in the Soviet Arctic offshore field and decided to use the bilateral institutions to enhance their competitive position, to funnel R&D investments to Arctic technology, and to enter novel niche markets.[28] To the Soviet Union, they offered their experience in ice-going vessels, willingness to engage in long-standing cooperation, and the possibility to channel Western technological expertise.[29]

The Soviet party of the Scientific-Technical Committee responded to the Finnish initiative in March 1976. Their attitude was positive. The Finnish Eastern traders, who were used to negotiations that could last years, the short reaction time was a surprise and interpreted as a sign of great interest.

The Soviet chair of the Scientific-Technical Committee D. M. Gvishian confirmed to his Finnish colleague Pekka Kuusi that the Soviets took the proposal seriously. According to Gvishian, the Soviets were already negotiating with the American company Brown & Root Inc., whose expertise he regarded as the best in the world, but noted that one 'had to be careful with Western companies—they all claim to know more than they actually know'. Finland, it appeared, was not included in this category of skilful but unreliable Western business partners.[30]

This comment captured the quintessence of the Finnish competitive edge in the Soviet planning economy. Finland was not the only possible channel available for the Soviet Union to obtain Western technology nor was it the most experienced partner in Arctic offshore explorations. Instead, it appeared as the most convenient partner for extensive scientific-technical cooperation.

Encouraged by the positive feedback, the Finnish shipyard managers prepared a dossier of the Arctic project for President Kekkonen to take on his fishing trip to the Soviet Union in the summer of 1976.[31] The Finnish practice of using the president as a courier in industrial diplomacy raises a question of the motivation of the state leader to engage in such an action. Like in Chapter 4, the industrial and political interests in Finnish–Soviet relations might not have been the same, but they were compatible: Acting as intermediators offered the high political figures a possibility to promote their personal political status as well as broader diplomatic goals of Finland. At this point, the Arctic project was not a priority for the state of Finland in a sense that its success would have been critical for the national well-being. However, it was an appropriate gesture of political goodwill in the Finnish–Soviet relations. If successful, it had the potential to create industrial vacancies and indirectly contribute to national welfare as well as demonstrate Finnish technological prowess for the rival Western companies.

After Kekkonen's visit, Gvishian confirmed to the Finnish delegation of the Scientific-Technical Committee that the Soviet Union agreed in cooperating with Finland on ice mechanisms, ice physics, and technical development of state-of-the-art equipment. It was only the actual oil explorations the Soviets wanted to keep Finland out.[32]

As a result, shipbuilding became a topic on its own right in the Finnish–Soviet scientific and technical agenda. In 1977, for the first time since the beginning of the cooperation, the minutes of the Finnish–Soviet Scientific-Technical Committee meeting recorded a significant number of studies initiated by the Finnish maritime sector: propulsion in heavy ice conditions, physics and mechanics between ship hull and ice, and winter navigation.[33] The busy shipbuilding directors now found time to participate in the non-commercial committee work. Wärtsilä's director, Tankmar Horn, was appointed as a member of the Scientific-Technical Committee in 1979. Tauno Matomäki, the director of the oil-rig builder Rauma-Repola, became the leader of the offshore working group.[34]

Within the Arctic project, the Finnish research organisations and industrial research laboratories collected annually a list of research topics related to Arctic offshore technology, ice-going vessels, and Arctic electrical engineering. Together with their Soviet colleagues, they also organised symposia in Helsinki and Moscow. The State Technical Research Centre in Finland (*Valtion teknillinen tutkimuskeskus*, VTT) was interested in the study of ice as a geophysical and technical problem and in ice forecasting methods; Wärtsilä was interested in the ice-mechanism in icebreaking; Rauma-Repola was concerned with ice pressure in offshore drilling structures. The Soviet researchers presented studies based on their experience of Siberian river transportation, Arctic seafaring, and ice research methods.[35] In 1982, almost 4,000 Soviet scientists participated in research cooperation in Finland while almost 3,500 Finnish scientists travelled to the Soviet Union.[36]

While the Arctic project was about scientific and technological cooperation, it had close links to economic cooperation coordinated by the Intergovernmental Economic Commission.[37] The chairs of the Arctic project represented scientific organisations, but the possibilities of translating the scientific and technical knowledge into economic products was a constant topic. For the Finnish shipbuilding industry, the Soviet Arctic promised a prosperous future.[38]

The long-term industrial interest also presented itself in the intergovernmental agreements and protocols. In the revised Long Term Programme (1981–1995), ice model tests and seafaring in heavy ice conditions were among the primary focus areas.[39] The annual plans for scientific and technical cooperation between 1981 and 1985 all mentioned Arctic maritime technology as a topic of utmost importance.[40]

After the Soviet invasion to Afghanistan in 1979, the mid-Cold War détente in East-West relations turned towards a new ice age. Like in the early 1950s, the tightening Western embargo on high technology benefitted Finnish companies in the Soviet Union, and facilitated the entrance into the market of oil drilling equipment and offshore technology.[41]

If Finland's geopolitical location in the proximity of the Soviet Union was politically uncomfortable, the special position had its economic value, too. This was demonstrated in a short serial of episodes related to the Nordic cooperation in the Soviet offshore technology.

In the spring of 1982, Soviet foreign trade official Juri Piskulov proposed the Nordic countries,—Norway, Finland, Sweden, and possibly Denmark and Iceland—to collaborate in the production, financing, and exports of Arctic offshore technology.[42] The proposal appears as a brainchild of Piskulov himself rather than a high-level policy target of the USSR, but it had its technical rationale. The Soviet Union needed a certain type of concrete oil drilling platform that would be capable of reaching hydrocarbon deposits over 300 metres below the surface. Compared to the conventional metal platforms, concrete structures endured better in ice. Casting these concrete structures required sheltered and deep water in conditions best found in Norwegian fjords. Rauma-Repola was currently building oil drilling vessels and platforms for the Soviet Union, but the Finnish manufacturers had open waters of no more than a hundred metres deep.[43]

It is easy to understand the proposal from the Soviet point of view: Norwegians had the expertise in building the concrete platforms that Piskulov was looking for. On the other hand, the Finns had the extensive experience in doing business with the Soviet Union. In addition, if the payments were channelled through the Finnish–Soviet clearing system, the Soviet Union could pay for its technology purchases without convertible currencies.[44]

From the Finnish point of view, the triparty cooperation with the Soviet Union and the NATO-member Norway in the strategically sensitive Barents Sea area was politically an uncomfortable idea.[45] Even more, the Nordic cooperation risked potentially the Finnish privileged position in the Soviet Arctic. Foreign Ministry official Jorma Inki noted in his memorandum, '[w]e have to remember the competition between Finland and Norway. Finland gains the best results within the framework of the bilateral trade'.[46]

As it appeared, the Norwegians disliked the joint technology proposal as much as the Finns. This was not because they hesitated to collaborate with the Soviets but because they were reluctant to cooperate with Finland. Since 1980, the Norwegians had put effort in increasing its machinery exports to the Soviet Union; they had organised joint offshore seminars and invited Soviet experts to visit Norwegian factories and shipyards.[47] Instead of Nordic cooperation, the Norwegian offshore companies founded their own consortium BOCONOR (Barents Off-shore Consortium of Norway) to coordinate their export and marketing efforts.[48]

Similar to the Finnish shipyards, which were unwilling to share their expertise in the Soviet trade with the Norwegians, the Norwegians saw no reason to assist the Finns in offshore technology. The chair of BOCONOR, Rolf E. Rolfsen, underlined in his meeting with the Finnish Ambassador Jaakko Blomsted that Norway needed no help from Finland in offshore technology. The only role that he could imagine for the Finnish industry was a minor subcontractor subordinated to Norwegian project managers. Afterwards, Blomsted reported to Helsinki: 'In my opinion it is clear that Rolfsen with his arrogant response wanted to clarify how close relations and frequent daily contacts they have with their [Soviet] partners'.[49]

The controversy surrounding the Nordic-Soviet technology cooperation revealed a juxtaposition that is utterly dissimilar to the traditional picture of the East-West confrontation. Instead of Nordic countries joining their forces to compete against the Soviet Union, the private industries accompanied by diplomats and politicians in Finland and Norway competed against each other for *closer* cooperation, boasting about their warm relationship with the Soviets. Although the Soviet-Norwegian affairs were far from unproblematic and proceeded far from smoothly, it demonstrated the Western interest in the Soviet Arctic.

In 1988 and 1989, the Finnish–Soviet Arctic project was still the third largest scientific and technical cooperation programme after agriculture and construction even though the trend of research exchange was slightly declining.[50] In October 1989, during his visit to Helsinki, Gorbachev signed an agreement on a joint development project on Kola Peninsula that was located close to the Finnish Northern border.[51]

But then, a couple of years later, the Soviet Union disappeared. The 40 years of Finnish expertise in navigating the hierarchical Soviet planning economy using the bilateral institutions to leverage their position lost its value. Scientific and technical cooperation were no longer a technopolitical tool to buy political goodwill among the Russian foreign trade officials. The technological aspects of the Finnish-Russian scientific and technical cooperation survived the end of the Cold War better. In particular, the research cooperation in the study of ice conditions and environmental circumstances in the Barents Sea continued into the next millennium.[52]

In that way, this study of the Finnish–Soviet Arctic cooperation supports the argument in the transnational Cold War studies that the social aspects of the scientific and technical cooperation were often more important and long-standing than the political ones. As scholars of West-East technology transfer in the Cold War computer science and forestry have pointed out, the most significant long-term result of the border-crossing cooperation projects was the social network of experts that expanded on both sides of the East-West divide.[53]

## Intra-industry trade: buying friendship and goodwill

In 1983, Rauma-Repola was offered to buy a pair of mammoth tusks found in Siberia. According to the Soviet trading company, the tusks were 'perfectly suited to be symbolic allusions to the Soviet trade, showing [Rauma-Repola] among the companies at the forefront of the Soviet trade as well as the prime trading partner of the Soviet Union'.[54] Those tusks were perhaps more curious than the offers the Finnish shipbuilding companies typically received from the Soviet Union in the name of good business relations, but they demonstrated the wide scale of the intra-industry trading in the end of the Cold War.

Before the mid-Cold War, the eagerness of the Soviet foreign trade politicians to diversify the bilateral trade structure by selling Soviet-made machinery to Finland had appeared in the Finnish shipbuilding industry only as a light pressure to import some products and goods from the Soviet Union. Besides the 'Eastern Trade Promotion Committee' in the 1950s and 1960s, however, there had been only a few efforts in the Finnish manufacturing industry to increase such imports. Figure 5.4 shows how the structure of the Finnish–Soviet trade had remained asymmetric. Finland exported machinery and industrial products and imported little else than raw materials.

The Soviet trade negotiators were usually not too interested in increasing the procurements from the Soviet Union either. Often the Soviet end-user organisations preferred Western components and machinery and the Soviet factories had few incentives to sell their products to Finnish shipyards.

In the mid-1970s, the Soviet business delegations started to show stronger interests in increasing machinery exports to Finland. As was typical for the

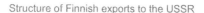

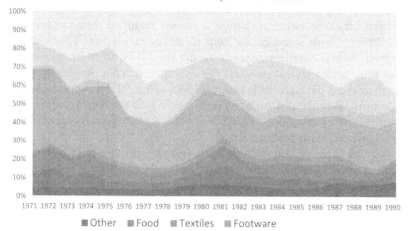

Structure of Finnish exports to the USSR

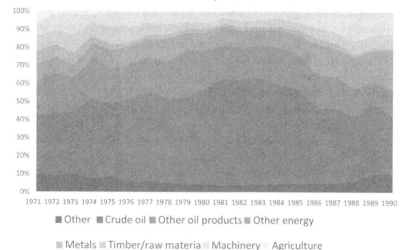

Structure of Finnish imports from the USSR

*Figure 5.4* Structure of Finnish–Soviet bilateral trade 1971–1990. Data: Bank of Finland.

Finnish–Soviet trade administration, the first reaction to changes was the establishment of a new committee. In 1975, the Finnish–Soviet Economic Commission organised a working group on ship equipment trade to examine and increase industrial cooperation in shipbuilding industry. Industrial co-operation at this point referred mostly to the 'counter purchases' —Soviet content in the ships the Soviet organisations ordered from Finland. Counter-purchases were not uncommon in Western trade either, but they were mainly required in major state procurements of arms and aeroplanes.

Within the Finnish–Soviet framework, however, the target was to include Soviet components in every project.[55]

There were four basic types of counter-purchases. The first type was a simple barter trade in which a Finnish company swapped their products or services directly with some goods from their Soviet partner. This kind of exchange trade was problematic because the shipyard and the buyer rarely had matching production structures. For example, when a Soviet company wanted to make a payment to Rauma-Repola using 50,000 tonnes of fish, which Rauma-Repola as a metal manufacturer had no means to process, the Finnish Foreign Ministry needed to contact an Icelandic fish processing factory to proceed with the transaction.[56]

The second type of counter-purchase was compensation trade. It was essentially a lighter version of barter, in which part of the price was paid in cash and the rest with different products. For instance, the Soviet Ministry of Fisheries proposed paying part of their ship repairs with fish. Besides the large amount of fish being difficult to liquidise, the prospects of this arrangement were further deteriorated by the poor quality of the fish. The Finnish shipyard would have preferred payments in a combination of fish and scrap iron but because iron and fish were under different branch ministries in the Soviet Union, this arrangement turned out to be too complicated.[57]

The third type of counter-purchase was a buy-back arrangement in which a Finnish company received part of the payments with products of the production facilities they had delivered to the Soviet Union. This was relatively rare in shipbuilding but pulp factories were occasionally partly paid for with pulp. Problem with these buy-back agreements was that they transferred the business risks to the Finnish company, as the value of future production was difficult to evaluate beforehand.

The fourth and the most common type of counter-purchase in the Finnish–Soviet ship trade was to require the shipyard to buy products from their Soviet counterpart as a prerequisite for signing the contract. Rauma-Repola was the only shipbuilding company that frequently installed Soviet engines in its ships. Other shipyards imported merely simple components such as anchor chains and radio-equipment to be installed in Soviet-ordered ships and miscellaneous other goods such refrigerators and bed linen to be used at shipyards for other production activities. The counter-purchase could also include objects and materials that had only a remote connection to shipyards, such as cars that were used to drive Soviet visitors from the railway station to the shipyard, and lathes that were donated for vocational schools.[58]

In addition to some useful components, the Finnish shipyards ended up with a stock of Soviet equipment with no demand outside the Soviet Union. Rauma-Repola, for instance, investigated the possibility to re-export Soviet-made craft tools to Southern Africa and reported that while 'the prices were very competitive, the quality was too poor to find customers'.[59] They also tried to re-export Soviet-made floating shipyards to India but these projects failed because of high price and inflexibility of the Soviet design.[60]

In 1975, the Finnish Shipyard Association (STTY) collected industrial attitudes towards increasing use of Soviet equipment and compiled a long and discouraging list. The Finnish shipyards reported technical and commercial problems with Soviet components related to unsatisfactory information about the product, poor quality or inaccurate standards, unpredictable type conversions, and too long or unspecified delivery times. Occasionally, the Soviet inspectors were themselves unwilling to accept the Soviet components as a part of the ship delivery.[61]

The problems that hampered any significant increase in the Soviet content in the Finnish ships appeared as matters of practicality rather than principles. In 1977, the ship equipment working group listed failed attempts to import Soviet equipment. The array of reasons varied from the wrong standards of the component to the wrong size or wrong specification. The machines had come with inadequate information and no spare parts. The Soviet partner might have never submitted a tender or the price had been too high. A quarter of a year had been the most accurate delivery window the Soviet factory could specify, fibreglass lifeboats had been made of aluminium, or floodlights had had poor luminous efficiency.[62]

At the state level, the Long Term Programme articulated as a joint target to increase the proportion of Soviet components in Finnish-built ships up to 10% from the current 4%–7%.[63] At the industrial level, it was significantly easier to sell products to the vast and technology-hungry Soviet economy than to purchase specific technological products from the centrally coordinated production system. The command lines in hierarchical planning were long and complex. Even the nuclear icebreaker project discussed in Chapter 3, that was to showcase the Finnish–Soviet industrial cooperation on a grand scale, suffered from insubordination within the Soviet industrial branches and required the intervention of both the State Planning Committee Gosplan and the Soviet Ministry of Foreign Trade to bind the ship import and steel export together.[64]

Officially, both sides of the Intergovernmental Economic Commission agreed that the Finnish–Soviet bilateral trade should not force the Finnish corporations to barter trade.[65] Soviet Deputy Minister Manzhulo reckoned that the Finnish shipyards exaggerated the burden of the required counter-purchases but simultaneously promised that the Soviet officials would refrain from making any 'insane' requests.[66] Other Soviet officials stated that it was not the policy of the Soviet central administration to make counter-purchases into prerequisites for ship contracts and asked the Finnish shipyards to report the 'most blatant' examples of such demands.[67]

At the industrial level, however, the increasing competition in the Soviet market in the 1980s made the Finnish companies willing to accept counter-purchases as a part of the Soviet trade.[68] In 1983, the marketing department of Rauma-Repola concluded that counter-purchases had become an established instrument in competition. In order to survive and to succeed in the future, the Finnish shipyards could no longer ignore the topic hoping it to disappear, but they had to create a proactive counter-purchase strategy.[69]

Rauma-Repola's counter-purchase strategy focused on business communications with the Soviet trade politicians to improve the corporate brand in the higher levels of the Soviet hierarchy. The marketing department instructed everyone to make frequent enquiries after Soviet products during trade negotiations. Even if the Soviet organisation had nothing to offer, it was not a valid excuse to avoid showing interest. No purchases should be made without the 'necessary publicity'. Special, unique, and extraordinary procurements that could be highlighted in advertisements were preferable. In addition to sending a couple of 'impressive trade delegations' to visit the Soviet factories every year, the company should also compose a common narrative to communicate 'Rauma-Repola's active and dynamic procurement policy'.[70]

The communication procedure passed beta-testing with real Soviets. During a conversation, the Soviet vice-commercial representative A. V. Tverdokhlebov admitted that he had come to the meeting with a negative attitude but changed his mind after hearing the Finnish assurances: 'I was aggressive when preparing for this negotiation. I had the impression that Rauma-Repola was categorically against purchases from the Soviet Union but now I understand that Rauma-Repola as a whole is dealing with the matter in a coordinated fashion'.[71]

Towards the end of the Cold War, the economic difficulties in the Soviet Union added to the pressures to increase sales. In 1986, Soviet negotiators raised their demand for Soviet content in ships to 15%. A while later, Sudoimport confirmed that they were not allowed to sign a trade contract without sufficient counter-purchases. In 1987, the official demand was expanded to 25%–30%, while in reality the share of Soviet technology was still below 8%.[72]

High Soviet content in the Finnish-built ships started to compete with domestic production. According to the semi-official rule in the Finnish Licensing Office, over 80% of the products sold via the Finnish–Soviet clearing trade system had to be of domestic origin in order to prevent other countries from benefiting at the cost of Finnish workers and companies. However, in these calculations, Soviet components were classified as non-foreign content. The more the Finnish ships had Soviet content, the less the Finnish manufacturers and subcontractors had opportunities to benefit from the trade.[73] In addition, the counter-purchases disturbed the markets when the shipbuilding companies accepted higher prices and lower quality products to fill their quotas. At worst, the Finnish Licensing Office complained to the shipyards, the Soviet components were priced up to 3–4 times above their market price.[74]

The elements of absurd theatre in the Soviet trade got amplified towards the dissolution of the Soviet Union when the decreasing volume of orders from the Soviet customers pushed the Finnish shipyards to invest in the political goodwill in Moscow. The contemporary actors tend to refer to the industrial cooperation with diminutive and derogatory nicknames or as 'a magical world that entitled to do anything funny'.[75]

However, the dusty stock of secondary Soviet goods abandoned in storehouses at the shipyards remained as emblems of the late Cold War ship trade.

The purchases appeared as irrational only after the dissolution of the Cold War shipbuilding. As long as there were any prospects of Soviet ship trade, tonnes of fish and mammoth tusks were not jokes but serious business.

## Industrial cooperation: playing the role of an active partner, 1988–1990

Despite all the controversies surrounding the counter-purchases and scientific-technical cooperation, they limited the transfer of concrete competitive advantages across the border. Joint production, in which Finnish companies contributed with their intellectual capital and technical know-how to establish manufacturing in the Soviet Union, could nurture new competitors.

Since the 1970s, the intergovernmental agreements and protocols about the development of economic relations expressed the Soviet interest in expanding industrial cooperation. The Finnish companies, understandably, had been unenthusiastic about replacing their own product exports with assistance for potentially rival production facilities abroad. Rauma-Repola's shipbuilding director concluded in 1980, that industrial cooperation with Soviet shipyards was not a realistic option; if it had been realistic, it would have already materialised.[76]

Towards the end of the Cold War, the urgency of industrial modernisation in the Soviet Union lifted the joint ventures to the top of the agenda. The revision of the Long Term Programme in 1988 placed industrial cooperation in shipbuilding as a priority in the bilateral cooperation.[77] As the previous chapters have described, the latter half of the 1980s was characterised by increasing competition and decreasing demand in the Soviet trade. To maintain the privileged position of the Finnish shipbuilding industry in the Soviet market, the bilateral clearing trade system, intergovernmental personal networks, or even increasing counter-purchases had proved to be inefficient, too bureaucratic, or too expensive. The joint production emerged as the last untested anchor to moor the Finnish shipyards to the Soviet sphere of interest. The turn of Finnish attitudes was abrupt and complete. In 1989, *Kauppapolitiikka*, the Ministry of Foreign Affair's publication on foreign trade reported that there were over 100 Finnish–Soviet joint venture projects in the pipeline waiting to be realised.[78]

One of them was Wärtsilä's initiative for cooperation in naval architecture, which captured the industrial rationales for increasing cooperation. Similarly to technology import from the Soviet Union, this proposal for a joint venture reflected the Finnish shipyards' efforts to maintain their competitive position as a close trading partner and to bypass the restrictions caused by the economic problems in the Soviet Union.

Wärtsilä Marine, Wärtsilä's shipbuilding subsidiary, submitted a proposal for a joint ship design office in the Soviet Union in the spring of 1988. In the proposal, the company listed benefits for the Soviet partners including transfer of skillsets critical for the production of special and complex ships, training in the use of digital CAD/CAM systems, foreign income for the Soviet partners paid in convertible currencies, increase in exports of Soviet components and machines, and an upgraded image of the participating Soviet shipyards thanks to the Western cooperation.[79] In short, the proposal contained all the aspects the Soviet negotiators had kept requesting from the Finnish shipyards, and all the kind of technical competitive advantages the Finns had previously been reluctant to hand to the Soviets.

The idea of the joint ship design office had been developed within a small group of Wärtsilä's shipbuilding engineers.[80] The earlier experiences of joint ventures in the Soviet Union had not been encouraging but resulted in bureaucratic problems without remarkable gains.[81] The main rationale behind the joint venture for now was to boost the company brand within the Soviet foreign trade circles and to provide a competitive edge for Wärtsilä over Western competitors.[82] As a memorandum coined: 'For the sake of our image we have to give something [to the Soviets]. We will play the role of an active partner'.[83]

The joint ship design office, then, appeared more as a performance than a concrete project: an unprecedented marketing campaign. The proposal was carefully carved to respond to the needs the Finnish shipbuilders anticipated the Soviet administration to have. Shipbuilding and particularly the knowledge-intensive ship design was expected to be a priority in the Soviet economic modernisation.

From the Finnish point of view, cooperation on ship design, instead of ship construction, required less capital and implied smaller financial risks. The only business risk was of losing leverage in price negotiations if confidential cost calculations would be leaked to the Soviet Union.[84]

According to the plans drafted in the summer of 1988, Wärtsilä Marine would found the joint venture together with the Soviet Ministry of Merchant Marines, Morflot, and the Ministry of Shipbuilding.[85] The majority of the venture was to be in Soviet hands: Wärtsilä Marine 30%, Ministry of Shipbuilding 30%, and Morflot 40%.[86]

Later in the year, the Finnish side upgraded its project plan to ambitious joint ship production that aimed at rationalisation of Wärtsilä's shipbuilding through a partial integration of Finnish and Soviet shipyards along the Gulf of Finland.[87] Modular construction and border-crossing supply chains had become common in shipbuilding. A long-term trend was carrying the shipyards away from multi-talented manufacturers towards streamlined assembly lines that outsourced an increasing share of production to specialised subcontractors. Against this backdrop, the motivation of the Finnish shipyards to increase cooperation with the low-cost Soviet shipyards in its immediate vicinity was logical.

In its internal documents, Wärtsilä Marine noticed the social risk of a political lobbying campaign in the *perestroika* era. The foreign trade reformations had just about to release Soviet companies from the state control. The risk was that these liberated organisations would experience the Finnish proposal not as a fresh wind of change but as a stuffy breath from the past. If the joint venture was taken as a political project, it could corrupt Wärtsilä's brand among the new Russian businessmen instead of polishing it.[88]

While recognising the new atmosphere in the Soviet business environment, the company opted for the traditional methods to maximise political impact. Wärtsilä employed its highest-ranking directors available to lobby the joint venture within their established networks in Moscow.[89] The company directors asked Finnish Foreign Minister Kalevi Sorsa to raise the project onto the agenda of the Economic Commission and Finnish Prime Minister Harri Holkeri to discuss the initiative with his Soviet colleague N. Ryzhkov.[90] The initial reactions in these political and administrative circles were encouraging enough to proceed with the planning.[91]

In the autumn of 1988, the Soviet Ministry of Shipbuilding appeared in the memoranda in parallel with the abbreviation BT referring to *Baltian Telakka*, Baltic Shipyard in Leningrad subordinated to the Shipbuilding Ministry.[92] While Wärtsilä had identified the potential partner it was interested in cooperating with, the Soviet shipyard shared not the enthusiasm: 'Although the advantages of the joint venture for the Soviet Union can be shown, the Soviet partner should also benefit from collaboration. Those benefits are still unclear', as the representative from Baltic Shipyard complained.[93]

The Finnish documents pictured the joint venture as an altruistic developmental project helping the Soviet shipyard to gain access to modern Western technology and develop its processes. Baltic Shipyard—one of the oldest Russian shipyard that had built cutting-edge submarines and icebreakers for the Soviet navy—replied promptly that it needed no help from its neighbour.[94]

The other Soviet partner, Ministry of Merchant Marines, Morflot, was the primary end-user organisation for the icebreakers built at the Helsinki and Baltic Shipyards. From its point of view, cooperation between its two suppliers was promising. It did not, however, want to be a partner in joint production that would build ships for third parties. According to Morflot, participation in such venture would only mean increasing costs without bringing new vessels to its use.[95] This contrasted with the view of the Soviet Ministry of Shipbuilding. It had no interest in cooperating with Finnish shipyards without the opportunity to earn convertible currencies through exporting ships to third countries.[96]

After December 1988, archival folders fell suddenly silent on the joint project. After piles of documents, letters, and memoranda, the project disappeared from the agenda. As one interviewee put it, 'some plans just fell through'.[97] In its all vagueness and obscurity, this may be the most accurate explanation available. At the turn of 1989, Wärtsilä Marine was already deep in economic problems and had no time or resources to invest in ambitious plans. The Soviet administration had its hands full of domestic reformations while navigating the turbulence of the socialist bloc. Baltic Shipyard, that had a history as the leading shipbuilder of a superpower, had no motivation for becoming a low-cost subcontractor for Finland.

And yet, Wärtsilä's initiative for the joint ship design office had been a very good plan. It was a perfect response to the economic priorities in the Soviet economic strategies about industrial modernisation and expanding exports. It was everything that had been called for in the intergovernmental agreements, plans, and programmes. It could have had an economic rationale. It certainly had technical and organisational rationales. It just did not align with its stakeholders' priorities at the moment.

The joint venture initiative was enlightening not because it had concrete results but because it showed us the industrial actors trying to find their way in the constantly changing maze of the Soviet foreign trade. In 1988, the shipbuilders hardly knew that the Soviet Union would collapse; they experienced its transformation but also knew that shipbuilding was going to go on in the Gulf of Finland:

> Even though the Finnish shipyard industry is going through difficult time of readjustments, there is one reliable element and direction − cooperation with our neighbor Soviet Union. Wärtsilä Marine has all preconditions to be a strong partner for Soviet organisations in the field of shipbuilding.[98]

Developing business in the turbulent environment was not so much about good or bad decisions but a struggle to find a navigable route forward when the passage was only illuminated by past experience.

## Conclusions

Philip Hanson has pointed out the paradox in the Soviet technology transfer policy: the extensive efforts to transfer and assimilate Western technology accompanied by the claim that the Soviet Union was technologically self-sufficient.[99] Through the scientific, technical, and industrial cooperation, the Finnish shipyards responded simultaneously both to the Soviet Union's need to acquire competitive technology and to its wish to receive recognition for its technological competence.

The Finnish shipbuilding industry practiced Soviet trade for economic reasons; the state-level bilateral framework provided the shipyards with irreplaceable opportunities to conduct stable, high-volume, and often profitable ship exporting without actually being bound to the rigidities and restrictions of the bilateral trade. During the first half of the Cold War, the Finnish industrial interest in maximising the export of goods had been compatible with the Soviet Union's interest in using the Finland primarily as a supplier of vessels and reparation services. In the 1970s, both the Soviet and Finnish attitudes changed in a way that underlined the primacy of the reciprocal exchange of technology and technological knowledge.

First and foremost, the Finnish shipyard companies perceived this non-commercial cooperation as a part of marketing to an authoritarian, centrally

planned economy. Their positive approach to scientific and technical cooperation smoothed over the ideological discomfort the dedicated communists
felt towards capitalist big business. While the state-level liturgy manifested
the peaceful co-existence, the industrial cooperation projects made the rhetoric concrete and real, and through that enforced trust between the Finnish
and Soviet actors.

Trust between partners decreased transaction costs and risks in future-
oriented planning. The special Cold War flavour came from the fact that
the Finnish shipyards invested in building trust not only with their business
partners, companies and organisations but also with the political leadership
and bureaucracy. While they certainly looked down on the quality of Soviet
technology, they also understood the value of standing out against the Western businessmen who addressed the Soviet industry with a mixture of pity
and condescension. The Finnish shipyards did not buy Soviet cars to carry
people but to polish their corporate brand.

The amount of time and money the big shipbuilding corporation invested
in the image marketing among the Soviet political hierarchy depicts how
tightly the Finnish shipbuilding industry was intermingled with the Finnish–
Soviet state relations. As a general trend, the more difficult it was to do
business with the Soviet, the further the Finns were ready to go with the
extra-curricular activities. Import trading, scientific and technical cooperation, and joint ventures exemplified how the Finnish shipyards became ready
to shift from their commercial role as ship exporters into active contributors
to technology transfer in order to nurture their privileged position in the
Soviet Union.

The Finnish rationales for cooperation were merely performative, but it
did have tangible consequences. The techno-scientific results of the Cold
War technopolitics, such as the Arctic maritime technology products, understanding of ice mechanics, and established scientific research networks,
withstood the dissolution of the Cold War shipbuilding system and formed
one of the building blocks of post–Cold War shipbuilding in Finland.

## Notes

1 Rentola, *Niin kylmää että polttaa*, 1997, 352.
2 Kohvakka, "Science, Technology and Changing Power Relations," 2011, 351.
3 Kohvakka, "Science, Technology, and Changing Power Relations," 352–353;
  Autio-Sarasmo, "Knowledge through the Iron Curtain," 2011, 68; Autio-
  Sarasmo, "Soviet Economic Modernisation and Transferring Technologies from
  the West," 2006, 105–107; Autio-Sarasmo, "Technological Modernization in the
  Soviet Union and Post-Soviet Russia," 2016; Hanson, *The Rise and Fall of Soviet
  Economy*, 2014, 60–61. See also Kuisma, *Kylmä sota, kuuma öljy*, 75–106; Kochet-
  kova, *The Soviet Forestry Industry in the 1950s and 1960s*, 2017.
4 Autio-Sarasmo, *Technological Modernisation in the Soviet Union and Post-Soviet
  Russia*, 2016, 81–82; Autio-Sarasmo, "Transferring Western Knowledge to a
  Centrally Planned Economy," 2018, 144–144.
5 Kohvakka, "Science, Technology, and Changing Power Relations," 2011.

6 Kohvakka, "Science, Technology, and Changing Power Relations," 2011, 258–259, 352.
7 Laurila, *Finnish-Soviet Clearing Trade*, 1995, 59. In 1977, the Finnish-Soviet Scientific-Technical committee started a thorough "methodological project" to study the cooperation between two economic systems. The project resulted in a three-volume study in 1980: *Suomi-SNTL: Tieteellis-teknisen ja taloudellisen yhteistyön vuorovaikutus. Raportti Suomen ja Neuvostoliiton välisen yhteistyön metodologiaa koskevasta tutkimuksesta osat I-III*, 1980.
8 Finnish-Soviet Scientific and Technical Committee XVIII joint meeting in Helsinki 23.5.1972–25.5.1972, f. TT-komitea pöytäkirjat, UMA.
9 Autio-Sarasmo, "Knowledge through the Iron Curtain," 2011, 71.
10 B. Långhjelm on "Eastern Trade Promotion Committee," 11.5.1959, f. "Idänkaupan edistämiskomitea," RR, UPMA.
11 Meeting between Rusk and Karjalainen, 1.6.1966, Vuosikirja 1996 UKA; PM on the Icebreaker Joint Venture, 23.4.1969; Founding of a consortium, MVR draft, 22.4.1969, WW 20, NA.
12 Landtman, "Finnish Icebreakers," *US Naval Proceedings*February 1969; Olavi Munkki to Christian Landtman, 10.4.1969, PM outlining the establishment of a consortium, MVR draft, 22.4.1969, WW 20, NA.
13 Coen, *Breaking Ice for Arctic Oil*, 2012, 37.
14 Coen, *Breaking Ice for Arctic Oil*, 2012, 39–40.
15 Coen, *Breaking Ice for Arctic Oil*, 2012, 159–160.
16 Ferreiro, *Bridging the Seas*, 2020, 116–133.
17 Aker arctic, *50-Years of Ice Model Testing. A Success Story of Finnish technology*. Available online https://akerarctic.fi/app/uploads/2019/04/50-Years-of-Ice-Model-Testing.pdf.
18 Matala, "Läpi kylmän sodan ja jään," 2015, 5–25.
19 Aunesluoma, *Vapaakaupan tiellä*, 2011, 361.
20 Hanson, *The Rise and Fall of the Soviet Economy*, 2014, 130–131.
21 Proposal for TT commission 30.3.1976, f. "Arktinen projekti II," Sere, UPMA.
22 Kuisma, *Kylmä sota, kuuma öljy*, 1997, 485.
23 Olsson, "Offshore som livboj," 1998, 205–229; Tenold, "Saving a Sector–But which One?" 2001.
24 *Prospect for Soviet Oil Production: A Supplemental Analysis*, 1977; *USSR: Development of the Gas Industry*, 1978; *Impending Soviet Oil Crisis*, Intelligence Memorandum ER 77-10147, 1977; Bergesen et al., *In Search of Oil and Security. Soviet Interests in the Barents Sea*, 1986.
25 PO 507 on the Arctic Sea 6.8.1980; From VTT to KTM on research facilities for Arctic shipbuilding and offshore technology in Finland 28.4.1980, f. Arktinen projekti 1976–1981," Sere, UPMA.
26 *OECD Observer* 92/1978.
27 Finnish Embassy in Moscow on the Arctic project 5.5.1977, f. Arktinen projekti II, Sere, UPMA.
28 PM on oil and gas in the Soviet Arctic continental shelf, 2.3.1983 f. Arktinen projekti 1982–1985, 43-2, UMA; Scientific and Technical Committee's meeting 31.5–2.6.1977 in Moscow; 15.5.1978–17.5.1978 in Helsinki, TT-komitea pöytäkirjat, UMA.
29 Finnish-Soviet negotiations on Arctic cooperation, 8.4.1976; Meeting of industrial leaders on Arctic project, 16.9.1976; Meeting in GKNT on Arctic project, 7.6.1976; Finnish proposal on Northern USSR Arctic offshore research cooperation to GKNT, 4.7.1979, f. Arktinen projekti, Sere, UPMA.
30 Meeting between D. M. Gvishiani and Finnish corporation managers on Arctic project, 26.10.1976, f. Arktinen projekti II, Sere, UPMA.

31  PM about oil and gas in the Soviet Arctic continental shelf, 2.3.1983. f. Arktinen projekti 1982–1985, 43-2, UMA.

32  Meeting between D. M. Gvishiani and Finnish corporation managers on Arctic project, 26.10.1976, f. Arktinen projekti II, Sere, UPMA.

33  Scientific-Technical Committee meeting 31.5.1977–2.6.1977 in Moscow and 15.5.1978–17.5.1978 in Helsinki, TT-komitea pöytäkirjat, UMA.

34  Scientific-Technical Committee meeting 15.5.1978–17.5.1978 in Helsinki; Long Term Plan 1990 working group 15.5.1980–16.5.1980, TT-komitea pöytäkirjat, UMA.

35  Arctic offshore technology symposium in Moscow, 28.12.1979; Academy of Finland Workshop on Promotion of Arctic research in Helsinki, 5.12.1979; PM on the current situation of the Arctic project, 3.1.1984; VTT proposals for cooperation projects, 29.7.1979, f. "Arktinen projekti," Sere, UPMA.

36  Records of Finnish-Soviet Scientific-Technical Committee's meeting 30.5. 1983–31.5.1983 in Moscow,TT-komitea pöytäkirjat, UMA.

37  KPO on oil and gas in the Soviet Arctic continental shelf, 2.3.1983, f. Arktinen projekti 1982–1985, 43-2, UMA.

38  "Telakoiden tuotannosta puolet Neuvostoliittoon Tilauskanta Euroopan kolmanneksi suurin," *Kauppalehti*, 2.6.1981; "Kansainvälinen telakkakriisi jatkuu: Suomi voimakkaana 1980-luvulle," *Suomenmaa*, 2.6.1981; "Suomen ja N-liiton uusi yhteistyöalue: Arktinen laivateollisuus?" *Savon Sanomat*, 28.5.1981.

39  Scientific-Technical Committee meeting 7.9.1981–8.9.1981 in Moscow, TT-komitea pöytäkirjat, UMA.

40  Scientific-Technical Committee meeting 1981–1985, TT-komitea pöytäkirjat, UMA.

41  Export Control working files 1-12/80, Brzezinski material, NSA 12, President Carter library. See also CIA memorandum, "Soviet Arctic Economic Activity," March 1984, GI M 84-10049, General CIA Records. CIA Electronic Reading Room. https://www.cia.gov/library/readingroom/docs/CIA-RDP85T00287R 001101390001-8.pdf.

42  KPO on oil and gas in the Soviet Arctic continental shelf, 2.3.1983, f. Arktinen projekti 1982–1985, 43-2, UMA.

43  KPO 69 on the Soviet so-called "Arctic project" and the Nordic countries, 8.4.1982; KPO 275 on Soviet Arctic continental shelf, 14.4.1982, f. Arktinen projekti 1982–1985, UMA.

44  KPO 275 on Soviet Arctic continental shelf 14.4.1982, f. Arktinen projekti 1982–1985, 43-2, UMA.

45  KPO on oil and gas in the Soviet Arctic continental shelf, 2.3.1983, f. Arktinen projekti 1982–1985, 43-2, UMA.

46  KPO on oil and gas in the Soviet Arctic continental shelf, 2.3.1983, f. Arktinen projekti 1982–1985, 43-2, UMA.

47  Finnish Embassy in Oslo 80 about Norwegian-Soviet trade and industrial relations, 21.4.1982, f. Arktinen projekti 1982–1985, 43-2, UMA.

48  Finnish Embassy in Oslo to Formin 22.4.1982 about oil exploration in Barents Sea; Finnish Embassy in Oslo 80 about Norwegian-Soviet trade and industrial relations, 21.4.1982, f. Arktinen projekti 1982–1985, 43-2, UMA; Gustafson, *Crisis amid Plenty*, 2014, 216.

49  Finnish Embassy in Oslo KRT-140, 10.6.1984, f. Arktinen projekti 1982–1985, 43-2, UMA.

50  In 1988, research exchange in the Arctic project included 70 scientists vising Finland and the Soviet Union. In 1989, 71 Soviet scientists visited Finland and 59 Finnish scientists travelled to the Soviet Union. Compared with exchange in construction (182 to Finland and 26 to the Soviet Union) and agriculture (91

to Finland and 101 to the Soviet Union), Records of the Scientific-technical committee, TT-komitea pöytäkirjat, UMA.

51 Finnish delegation of the Economic Commission, meeting on Kola project, f. 66, 43-2, UMA; Finnish-Soviet Treaty on Cooperation on the Kola Peninsula, SopS 84/1989.

52 Interview G. Wilkman 16.1.2014, Espoo; Pauli Jumppanen 23.1.2014 Espoo.

53 Kaataja, "Expert Groups Closing the Divide," 2015; Kochetkova, *The Soviet Forestry Industry in the 1950s and 1960s*, 2017, 70.

54 Nastradining Co to Rauma-Repola 23.8.1983, f. "RR Vastaostot," UPMA.

55 Programme for Finnish-Soviet Working Group on Ship Equipment Trade under the Economic Commission, 8.9.1975, STTY 37, ELKA.

56 RR on counter-purchases 31.7.1984 PM on counter-purchases, 18.9.1984, Vastakaupat II, RR, UPMA; From Finnish Embassy in Reyjavik to Helsinki ID 294/1988 on clearing trade involving the governments of the Soviet Union and Iceland, Icelandic state fish factories and Rauma-Repola, f. Suomi-NL 1.1.1988–30.6.1988, 43.41, UMA.

57 WM on problems with trading, 17.5.1988, WM 30, ELKA.

58 Shipyard purchases from the Soviet Union, collected by the STTY, 1982–1986, STTY 37, ELKA.

59 RR on counter-purchases from the USSR, 14.3.1985, f. Vastaostot II, RR, UPMA.

60 RR on counter-purchases from the USSR, 14.3.1985, f. Vastaostot II, RR, UPMA.

61 STTY on shipyards increasing purchases from the Soviet Union, 12.12.1975, STTY 37, ELKA.

62 Ship Equipment Working Group, list of products discussed but not purchased 13.1.1977, STTY 37, ELKA.

63 Meeting of the Finnish-Soviet Economic Commission Machinery Division Shipbuilding group 4.9.1979–5.9.1979, STTY 1, ELKA; Programme for industrial cooperation to implement the measures decided in the 16th Meeting of the Machinery Division as a part of the PAO protocol 12.11.1980, STTY 38, ELKA; Uola, *Meidän isä on töissä telakalla*, 1996, 249–252.

64 Haapavaara, *Iso-Masa laivanrakentaja*, 2002, 92. Interview Saarikangas 5.2.2014.

65 RR Executive Board meeting 6.1.1983; RR on trading and counter-purchases, 28.4.1983; KPO 495 on counter-purchases in Finnish-Soviet trade 6.10.1983, f. Vastaostot, RR, UPMA; RR on counter-purchases in Finnish-Soviet ship trade, 4.10.1984; KPO to Teollisuuden keskusliitto 14767 on counter-purchases in the Finnish-Soviet trade, 4.7.1984, f. Vastaostot, RR, UPMA.

66 KPO 497 on the visit of Deputy Minister Manzhulo in Helsinki 20.9.1983–24.9.1983, f. 50, 4741, SPA.

67 RR on counter-purchases in Soviet trade, 13.7.1983; KPO 14767 to Teollisuuden keskusliitto 4.7.1984 on counter-purchases in the Finnish-Soviet trade, f. RR Vastaostot, UPMA.

68 PM RR/Kari Ketola "yrityskohtaiset vastaostot Neuvostoliiton kaupassa" 13.7.1983; Åke Wihtol/UM 14767 to Teollisuuden keskusliitto 4.7.1984 on counter purchases in the Finnish-Soviet trade, f. "RR Vastaostot", UPMA.

69 RR on trading, 3.1.1983; RR on counter-purchases 31.7.1984; Director Stefan Widomski's Speech in the SNS 40-anniversary seminar in Espoo 11.2.1985, f. "RR Vastaostot," UPMA.

70 RR on purchases in the Soviet trade, 26.8.1983, f. Vastaostot, RR, UPMA.

71 Meeting in the Soviet Commercial Embassy, 18.8.1983, f. Vastaostot, RR, UPMA.

72 Economic Commission Working Group for Shipbuilding, meeting 26.10.1987–30.10.1987, WM 34, ELKA.

73  L. Jakobsson to Pekka Laine, 19.11.1987, WM 30, ELKA.
74  From Licensing office, forwarded by STTY to its members companies, 15.10.1986, STTY 14, ELKA.
75  Interview K. Ketola & H. Eskelinen 26.3.2014.
76  RR on finding a shipyard for joint cooperation, 11.12.1980, f. 589C, UPMA.
77  Finnish-Soviet Long-Term Program 1990, SopS 10/1988.
78  "Suomalaisinvestoinnit yhteisyrityksiin helpottuvat Neuvostoliitossa," *Kauppapolitiikka* 3–4/1989.
79  WM proposal, 11.6.1988, WM 30, ELKA.
80  WM on joint ventures in the USSR, 15.7.1988, WM 40, ELKA; Meeting in MVT, 27.12.1987, WM 29, ELKA.
81  Meeting in MVT, 27.12.1987; WM on Perestroika Working Group, WM 29, ELKA.
82  WM on joint ventures in the USSR, 15.7.1988, WM 40, ELKA.
83  WM on joint ventures, 10.6.1988, WM 30, ELKA.
84  Letter draft 29.9.1988 C. E. Lindfors to Minister Jo. M. Volmer on new generation nuclear icebreaker, WM 40, ELKA.
85  WM proposal 11.6.1988, WM 30, ELKA.
86  WMH on a joint venture's business plan, 25.9.1988, WM 4; WM on joint ventures, 10.6.1988, WM 30, ELKA.
87  WMH on a joint venture's business plan, 25.9.1988, WM 40, ELKA.
88  Letter draft 29.9.1988 C. E. Lindfors to Minister Jo. M. Volmer on new generation nuclear icebreaker, WM 40, ELKA.
89  WM on joint ventures in the USSR, 15.7.1988, WM 40, ELKA.
90  Letter draft 29.9.1988 C. E. Lindfors to Minister Jo. M. Volmer on new generation nuclear icebreaker, WM 40, ELKA.
91  According to a note that had found its way from the UM to WM through several intermediaries, Ryzhkov had promised "to think about it" L. Jakobsson to K. Airaksinen, 28.9.1988, WM 30, ELKA; PM WMH on WM's joint venture in the Soviet Union, 29.9.1988, WM 40, ELKA.
92  PM WMH 29.9.1988 on a suggestion for WM's joint venture in the Soviet Union, "Ehdotus WM:n yhteisestä suunnittelutoimistosta NL:ssa," WM 40, ELKA; Letter draft 29.9.1988 C.E. Lindfors to Minister Jo. M. Volmer "Yhteistyöehdotus uuden sukupolven atomijäänmurtajasta," WM 40, ELKA.
93  Meeting Moscow 6.12.1988, WM 40, ELKA.
94  WMH on a joint venture 25.9.1988, WM 40, ELKA.
95  Meeting in Morflot 1.9.1988, WM 40, ELKA.
96  Meeting in Moscow 7.12.1988, WM 40, ELKA.
97  Interview P. Jumppanen 23.1.2014.
98  *Kauppa ja kansojen etu*, 1987, 144.
99  Hanson, *The Rise and Fall of the Soviet Economy*, 2014, 61–62.

# 6 From consensus to competition

## Reorganisation and rationalisation in shipbuilding

Ships have no breaks, just momentum. When a vessel that has been travelling full speed ahead suddenly experiences an engine failure and loses all forward thrust, it takes miles to bring it to a standstill. The same goes with large shipyards. Gargantuan shipbuilding facilities tie capital in their concrete building berths, cranes, and uncompleted hulls that are hard to liquidate. Complex, specialised organisations are sluggish to rescale in reaction to cyclical demand. The combination of rigid production, large-scale effects on employment, and volatile shipbuilding market brought national governments to the frontline when the tidal waves of globalisations first hit the traditional manufacturing in Europe. The stakes were high, and the chosen policy had permanent impact on shipbuilding communities. Like a ship once sunken to the bottom of the sea, a shipyard once closed was unlikely to be opened again.[1]

The shipyard crisis arrived Finland later than elsewhere, but when it did, it threw the industry and the state into a whirlwind that redefined the foundation for the Finnish shipbuilding policy. This and the following chapter approach the Finnish shipbuilding companies renegotiating their relationship with each other and with the state. This chapter does that through the analysis of the processes that led to the industrial reorganisation and descaling; the next chapter focuses on the state aid and financing. Together, these two parallel chapters present the Finnish account of the state response to the European shipyard crisis.

The European shipyard crisis stemmed from the twin menace of dwindling competitiveness against Asian shipyards and diminishing demand in the global markets. In Finland, as the previous chapters have pointed out, the technical specialisation and bilateral trade with the Soviet Union decreased the direct cost-competition against the Far East and buffered against the market fluctuation. This chapter introduces two more elements of stability: the shared mission of expanding shipbuilding industry that tied the state and the industry together and the consensus-oriented practices within the shipbuilding companies that coordinated the domestic competition.

Cooperation and coordination are overarching themes in the modern economic history of Finland referred to as 'cooperative capitalism', 'consensus capitalism',[2] 'national capitalism' (*kansallinen kapitalismi*),[3] 'negotiation economy' (*neuvottelutalous*),[4] or 'consensus politics'.[5] Historians use different concepts, but generally agree that the Finnish industrial development in the 20th century was shaped by the active contribution of state to industrialisation and close interaction between political and business elites.[6] Companies engaged in official and unofficial cooperation with each other, governmental bodies, and labour market organisations to negotiate wages and industrial policies.[7] An overarching theme in this chapter is the dismantling of this old sense of consensus and the renegotiations over a new basis of the intra-industry and state–industry relations.

For most part, downscaling of the Finnish shipbuilding capacity took place as a result of industrial reorganisation process during the long 1980s: the negotiations were sparked off by the crisis talk in the late 1970s, and the tail of the process continued to the early 1990s. The Cold War presents itself as a framework in which the political and industrial actors assessed their expectations of the future shipbuilding and adjusted their strategies according to the expectations. The economic difficulties—which were concurrent or forecasted—forced the state and the industry to reimagine the future of shipbuilding without the static context of the Soviet trade.

## Cooperation, consensus, and concentration

After the war, Wärtsilä was clearly the largest and most experienced in building relatively sophisticated steel vessels; it had the strongest negotiation power and ability to cherry-pick orders according to its technology and business strategy. In 1948, the smaller, often newly founded wooden ship producers founded a cooperative body, the 'Finnish Wooden Ship Industry' (*Suomen Puulaivateollisuus—Finska Träfartygsindustri ry*), to coordinate their relations with the state and the Soviet customers, and to increase their bargaining power against Wärtsilä. After the war reparations, the association removed the reference to wooden hulls, renaming itself the 'Shipyard Association' (*Telakkayhdistys*). The change of name did not change the fact that the association was essentially a cartel. It established uniform pricing and controlled the shares of the Soviet orders that each of its member shipyards could receive.[8]

Export cartels were neither uncommon nor illegal in Finland at that time. They were even preferred over destructive price competition between domestic companies. Forestry, the leading export industry, had been entirely cartelised in the inter-war period. Finland introduced the first antitrust law in 1957, but until the 1980s, the legislation focused on monitoring and controlling instead of the prohibition of cartels.[9] From the narrow national point of view, export cartels did not harm domestic customers but increased the competitiveness of the small country in international markets.[10] The Shipyard Association differed from the better-known forestry cartels as its prime motive was not to establish a nationwide cooperative network to gain competitiveness abroad. Instead, it was an instrument for minor shipyards to coordinate their mutual competition for the Soviet orders.

The Shipyard Association did not last long. The mutual interests, that had joined the rival companies together at the turn of the 1950s, vanished towards the end of the decade. The Soviets refused to negotiate with a cartel seeing it ideologically deprecating as a symbol of exploitative capitalism. The association also suffered from growing internal conflicts of interest. One founding member, Rauma-Repola, had outgrown the other participants, which made the negotiations asymmetric and troublesome. The members agreed to dismantle the Shipyard Association in 1962.[11]

In the course of the first 10–15 years of the Cold War shipbuilding, the Finnish shipyard industry concentrated on fewer but bigger units. After the war reparation, there had been 15 shipyards of various sizes and technical competence; in the 1960s, only four or five shipbuilding companies coordinated the domestic industrial dynamic.[12] This concentration facilitated official and unofficial cooperation among the major shipbuilding companies and their managers.

In 1967, the seven industrial leaders—Wärtsilä, Valmet, Rauma-Repola, Laivateollisuus, Hollming, Reposaari Machine Shop (*Reposaaren konepaja*), and Uusikaupunki Shipyard—founded their own group under the Finnish employers' union for metal industries, *Suomen Metalliteollisuusyhdistys*. In 1975, after Rauma-Repola had acquired Reposaari and Uusikaupunki Shipyards, and Valmet bought up Laivateollisuus, the remaining five shipbuilding companies created an independent interest group, the Finnish Shipyard Association (*Suomen Telakkateollisuusyhdistys*, hereafter STTY), to represent the industry in the negotiations with the state and to maintain the industry's public image. Within STTY, the companies cooperated on several issues such as translating Russian technical specifications and coordinating the education and training of shipyard workers.[13] In the spirit of the corporatist tradition of the Finnish welfare state project, the shipyards also collaborated in investigating job satisfaction and workplace safety to deal with the high turnover of the shipbuilders and bargain over wages.[14]

One of the few sources of constant friction between the shipbuilding industry and the state was unstable employment situation at the shipyards. Shipbuilding was project-based business, and a large number of short-term contracts had the potential to cause short-term unemployment.[15] The STTY wanted to protect the industrial image as a good employer and also to tackle the Nordic 'immigration problem' referring to the problem with skilled workers moving from Finland to Swedish shipyards in search of better employment. To avoid the situation in which news of labour shortage would put pressure on wage increase, the STTY member companies agreed not to recruit workers from other shipyards, not to publish salaries in newspapers, and not to advertise vacancies more than once in a month.[16]

The Finnish Cold War shipbuilding was not immune to international fluctuation or domestic competition. Yet, it was often able to compromise over the disagreements without making the conflicts of interests public in a way that would damage the industrial image as an employer.

The STTY was the public façade of the cooperation but not its hearth. From the early 1960s until the mid-1980s, the shipbuilding companies coordinated their actions unofficially within an informal group of top managers who were tied together by personal relations, similar backgrounds, and mutual trust. This 'Club of Five'[17] functioned effectively like an export cartel in the Soviet trade. The five shipbuilding directors divided the Soviet orders to the shipyards based on their established production structures and market shares. Competition for new types and ship classes was open, but once a company had caught one contract, invested in its design, and development, the other companies would be restrained from entering into serious price competition for following orders of the type. In practice, as Figure 6.1 shows, the unofficial cooperation managed to freeze the market shares of the leading Finnish shipbuilding companies.[18]

The aim of this coordinated competition was to prevent the Soviet Union from benefitting from price competition between Finnish companies, support technical specialisation at the shipyards, and decrease costs of production through longer series. The cooperation was kept unofficial and secret. Though export cartels were not illegal, the collaboration within the shipyard directors had also an effect on domestic competition. Even more so, the secrecy was imperative because the Soviet disapproval against cartels was well-known.[19]

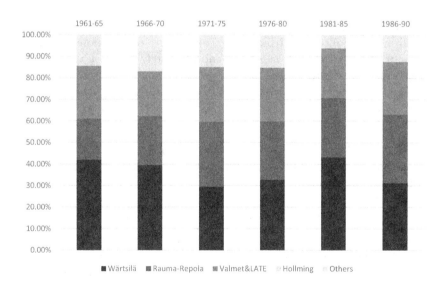

*Figure 6.1* The shares of the Finnish shipbuilding companies in the Finnish–Soviet trade in five-year periods 1960–1990. Data: Uola, *Meidän isä on töissä telakalla*, 1996, 577.

## Riding the waves of despair and prospects: First Shipbuilding Committee, 1977–1982

The rapid industrialisation in the first half of the Cold War had conjoined the Finnish state and shipbuilding industry together by common interests in national security, social stability, and economic growth. Industrial expansion promoted the national security through the Soviet trade, national welfare through the industrial employment, and national prestige through showcases of technological prowess. In the apogee of the Finnish shipbuilding in the 1970s, it seemed to have gained an unstoppable momentum.

Elsewhere in European shipbuilding countries, the 1970s was a turbulent decade. The OPEC shock crashed demand for crude oil carriers first. Then the demand for other cargo types followed the downturn reacting to the depressed economic prospects. Governments in Western Europe adopted different national shipbuilding strategies combining nationalisation, down-scaling, shipyard closures, and financial support for industrial restructuring in the hope of preserving a fraction of the competitive shipyards for the future upswing.[20] State acquisitions and interventions raised social tensions to the surface of national shipbuilding policies but an ostensible unanimity prevailed in Finland. Political historian Pauli Kettunen has described the 1970s as 'the strikingly grey decade'—the decade when elderly men in grey suits led the country and the national political debates in foreign affairs and economic policy turned into seemingly apolitical consensus.[21] In Finnish shipbuilding policy, the seemingly grey, apolitical consensus covered an undercurrent of a conflict underneath.

In 1977, social democratic Prime Minister Kalevi Sorsa invited represent-atives from the political and industrial stakeholders to a remotely located Korpilampi-hotel to discuss, negotiate, and ultimately arrive at a consensus over the new economic policy. *Suomen Kuvalehti* reported from the event making an allegorical comparison to the historical labour market agreement in 1939, when the crisis of national survival on the eve of Winter War over-ruled all the ideological differences:

> They were 350. They were like a sort of board of directors in the company called Finland Ltd. (Oy Suomi Ab) that has over four and half million employees [...] almost as important as what was said was who was invited and how they were seated: an industrial tycoon next to a communist poli-ticians, trade union activist next to a spokesperson of agriculture.[22]

The concurrent economic problems created a sense of national emergency and motivated stakeholders to compromise in order to contribute to the com-mon national goal in the 'spirit of Korpilampi'. That consensus placed the priority to industrial competitiveness over full employment.[23]

After the shipyard directors returned from Korpilampi conference, the Finnish shipbuilding industry changed its public communication to crisis talk. 'The shipyard crisis is reality', headlined the maritime monthly *Navigator* as to signal the urgent distress of the industry in September 1977.[24] The reason for the outcry was that some shipyards had got no new orders in a year, and many locations had announced the possibility of redundancies. In the international comparisons, however, the Finnish shipbuilding industry was still doing well. The four major shipbuilding companies employed directly over 18,000 shipyard workers at 12 shipyards, and the trend was rather upward than downward.[25]

The discussion of the Finnish 'shipyard crisis' surfaced in 1977 when the cycles in Western and Eastern trade occurred coincidentally. The cyclical downswing in the Soviet five-year planning cycles was typical at the point when the shipyards had completed their orders in hand and the Soviet Union had not yet started to make new orders to fulfil the next five-year plan. This time, however, the Eastern upturn was delayed while the Western trade had remained sluggish (Figure 6.2).

Domestic challenges in Finland were accompanied by depressing international news. The monthly press reports at Wärtsilä Turku Shipyard give some insights into the atmosphere: the United Kingdom had implemented hard protectionist measures to protect its shipyards (*Fairplay* 18.12.1975), CMEA countries, too, suffered from a tanker surplus and were looking for new markets in the West (*Seatrade* 12/1975), shipyard closures were planned in Sweden (*Svensk sjöfarts tid* 7/1976), the British shipyard crisis had already lasted a decade and despite state interventions, productivity had not improved (*Economist* 14.2.1976), the United States increased its support for shipyards to compete against Japan (*Economist* 13.3.1976), West Germany subsidised domestic orders by 16% (*Fairplay* 5.8.1976), and the Netherlands by 23.75% (*Lloyds List* 7.10.1976).[26]

The domestic and international problems together amplified the crisis mentality that pressed for re-engineering both shipbuilding and shipbuilding policy in Finland. Insecurity made everyone nervous. From the company's point of view, the inability to provide steady employment for skilled workers hampered the future recruitment and led to sunk costs in workers' education.

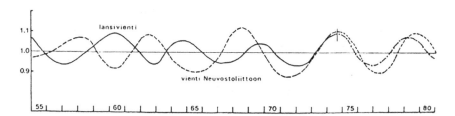

*Figure 6.2* Cyclical fluctuation in the Finnish Eastern trade (dash line) and Western trade, drafted by the Finnish Labour Institute for Economic Research and circulated among the shipyard managers with a note: 'It may be better to avoid underlining the stability and counter-cyclical effect of the Soviet trade—at least in the company of experts'. Circular letter from Rewell/Wärtsilä to Forsgren/STTY 20.3.1980, STTY 48, ELKA.

For the Finnish government, a mass of unemployed metal workers was a distressing image.[27]

Nobody could possibly tell how long the international depression in shipbuilding might last. Nobody wanted to follow Sweden and the United Kingdom along the path to a prolonged crisis, where only state interventions and funding kept uncompetitive shipyards alive.

Potential de-industrialisation in Finnish shipbuilding had a tangential but well-recognised connection with national security as it could cause discomfort in the Finnish–Soviet relations. The Finnish shipbuilding companies had recently modernised and expanded shipyards, counting on that the returns from the ever-growing Soviet trade would cover the investments as outlined in the Finnish–Soviet intergovernmental protocols and speeches. Closing the shipyards, that had just been erected to fulfil the Soviet demand, could be taken as a sign of distrust in the Soviet Union.[28]

To address the industrial distress, the Ministry of Trade and Industry appointed a Shipyard Committee in 1977. The chair was a civil servant Pentti Viita from the Ministry of Trade and Industry, and the other members were representatives from ministries, industry, and labour unions. The task was to examine the future prospects for Finnish shipbuilding and to suggest strategic measures for how to overcome the current challenges.

The Shipyard Committee started its work under gloomy future expectations when the Finnish shipyards reported empty order books. At the end of the year, the Shipyard Committee proposed a 25-point action plan to save the Finnish shipbuilding industry with the emphasis on governmental measures to support companies and facilitate structural changes.[29]

To avoid future crises and to increase protection against international jolts, the committee proposed building the future shipbuilding on the foundation of two pillars: Soviet and domestic trade. In ideal circumstances, according to the Shipyard Committee, domestic orders would cover up to 20% of the Finnish ship production and Soviet orders 60%–70%.[30] To adjust the industry in the new market situation and to ease price-competition, the committee proposed 20% cuts in shipbuilding capacity.[31]

To tow the shipyards up from the slump, the committee proposed state actors to take initiative to push the Soviet Union to contract for new ships during the ongoing five-year period 1976–1980, or re-schedule orders in the next five-year period 1981–1985. These additional ship orders would be funded through the bilateral trade by increasing the imports and the transit trade of oil and gas. Second, the committee proposed the state organisations to reschedule their future orders for icebreakers and naval ships to provide immediate remedy for the struggling shipyards. Finally, the committee brought up the possibility to subsidy certain domestic orders to support shipyard employment until the next upswing.[32]

The fear of mass unemployment, even if temporary, prompted the government to appropriate subsidies for shipyards worth of FIM70 million in total in years 1978 and 1979.[33]

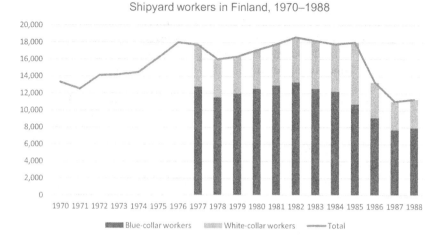

*Figure 6.3* Workforce employed directly by the Finnish shipyards. Data: Shipyard Committee 1984; STTY; Tuominen (1988).

With hindsight, this appears as an obscure transition period. The priorities in industrial policy had already started to move from the full employment towards international competitiveness, but the policy measures were still propelled by arguments for domestic employment: When the shipbuilding directors wrote letters to the Ministry of Trade and Industry asking for financial support, they justified their requests by the difficult employment situation.[34] When the civil servants prepared the shipyard subsidy plans for the government, they carefully estimated how many man-years the state would receive in exchange for the financial aid.[35] Sometimes, the companies saved the administration from the mathematical troubles and calculated the appropriate scheme based on the subsidy/man-year ratio.[36] When the government proposed new state-aid schemes, it justified it as being cheaper for the public sector than the unemployment benefits.[37] When members of the Parliament raised critical questions about the government's inaction on the issue of potential low season at shipyards, they, too, invoked to the distress of the workers and their families.[38] When the Parliament appropriated FIM20 million in a supplementary budget for domestic ship orders in the spring of 1978, it justified this as a support for shipyard workers.[39] The state aid to private shipyards was translated, in effect, into social benefits.

The Shipyard Committee published its final report in December 1977. At that time, its gloomy, pessimistic content contrasted already with a new dawn at the shipyards. The Soviet Union had placed new orders, several shipyards announced new contracts, and the attention turned towards the next upswing. At the turn of the 1980s, the Finnish shipbuilders shared again a highly optimistic outlook. All domestic newspapers joined the *Navigator* in circulating positive news of the prosperous industry.[40]

Instead of industrial downscaling, quite the contrary occurred. The Shipyard Committee 1977 had suggested decreasing the shipbuilding workforce by 12%, but, eventually, the shipyards increased their staff by 12% (Figure 6.3).[41] In an upswing like this, state subsidies and other measures were no longer critical to industrial survival, but they were, as Mikko Uola has articulated, 'morally supporting'.[42] They articulated state commitment to the shipbuilding.

Only one Finnish company, Navire, abandoned shipbuilding at this point. It had already contracted with Norwegian Kvaerner on selling its facilities including the shipyard in Naantali, but the trade was not realised. Foreign acquisitions required permission from the Bank of Finland, and the central bank refused to give it. Instead, to prevent the entrance of a Norwegian competitor to their home market, Wärtsilä and the escalator company Kone bought Navire's properties.[43]

*Figure 6.4* Should the profits of the Finnish–Soviet ship trade be accredited to the political or industrial actors? The Finnish ship trade with the Soviet Union used to be so profitable that many interest groups wanted to take the credit from it. In 1984, Wärtsilä Turku Shipyard refused the visit of the social democrat Prime Minister Kalevi Sorsa. The party newspaper of the Social Democratic Party commented the issue with a cartoon of Wärtsilä's director Tankmar Horn arrogantly turning down Minister Sorsa who, as the chair of Finnish–Soviet Economic Commission, tried to bring to Wärtsilä 'Easter trade, ship contracts, and icebreakers'. *Suomen Sosialidemokraatti* 12.9.1984, original Stefan's collection 1984:104, TVA. Used with permission by Työväenarkisto.

The first wave of shipyard crises in Finland resulted in intense state-industry dialogue but not much of a strategic change. From 1977 to 1982, the shipbuilding interest groups utilised the crisis mentality to lobby for an advantageous shipbuilding policy (Figure 6.4). In contrast to Sweden and the United Kingdom, where state interventions had a negative reputation as expensive and inefficient attempts to prevent the inevitable, in Finland the shipyards communicated the crisis only as a temporary nuisance. The survival of the industry was not in danger, only the full employment was. While the current problems made the state support necessary, the positive future prospects made it rational. Rhetorically, the Finnish shipbuilding industry balanced on the breaking point between a successful future and difficult present.

## The turn of the tide: towards radical reorganisation, 1983–1986

'Shipyards on the threshold of a new crisis' alerted the *Navigator* in the autumn of 1983. The events in 1977 seemed to repeat themselves. The shipyards were finishing their last orders in hand without new contracts on the horizon. Once again, Ministry of Trade and Industry appointed a Shipyard committee that had the same task, the same chair, and even the same name as the previous committee. As an echo to its namesake six years earlier, the Shipyard Committee proposed some policy measures and industrial cooperation to reduce capacity. Again, the publication of the committee report occurred coincidental with an upturn when new orders from the Soviet Union started to refill the order books.[44]

Ostensibly, the second Shipyard Committee yielded no more results than the first one. Behind closed doors, nevertheless, the four biggest Finnish shipbuilding companies, Wärtsilä, Rauma-Repola, Valmet, and Hollming, entered into consultations about a radical reorganisation. The ambitious aim was nothing less than the merger of all Finnish shipyards into one governmentally supported company.[45]

The negotiations of reorganisations marked a watershed in the way the Finnish shipbuilding companies coordinated their relations. The prevailing consensus-oriented culture of the Finnish shipbuilding industry had been maintained by the cooperative practices of the top managers. Between 1983 and 1984, three out of four top shipbuilding directors retired or moved to another company. The new members that replaced the old managers in the unofficial coordinating body the 'Club of Five' were not committed to the compromises of their predecessors. Rauma-Repola calculated that it had the potential to gain over 35% of the Soviet ship orders from Finland in open competition, instead of the 15%–20% that it had been used to under the coordinated competition.[46] The Club started to unravel and finally broke up in 1985.[47]

On December 5, 1986, the company directors decided also to break up the Finnish Shipyard Association STTY invoking the increasing costs and decreasing benefits of the cooperation.[48] The operational board of the

STTY was surprised to learn about the directors' decision at their meeting.[49] Unable to find arguments to explain the decision, the board members noted that none of the directors had been close to the association and they knew only a little of the work it did on translating the industrial standards and cooperating in education. The costs of cooperation could hardly be blamed, as the membership fees were decided by the member companies themselves. Moreover, the association had FIM450,000 in its bank account, which was enough for STTY to operate some years without collecting any new membership fees.[50] The STTY board members also noted the potential harm to the international credibility of the Finnish shipbuilding industry if it was left without a national shipyard association: 'AWES countries have experienced various problems in recent years, but no one has started the industrial reorganisation process by closing down the industry's own association'.[51]

The arguments for industrial cooperation were in vain. In February 1987, the STTY decided to close down itself.[52]

Parallel to the process of running down the cooperation organisation, the shipbuilding companies continued their negotiations on a merger. The two West Coast shipbuilders, Rauma-Repola and Hollming, left the negotiation table while Wärtsilä and Valmet managed to reach an agreement over reorganising their shipbuilding and paper machine production into two new subsidiaries.[53]

The merger of Wärtsilä's and Valmet's units was published on July 30, 1986. It was a great surprise to anyone not directly involved in the negotiations. *Navigator* described the 'the most carefully guarded secret of Finland' as the 'most radical rationalisation in history'.[54] Indeed, still in June 1986, when Wärtsilä and Valmet already prepared their organisations for the future merger, Wärtsilä's director Tor Stolpe had claimed to the Finnish business magazine *Talouselämä* that there were no reorganisation plans on the horizon.[55]

The merger contradicted Wärtsilä's and Valmet's histories and public images. Wärtsilä was one of the biggest privately owned conglomerates in Finland. Valmet was a state-owned company founded to counterbalance Wärtsilä's dominance in shipbuilding. The 'unlikely Finnish connection', as the *Journal of Commerce* headlined, received attention beyond the national borders. Commentators asked why the 'unholy alliance' or 'unorthodox merger' was necessary, but approved the resolution as a prime example of how cold-headed managers prepared their business for the future.[56] The atmosphere in the mid-1980s was in favour of bold moves.

Both Wärtsilä and Valmet were traditional, large multi-branch conglomerates. They appeared as heavy and inefficient in the eyes of new corporate management that put the priority on specialised and streamlined production structure. In 1984, Valmet's strategy paper had metaphorically compared portfolio management with trimming fruit trees: 'If branches are never cut, the tree may grow big, but won't bear fruit'. Shipbuilding, the strategy paper continued, was a particularly risky branch that involved high fixed costs and volatile demand.[57] Similar considerations had taken place in Wärtsilä, which had branches ranging from diesel engines to lavatories and from security systems to art glass. Wärtsilä was listed on the Stock Exchange in Stockholm and London in 1984, which increased the need of showing steady profitability to the shareholders across the corporate group.

Wärtsilä and Valmet shared the ownership of the new maritime company based on the size of their shipbuilding sectors, 70% for Wärtsilä and 30% for Valmet. Thanks to its majority, Wärtsilä dominated the new shipbuilding company which was also indicated in the new name: Wärtsilä Marine. It was clear that the marine technology was more important for Wärtsilä than it was for Valmet. Ships generated more than half of Wärtsilä's results.[58] Even though Wärtsilä's shipbuilders would never have admitted that they had anything to gain from cooperation with Valmet, the merger eased competition in the certain specialised niches that were important to Wärtsilä. Valmet had shown clear inclinations towards entering into Wärtsilä's core business of ice-going vessels and passenger ships, and managed to get its first orders—a nuisance if not a threat to Wärsilä's marketing.[59]

Another motivation for the reorganisation was that the shockwaves of the merger would make the painful rationalisations easier to implement with minimal impact on corporate brand. The Finnish shipyard managers were well aware of the need for profound re-engineering in working culture (Figure 6.5). The shipyard committees had pointed the finger at hierarchical organisations, inflexible processes, rigid job specifications, and the strong presence of labour unions at yards that created resistance to change, inefficiency, and strikes.[60] Wärtsilä Marine's core competence was hard technology, as was revealingly expressed in preparatory negotiations between Wärtsilä and Valmet in the summer of 1986: 'It is the technology that generates profits, not the labour'.[61] The concrete aim was to decrease capacity from 10,000 to 6,000 shipyard workers.[62]

The Finnish government supported the merger by passing a law of industrial tax reliefs in the case of merger. 'Lex Wärtsilä Marine' was not a bureaucratic detail, but a measure of significant state support that eliminated taxes worth FIM700 million that the parent companies Wärtsilä and Valmet would otherwise have been obliged to pay and therefore decreased the financial risks involved in the reorganisation.[63]

In the parliamentary debate, a small group of extreme left-wing politicians railed against the arrangement on the grounds it meant privatisation of shipbuilding, increasing unemployment, and would also damage the Finnish–Soviet relations by decreasing Finland's ability to build ships for the Soviet Union. The vast majority of the Parliament, however, backed the proposal.[64] Instead of privatisation or killing off the state shipbuilding, the supporters argued for the tax reliefs as reasonable policy instrument to facilitate industrial restructuring. For this majority, the question was no longer whether the Finnish shipbuilding required rationalisation or not, but how the state could best facilitate the industrial adaptation to the global competition.

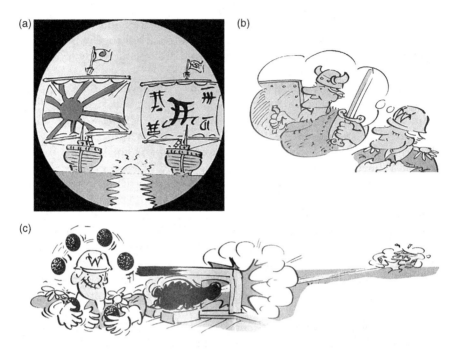

*Figure 6.5* To improve workplace culture, Wärtsilä published an allegorical cartoon of two sailors who fight against cost-efficient Asian and government-subsidised European enemy ships. While Sailor Precise (Merimies Jämpti) understood that he has to take immediate action, to forget old rigid practices and to apply new methods to win the war, Sailor Stupid (Merimies Mäntti) focused on nostalgic day-dreaming and complaining about the unfair situation. The story ends with Sailor Stupid realising that he had to change his attitude to survive upcoming battles. Brochure 'Tartu Ongelmaan – Meritaistelu tarvitsee merimies Jämptiä' (Undated, Wärtsilä Telakkaryhmä), WM 43, ELKA.

That even the majority of left-wing parties were ready to accept lay-offs in exchange for economic growth was a reflection of the prevailing consensus over liberalisation and deregulation across the political spectrum.[65] The shipyard companies definitely took the 'Lex Wärtsilä Marine' as an indicator of state support for shipbuilding rationalisation.

## Bargaining over state interventions, 1987–1988

Wärtsilä Marine's new CEO Pekka Laine (1937–) was a professional change manager. He had a degree in social sciences, work experience in paper industry, and reputation as a cold-blooded leader of industrial rationalisation. His public nickname, Black Peter (*Musta Pekka*),[66] fit well with his self-understanding as a determinate strategic manager he describes in his memoirs:

'It was extremely important not to stand still but to discover a way forward and follow it with determination'.[67]

The newly appointed management outlined the 'super flexible business strategy'[68]. The strategy was to gain competitive advantages in specialised vessels, to survive the recession through aggressive marketing, and to adapt to the low price level by cutting costs.[69] The business plan was bold, future-oriented, and in the borderland of impossibility. Wärtsilä Marine's marketing material boasted of competitiveness and promised 'prototypes and one-offs with the price level and delivery time of the serial production', but the price level dropped close to break-even point.[70] Important pioneering customers in the USSR ministries and offshore industries were plunged into economic difficulties and hesitant to place new orders.[71] Organisational reengineering, that was expected to reduce the construction costs by 20% and delivery time by 30%, failed to meet its ambitious goals.[72] The aggressive marketing strategy managed, however, to fill the order books, as shown in Figure 6.6.

The main instrument in the rationalisation was to cut costs by decreasing capacity. In January 1987, Wärtsilä Marine decided to run down Valmet's Vuosaari Shipyard. Closing a large shipyard that had been opened to respond to Soviet demand only 13 years earlier was a sign of distrust in the Soviet trade and thus an uneasy topic in the Finnish–Soviet meetings. Yet, besides some grumble in private, Sudoimport or the Soviet customers showed no interest in creating a political uproar against the closure.[73]

Vuosaari Shipyard closed its gates in 1987. Valmet Laivateollisuus Shipyard in Turku did the same in the following summer. Two years after the merger, Valmet's newbuilding shipyards no longer existed. Those who had portrayed the founding of Wärtsilä Marine as the manifestation of privatisation pronounced now the end of state-owned shipbuilding in Finland.[74]

*Figure 6.6* The Finnish Shipbuilding order-book end of the year (GT). Data: Association of West European Shipbuilders and Shiprepairers Awes, Annual reports, MTA.

Wärtsilä Marine made loss in its first year in operation, but that was expected and accepted as an inevitable drawback of industrial restructuring.[75] However, the incomplete organisational change, unprofitable orders, and haphazard decision-making continued to hamper the work at the shipyards. The shipyard closures did not deliver the expected cost savings but rather increased shortage of skilled workers that, together with frequent strikes, put pressure to the management to raise salaries rather than to lower them.[76] The gap between calculated and realised costs grew larger. In November 1988, the company forecasted accumulated losses of 1.250 billion before the end of 1990.[77] Cash flowed out of the company faster than it came in, Wärtsilä Marine drifted close to insolvency. Yet, it still had parent companies with strong balance sheets and well-established cash reserves to carry it through the difficult first years.[78]

The West Coast shipbuilders, Rauma-Repola and Hollming, who had opted out from the reorganisation plans in 1986, were faced with the same difficult circumstances of low demand, subsidised price-dumping, and dire market predictions. In the spring of 1988, a leading daily newspaper *Helsingin Sanomat* announced that Rauma-Repola and Hollming had returned to negotiations with Wärtsilä Marine: 'The reason for reorganisations is that neither of the companies has got any new ship orders from the Soviet Union. Because of the reduction in volume, the operations will be reorganised'.[79]

The newspaper did not disclose the source of information, but the piece of news was consistent with the business scenarios drafted in Wärtsilä Marine. The shipbuilding strategy placed its trust in an upcoming dawn in the Soviet trade, but even the next upturn was not expected to bring all the shipyards on an even keel. Under the worst-case scenario, only three shipyards would survive: Wärtsilä Perno Shipyard building large ships, Hollming Rauma Shipyard focusing on small vessels, and Kotka Shipyard doing all the repairs. The most optimistic scenario was almost as bad as the worst case, but the Wärtsilä Helsinki would continue building ice-capable tonnage.[80] The shipyard closures could be avoided only if the Soviet Union would multiply its orders, the oil market price would hike to the peak level of the oil crisis, and the international cost-competition for Soviet orders would come to an end.[81] The Finnish shipbuilding should, in sum, return to the circumstances in the mid-1970s.

Directors of Wärtsilä Marine, Rauma-Repola, and Hollming launched negotiations in the autumn of 1988. On the table was a plan to merge all the Finnish shipyards into one state-supported company. The rationale was to increase control over domestic competition and to support technical specialisation.[82] In essence, the negotiations had exactly the same goals as what they had previously enacted through the STTY, but now, the context was different. The Club of Five had controlled cooperation under circumstances when the production expanded and the Soviet orders provided a relatively static basic load for the five or four big shipbuilders. Now, the negotiations were about controlling the competition to save at least the competitive core of Finnish shipbuilding for the international market. Competition between the Finnish companies after the dismantling of the coordinated competition had been devastating for everyone involved. Wärtsilä Marine struggled with an excess load while the other Finnish shipyards suffered from an underload. Without coordination, all shipyards would close their gates in a random order when they ran out of money. The destruction would be detrimental, instead of creative, and leave nothing behind.

On December 1988, the shipbuilding companies emerged with a plan to consolidate all the Finnish shipyards into a single company with the working name of 'Finnmarine'. According to sketches, Wärtsilä would still be the biggest shareholder with a share of 35%, Rauma-Repola the second biggest with 20%, and Valmet refused to have more than 15%. Hollming would receive 10% due to its smaller size, and the state would participate with a 20% share.[83]

The Ministry of Trade and Industry appointed the third joint shipyard committee to prepare the merger. Its composition was similar to the two previous committees in 1977 and 1983, but it had a new chair, the Permanent Secretary at the Ministry, Bror Wahlroos (1928–2007). Since his move from the private sector to the Ministry in 1969, Wahlroos had been involved in developing Finnish Western trade policy and management of state-owned companies. As an active public debater with strong opinions, he was a controversial and colourful figure among the Finnish civil servants.[84]

What had changed dramatically after the second Shipyard Committee in 1983–84 was the future expectation. In terms of numbers, the target was now to descale the Finnish shipyard production from 10,000 workers to only 3,000 workers.[85] The practical goal of the third Shipbuilding Committee was to agree on the reorganisation, but it became an arena to debate the principles of state interventions as well.

For all companies except Hollming, the state ownership was a critical precondition to increase the credibility of the new company and to signal to financers and customers that Finland was not going to abandon its shipyards.[86] In addition, the industry asked for low-interest loan of half a billion that could be partly settled against the shipyard closure expenses, state guarantees for external financing, and a law of tax reliefs similar to 'Lex Wärtsilä Marine'.[87]

In discussions with state representatives, the companies did not try to conceal or downplay the risks. Rather, the industry used the high business risks as their key argument for state ownership:

> Companies have suffered considerable losses in competition against subsidised [foreign] industry and consider that as long as the future prospects of the industry remain insecure and the competition situation is unhealthy, the state should come to share the risks of the [shipbuilding] industry in Finland.[88]

In the early phase of industrialisation in Finland, the government had adopted an active entrepreneurial role and taken initiative in risky branches of national importance. Now, it was offered a role of the risk carrier for a mature industry with the strange consolation that 'if the risks are not realised, the state's financial losses from this venture remain small'.[89] Industrialisation was, again, a national project: 'Because the issue concerns the Finnish industrial and labour policy as a whole, it cannot be left for private companies to tackle alone'.[90]

Wahlroos presented the reorganisation plan to the Ministerial Committee on Economic Policy in December 1988. In Finland, ministerial committees were not formal decision-making bodies but confidential arenas for discussion. Nevertheless, the consensus among the committee members, the Prime Minister, the Minister of Finance, the Minister of Trade and Industry, and the Minister of Labour usually outlined the will of the government as a whole.[91] The minister in charge was Ilkka Suominen (1939–), the chairman of the conservative National Coalition Party that had formed the government with social democrats. In its foreign affairs, the 'blue-red' coalition still made the traditional reference to the FCMA treaty and the priority of Finnish–Soviet trade, but in its economic policy, the non-socialist parties pushed for a liberal economic platform.[92]

Wahlroos warned the Ministerial Committee against following the route trod by Sweden and the United Kingdom where the governments had not managed to save shipyards from the downfall but only encouraged companies to ask for more money.[93] According to the notes of Valmet's representatives in the Shipbuilding Committee, Suominen had not previously been categorically against the state ownership, but at the Ministerial Committee meeting, he chimed in with Wahlroos speaking out against increasing stakes in shipbuilding.[94] Anything else on the list was negotiable to him from the tax reliefs to subsidised financing. The policy aim was to descale the Finnish shipbuilding industry at minimal expenses for the public sector.[95] Yet, the ministers seemed to share Wahlroos' sceptical attitude towards the shipyard crisis. Instead, they suspected that the company directors exaggerated their difficulties and bluffed when they claimed that the state ownership was non-negotiable.[96]

The main dilemma in the governmental discussion was to formulate the policy in the way that would give the right impression domestically and internationally. Due to the global overcapacity, each shipyard closure was a step towards healthier market competition and benefit for those who survived. The Finnish government did not want to promise to the Finnish industry unconditional state support, but neither wanted it to imply to the international audience that Finland would withdraw its support for shipbuilding.[97]

In January 1989, the government approved all the other conditions the third Shipyard Committee had set for the reorganisation but refused to invest any venture capital in the new shipbuilding company. Without the state as a shareholder, Wärtsilä opted out of the merger. The other companies followed Wärtsilä and left the negotiation room.[98]

## Big bankruptcy changes the atmosphere, 1989

In the spring of 1989, Wärtsilä Marine sunk deeper into economic difficulties. In the summer, it ran out of cash. An interim financial statement
forecasted FIM1.225 billion accumulated losses by the end of the year.[99] In
July 1989, Wärtsilä Marine's directors and owners contacted Ministers Ilkka
Suominen and Erkki Liikanen asking for public intervention to bail out the
company.[100]

The state and the company shared a common interest to avoid bankruptcy until the shipyards had delivered the ships that were currently under
construction. Wärtsilä and Valmet had both expressed their intentions to
abandon their shipbuilding branch as soon as possible and had interest in
minimising their costs. The aggressive marketing had filled Wärtsilä Marine's building berths, but now the 'best-looking order book in the country' looked increasingly as a liability. Uncompleted ships tied a lot of capital
and were difficult assets to liquidate.[101] The state had considerable financial
commitments at stake since the state-owned export credit organisations had
granted credits without sufficient collaterals.[102] The government that had
strived for minimal involvement in the public sector, then, was in the deadlock position forced to take responsibility for the private company thanks to
its own organisations.[103]

The main problem was reliability: the reliability of the government and its
shipbuilding policy on the one hand, and the reliability and credit rating of
Wärtsilä Marine on the other hand. Without confidence, widespread panic
might break out and frighten off the subcontractors and financiers. As Minister Liikanen noted, 'the presence of a dead body changes the atmosphere'.[104]

The state, represented by Bror Wahlroos, invited the parent companies,
Wärtsilä and Valmet, and the main financers, Suomen Yhdyspankki (SYP)
and Postipankki (PSP), to negotiations with the sole aim to keep the shipyards running until they had completed the orders in hand.[105] In August,
the negotiators published a rescue package that divided out half of the financing responsibilities to the public sector, while the parent companies and
commercial banks were responsible for the quarter each. To increase trust in
Wärtsilä Marine, the state and commercial banks took over the directorate
and appointed Wahlroos as the chair of the board. Wahlroos was the 'man
of a transition period'. As a high-ranking civil servant leading the privately
owned company, he was a personification of the complex state-industry he-
lix. Wärtsilä Marine, which founding had been seen to manifest privatisation
and the end of state-owned shipbuilding, looked now like a state-owned
company.[106]

The negotiators had formulated the first part of the financing package to
increase public trust in the company. The agreement performed as it was
meant to restoring confidence among subcontractors and customers in that
the projects of Wärtsilä Marine were taken care of. Subcontractors returned
to the shipyards, the production went on.

But the agreement also had another, undisclosed part. The second part restricted the liability of the commercial banks if the costs exceeded FIM700 million. Those losses were to be covered by the state and the parent companies at a ratio of two to one.[107] Consequently, the secret protocol committed the government to the policy it had tried to avoid, having financial liability for shipbuilding without limit.

On October 11, Wärtsilä Marine published a new financial statement. No matter how pessimistic its estimations in the summer had been, three months later, they proved to have been optimistic. Figure 6.7 shows how the forecast was roughly a billion FIM worse than what had been previously expected.

The Wärtsilä Marine directorate, that is the state, the banks, and the two parent conglomerates, had two options on the table. The first option was to continue financing until the shipyards had delivered their ships under construction to the buyers. First to be completed was a ferry *Cinderella* for the Finnish shipping company SF Line, next in the array was a cruise ship *Fantasy* to the Miami-based Carnival Cruise Line. Once left the ship dock, they would decrease the liabilities. Before that, the debt would accumulate seemingly without limit. The second option was to discontinue the financing package and to declare the company bankrupt. Thousands of unemployed metalworkers and an array of bankrupted subcontractors were politically an unpalatable scenario. The probability that the debtors would get the invested money back in liquidation was not high.[108]

On November 11, the commercial banks SYP and PSP announced to the government that they would stop financing if the state did not promise to offset their losses.[109] This changed the tone of the government. At that point, the government had little trust in numbers coming from Wärtsilä Marine. Neither did they trust the commercial banks nor their parent companies, but they suspected them playing on nerves waiting for the state to surrender and accept a larger share of the liabilities.[110] Politically, going on according to the route map drafted in August meant the same as the state opening a checking

*Figure 6.7* WM's results as estimated in the interim financial statements in 30.6.1989 and 11.10.1989, MFIM. Source: Parliamentary Auditors' Report, B1 K3 vp1990.

account without a credit limit for expenses no one could reliably estimate: 'If we continue negotiating with the banks and Wärtsilä, it will go public and give an impression that more [public] money is coming and that the government has miscalculated the odds', Minister Suominen pondered, 'then if we won't give the money, it will show us irresolute'.[111]

The financing package, that was meant to prevent bankruptcy, now became the prime reason for the government to opt for bankruptcy. Increasing unemployment was politically easier for the government than unlimited public financial support for the company no one trusted.[112]

The Helsinki Court House declared the bankruptcy on October 23. The press greeted the news astonished as a 'national tragedy' and also credited the government for demonstrating determination against big business: 'the sheep finally showed its teeth', *Suomen Kuvalehti* titled its editorial.[113]

At Helsinki Shipyard, the bankruptcy was announced by Wärtsilä Marine's Vice-president Martin Saarikangas straight after the court decision. Saarikangas was a shipbuilder by education and had worked at Helsinki Shipyard since 1959. After 1987, he had mainly stayed in the United States as a sales manager promoting Wärtsilä's cruise ships but returned in August 1989 to replace the manager of Helsinki Shipyard who had accidentally died during a running race around the shipyard. During his time in the States, Saarikangas had become familiar with the American bankruptcy code that permitted the bankruptcy trustees to reorganise the business and operate it to minimise total losses. Saarikangas's plan was to interpret the Finnish law in the American spirit and to continue shipbuilding at Wärtsilä's Shipyards.[114]

There had been rumours circling around the shipyards about intentions to renegotiate the loss-making contracts, but general attitude was sceptical about the possibilities to get American buyers to increase their contract prices.[115]

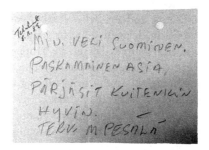

*Figure 6.8* Primary sources on communication after Wärtsilä Marine's bankruptcy in available archival collections are extremely limited. The silence of archives may indicate two things: either the event was too insignificant to write about or it was too sensitive. The few available notes related to the Wärtsilä Marine indicate that the latter was the case. In this brief note with a terse style (apparently from the Member of Parliament Mikko), Pesälä compliments Minister Suominen on his good work, Collection of Ilkka Suominen, folder 80, PTA.

The confusion after the bankruptcy built up momentum for Saarikangas to occupy a central position in the negotiations over the Finnish shipbuilding. Saarikangas was close to Helsinki Shipyard and also able to claim distance from the Wärtsilä Marine's management. He had good personal connections with Wärtsilä Marine's biggest customer CCL, which now had three unfinished luxury cruise ships waiting to be completed in Helsinki and Turku. Most importantly, he came up with a clear direction at the time of turmoil.

Negotiations between Saarikangas, ship buyers, and the banks proceeded rapidly. In a week, the SYP bank and most of the customers joined negotiations for a new shipbuilding company that would complete the projects with Saarikangas as its director and shipping companies, SYP, and the state as shareholders. The economic rationale to continue the production as fast as possible was an imperative for all. The shipyard workers had been dismissed with a two weeks' notice after the bankruptcy, supply chains, and subcontractor networks were falling apart.[116]

Saarikangas registered the new shipbuilding company 'Masa-Yards' on November 11. It had a share capital of FIM570 million comprising 100 million from SYP and state and 170 million from ship buyers. In addition, it received FIM200 million unsecured credit from Wärtsilä.[117] Valmet, apparently disappointed with Wärtsilä and shipbuilding in general, declared promptly that it had nothing to do with the new company.[118] On November 8, a day before the work was to end after Wärtsilä Marine's bankruptcy at the shipyards, the creditor meeting authorised the bankruptcy estates to rent out Helsinki and Turku Shipyards and to sell the unfinished ship hulls to the new company.[119]

After all, shipbuilding continued in Helsinki and Turku without interruptions.

As Minister Liikanen had anticipated during the financing negotiations in August, the bankruptcy, 'the dead body', changed the atmosphere completely. On the one hand, it created a shared understanding of emergency that made the old structures malleable and erased several organisational and mental rigidities that had previously delayed structural transformations. It enabled determinate actors like Saarikangas to seize an opportunity, to re-launch negotiations with a clean table, and to unite the state, customers, and workers against a common threat. The new shipbuilding company, Masa-Yards, continued with the production, shipyards, and staff of the old company, but it was able to renegotiate the loss-making contracts, reduce the compensations to the subcontractors, and introduce a new organisation structure with hand-picked staff.[120] For a short period of time, the Helsinki and Turku Shipyards, traditionally famous for troubled industrial relations and frequent strikes, became prime examples of collaboration and flexible negotiations.[121]

On the other hand, when things were moving fast with the momentum breaking old practices and alliances, the destruction was not only creative but also destructive. In particular, the bankruptcy left deep wounds in the trust between the subcontractors and the state-supported shipyards that took time to recover.[122]

## At the crossroad of national and international, 1990–1992

In the history of Finnish shipbuilding, Wärtsilä Marine's bankruptcy was an explosion that marked the end of the Cold War era. The light of its flames illuminated the surroundings and helped the state and the public audience see clearly the scale of the structural change. At the same time, the blast overshadowed what was happening elsewhere in the Finnish shipbuilding industry.

In December 1989, when Wärtsilä Marine's bankruptcy estate organised the first bankruptcy sale to liquidate the shipyard facilities and uncompleted ships, the West Coast shipbuilders Rauma-Repola and Hollming allied with the state and entered into competition against Masa-Yards. The aim was to complete the reorganisation of the Finnish shipbuilding industry by bringing all the shipyards under the same management. It would, then, execute the final rationalisation of the industry.[123]

Rauma-Repola and Hollming operated under the same circumstances than Wärtsilä Marine, but they were slightly different kinds of actors. Rauma-Repola was, like Wärtsilä, a large multi-branch conglomerate, but marine technology compromised significantly smaller share of its business. That had put less pressures on it to accept unprofitable contracts. Hollming was a significantly smaller and family-owned enterprise which made it some-times to stand out among the big business. From the point of view of the West Coast shipbuilders, the merger into just one Finnish shipbuilding company with the state as a shareholder would increase their leverage in negotiations so that the shipyard closures would start with Helsinki Shipyard, not in Rauma.

Who was the state in these negotiations was a more complicated question. In the creditors' meeting, the state organisation that was allied with the West Coast shipbuilders was the Export Credit ltd, Minister Ilkka Suominen in its board of directors. On the other side of the bargaining competition in the bankruptcy sales, the state was also a shareholder in Masa-Yards.

The West Coast alliance, Yhtyneet Telakat (*United Shipyards*), failed to win the majority in the creditors' meeting, but the competition forced Masa-Yards to increase its offer for Wärtsilä Marine's bankruptcy estates and to promise Rauma-Repola subcontracting work.[124]

In October 1990, the decision over Masa-Yards' ownership raised the reorganisation of shipbuilding back to the governmental discussion. The SYP bank, which had become an involuntary owner of Masa-Yards after the bankruptcy, was looking for a buyer for its shares. That gave an opportunity for the Ministry of Trade and Industry to continue with the reorganisation of the domestic shipbuilding. Minister Suominen presented to the Ministe-rial Committee on Economic Policy a plan to merge Rauma-Repola's and Hollming's shipyards under the management of Rauma-Repola's director Tauno Matomäki and to incorporate Masa-Yards into this new shipbuild-ing company in which the state would be a shareholder. From the point of view of the Ministry of Trade and Industry and the West Coast shipbuilders, the rationales behind the merger were the same as before: to coordinate the reorganisation and rationalisation in the Finnish shipbuilding industry in a way that prioritised the West Coast shipyards over Helsinki Shipyard.

The strongest opposition to Suominen's proposal came from the social democratic Ministry of Finance Matti Louekoski. He questioned the 40% profits SYP would receive from selling the shares it had not wanted in the first place, and criticised the state involvement in the new shipbuilding company as a whole.[125] The government failing to reach consensus upset the plan and resulted in a curious situation in the press: The conservative National Coalition Party, which had won the elections on the platform of economic deregulation and liberalisation, articulated its upset of the failed state intervention, while Social Democratic Party complained about the state having too big role in market economy.[126]

In January 1991, SYP had found a new buyer for its shares. This made it a decision between two alternatives: the domestic alliance led by Matomäki, and the international option with Norwegian Kvaerner. Because foreign acquisitions required authorisation in Finland, the government found itself once again in the position of the final decision-maker in shipbuilding reorganisation.

Formally, the decision whether to allow the direct foreign investment in Finnish shipyards was about international relations and Finnish economic policy. The government was not afraid of Norway to launch a full-scale trade war even if Kvaerner's offer was declined, but it was concerned about the damage this kind of a protectionist act could cause to the Finnish international image. At the time, Finland was negotiating on the participation in the European Economic Area, and declining foreign acquisitions did not go well with the economic liberalisation and international cooperation.[127]

There were also economic aspects to consider. The domestic option required the state investing new venture capital in the new shipbuilding company, which would bind the state to the shipyards for an unpredictable period of time. If Norwegian Kvaerner bought the shares, instead, it would set the Finnish state immediately free from shipbuilding and even generate some profits from its investments in Masa-Yards.[128] As the ministers noted, the 'logic on the whole supported selling' Masa-Yards to Norway, but the decision was far from easy for the ministers who claimed their 'hearts beating for the domestic solution'.[129] For the first time in Finnish business history, however, the government ended up to support the selling of the majority of a strategically important export industry abroad.[130]

Foreign ownership at Helsinki and Turku Shipyards put an end to the plans to integrate the Finnish shipbuilding into just one company but the cooperation between the West Coast shipbuilders continued. In October 1991, the alliance of Rauma-Repola and Hollming won the contract for the two multipurpose icebreakers ordered by the Finnish Maritime Administration (Figure 6.9).[131] That the shipyards with no previous experience in building large icebreakers eventually beat Helsinki Shipyard, which had specialised in icebreakers for decades, was unexpected. It sparked speculations over

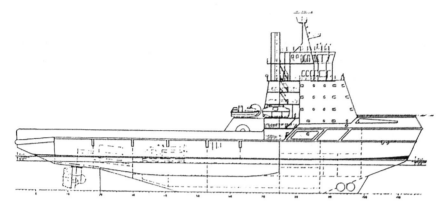

*Figure 6.9* Late 1980s, the Finnish Maritime Administration launched a project to
replace the old Tarmo–class (1963) icebreakers. During the design process, the conventional Baltic icebreaker transformed into novel-type
multipurpose vessels that could be leased out for Arctic operations in
the summer. This is an early draft of the 'Tarmo 2' project, designed
by a Finnish engineering company to accommodate requirements of the
Norwegian offshore company Ugland, which eventually became the first
private contractor for the Finnish multipurpose icebreakers that were
built by Finnyards in Rauma. Arctia Shipping archive, ILS report 'Tarmo
2-luokan jäänmurtaja Supply-versio' 9.1.1991.

the contract being a measure in regional and industrial policy. Indeed, in
November 1991, the two West Coast shipbuilding companies published their
plan to merge and established a new company 'Finnyards', Hollming's director Aarno Mannonen as CEO.[132] State came to the company as a minority
shareholder with 13% share. In addition, the state supported the merger with
granting guarantees for domestic and foreign loans.[133]

Only a minor epilogue is left of the reorganisation of the Finnish Cold
War shipbuilding industry before we reach the chronological border of this
study. In August 1991, Rauma Yards decided to close Uusikaupunki Shipyard. It provoked an outcry in the Parliament. A group of social democrats
demanded the state to subsidy Uusikaupunki Shipyard rather than paying unemployment benefits for the shipyard workers, and called for governmental
actions to support the Soviet trade 'through new credits, trade exchange, and
financing arrangements'.[134]

These suggestions, the translation of the social security expenses into shipyard subsidies and the support to the Soviet trade, had constituted the solid
foundation of the Finnish shipbuilding policy in the 1970s. In 1991, however,
the Minister of Trade and Industry Kauko Juhantalo refused the state aid to
Uusikaupunki on the grounds it would be a state-intervention in private
business. Regarding the problems in the Finnish–Soviet trade, he continued

that they 'were primary Soviet domestic problems which were not under the Finnish government's power to solve'.[135]

In 1991, Finland had gone into a deep recession. The government had to prioritise its spendings in a restricted framework. None of the smaller shipyards had enough political gravity that would attract state assistance in their difficulties. Nor was the Soviet trade anymore a priority in the Finnish trade and industrial policy.

Because of the local importance, the city of Uusikaupunki bought the shipyard from Rauma Oy. In 1993, the shipyard went bankrupt, but the atmosphere had changed since the 1980s so much that the shipyard went down without provoking a nationwide public outcry.[136]

## Conclusions

Big business turns slowly. There had been more than 15 shipyards competing for the Soviet orders at the beginning of the Finnish Cold War shipbuilding. In the 1970s, only four large shipbuilding corporations coordinated the competition. At the same time, industrialisation of the Finnish society accelerated. Finnish shipbuilding industry gathered momentum from its contribution to the national welfare through the employment and exports. The state and industry were perhaps not in the same boat, but they were travelling together. They had different destinations but same interest in the predictability of the Soviet markets, social stability at the shipyards, and expansion of the exports.

Unlike many other European countries, Finland survived the 1970s oil crisis without fatal damages to its shipyards. Propelled by the Soviet orders, the shipbuilding industry expected it to be able to navigate waters too shallow for other shipbuilders. When the problems arose and the shipbuilding directors recognised the need to turn the course, the momentum made the shipyards slow to respond.

The shipyard crisis did not arrive in Finland unannounced. The shipbuilding policymaking after 1977 was merely management of everlasting crisis; the past, the present, and the predicted. The choice of the new course depended on the expectation: whether the crisis marked a culmination point to the worst or to the recovery.

In the Finnish version of the shipbuilding crisis, first to break down was the traditional consensus. The crisis created a sense of being on the threshold of a new era, where old practices and conventions were to be renegotiated. It allowed the shipbuilding directors and political leaders to abandon the full employment as their shared target and to open up the possibility of capacity reductions.

The long 1980s from 1977 to 1992 captured the competitive capitalism overcoming the traditional model of cooperative capitalism in Finland, but the route was not clear or direct. Ministers tried to balance unemployment and rationalisation, structural change and minimising costs, and patriotism and internationalisation. The process was full of conflicts, hasty decision-making, and complex arrangements. New alliances and new enemies were made. As a result, the state involvement in shipbuilding initially increased.

The end of consensus did not remove the need for coordination. When the bulk of Soviet orders diminished and there was less to share out between the shipyards, coordination increased in importance. The political and industrial actors tried to control the de-industrialisation process to save the competitive core of the shipyards. In 1991, there were no more than two major shipbuilding companies both competing in the international markets.

Industrialisation had been imperative to the welfare of Finland at the beginning of the Cold War, and it remained to be so at the end of the period. However, the national focus shifted from industrial employment to international competitiveness. When the state negotiated with the industry about the reorganisations, it coupled the question of rationalisation with the question of state aid. Financing had become critical for the internationally competitive shipbuilding industry but public resources were limited and subject to political struggles. The next and final empirical chapter of this study will explore the relations between the international industry and national competitiveness.

## Notes

1 The discourses of shipyard crisis focus on the end of shipbuilding and rarely recognise the possibility that closed shipyards sometimes became important sites for industrial activities other than shipbuilding. Roslyng Olesen, *Da værfterne lukkede. Transformationen af den danske værtsindustri 1975–2015*, 2016.
2 Siltala, *Puu-Valion nousu ja uho: Murtuva yhteistyökapitalismi ja osuusaate 1982–2004*, 2013, 28–32. The concept is adopted from Chandler, *Scale and Scope*, 1990.
3 Kuisma, *Kahlittu raha, kansallinen kapitalismi*, 2004.
4 Kuusterä & Juha, *Suomen Pankki 200 vuotta II*, 2012, 12.
5 Paavonen, *Vapaakauppaintegraation kausi*, 2008, 42–44.
6 Kuisma, *Kahlittu raha, kansallinen kapitalismi*, 2004, 11–12; Alasuutari, *Toinen tasavalta*, 1994, 74–76; 266; 280; Ojala & Karonen, "Business: Rooted in Social Capital over the Centuries," 2006, 98–99.
7 Bergholm, *Sopimusyhteiskunnan synty II*, 2007.
8 Records of the Shipyard Association 1948–1960, Suomen Puulaivateollisuus—Finska Träfartygindustrin Ry, Suomen Telakkayhdistys—Varvsföreningen r.y, hallituksen kokousten pöytäkirjat 1948–1960, NA; Id & Peter, *Innovation and Specialisation*, 2017, 26; Uola, *Hollming 1945–2000*, 2001, 74–75; Sahari, *Valtio ja suurteollisuuden synty*, 2018, 253.
9 On the Finnish competition laws during that period, see Fellman, "Kilpailupolitiikka koordinoidussa markkinataloudessa," 2010.
10 Finnish cartels are studied best in the forestry industry. See Heikkinen, *Paper for the World: The Finnish Paper Mill's Association—Finnpap 1918–1996*, 2000; Jensen-Eriksen & Ojala, "Tackling market failure or building a cartel?" 2015; Siltala, *Puu-Valion nousu ja uho*, 2013; Kuisma, "Government action, cartels, and national corporations," 1993; Kuorelahti, "Boom, depression and cartelization," 2015; Jensen-Eriksen, "A Potentially Crucial Advantage," 2013. Pricing coordination continued in Western Europe when the private paper companies

cooperated as a form of "private protectionism" to respond to the intergovernmental free trade processes within the OEEC, EEC, and EFTA. Jensen-Eriksen, "Industrial Diplomacy and Economic Integration," 2011.

11  Records of the Shipyard Association 1948–1960, Suomen Telakkayhdistys, hallituksen kokousten pöytäkirjat 1948–1960, NA; Id & Peter, *Innovation and Specialisation*, 2017, 26; Uola, *Hollming 1945–2000*, 2001, 133–134.

12  *Statistical Yearbook of Finland 1976*, table 95 establishments in manufacturing by the size of their personnel in 1974, item 3841, shipbuilding, and repairing according to SIC classification.

13  Uola, *Meidän isä on töissä telakalla*, 1996, 479; Landtman, *Minnen från mina år vid Wärtsilä*, 2011, 164.

14  Kauppinen, *Laivanrakentajien vaihtuvuus. Tutkimus seitsemällä Suomen telakalla laivanrakentajien vaihtuvuuteen vaikuttavista seikoista*, a study ordered by STTY shipyards, 1973; Suomen Metalliteollisuusyhdistys, press release on the publication 31.5.1973; "Study on Shipbuilders High Turnover," MTA.

15  Martti Rewell to Aarno Mannonen 24.4.1980, STTY pöytäkirjat 1, ELKA.

16  STTY on a labour market agreement 26.8.1980; STTY on PTT—working group meeting at Pansio Shipyard 7.5.1980, STTY pöytäkirjat 1, ELKA.

17  *Viitosklubi*. Name refers to the original number of participants. Another name, *Kopplakunta*, was a reference to Beagle Boys (*Karhukopla*) in the then very popular *Donald Duck* magazine. Mikko Uola has used "Karhukopla" to refer to the cooperation between Uusikaupunki shipyard and Hollming in designing and building timber cargo vessels to the Soviet Union. Uola, *Meidän isä on töissä telakalla*, 1996, 345. Pekka Sutela refers to "Kämp Club," named after the high-end hotel in Helsinki, where the group was known to meet as they were unable to use shipyard facilities for the informal and secret cooperation Sutela, *Trading with the Soviet Union*, 2014, 67.

18  Landtman, *Minnen från mina år vid Wärtsilä*, 2011, 164–165; Uola, *Meidän isä on töissä telakalla*, 1996, 482–485; Interview of C. Landtman 21.2.2014; Interview M. Törmä 19.2.2014.

19  Landtman, *Minnen från mina år vid Wärtsilä*, 2011, 164–165; Uola, *Meidän isä on töissä telakalla*, 1996, 482–485; Interview of C. Landtman 21.2.2014; Interview M. Törmä 19.2.2014.

20  Case studies on different national crisis-strategies in shipbuilding: *Shipbuilding and Ship Repair Workers Around the World: Case Studies 1950–2010*, eds. Raquel, Murphy & van der Linden, 2017; Bruno & Tenold, "The Basis for South Korea's Ascent in the Shipbuilding Industry, 1970–1990," 2011; Stråth, *The Politics of De-industrialisation*, 1987.

21  Kettunen, *Historia petollisena liittolaisena*, 2015, 169; Alasuutari, "Suunnittelutaloudesta kilpailutalouteen," 2004.

22  Kyheröinen, "Niin korpi vastaa, kun sinne huudetaan," *Suomen Kuvalehti*, 37/1977.

23  Outinen, *Sosiaalidemokraattien tie talouden ohjailusta markkinareaktioiden ennakointiin*, 2015, 85; Wuokko, *Markkinatalouden etujoukot*, 2016. Rainio-Niemi, "A Nordic Paradox of Openness and Consensus?" 2014; Kettunen, "The Transnational Construction of National Challenges," 2011.

24  "Telakkakriisi tosiasia," *Navigator* 8/77.

25  *Tuotantotavan muutos Suomen laivarakennuksessa*, 1995, 9–12.

26  Ab Crichton-Vulcan Oy collection, HE:1, HE:2, HE:3, HE:7, National Archive (Turku).

27  Only in 1975, the Finnish unemployment had peaked and provoked talk of a national state of emergency. Kuusterä & Tarkka, *Suomen Pankki 200 vuotta II*, 2012, 414; 428; Tiihonen, *The Ministry of Finance*, 2012, 181.

28  Including: the Treaty of Commerce between Finland and Soviet Union 1947, SopS 13/48; Agreement on Friendship, Cooperation and Mutual Assistance

(YYA) 1948, SopS 17/48; Founding on standing Intergovernmental Economic Commission 1967, SopS 45/67; Agreement on Constant Development of the Economic, Technical and Industrial Cooperation 1971, SopS 64/71. The 1977 signed Finnish-Soviet Long Term Agreement, SopS 54/1977.

29  Telakkatoimikunnan mietintö [Shipyard Committee Report], 1977.
30  *Shipyard Committee Report*, 1977, 26.
31  *Shipyard Committee Report*, 1977.
32  KTM/Pentti Viita to Formin 107/070/77, 13.9.1977 on ship trade during the five-year period 1976–1980; PM KTM/Shipyard committee 7.10.1977, summary of proposals for the measures that are related to the Soviet trade and shipyard employment 1978–1980, f. 163, 58 B1, UMA.
33  Table on shipyard subsidies 9.9.1981, EAB1 telakka-avustukset, KTM, NA; Laivatilaustyöryhmän muistio, luonnos 12.1.1983, Työryhmämuistiot VM 1, Valtiovarainministeriö 1983 (*Ship Contract Working Group*, Ministry of Finance, draft 12.1.1983, original classified, 1983), Valtionvarainministeriö, komiteat. Laivatilaustyöryhmän arkisto 1, NA. The Shipyard Committee Report had proposed that the state would appropriate FIM60 million for shipyards during the expected depression from 1978 to 1980 as an alternative to unemployment benefits. Compare with Shipyard Committee Report, 1977, 82–83.
34  Tankmar Horn to KTM 10.3.1978; Horn to KTM 31.8.1978; Rauma-Repola to KTM 21.2.1979; Enso-Gutzeit to KTM 25.6.1979, EAB1, KTM, NA.
35  Proposal for Ministerial Committee on Finance and Preparatory Work 1.3.1978; KTM 27.2.1978, EAB1, KTM, NA.
36  Tor Stolpe to Pekka Rekola 2.15.1979, PM on Oy Silja Line Ab's ferry project 2.15.1979; Tor Stolpe to KTM 19.4.1979, EAB1, KTM, NA.
37  Proposal for the government 28.6.1979; KTM on state aid for Wärtsilä/Suomen Höyrylaiva OY 19.6.1979, EAB1, KTM, NA.
38  Written question to the Minister of Trade and Industry on employment at Perno Shipyard, KK 375, 1978 vp.
39  KTM 20.4.1978 on state subsidies for shipyards, EAB1, KTM, NA.
40  "Tilauksia ja töitä riittää," *Uusi Suomi* 2.6.1981; "Telakoilla menee hyvin," *Suomen sosiaalidemokraatti* 2.6.1981; "Tilauskanta Euroopan kolmanneksi suurin," *Kauppalehti* 2.6.1981; "Kansainvälinen telakkakriisi jatkuu: Suomi voimakkaana 1980-luvulle," *Suomenmaa* 2.6.1981; "Suomen ja N-liiton uusi yhteistyöalue: Arktinen laivateollisuus?" *Savon Sanomat* 28.5.1981; "Horn, Wärtsilä: Telakkateollisuus näkee hyviä aikoja," *Hämeen Sanomat* 5.5.1981; "Suomi on nyt varteenotettava laivanrakennusmaa," *Etelä-Suomi* 5.5.1981; "Suomen laivanrakennus kolmantena," *Keskipohjanmaa* 6.5.1981; "Telakkateollisuudella Suomessa hyvät asemat," *Etelä-Saimaa* 5.5.1981; "Suomi vahvistaa asemaansa laivanrakennusmaana," *Etelä-Suomen sanomat* 5.5.1981.
41  In 1977, the Finnish shipyards employed approximately 16,000 people. The committee report suggested decreasing this number to 14,000, but it increased to 18,000 in 1983. Shipyard statistics, STX Turku.
42  Uola, *Meidän isä on töissä telakalla*, 1996, 459.
43  *Wärtsilä* personnel magazine 1/82.
44  Shipyard Committee 84 Report, KTM 53, 1984.
45  Interview C. Landtman 21.2.2014 Helsinki; Uola, *Hollming 1945–2000*, 2001, 245–246.
46  Landtman, *Minnen från mina år vid Wärtsilä*, 2011, 170–171; Uola, *Meidän isä on töissä telakalla*, 1996, 484.
47  Landtman, *Minnen från mina år vid Wärtsilä*, 2011, 262.
48  STTY meeting 5.1.1987, STTY Kirjeenvaihto 14, ELKA.
49  STTY board meeting 10.12.1986, STTY pöytäkirjat 3; STTY meeting 17.12.1986, STTY Kirjeenvaihto 14, ELKA.

50  STTY meeting 17.12.1986, STTY Kirjeenvaihto 14, ELKA.
51  STTY meeting 17.12.1986, STTY Kirjeenvaihto 14, ELKA.
52  Records from the STTY board meeting 11.2.1987, STTY 37; Records from STTY board meeting 18.3.1987, STTY Pöytäkirjat 4, ELKA.
53  According to Uola (*Hollming 1945–2000*, 2001, 245–246), Wärtsilä had insisted that all participants decrease their dependence on the Soviet trade, which Hollming and Rauma-Repola did not want to accept.
54  "Historian ronskein rationalisointi," *Navigator* 9/1986.
55  Anu Linnanahde, "Telakkakriisi tulee sittenkin," *Talouselämä* 34/1985.
56  Albert Axebank, "An unlikely 'Finnish connection'", *Journal of Commerce*, 29.10.1986.
57  Strategy Proposal 4.6.1984, Valmet keskushallinto 637, ELKA.
58  Anu Linnanahde, "Telakkakriisi tulee sittenkin," *Talouselämä* 34/1985.
59  Strategy meeting of Valmet Shipbuilding division 30.6.1980, Valmet keskushallinto 624, ELKA. Landtman, *Minnen från mina år vid Wärtsilä*, 2011, 250.
60  Wärtsilä Turku Shipyard was particularly famous for its strikes that frequently stopped the work usually in protest to raise wages, but sometimes also as a response to disagreements over workplace safety or foreign affairs. About this "striking culture," see Pääkkönen, *Turun Pernon telakan lakkokulttuuri*, 2016; Shipyard Committee Reports 1977 and 1984; Niemelä, "Työelämän suhteet ja työn uudelleenorganisointi Masa-Yardsissa," 1992.
61  Wärtsilä—Valmet negotiations 16.6.1986, Valmet HT 221, ELKA.
62  Tuominen, *Valmet-Wärtsilä*, 1988, 33–34.
63  Government's Decision in Principle, 5.6.1986, Vp 1986; Tuominen, *Wärtsilä-Valmet fuusio*, 34–35.
64  The bill was approved by the 85% of the votes.
65  Parliament records of plenary session, Vp1986 7.11; 11.11; 14.11; 18.11; 21.11; 27.11; 28.11; SäädK 907/86.
66  As a reference to a Finnish card game (with rather racist original connotations) in which whoever has the 'Black Peter' at the end of the game loses.
67  Laine, *Minusta tuli Musta-Pekka*, 2014, 132.
68  W–V strategy project memorandum, 6.10.1986. WM strategy folder, private collection Matti Törmä, STX-Turku.
69  Strategy draft 10.2.1987, WM Strategy folder, Private collection Matti Törmä, STX-Turku; *Navigator* reprinted in English 1987; "Voimat yhteen," *Navigator* 6/86.
70  W–V strategy project memorandum, 6.10.1986. WM strategy folder, private collection Matti Törmä, STX-Turku; Memorandum on marketing strategy 17.6.1988, WM strategy folder, private collection Matti Törmä, STX-Turku.
71  Strategy draft 10.2.1987, WM Strategy folder, private collection Törmä, STX-Turku.
72  Landtman, *Anförande för oy Wärtsilä AB:s styrelse 90/01/05*. Landtman's private collection; Strategy draft 10.2.1987; Memorandum 14.6.1990 (Törmä), *Miten Wärtsilä meriteollisuus saatettiin konkurssiin?* Matti Törmä, private collection; Interview M. Niini 16.4.2014, M. Törmä 19.2.2014.
73  Minutes WM/L. Jakobsson from a meeting 12.5.1987 in Sudoimport, WM 29, ELKA.
74  "Loppu valtiolliselle laivanrakennukselle," *Navigator* 2/1987; Ristilehto, *Liiketoimintashokki*, 2004, 91; 94. On the necessity to reduce capacity also in *Navigator* 5/1986.
75  Expected result in the first three years: −441.8 million, −30.6 million, and +342 million. *Parliamentary Auditor's Report on Wärtsilä Marine*, B1 K3, VP 1990.
76  VHT board meeting 2.3.1987, Valmet 221, ELKA; Törmä, *Miten Wärtsilä meriteollisuus saatettiin konkurssiin?*.
77  *Parliamentary Auditor's Report on Wärtsilä Marine*, B1 K3, VP 1990.

78 Ristilehto, *Liiketoimintashokki*, 2004, 92–94; Ranki, *Haltia vai haltija*, 2000, 313; *Parliamentary Auditor's Report on Wärtsilä Marine*, B1 K3, VP 1990.
79 HS 12.5.1988.
80 PM WM on perspectives to the developmental possibilities in shipbuilding 26.1.1988, Valmet keskushallinto 714, ELKA.
81 PM WM on perspectives to the developmental possibilities in shipbuilding 26.1.1988, Valmet keskushallinto 714, ELKA.
82 PM which Valmet presented to the shipyard committee 19.12.1988, Valmet keskushallinto 714, ELKA.
83 Development of the shipyard industry 17.11.1988, Valmet keskushallinto 714, ELKA.
84 *Telakkateollisuustyöryhmä 1988* [Shipbuilding Industry Committee report 1988], 1989, unpublished, UCC: 30, KA; Vesikansa, "Bror Wahlroos," Kansallisbiografia, SKS. Published in 2007 at www.kansallisbiografia.fi.
85 Finnish shipbuilding reorganisation 8.12.1988, Valmet keskushallinto 714, ELKA.
86 PMs on reorganisation of shipbuilding 9.12.1988; 22.11.1988; 17.12.1988; 29.11.1988,Valmet keskushallinto 714, ELKA; *Shipbuilding Industry Committee report*, 1989, 3–4.
87 Conditions regarding the negotiation results 19.12.1988; reorganisation of the Finnish shipbuilding industry 19.12.1988, Valmet keskushallinto 714, ELKA.
88 Reorganisation of the Finnish shipbuilding industry 19.12.1988, Valmet keskushallinto 714, ELKA.
89 Reorganisation of the shipbuilding 19.12.1988, Valmet keskushallinto 714, ELKA.
90 Reorganisation of the shipbuilding 19.12.1988, Valmet keskushallinto 714, ELKA.
91 Due to the informal role of the Ministerial Committee, the protocols were not public documents. However, a high-ranking civil servant in the Ministry of Trade and Industry, Risto Ranki, published his notes from the ministerial committee meetings as a part of his dissertation in 2000. Ranki, *Haltia vai haltija*, 2000.
92 Harri Holkeri's Government Programme, 30.3.1987. Available at: https://valtioneuvosto.fi/en/-/64-paaministeri-harri-holkerin-hallituksen-ohjelma.
93 Ranki, *Haltia vai haltija*, 2000, 314–315.
94 Valmet's report on restructuring of shipbuilding, 22.11.1988, Valmet keskushallinto 714, ELKA.
95 Ranki, *Haltia vai haltija*, 2000, 315, 317–318.
96 Afterwards, the report of the Shipbuilding Industry Committee 1988 was a central piece of evidence in Supreme Court of Finland of that the Finnish Board of Export Guarantees, which member Bror Wahlroos was, were aware of the economic risks involved when the board granted financing for Wärtsilä Marine without sufficient collateral in February 1989. According to Wahlroos' defence, he had been convinced that the shipbuilding industry only exaggerated their difficulties to get state support. *Supreme Court decision*, diaari R94/179, 107:1995 KKO; "Meriteollisuuden takuupäätöksestä varoitus kahdelle virkamiehelle," HS 15.6.1995.
97 Ranki, *Haltia vai haltija*, 2000, 314–320; 331; 334.
98 WM internal note 20.1.1989, Valmet keskushallinto 714, ELKA; Letter of Intend 3.1.1989, Valmet keskushallinto 714, ELKA.
99 *Parliamentary Auditor's Report on Wärtsilä Marine*, B1 K3, VP 1990.
100 Meeting of WM's board of directors 10/1989, 7.8.1989, folder 80, collection of Ilkka Suominen, PTA; Ranki, *Haltia vai haltija*, 2000, 321.
101 Notes from the meeting of Ministerial Committee on Economic Policy, 3.8.1989, Suominen 80, PTA.

102  A practice that had privileged WM over other shipbuilding companies Rauma-Repola and Hollming, who were required to put assets as collateral against debt obligations. *Suomen Kuvalehti* 35/1989.

103  *Parliamentary Auditor's Report on Wärtsilä Marine*, B1 K3, VP 1990, 27, 34.

104  Ministerial Committee on Economic Policy meeting 3.8.1989, Suominen 80, PTA.

105  Copy of contract, Koivisto 13, NA; Ristilehto, *Liiketoimintashokki*, 2004, 95–96.

106  "Siirtymäkauden mies," [Man of the transition period] *Navigator* 7–8/1989; "Valtio pelastaa Wärtsilän telakat" [The state saves Wärtsilä's shipyards] HS 10.8.1989; "Käytännössä Wärtsilän Meriteollisuus näyttää tästedes valtiolliselta" [In principle, WM looks like a state-owned company], US 11.8.1989.

107  Timo Anttila, "Marinen salaiset siirrot" [Secret moves of Marine], SK 35/1989.

108  Ministerial Committee on Economic Policy meeting 13.10.1989, 17.10.1989, and 20.10.1989, Suominen 80, PTA.

109  Ministerial Committee on Economic Policy meeting 10.10.1989, Suominen 80, PTA.

110  The Ministerial Committee exercised extra care when handling the Wärtsilä Marine case. The members of the committee received no written memoranda in the meetings or they were collected back. Besides Risto Ranki's publication and the discussion notes in Ilkka Suominen's collection in PTA, there is not much first-hand information from the discussions. Juhani Kivelä, high-ranking civil servant in the Ministry of Finance, made hand-written notes on the margins of the meeting agenda. These notes are generally consistent with the Ranki's notes. Juhani Kivelä's copy of the agenda of Ministerial Committee on Economic Policy meeting 27.10.1989, Ministerial Committee on Economic Policy meeting agenda 27.10.1989, UAC:11, NA; PM 3.11.1989, Koivisto 13, NA.

111  Ministerial Committee on Economic Policy meeting 13.10.1989, 17.10.1989, and 20.10.1989, Suominen 80, PTA.

112  Ranki, *Haltia vai Haltija*, 2000, 320–338; US 24.10.1989.

113  "Lampaan hampaat" [The teeth of the sheep], SK 45/1989.

114  Saarikangas interview 5.2.2014, Haapavaara, *Iso-Masa*, 127–143.

115  Ministerial Committee on Economic Policy 27.10.1989, Suominen 80, PTA; Haapavaara, *Iso-Masa*, 128.

116  WM internal announcement 23.10.1989, WM 30, ELKA; PM 3.11.1989; Valtion Takuukeskus VTK [The Finnish Board of Export Guarantees] to Ministerial Committee on Economic Policy 30.10.1989; PM 3.11.1989; Notification from SYP and Wärtsilä and VTK's answer to those, both 1.11.1989, Koivisto 13, NA.

117  SYP on shipyard crisis after 27.10.1989 and 14.11.1989, Koivisto 13, NA.

118  Valmet on its conditions concerning WM's financing package 1.11.1989, Koivisto 13, NA.

119  PM WMkp 27.9.2013 on creditors' meetings, WMkp.

120  Ristilehto, *Liiketoimintashokki*, 2004, 99–101; Niemelä, "Kriisin kautta joustavaan tuotantoon," 1998.

121  Malinen, *Ostaa, Myy, vaihtaa ja valmistaa*, 1998; Niemelä, "Työelämän suhteiden ja työorganisaation muutos," 1995; Niemelä, "Miksi telakoilla ei enää lakkoilla vanhaan malliin?" 1994.

122  Ristilehto, *Liiketoimintashokki*, 2004, 99–100; Malinen, "Telakkatoimittaja ja telakka – suhde eri ajanjaksoina," 1995; HS 7.11.1989; Pusila, "Telakat paikallisilla työmarkkinoilla," 1995, 47; Toivonen, Telakoiden ja alihankkijoiden välisten suhteiden kehittyminen, 1995, 77–124.

123  *Telakkatukityöryhmän muistio* 27:1989 [Committee report of the Working Group for Shipyard Subsidy], 1989.

124  PM WMkp 27.9.2013 on creditors' meetings, WMkp; H. J. Perälä to Ilkka Suominen 2.1.1990, Suominen 21, PTA; "Ministeri Suominen karsastaa

telakoiden pakkoavioliittoa," HS 9.1.1990; "Suominen vääntää Masa-Yardsin ja SYP:n kättä valituskanteen avulla," HS 13.1.1990; "Ei se niin ollut, Masa!," HS 18.1.1990; Uola, *Meidän isä on töissä telakalla*, 1996, 467.

125 Ranki, *Haltia vai Haltija*, 2000, 339–342; Uola, *Meidän isä on töissä telakalla*, 1996, 468.
126 "Telakkafuusio kaatui," HS 25.10.1990.
127 Ranki, *Haltia vai haltija*, 2000, 350.
128 Ranki, *Haltia vai haltija*, 2000, 341–342.
129 Ranki, *Haltia vai haltija*, 2000, 349–352.
130 "Kværner osti Masa-Yardsin," HS 10.11.1990.
131 *Monitoimimurtajien hankinta ja kaupallinen toiminta, tarkastuskertomus* [Auditors' report of the procurement and use of multipurpose icebreakers], 43/2003.
132 "Rauma-Hollmingin tarjous oli edullisempi kuin Masan," HS 12.9.1991; "Monitoimimurtajan hintaan tulee yli 200 mmk korkoja," HS 22.10.1991; "Rauman telakat yhdistyvät," HS 8.11.1991.
133 Government proposal to the Parliament HE 61, 1992 vp; Commerce Committee of the Parliament Report TaVM 22, 1992 vp; Records of the parliament PTK 72, 1992 vp.
134 Written question and reply, KK 104, 1991 vp.
135 Written question and reply, KK 104, 1991 vp.
136 Uola, *Meidän isä on töissä telakalla*, 1996, 374; 523.

# 7   National competitiveness and international economy

## Shipyard financing and state aid

No ship has been built without money. In the Cold War era, the availability and terms of financing became critical in the competition for ship contracts. At an accelerating speed after the 1970s oil crisis, state-funded financing schemes and subsidies became normal procedures when state pitted against state to support locally important industries in the conditions of global over-capacity. The Organisation for Economic Co-operation and Development (OECD) recognised seven main categories of government assistance for ship-building: the protection of national markets through custom duties, import restrictions and government purchasing, direct subsidies or fiscal assistance for shipyards, support for R&D activities and restructuring, general facilities for financing shipyards on favourable terms such as public guarantees for loans, and assistance for domestic ship purchases.[1]

The Finnish Cold War ship financing institutions grew up in the divided world and adapted to the differences between the international ship market and the trade with the Soviet Union. Chapter 4 examined the bilateral clearing trade and payment institutions in the Finnish–Soviet ship trade and described how it decreased the need for external financing. This chapter focuses on the other side of the story, the ship financing in the domestic and Western shipbuilding markets.

Finnish shipyard financing policy travelled along a distinct trajectory until the 1980s. When the large maritime countries erected institutions for state support for shipyards, the state and the shipbuilding industry in Finland were united in their opposition against shipyard subsidies. In the polarised Cold War business environment, the Finnish shipyard financing policy turned out to be peculiar and often unrecognised within the OECD framework. The array of state financing arrangements in Finland was perhaps shorter and certainly different than in many other countries, but the role of state in the shipyard financing was substantial, nevertheless.

Much of this chapter examines the transformation of the Finnish shipyard financing policy in the face of the European integration process at the end of the Cold War era. Like the ship financing in the Finnish–Soviet trade, the shipbuilding financing policy in the Finnish–EC relations was a part of both domestic industrial policy and foreign affairs. Even though the European integration in Finland was mainly understood in terms of economic liberalisation and deregulation, the process initially increased the direct state subsidies to Finnish shipyards. It compelled the Finnish government to reconsider the role of state in supporting increasingly international, yet locally important industry, and choose which shipyards and which types of ships would be entitled to the state aid.

In this chapter, the disintegration of the Cold War world order and the downfall of the Soviet trade present themselves as external jolts to the domestic political practices. They re-politicised certain instruments of state support that had been established as ordinary, which forced the state to re-assess the value of the domestic and Western markets that had previously been subordinated to the Soviet ship trade.

When Finland introduced direct state subsidies to shipyards in accordance with the EU shipbuilding directive in 1996, it could no longer claim that it had no permanent state-aid schemes for shipbuilding. The Finnish shipbuilding policy had abandoned the unique features that once made it distinctive in European comparisons. In that sense, then, Finland stopped being a Cold War special case in shipbuilding and became a normal European country.

## Emergence of export financing and guarantees

The two critical problems in the Finnish economic policy during the Cold War were the balance of payments and inflation. It was natural, even necessary, for a small economy to expand exports to create employment for industrial workers and to bring in revenues to pay for the imported goods and raw materials that were not available domestically. This endorsed the priority of exports and export industries in domestic trade and industrial policy. The industrial competitiveness in the export markets was closely connected to the problem with inflation that tended to be faster in Finland than in the competing countries. The rapid increase in wages and production costs was fuelled by the social transformation from a low-cost agrarian country into a high-cost industrialised country and resulted in a difficult inflation-devaluation cycle in the Finnish economy.[2]

The two main elements in the Finnish Cold War ship financing policy in the early Cold War period addressed these critical problems: the cost compensation systems provided public reimbursement for the shipyards to offset the increasing costs during the production period in all export trade, and the state-supported export credits facilitated exports of capital goods to other countries than the Soviet Union.

The first dedicated measure in the Finnish Cold War ship financing policy was the Export Compensation System (*Vientikorvausjärjestelmä*). It was introduced in 1950 to support domestic employment by reducing the risk of cost increase in the Soviet trade.[3] At that time, the bilateral trade with the Soviet Union dominated the Finnish ship exports, but the fixed contract prices and long delivery times exposed the revenues to inflation. The Export

Compensation System allowed companies to receive compensation for the domestic increase in prices so that the contract price, which had been calculated during the contract negotiations based on the concurrent production costs, would be sufficient to cover the costs of construction accumulated by the time of delivery. The mechanism was targeted at the production of large, individualised capital-intensive products with the minimum time of delivery from six to ten months, namely ships and paper machines.[4]

The rationales behind the Export Compensation System were related to the national security and social stability. This was coined by the Prime Minister Kekkonen in his answer to the critical voices that referred to the state-supported ship exports to the Soviet Union as 'the second war reparation project'. Kekkonen advocated the Export Compensation System on the ground the compensations to the export companies repaid themselves with added predictability and security in industrial jobs and warned against tarnishing the Finnish–Soviet economic relations:

> This is the only available way to keep the metal manufacturing and ship-building industry occupied and to provide work for thousands of workers. The rumour campaign about "the new war reparations" is factually false; the rumours damage the foreign affairs and trade policy of our country.[5]

The Exports Compensation System was a collective risk-sharing mechanism, not unusual in the international trade. In principle, the different state guarantees were not considered as state subsidies if the insurance fees collected from the companies covered the compensations that were paid out. The Finnish Export Compensation System was, however, free of charge for the companies. While not being a clear case of direct state subsidy, it was not a cost-neutral insurance policy either. It reallocated part of the business risk to the public sector for political reasons.

The Export Compensation System smoothed away part of the negative impact of the rapid industrialisation when the wages increased faster than the productivity of the industry. It cleared the way for consensus-oriented labour market negotiations. On its behalf, the Export Compensation System was an element that lubricated the co-development of the industrialised welfare state, shipbuilding industry, and the Finnish–Soviet trade.

At the beginning, the public expenses for providing the export industry with insurance against inflation remained reasonably low. Between 1950 and 1957, the costs of the Export Compensation System totalled FIM1.4 billion, which was only 1.25% of the exports that had been covered by the arrangement. In 1959, the Industrial Advisory Board estimated that the system had benefitted indirectly over 10,000 industrial workers and was clearly a cost-effective public measure.[6]

The costs of the Export Compensation System increased substantially after the devaluations of the Finnish markka, first in 1957. From the industrial point of view, the combination of the partial compensations against domestic inflations and the devaluation of the currency was highly advantageous. Afterwards in 1976, the Ministry of Trade and Industry estimated that the Export Compensation System had covered approximately half of the domestic inflation for export companies.[7]

The main advantage of the Export Compensation System was that it allowed the shipyard companies to contract for long-term projects without having to worry about the cost increase, which increased predictability at the shipyards. The downside was the increased economic dependency on the Soviet Union.

To support ship exports to other countries, Finnish metal engineering corporations and commercial banks co-founded the export credit agency, Vientiluotto Oy, in 1956. The Ministry of Finance and the Bank of Finland were represented on the board, but the state became a majority shareholder only in 1962. Conservative newspapers suspected that the state involvement in export financing was a sign of emerging nationalisation and possibly even a baby step towards socialism. In retrospect, the introduction of state-supported export financing appeared rather as an expression of economic nationalism.[8] The government justified the state participation in export financing not as a support for big business but as salient for national welfare:

> In the process of industrialisation the role of exports has become even more important for our economy and its development requires more attention because only extensive exports support the development of our living standards and employment. At the time of intensifying international competition, the state [...] has to create conditions for the [domestic industry for] competition with foreign countries in equal terms.[9]

In 1963, the export credit agency renamed itself Suomen Vientiluotto Oy—Finlands Exportkredit Ab (hereafter Finnish Export Credit, SVL).[10]

The state-supported export financing was essential for the increasing ship exports to the non-socialist countries in the 1960s and 1970s. The interest-subsidised export credits enabled Finnish shipyards to sell ships with a higher share of credit, longer payback time, and lower interest rate than what would be possible if the financing had come from the Finnish commercial banks. At the end of the 1960s, as Figure 7.1 illustrates, the majority of the export credits that were granted by the Finnish Export Credit Ltd were to the exports of vessels and oil-drilling rigs.[11]

A small country with low cash reserves could not compete against bigger countries with deeper pockets in ship financing. Thus, it was of Finland's interest to support international cooperation to regulate the state support in export credit conventions. The main arena for the international ship financing debate was the OECD, an intergovernmental organisation committed to stimulating economic growth by advancing fair markets and democracy. Because the OECD had its roots in the Organisation for European Economic

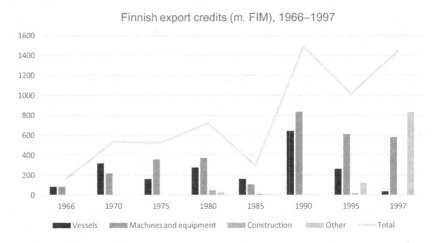

*Figure 7.1* Export credits granted by Finnish Export Credit Ltd. (million FIM in 2004 value). Data: Suomen Vientiluotto, Herranen, 2009, 409.

Co-operation (OEEC), a Western European organisation coordinating American post-war financial aid, Finland had refrained from joining it until January 1969.[12]

In the same year, the OECD Council reached a compromise on subsidised shipbuilding credits in export trade. As the title of the protocol implies, 'Understanding on Export Credits for Ships,' it was not a binding accord but merely a gentleman's agreement. It outlined the maximum level for support that national governments were allowed to offer for their export credit organisations in fair competition: maximum duration of eight years for the maximum of 80% of the ship price and a minimum net interest rate of 6%.[13] The Finnish Export Credit Ltd adjusted its export credit schemes for shipbuilding according to this OECD convention. Even though the OECD's intention had been to halt the subsidy race, the 'OECD export credits' came to be widely understood as the generally accepted and expected zero level of subsidised financing.[14] The OECD Understanding of 1969 was complemented by the OECD General Arrangement for the Progressive Removal of Obstacles to Normal Competitive Conditions in Shipbuilding Industry (1972) and the General Guidelines for Government Policies in the Shipbuilding Industry (1976). They articulated the shared interest in restraining the state support and restoring healthy conditions for fair competition but had limited effectiveness.

In Finland, the reformation of the export financing came with the establishment of the state export credit guarantees. In 1962, the Finnish Board of Export Guarantees (Vientitakuulaitos, VTL) was founded under the Ministry of Trade and Industry.[15] Guarantees are insurance-like countersecurity provided to export credit agencies to cover the risk of credit losses. For example,

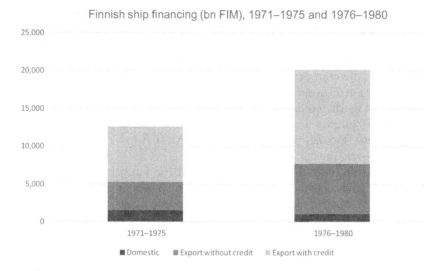

*Figure 7.2* Finnish ship deliveries based on financing, billion FIM (in 1975 value).
Data: *Export Credit Committee report*, 1976, 4.

Credit Risk Guarantees (*Luottoriskitakuu, L-takuu*) and Finance Guarantees (*Rahoitustakuu, R-takuu*) were considered as a normal part of institutional state support for commerce in market economies, and were available for all export companies.[16]

The Cost Guarantee System (*Kustannustakuujärjestelmä, K-takuujärjestelmä*), on the other hand, was an instrument targeted only at shipbuilding and paper machine industries. Only the 'domestic industrial products that could be clearly itemized' and had a long delivery time were eligible for the guarantees. Although the product was denoted as a 'guarantee', the Cost Guarantee System was a sophisticated version of the Export Compensation system which it replaced. Essentially, it offered the export companies state-supported protection against high inflation.[17]

Like the other export guarantee products, the Cost Guarantee System was supposed to be a self-supported mechanism for risk-sharing on occasions when business risks were unpredictable or abnormally high. While the Export Compensation System had been free of charge, the cost guarantees were subject to a charge that initially totalled 0.01% of the contract price for each month (from 1975, 0.04% in a month). Unlike the Export Compensation System, the cost guarantees never covered the whole contract price.[18] The amount of compensations was calculated by a formula which had multiple variables including the delivery time, the cost-increase, and the definition of the 'abnormally high' inflation rate. For example, in 1967, the Cost Guarantee System compensated the Finnish shipyards for the part of cost-increases that exceeded 6% in a year.[19]

The line between a state subsidy and a normal, state-supported risk-sharing instrument was fuzzy and open to interpretations. A central difference between a public export guarantee and an export subsidy was that subsidies were disproportionally profitable for companies. How advantageous the Cost Guarantee arrangement was for the shipbuilding companies depended on the share of the contract price that was valid for reimbursement, the index series used to determine the cost increase, the realised cost increase that were experienced by the company, the company's ability to include the predicted inflation in contract prices, and the companies' chances to cash in on the currency rate fluctuation and devaluations. All these variables were subject to changes over time.[20]

First time in 1972, the compensations that the Finnish Board of Export Guarantees paid to the companies surpassed the amount of fees the companies had paid for the guarantee products. After the oil crisis skyrocketed the energy prices, the inflation rate and the cost guarantee disbursement for the shipbuilding industry multiplied at a high speed.

In the mid-1970s, the Cost Guarantee System was no longer a self-funding, cost-neutral risk-sharing apparatus. Before the 1970s, the Cost Guarantee compensations had totalled few millions; in 1974, the costs had hiked to 150 million, and in 1976, to 610 million FIM (Figure 7.4).[21] Most of these compensations were paid to the ship exporting companies.[22]

Even though the terms of the Cost Guarantee System were unchanged, the external jolts transformed the previously neutral state guarantee system into a controversial state subsidy. It sparked up a debate over the state role in maintaining a competitive business environment. Opinions on the Cost Guarantee System ranged from one extreme to another. Like in the early 1950s, the general public received it as an increasingly expensive mechanism that nationalised business risk and allocated public money for private business at the time when working-class people were left to struggle with inflation by themselves. The Finnish shipbuilding directors were—understandably—strongly in favour of the arrangement and defended it against accusations that such reimbursements for inflation should be paid for workers instead of big corporation.[23] Wärtsilä's director Tankmar Horn articulated in 1975, that

$$\frac{b-a}{a} \times 150 + \frac{c-a}{a} \times 250 + \frac{d-a}{a} \times 350$$

$$./. \ t \ x \ ov \ - \ \% \ x \ 1.000$$

*Figure 7.3* Cost Guarantee System had several variables. This equation is an example that the Cost Guarantee Committee used to illustrate the reimbursements in 1976. The exemplary contract price is 1000 of which the guarantees cover 75%. A represents the cost increase index, B, C, and D represent the mean value of cost increase during the quarter, and 150, 250, and 350 represent the cost accumulation during the last three-quarters of the project turnout time. *Cost Guarantee Committee report* 1976, 6.

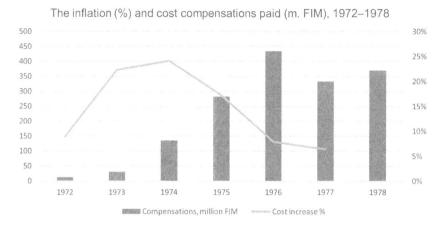

*Figure 7.4* The compensations paid to the Finnish shipbuilding industry based on the Cost Guarantee System. Data: *Shipyard committee report* 1977, 19.

the Finnish shipyard industry did not need state aid but moderate inflation. If the state was unable to control inflation, according to Horn's reasoning, it was only fair to receive such compensation.[24] Of the governmental organisations, the Ministry of Trade and Industry wanted to maintain the terms of Cost Guarantees as they were, while the Ministry of Finance advocated a less expensive policy.[25]

In the face of public criticism, the Finnish government appointed the Cost Guarantee Committee to investigate the export guarantees and propose policy measures. The committee was chaired by Klaus Waris, Professor Emeritus in Economics and former director of the Bank of Finland, who had been active in export financing discussions in the 1950s. The other members were civil servants from different ministries and the Bank of Finland, but the committee had no industrial representation.

The committee's conclusions were in support for the continuation of the Cost Compensation System.[26] The committee report justified the inflation compensations by invoking the nation-wide socio-economic problems that had forced the shipyards to raise wages to persuade the skilled workforce not to move to Sweden.[27] In previous years, Finland had suffered from unemployment rather than labour shortage, but the argumentation underlined the overall conclusion that the Finnish shipbuilding industry was a responsible employer in a difficult situation. The shipyards were contributors to the national projects of security and welfare, they were not gamblers playing with public money. The Cost Guarantee Committee recognised the risk that the public risk-sharing mechanisms could encourage risky business behaviour, but stated that this was not the case in Finland. The committee did, though, propose adjustments that would decrease the cost of the Cost Compensation

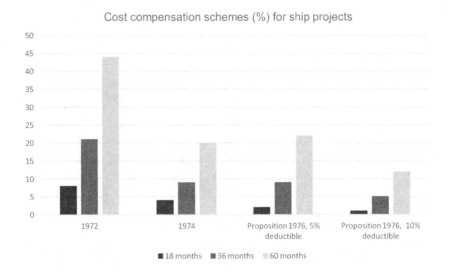

Cost compensation schemes (%) for ship projects

■ 18 months   ■ 36 months   ▨ 60 months

*Figure 7.5* Cost Guarantee compensations in 1972 and 1974, and two scenarios for
1976 presented by the Cost Guarantee Committee. Data: *Cost Guarantee
Committee report*, 1976, Appx. 2.

System to the public sector and allocate most of the compensations to the
long-term projects that needed inflation protection the most (Figure 7.5).[28]

Advised by the Cost Guarantee Committee, the government concluded
that a public mechanism to share the risks of unpredictable inflation was
compatible with market capitalism. However, the system, that overcompen-
sated business risks for only a few industrial branches, was not. While the
general operational principles of the Cost Guarantee System remained, it became a more flexible policy instrument. The sitting government received
now the right to adjust the terms of the Cost Guarantees without having
to consult the Parliament or amend the law. The most effective adjustments
were the governmental decisions over the guarantee fees and the share of the
cost increase companies had to cover by themselves.[29]

In 1980, shipbuilding companies received compensation for the inflation
that exceeded 9%. In 1982, it was lowered to 7%. Industrial interest groups
complained about the changes arguing that they degraded the competitiveness of the Finnish shipyards against countries where inflation was lower, but
the governments refused to return to the pre-oil crisis terms.[30]

The Cost Guarantee System lost its momentum in the mid-1980s. As a
result of cost escalation after the oil crisis, the mundane kind of export guarantee arrangement became politicised. First, the Cost Guarantees became
deeply unpopular with the public, and after the governmental measures, less
profitable for the industry. In 1986, Finnish shipyards applied for Cost Guarantees for the last time. In 1988, the system was dismantled.[31]

**Foothold on the home market**

In the post-war years, the Finnish shipbuilding industry was propelled forward by export trade instead of domestic demand. The development of the state financing institutions took shape alongside the export orientation. In the 1950s, the Finnish shipping industry had started to renew its aging tonnage but relied mostly on foreign shipyards or second-hand ships.[32] Due to the generous export credit schemes available at the foreign yards, the domestic yards rarely succeed in winning domestic contracts even if their costs were at the same level.

The inability to compete in domestic market made the shipyards dependent on exports. Bertel Långhjelm, Wärtsilä's deputy manager (1951–1961, general manager 1962–1970) pointed this out in his lengthy article in 1956. Without the home market, the Finnish shipyards were exposed to foreign economic fluctuation and were thus vulnerable to mass-unemployment. In the 1950s context, the mass-unemployment translated directly as the danger of communism. Competitiveness at home, therefore, contributed to social stability and ultimately to national welfare and security.[33]

To facilitate domestic ship purchases, the Finnish government introduced a new tax law in 1956 commonly known as 'Lex Långhjelm'. It enabled shipyards to offer better terms of payments for their domestic customers by making the interest revenues that accrued on the basis of the supplier credit tax-deductible up to 4% each year.[34] Perhaps it was fitting that Långhjelm, who was portrayed as 'an intelligent man with an economic mind-set but lacking [Wärtsilä's director Wilhelm] Wahlforss's enthusiasm',[35] remained best known among the maritime historians for the financial arrangement that had significant economic benefits for the Finnish shipbuilding, but which never awakened any excitement in the public.[36]

In addition to taxation, the public sector supported domestic shipping through rewards for better ice-classes; the ships with higher ice-classification paid lower navigation fees. The main target was to increase the share of ice-strengthened vessels in the Finnish merchant tonnage. Even though the rewards were not conditional on buying Finnish-built ships, as Figure 7.6 indicates, it indirectly supported the Finnish shipbuilding industry and its competitiveness in building these reinforced vessels.[37]

In the first half of the Cold War, the home country was only the third most important market for the Finnish shipyards. It came after the Soviet orders, which were crucial for shipbuilding volume and political relations, and the Western market, which counterbalanced the cycles in the Soviet trade and demonstrated to the world that Finnish shipbuilding was *not* dependent on the Soviet orders. Between 1966 and 1976, less than 15% of the Finnish-built ships remained in Finland.[38] Even state-owned shipping companies were not required to buy Finnish ships.[39]

In December 1976, the Ministry of Trade and Industry appointed a Ship Working Group to examine policy measures to increase the competitiveness

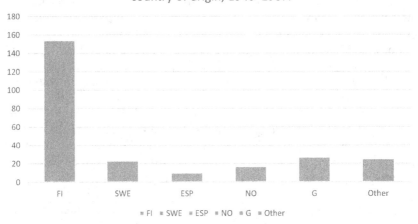

*Figure 7.6* Number of ships in the Finnish Mercantile Marine Database by country of building, with ice class of 1A or 1A Super, 1947–1987. Data: The Finnish Mercantile Marine Database, http://kauppalaiva.nba.fi/.

*Figure 7.7* The geographical distribution of the Finnish shipbuilding. Data: SM database for ships completed in Finland, 1975–1996. Data: Author from various sources.

of Finnish shipyards for Finnish-flagged ships.[40] The Committee chair was Pentti Viita, the same civil servant from the Ministry of Trade and Industry that later chaired both shipyard committees described in Chapter 6. Other members of the Committee represented the Finnish Shipyard Association STTY and the Finnish Shipowners' Association (*Suomen varustamoyhdistys*).

The reawaken interest in the domestic competitiveness stemmed from the international recession in shipbuilding. It made the Finnish shipyards eager to secure a stronger foothold at home market as a protection against the international downturn that had decreased Western orders for newbuilding tonnage (Figure 7.7). Ship buyers and shipbuilders were not united in their interests, quite the contrary. Shipyards needed profitable orders, and ship buyers wanted inexpensive vessels.

Finnish shipping companies were used to buying the majority of their tonnage from the large shipyards in Sweden, Spain, and West Germany, where they got good-quality ships with lower price, shorter delivery time, and better terms of financing than what was available in Finland.[41] The shipping companies operated in the internationally competitive market. Nationalistic feelings and concerns over domestic employment did not inspire them to place orders from domestic shipyards. There was, however, one thing both shipbuilding and the shipping industries agreed on: that the domestic trade should be equal to foreign trade in terms of financing.[42]

Table 7.1 shows the different credit schemes available for domestic and foreign ship buyers. For ship exports, the Finnish Export Credit Ltd provided credits based on the OECD convention on export financing. For domestic orders, a Finnish shipyard could get Domestic Supply Credit (*Kotimaisen Rahoituksen Tuki, KTR-luotto; hereafter KTR credit*) after the delivery. While Export Credit Ltd was a company in which the state held a share majority, money for KTR credits came from the Bank of Finland and commercial banks.[43]

*Table 7.1* Comparisons of state financing schemes for domestic ship trade (Finnish shipyard selling a ship to a Finnish shipping company) and export trade (Finnish shipyard selling a ship to a foreign buyer)

|  | *KTR financing schemes for domestic purchases* | *Export credits (OECD)* |
|---|---|---|
| **Payments at the delivery** | 20% | 20%–30% |
| **Interest rate** | Not fixed, in 1977: 9.25% | 8% |
| **Term** | Two to eight years | Seven years (1977) 8.5 years (1984) |
| **Credit fee** | 0.25% | No |
| **Stamp tax** | 0.90% | No |
| **Security deposit** | Bank guarantee, mortgage, state guarantee | State export guarantee, mortgage |
| **Cost guarantees** | No | Yes |
| **Guarantee fee** | Buyer pays 1.5%/year | Seller pays 0.37% |

Data: *Ship Working Group Report* 1977, 25; *Shipyard Committee 1984 Report*, Appendix 1.

The key differences between the credit schemes for domestic and export orders were that the Cost Guarantees were not available for domestic contracts, and the KTR credits had a variable and generally higher interest rate. The Ship Working Group calculated that a ship of equal price and technical qualities would cost 26% less for the Finnish ship buyers if it was imported from abroad in comparison with a domestic purchase. This meant, the working group concluded, that the Finnish ship financing instruments discriminated against Finnish shipyards in favour of foreign builders.[44]

The Ship Working Group report in 1976 opened the discussion on ship financing policy but yielded no imminent results. The maritime sector being divided in their interests failed to gain bargaining power to muster political support for domestic ship purchases. The Finnish shipbuilders and shipowners found a common ground on passenger ships and ferries only a couple of years later in 1978. This took place when, as described in the previous chapter, the coincidental downturns in both Eastern and Western markets sparked up the crisis talk in the Finnish shipbuilding.

Passenger ferries crossing the Baltic Sea had an important role in creating and maintaining economic and cultural connections between the Nordic countries. The volume of the goods transported on wheels in the car ferries was modest in comparison with the cargo carried by large tankers and bulk carriers, but the value of this small-sized mixed cargo was significant for the Finnish economy.[45] The passenger ferries stood out also in the structure of the Finnish commercial fleet. In absolute numbers, Finland's passenger tonnage was roughly equal to Sweden and Denmark, but the low number of other cargo tonnage highlighted the relative importance of Finnish ferries.[46]

After the oil crisis, all freight rates had plummeted, but the profitability of ferry lines less so. At the same time, the market prices for standard cargo types dropped, but the tailor-made, high-quality passenger ships provided some leverage in price negotiations.

In 1978, when the first Shipyard Committee proposed financial measures to support shipyards through the temporary difficulties, the main attention turned to the domestic ferry companies.[47] In the gloomy circumstances, passenger ships glowed dim light at the end of the dark tunnel promising some revenues for Finnish shipping and profit-generating orders for shipbuilding.[48]

Following the Shipyard Committee's recommendation, the government appropriated direct shipyard subsidies of FIM20 million.[49] A test-case for this emergency-funding policy was a ferry project that the Finnish shipping company SF-Line was about to order from Japan. It was not an ordinary project but planned to be the largest flagship in the Finnish–Swedish traffic with 10,605 GT and capacity for 1,700 passengers.[50]

The argument for using state funds to win the exceptionally large contract to Finland was a combination of national competitiveness and uncompetitiveness. On the one hand, the contract was of paramount importance for Wärtsilä Turku Shipyard, which had a relative competitive advantage in the niche having previously completed several cruise ships and ferries. In particular, Wärtsilä did not want to let the Japanese shipyard get the valuable experience from building passenger ships and enter the narrow market niche of the Baltic ferries. On the other hand, the Finnish cost-competitiveness was strikingly worse in comparison with Japan. The Japanese shipyard had outbid Wärtsilä's best offer by FIM29 million. In his letter to the Ministry of Trade and Industry, director Tankmar Horn underlined that the company had made everything it had in its power to get the order to protect the employment but in vain: 'Our chances to get other contracts of this size are small. For that reason, we have bidded for these ships at loss-making price. Still, it seems, our price is too high'.[51]

Large passenger ships in the popular Finnish–Swedish route were public figures. They were rare exceptions in merchant shipping as being well-recognised vessels to which the ordinary people had a personal connection. The ferries of the 1980s took leaps from just being carriers of people and cars into being floating entertainment centres on the Baltic. Every new ship was larger and longer, each new ship provided more spacious cabins for the passengers to sleep in, and more shiny restaurants and bars to enjoy themselves (Figures 7.8 and 7.9). The Finnish maritime monthly *Navigator* did not save pages or superlatives when it described the new design solutions of the new 'show boats' and 'love boats'.[52] The synergy between ferries and cruise ships nurtured the kind of naval architecture, technical know-how, and subcontractor networks that provided competitive advantage in the narrow niche of passenger ships in comparison with shipyards that only had experience from cargo types.

In 1978, therefore, the mass-scale layoffs looming large at the shipyards provoked a public uproar over the possibility to let this kind of a special ship go to Japan. As a result, the Bank of Finland, which controlled the international monetary transactions in the Finnish regulated financial market, refused to approve foreign funding for SF-Line and effectively blocked the Japanese shipyard from getting the contract. Instead, the government agreed to allocate 17 million to offset 15% of the production costs, and to win the ferry order to Finland. Later, an additional 3 million was granted to the building of the second ship of the class.[53] Together, *Turella* and her sister-ship *Rosella* received all of the 20 million sum that the government had originally appropriated to support the Finnish shipyards over the crisis.

The state support for SF-Line inspired other shipping companies to ask for similar support for their newbuilding projects.[54] In the aftermath of the 1977–1978 shipyard crisis, the government subsidies totalled FIM65 million. It was more than triple the original subsidy reserve, but still moderately low in comparison with the huge scale of the big ship projects— *Turella* alone had been worth more than the state subsidies in total. Of this 65 million, a small inland shipyard in Savonlinna received half a million and Rauma-Repola 2.5 million for a project of two cargo ships. The vast majority of these funds were, however, assigned for Wärtsilä's different passenger ship projects.[55]

In November 1979, the central organisations of Finnish shipbuilders and shipowners invited representatives from the Ministry of Trade and Industry, Ministry of Finance, and Bank of Finland to embark *Turella*—the first ferry to receive state aid—and to participate in a seminar about the future of the Finnish maritime cluster. The lengthy presentations in the world-class floating conference room described to the governmental actors the difficult position of the nationally important industry in the international market. The Finnish companies depended on a national ship financing policy. The policy should provide the companies with fair operational conditions compared to companies in other countries. If the state failed to support the industry in the international competition, the nationally important maritime service function, shipping, would be taken over by foreign-flagged ships.[56]

This argumentation set the tone for the shipyard financing discussion. The first direct shipyard subsidies 1978–1979 were exceptional measures implemented in a crisis atmosphere to assist the shipyards to the next upturn. In the 1980s, the domestic market competitiveness became elementary for the long-term survival.

In the autumn of 1982, the Finnish passenger ferries reappeared on the political agenda. The Finnish–Swedish ferry company Silja Line planned to purchase two new vessels for the Turku-Stockholm route.[57] Japanese Nippon-Kokan had submitted the lowest tender. Wärtsilä's offer was 20%–30%, roughly 100 million, more expensive. At that particular moment, the Finnish shipbuilding industry was doing relatively well. Wärtsilä's shipyards were not in dire need of new contracts but instead had difficulties in scheduling new ferries in their fully booked yards.[58] According to Silja Line's Finnish partner, EFFOA, Wärtsilä had not even shown much interest in the project.[59]

This time it was the shipyard workers' organisation that first raised its voice to muster forces to win the ship to Finland.[60] The chair of the Finnish Metal Workers Union (*Metallityöväenliitto*) Sulo Penttilä warned the Finnish Shipyard Association STTY against letting the Japanese shipyard win the ferry contract: 'The Japanese would obtain such a good reference from these projects that it would hamper Finnish shipyards far into the future'. In his correspondence with the Ministry of Finance, Penttilä justified his outcry by the unfair competition situation in international shipbuilding: 'We know that Wärtsilä is one of the leading builders of ferries and passenger ships, according to our Union's opinion this [Japanese competitiveness] is about price-dumping or state-subsidised exports'.[61] The STTY could do nothing but chime in with the labour union requesting the Ministry to investigate whether the Japanese offer violated principles of fair trade.[62]

In November 1982, Minister of Foreign Trade Jermu Laine nominated Ship Order Working Group to examine the price dumping accusations.[63] In international trade, unfair price dumping referred to a form of discrimination in which a country sold products at the price that was lower than the fair market price level to enter a market or outrun competitors. The latest GATT Tokyo Round Code 1980 had recently specified the definition of dumping, and that definition had also been implemented in Finnish legislation. Dumping charges were serious issues in international affairs that would involve the international inspectors from GATT.[64]

The Finnish civil servants did not question accusations of unfair competition but were hesitant to press charges against the Japanese price dumping. On the one hand, they had no means to prove that the Japanese offer was really too low. Tailor-made passenger vessels had no clear market price, and the shipyard's cost-structure was a company secret. On the other hand, the full-booked shipyards in Finland made it a difficult case to demonstrate that the alleged dumping had damaged the Finnish shipbuilding.[65]

The buyer of the ship, EFFOA, was irritated by the public outcry that had arisen out of its investment plan. CEO Harry Österberg expressed his profound disappointment that the public accusations challenged the right of the private company in the capitalist country to make a legal investment based on economic rationales.[66] Moreover, the bureaucratic pondering at the ministries was about to delay the contracting so long that the Japanese shipyard could cancel or raise the lucrative offer.[67]

The draft of the Ship Order Working Group report has been dated January 12, 1983, indicating that the working group had concluded its work during the first weeks of the year. The report itself revealed nothing surprising for

*Figure 7.8 Finlandia* leaving from Helsinki to Stockholm 1982. Photo: Volker von Bonin, Helsinki City Museum.

anyone working with international shipping and shipbuilding at that time. Overall, the working group was sceptical about the prospects of pressing dumping charges against Japan and was not optimistic about alternative ways to win the contract for Finland. The price difference between the Finnish and Japanese offers was too wide to be compensated by domestic financial arrangements. The working group pointed out the possibility that the Bank of Finland could deny EFFOA from getting foreign credit due to monetary policy reasons. It concluded, however, that applying a monetary excuse for industrial policy aims was not reasonable and probably not effective, either, because the Swedish partner in Silja Line could buy the ferry on behalf of EFFOA.[68]

For tactical reasons, the Ship Order Working Group decided not to publish the report immediately in January. Instead, it told the journalists and EFFOA that the committee needed more time to investigate the pricing at the Japanese shipyards.[69] Before this announcement, the chair of the working group had felt compelled to ask for moral support from the minister in charge for telling the public audience and the shipping company something that 'was not completely true'. In his letter to Minister Laine, the chair described his strategy to invoke legal complications that had delayed the working group from determining whether the ministry was to initiate dumping investigations. In addition, he expressed moral considerations about having to deceive EFFOA:

> Lying to Silja-Line is morally not very comfortable and can result in harsh investigation afterwards if the tactical plans are ever leaked. In this situation, however, the truth would increase the risk that the ferries would be ordered from Nippon-Kokan.[70]

Silja Line wanted the new ferry operational in the high season of 1985, and its negotiation advantages decreased when time run short. Contracting with the Japanese shipyard without knowing about the possible dumping charges risked at having to pay penalty tariffs.[71]

The chair of the Ship Order Working Group described in his letter to Minister Laine, how EFFOA's director Österberg had reacted to the new delays in the dumping investigation in January 1983: 'He left from the meeting as uninformed, resentful, and miserable as he was at his arrival. We may conclude that this communication accomplished its purpose, as awkward and uncomfortable as it was'.[72]

The Ship Order Working Group's tactical procrastination reached its target. It managed to suspend Silja Line from contracting with the Japanese shipyard until Wärtsilä had the capacity to contract for the project and the state had time to negotiate on subventions. In February 1983, Silja Line contracted with Wärtsilä Turku Shipyard for the new ferry and completed the contract for its sister-ship later in the spring. Wärtsilä had bargained down its offer so that it was slightly below production costs and reorganised its other projects with Finnish subcontractors to make room for the ferries.[73] At the same time, the government authorised the Export Credit Ltd to grant exceptionally advantageous credits for over 90% of the contract price. The fixed interest rate was 8% and thus in line with the OECD export credit convention for not to draw uncomfortable attention in international comparisons. The payback time, however, was 12 years and generous compared to the normal credit arrangements in Finland at that time.[74]

The new ferries, *Svea* and *Wellamo*, started their operation in 1986. Upon the delivery, *Svea* was the largest ferry in the Baltic region. 168 meters long and 33,829 GT, but it was not the size or the sophisticated interior décor that made them remarkable vessels.[75] What was remarkable was that the government decided to use export credits to support a domestic order. The funds for the KTR credits for normal domestic ship orders came from the Bank of Finland, which was not directly subordinated to the political governance. The Export Credit agency, instead, was under the Ministry of Trade and Industry. The terms of export credits were also more advantageous for the industry and easier for the government to upgrade. Because the normal market interest rate was around 12%, the state subvention totalled 28.8% of the contract price. For comparison of the normal terms of the export credits at the time—80% of the contract price, payback time of eight years, interest rate of 8%—the subsidies were 14.4% of the subsidies, while the normal KTR-credits for domestic orders equalled only a 12.5% direct subsidy.[76]

The government did not want the Silja Line case to set the pattern the other domestic ship orders would follow.[77] The only enhancement of the KTR credit scheme in 1983 was the possibility to negotiate for a two-year payback time without mortgages.[78] In 1984, the shipyards estimated that for a Finnish ship buyer, the costs of domestic financing through the KTR-credit were 6% more expensive in comparison with the financing the shipyard could get as export credit when selling a ship abroad.[79]

Only two years later, in December 1985, the government decided to align the domestic ship financing schemes with export financing in accordance with the exception first made with *Svea* in 1983. The new legislation allowed the Export Credit Ltd to grant interest subsidy loans for Finnish ship buyers when they placed an order from a Finnish shipyard, using the financial terms that corresponded the OECD guidelines for ship export credits. In terms of financing, the domestic ship buyers became now equal to export trade. The Ministry of Foreign Affairs estimated that the subsidised interest rate was worth a 16% direct subsidy of the ship contract-price.[80]

The change of policy was implemented through an amendment of the Act on Interest Subsidy Loans for Domestic Purchases of Ships. The aim was to avoid an impression of a policy change that would open the floodgates for increasing state aid. No one wanted to risk the Finnish international image of a subsidy-free country. The allegedly state-free shipbuilding in Finland was a valuable asset in international negotiations and thus carefully nurtured by industrial and state actors. It became even more important when Finland entered negotiations with the EC for European-wide ship financing policy.

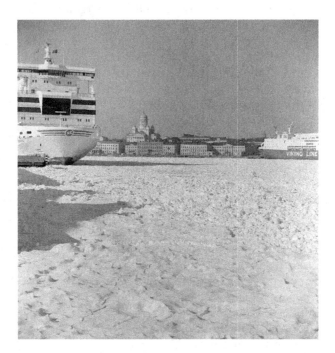

*Figure 7.9* *Svea Regina* and *Viking Saga* waiting for passengers in the front of Helsinki.
Photo: Bonin von Volker, 1985, Helsinki City Museum.

## International competitiveness on the threshold of Europe

During the Cold War, Finland's approach to the European integration pro-
cess had been characterised by the constant balancing between the West and
East; economic necessities and political possibilities. On the one hand, European economic integration and access to the Western European markets were
imperatives for the Finnish Western-oriented exports, especially the forestry.
On the other hand, participation in European political integration, such as
European Economic Community EEC, was out of the question. The Soviet
Union would interpret it as rapprochement with West Germany and NATO
countries that would violate the peace treaty, damage the Finnish–Soviet
relations, and destroy Finland's policy of neutrality.

Finland's acrobatic manoeuvring in its foreign trade policy resulted in curious special arrangements that granted Finland access to the European free
trade area while allowing it to preserve its special relations with the socialist
countries as well. These included the FINN–EFTA agreement in 1961, when
Finland joined the EFTA (European Free Trade Association) as an associate
member, and the free trade agreement with EEC in 1973, which granted
Finland the access to the European common market without supranational
political obligations.[81]

The EC shipbuilding policy was formulated in the aftermath of the oil crisis, shaped by the cross-currents between economic liberalism and national protectionism. The three main objectives of the EC shipbuilding policy were to facilitate structural adjustments, to restore a healthy and competitive ship-building industry, and to ensure that intra-community competition was carried out on an equal basis in all community yards.[82] In principle, the European integration process aimed at removing obstacles from free trade and international competition. Yet, in the face of global overcapacity and disruptive competition, the EC shipbuilding policy acknowledged national subsidy schemes as the only way to slow down the de-industrialisation in Europe. Therefore, the EC Fourth Shipbuilding Directive allowed national governments to grant direct shipyard subsidies for maximum 30% of the contract value, the Sixth Shipbuilding Directive brought the limit slightly lower to 28%.[83]

The common enemy that mustered the EC countries in defence was the industrialising Far East. The EC Commission stated in its report in 1989:

> The Commission will continue to work with its Far Eastern competitors for the normalization of the world market, as stated at the Tokyo meeting of the OECD Working party no 6 in November 1988. As aids given in the member States are a direct consequence of the selling of ships by Far Eastern countries at prices that do not cover costs, the Commission will focus its efforts on and overall elimination of abnormal pricing and distortions, and on the establishment of healthy market.[84]

Finland had a free trade agreement with the EC but was not a member of the community. In the application of the shipbuilding directive, it was an outsider and belonged to the category of third countries like Japan and Korea.[85] Finnish shipyards noticed to be left on the threshold of the integrating Europe: almost inside when it came to customs and tariffs, yet out from the decision-making when it came to shipbuilding competition. In competition against Western European shipyards, Finland's position almost, but not quite, in EEC meant that the rival shipyards could receive 28% edge in competition for orders in the form of state aid.[86]

In shipbuilding policy, Finland's aim was to be treated as a full member in EC against which the other members could not use state subsidies in competition.[87] As long as Finland was an outsider to the EC, it could only speak in favour of fair competition at public forums but not enter the negotiation tables. For example, in 1985, Prime Minister Kalevi Sorsa visited a maritime exhibition in Hamburg to find an ally in West Germany in the fight against the state aid for shipbuilding.[88]

Previously, Finland had participated in the economic integration that concerned mainly tariffs and custom barriers. Securing the competitive position of the Finnish shipyards in European market went beyond this, because it necessitated negotiations on domestic industrial policies. While the Finnish political leaders remained cautious not to risk the policy of neutrality by entering the political integration process, the shipyard financing became an arena where Finnish negotiators tried to relocate the country within the integrating Europe.

The Finnish government and shipyards were under the impression that the large EC shipbuilders subsidised their shipyards up to the maximum ceiling. They did not know, however, the accurate level of the state-aid schemes in different countries. Their information came from newspapers, diplomatic rumours, and customers who occasionally revealed terms of competitive tenders to get Finns to raise their offer.[89] Every shipyard had an incentive to present itself as a competitive producer in an otherwise unfair competition. Every government had reasons to mispresent or understate the level of the state aid to protect the locally important employers.

Between 1985 and 1987, the Finnish Ministry of Foreign Affairs investigated cases in which Wärtsilä competed for passenger ferries against the Western European shipyards that had outbid the Finnish offers with suspiciously low prices. In 1985, Wärtsilä lost an option for two passenger ships for Norwegian Royal Caribbean Line, roughly worth $175 million. The Norwegian buyer placed the order at a French shipyard which Wärtsilä claimed to have received over 40% of the contract value from the state as direct employment aid. The Finnish civil servants did not question the state-aid accusations. Instead, they reminded Wärtsilä that the EC directives allowed state aid for employment in a crisis situation if it did not increase capacity in a long term. Moreover, the Finnish-EC free trade agreement did not clearly specify

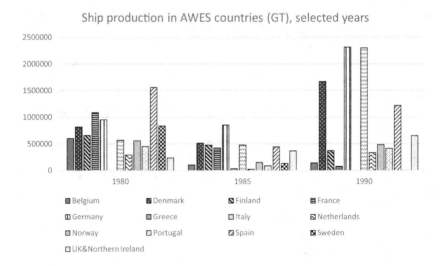

*Figure 7.10* The distribution of Western European merchant shipbuilding between AWES countries (GT). Volume of order book at the end of the year, ships over 100 tons, warships excluded. Data: Association of European Shipbuilders and Shiprepairers Awes, Annual reports, MTA.

terms of competition for orders in third countries, in this case in Norway.[90] As a conclusion, the Ministry recommended against blaming France for unfair competition because it was not worth the political risk: it 'would not be appropriate, and it would not give the lost ships back to Finland'.[91]

Another momentous case arrived at desks in the Foreign Ministry in 1987. Wärtsilä was in competition against Yugoslavian and West German shipyards for the new ferry contract to the Åland-based shipping company SF-Line. SF-Line had recently ordered its previous ferry, *Amorella,* from a Yugoslavian shipyard which had come as an utter surprise to the Finnish politicians, labour unions, and shipbuilders. That motivated the government to raise stakes to prevent Yugoslavia from winning this contract, too.[92] At the same time, it did not want to signal the EC countries that Finland subsidised its shipyards. This was salient in the competition against the German shipyard because the federal-level legislation allowed direct shipyard aid only if the competing yard was subsidised as well.[93]

The Finnish interests in this situation were somewhat conflicting. The first aim was to demonstrate to Yugoslavia that Finland was not going to allow price dumping without taking drastic measures. The second aim was to underline to Germany that the Finnish shipyards did not receive direct state aid.[94]

In October 1987, the recent failures to win orders against European shipyards pushed the government to increase public support for Finnish shipyards. This was accomplished through an amendment of the Shipbuilding Financing Act. The amendment enhanced the terms of interest subsidies and permitted the government to grant export credits that exceeded the OECD convention.[95]

The Act provided the government with financial instruments that could be used to support nationally important contracts without obligating the public sector to support all domestic ship orders. The selective process and conditional formulation of the Act enabled the government to concentrate its support on passenger ships and ferries, which were clearly stated in the documentation:

> The Government has kept as its starting point that unfair competition should not be allowed to damage the industrial branch that has successfully went through a difficult adjustment process, developed new technologies without state support and specialised in certain types of vessels.[96]

The tame title and dreary text of the Amendment of the Shipbuilding Financing Act camouflaged radical changes in the Finnish shipbuilding policy. It declared to the international observers that Finland was ready to cross the fine line between 'fair' export credits based on the OECD consensus and 'unfairly' subsidised export credits that exceeded the OECD terms. At the same time, all the diplomatic correspondence underlined that the Act implied no changes in the Finnish shipbuilding policy that remained to be against state aid: Finland supported only competitive industry and continued its mission to reject all disruptive public shipyard subsidies. The unspoken accusation against the European colleagues was that the Finnish government was forced to intervene in private business only because the EC countries continued to disturb free competition in shipbuilding.[97]

In December 1988, Prime Minister Kalevi Sorsa initiated Finnish–EC negotiations on shipbuilding subsidies. His argument was that Finland was a European country with European cost structure. The public shipbuilding subsidies, anomalies in the general trend against state interventions but justified because of Asian unfair price-dumping, were not fair when used against Finland.[98]

Finnish Ministry of Foreign Affairs was pessimistic about Finland's leverage in compromising with the EC on special treatment.[99] The first problem was Finland's relation to the European integration process. Officially, the EC Commission invoked bureaucratic obstacles that prevented the community from including a non-member country in a Community directive.[100] According to Finnish negotiators, these difficulties were political rather than technical: 'The EC should make a political decision to approve [increasing competition in European shipbuilding] and it would be a difficult decision'.[101]

The second problem was Finland's relationship with the Soviet Union. Some EC countries saw the bilateral trade with the Soviet Union as an unfair competitive advantage for the Finnish shipyards. As the Finnish representative in Brussels messaged to Helsinki, the Finnish–Soviet trade had 'had a bad psychological effect on member states that had watched the growth of shipbuilding capacity in Finland during the depressed 1970s'.[102]

To strengthen Finland's somewhat vague position as a European country, Sorsa promised that Finland would support the EC in the international shipbuilding negotiations between the EC, Japan, and South Korea: 'It would be a clear sign to others that *we Europeans* are unified and prepared to fight against state aid'.[103]

Finnish negotiators first tried to trade their support for the EC against Asian countries in exchange for the removal of state subsidies in the market segments in which the Japanese and Korean competition was not that intense: ferries, passenger ships, and the Soviet trade.[104] The EC countries categorically refused to abandon shipbuilding aid, their best advantage, before reaching an agreement with the Asian competitors.[105] Finnish participation in the EC delegation pushed the agenda further away from Finland's policy goals that were to get rid of the state aid. It would have been, though, a symbol to align Finland with the other Western European countries. Eventually, Finland became the only country that announced its readiness to launch international negotiations on shipbuilding financing. Japan and Korea hesitated, and the EC failed to get authorisation from the national governments.[106]

In 1988 and 1989, Finnish shipyards kept losing contracts in competition against the EC shipbuilders.[107] The Finnish shipyards estimated that their production costs exceeded the prevailing subsidised price level by 10%–30% for special purpose vessels and over 50% for standard ship production.[108] The

Finnish–EC negotiations, that Finland had once opened with a bold attempt to remove all state subsidies, ended with Finland establishing its own state subsidy system. In the fall of 1989, Finland and the EC Commission agreed on a common framework that regulated the competition between shipyards from Finland and EC countries. According to the procedure, the competing parties would case by case mutually agree on the level of state aid that would be allowed in any competitive bidding.[109] Mechanism like that was only possible if Finland had the possibility to grant state subsidies.[110]

That special mechanism to coordinate and compromise over state aid in shipbuilding competition between Finland and the EC countries, however, became outdated before it came into force. In December 1989, Finland started to negotiate on joining the European Economic Space (EES). As a merely economic arrangement that secured the access to European internal markets without an EC-membership, EES was said to be tailor-made for neutral countries like Finland: it had all the economic benefits without political obligations.[111] In particular, it would solve the problem with European ship subsidies because EES would parallel the EFTA countries with the EC members in the application of the Shipbuilding Directive and define Finland as a country against which the EC countries were not allowed to employ state aid.[112] This kind of special arrangement to ensure economic benefits without political commitment was well in line with the Finnish Cold War integration policy. As such, it became the last of the kind.

## Into a normal European country

In the Cold War era, the proximity of the Soviet Union constrained Finland's room to manoeuvre in foreign relations. In 1991, the dissolution of the socialist empire and the end of the Soviet Union removed the geopolitical straitjacket that had prevented Finland from fully participating in the European integration. In the spring of 1992, Finland submitted the application for EU membership.[113] The final phase in the Finnish shipyard financing policy transforming from the Cold War special case into a normal EU country took place during the membership negotiations, 1992–1995. At this stage, Finland was no longer balancing between the East and the West. Yet, before it became formally a member in 1995, it was not quite inside the European Union, either. Finland eventually adjusted its shipbuilding policy according to the EC standards but that took place as an incremental process and not as one big leap.

The horizon of expectation in the Finnish shipbuilding at the turn of the 1990s looked utterly confusing. The bankruptcy of Wärtsilä Marine in 1989 and the drastic industrial reorganisations and rationalisations described in the previous chapter, had forced the state to accept liabilities for shipyard employers and subcontractors against its preferences. The collapse of the Soviet trade and the termination of the bilateral trade system in 1990 broke down the most important market of the Eastern-oriented big business and were estimated to have caused the loss of 150,000 jobs.[114] At the same time, the Finnish economy as a whole went into the deepest recession since the 1930s.[115] The government had no extra energy, less goodwill, and a few financial resources to support the shipbuilding industry that might not be internationally competitive.

One element of the Finnish maritime policy that survived the end of the Cold War was the support for ice-strengthened tonnage. The national capability for winter navigation and the domestic competence in building ice-capable ships were considered critical for the security of supplies in a crisis situation, and therefore had a direct link to the post-Cold War national security considerations. The tax deductions and reductions in navigation fees continued to reward shipowners for high ice classes.[116] The Ministry of Transportation evaluated afterwards, that the costs of Finnish shipbuilding subsidies, consisting of interest subsidies for domestic vessels and support for high ice classes,[117] varied between FIM 22 and 134 million in 1990–1996.[118] It was less than the prevailing state support for the domestic shipping industry and less than the estimated level of subsidies in rivalry countries, but still clearly more than no subsidies at all. In the era of globalisation, domestic industrial competence remained a national challenge.

In November 1994, Finnish representatives at the EC complained that they were not fully able to participate in European shipbuilding policymaking as a future member country and that they were still outsiders to the European Community: 'Considering that the Finnish membership [in EU] in 01.01.1995 is practically certain, this perception of the Council is curious'.[119]

*Figure 7.11*  Cruise ships under construction at Helsinki shipyard in the early 1990s. After that, the sheltered building basin has become too narrow for the largest, post-Panamax cruise ships. Photo: Aker Arctic Inc.

To improve its position as a truly European country, Finland aligned itself with the EC shipbuilding policy in the international shipbuilding negotiations within the OECD. The US government had invited the world-leading shipbuilders, the EC, Norway, Finland, Japan, and South Korea, to compromise over a new discipline for state support for shipbuilding, and to create a level playing ground for all shipyards. Finland was in disagreement regarding the EC subsidies and participated in the negotiations formally apart from the EC delegation, but supported its platform to express loyalty to EC.[120]

The OECD negotiations progressed slowly. The critical bottleneck was the US 'Jones Act', a federal statute requiring all cargo ships operating in the coastal trade between two US ports to be constructed in the United States. As long as the Americans refused to open the cabotage for other than US-flagged and US-built ships, the EC countries were not willing to withdraw from state subsidy policy.[121] In December 1994, the negotiating parties—the Commission of the European Community, Finland, Japan, South Korea, Norway, Sweden, and the United States—signed the ship financing pact with the descriptive title 'Agreement Respecting Normal Competitive Conditions in the Commercial Shipbuilding and Repair Industry'. The agreement was ambitious and had the potential of becoming a watershed in global shipbuilding as the *OECD Observer* described:

> It is expected that the Agreement will prove of sustained benefit to the international shipbuilding market by eliminating the long-standing plague of government support and by deterring the dumbing practices that are widely believed to have been damaging to builders. That will in turn bring to light the competitive edge of countries in shipbuilding and reveal the true economic performance of individual shipbuilders.[122]

Unlike the previous OECD agreements on state subsidies for shipbuilding, this one was to be legally binding after the participating countries had completed their national ratification processes. Another breakthrough was that the agreement regulated both direct and indirect state aid for shipyards including injurious pricing practices. Only four types of state support were permitted under the agreement. First, the moderately subsidised export credits up to 12 years repayment period were allowed, but not the fixed, subsidised interest rate. Second, the support for domestic buyers was permitted if the foreign and domestic buyers were treated equally. Third, the state support to facilitate structural change at the shipyards was temporarily allowed. Finally, state assistance in research and development was allowed and it was to be the primary form of state support.[123]

The Finnish Parliament expressed strong support for stringent international discipline that would restrain state governments from shipbuilding competition and to restore the competition between shipyards based on technical and economic merits. The Parliamentary Finance Committee concluded in its statement that 'the agreement and the decree are central to safeguarding the competitiveness of the Finnish shipbuilding industry because Finland does not pay direct shipyard subsidies'.[124]

It is rather striking that still in 1994, after over 15 years of negotiations on state aid for shipbuilding in Finland, the Parliament justified its policy platform with the old argument that Finland did not subsidise its shipyards. It demonstrated the strength of the self-perception that the Finnish shipbuilding industry had been a special case in the European comparisons.

As a disappointment for the Finnish negotiators, the OECD agreement never came into force. The US Senate refused to ratify it on the ground that it removed the American protection for domestic shipyards and shipping. Without international consensus, the EC Commission, too, retained its policy of state aid. The EU policy on ship financing continued to regulate the state-aid ceilings instead of eliminating the subsidies.

The Finnish diplomats in the EU negotiations expressed their frustrations over this decision: 'We feel that state subsidies have distorted competition to a significant degree both on the world market and in Europe. We would have preferred to join a Union where this was no longer the case'.[125]

Finland joined the EU in 1995. In 1996, the Finnish government decided to start granting direct subsidies for shipbuilding. The level of the direct state aid for shipyards, which was up to 9% of shipbuilding contract prices, was relatively low, but it marked a policy change. Finland could no longer claim that it had no standing policy for shipbuilding subsidies.[126] New rules for shipbuilding aid in EC member countries, known as the 1540/98 Regulation, came into force in 1999. That outlined a shift away from contract-related aid towards support for investments and innovations but international competition in shipbuilding continued to rely on national financing arrangements.[127]

## Conclusions: state and national competitiveness

In January 1989, the Finnish maritime monthly, *Navigator*, described the Finnish shipbuilding industry on the watershed:

> The shipyards had been built on the political foundation of the continuance of the Eastern trade and were not able to adapt to the world market in time. The global overcapacity, subsidies, and price dumbing have slumped the international prices so low that, at the moment, ships should not be built but only bought.[128]

In the past, Finland had adapted to the dualism of the Eastern and Western markets that had balanced each other and provided the shipyards with relatively stable competitive environment for technical specialisation. In the future, it had to find its relative competitive advantages and survive the international competition. For the moment, Finland was adapting to two different futures at the same time: the one with the changing Soviet Union and one with the integrated Europe.

Under these circumstances, ferries and cruise ships ushered in the post-Cold War shipyard policy in Finland. Passenger ships were marginal in the global shipbuilding, but for Finland, they were salient. Being relatively important for Finnish-flagged shipping and a relative competitive advantage for shipbuilding, they provided a common platform for the Finnish maritime cluster and tangible objects for Finnish politicians to reassess the role of state in international competition.

Baltic ferries were large, expensive, and points of public interest. Their flashy lights made them stand out from the mundane cargo ships. The competitiveness in this narrow niche was about the combination of technical competence and artistic creativity; pragmatic functionality and illusion of extravagance. This chapter has focused on the aspect that the passengers of these cruise ships and ferries were least interested in: the minutiae of ship financing. State interventions centred on the seemingly bureaucratic administrators, who were short of the charisma of front-row politicians, and on technical details, that lacked the attraction of shiny new passenger cruise ships.

The politics of financing was sometimes hidden behind the tedious talk about interest rates and percentages, but it brought under the spotlight the financial imperative of the maritime economy. To succeed, shipyards had to master the steel and design, but also the money.

Until the 1980s, the Finnish shipbuilding industry promptly stated that it did not need nor want state aid but fair competition. The 'no subsidy' policy was possible, thanks to the three features that stemmed from the Cold War context in Finland. First, the bilateral trade system with the Soviet Union provided the shipyards with the basic load and ample cash reserves that buffered against risks in the Western exports as described in Chapter 4. Second, the coordinated competition between Finnish shipyards, described in Chapter 6, had facilitated technical specialisation in narrow market niches that were less exposed to fierce competition against low-cost shipyards. Third, the regulated economy allowed the government to establish alternative arrangements for state support that were not recognised by the international regulation against shipbuilding state aid, as discussed in this chapter. One such special arrangement was the Cost Guarantee System that equipped the shipyards to hedge against domestic inflation. In the Finnish Cold War shipbuilding, it contributed to the social stability by lubricating negotiations between labour market organisations on wage increases. It also increased predictability and stability at the shipyards by enabling the companies to make long-term contracts.

By the mid-1980s, the business environment experienced turbulence that was beyond the control of the Finnish companies. The importance of the domestic and Western shipbuilding markets increased while the advantages of the Soviet trade decreased. The new circumstances forced the Finnish government to introduce a new shipbuilding policy.

Policymaking on the threshold of a paradigmatic change was not about grand statements. The Finnish shipbuilding policy at the end of the Cold War took shape through *ad hoc* decisions that were specific, exceptional, and made in haste. Instead of creating a new national strategy, the governments made one-off decisions to counteract the effects of the global competition and to bring passenger ferries back to Finland one ship at a time.

In Finland, the European integration process had been primarily understood in terms of economic liberalisation, deregulation, and free trade. The shipbuilding policy opened up a process in which national welfare and national competitiveness were always in conflict.

## Notes

1  Stråth, *The Politics of De-Industrialisation*, 1987, 13–14.
2  Hjerppe, "Finland's Foreign Trade and Trade Policy in the 20th Century," 1993, 73–74.
3  Act on Securing the Export of Metal Manufacturing and Shipbuilding Products, SäädK 636/1950.
4  Herranen, *Valtion raha vauhditti*, 2009. Government proposal HE 88/1952, vp. 1952, 2165, 2816; See also: *K-takuukomitean mietintö* [Cost Guarantee Committee Report] 28:1976, 3.
5  Kekkonen,"Itäkaupan takuuolosuhteet", *Kyntäjä* 10/1952.
6  *Teollisuusneuvottelukunnan mietintö* [Industrial advisory board committee report], 4:1959, 89.
7  *Cost Guarantee Committee Report*, KTM 28, 1976, 3–4.
8  Kuusterä & Tarkka, *Suomen Pankki 200 vuotta II*, 2009, 45; Jensen-Eriksen, "Business, Economic Nationalism, and Finnish Foreign Trade during the 19th and 20th Centuries," 2015.
9  *Vientitakuutoimikunnan mietintö* [Committee of Export Guarantees Report], 7:1962.
10 In 1963–1981, the state owned 55.6% of the shares, three commercial banks together 26.6% and big export-oriented corporations 17.8%. Herranen, *Valtion raha vauhditti*, 2009, 36–47, 50.
11 Herranen, *Valtion raha vauhditti*, 2009, 66–67; *Export Credit Committee Report*, KTM 32, 1976, 3–4.
12 The Soviet Union's hostile attitude towards Finland accepting American aid through the Marshall Plan and attempted membership in OEEC in 1957 resulted in Finland opting out. Aunesluoma, *Vapaakaupan tiellä*, 2011, 104–109; 171–176.
13 Later, this was changed to 7.5% and 8%.
14 *OECD Observer*, 41, 1969, 11.
15 Act on Export Guarantees, SäädK 479/1962.
16 Credit risk guarantees were needed especially when exporting to developing countries. They were insurance-like guarantees for the company if the buyer did not pay back their debt. Finance guarantees were provided for small companies which had not sufficient assets to be used as guarantees to get export credits. Herranen, *Valtion raha vauhditti*, 2009, 80–90.
17 *Cost Guarantee Committee Report*, 1976, 5.
18 Herranen, *Valtion raha vauhditti*, 2009, 91–92; *Cost Guarantee Committee Report*, 1976, 8.
19 VTL on Cost Guarantee System, 2.12.1976, MTA.
20 For instance, originally the cost increase was based on an outdated special series of the Finnish whole share price index that was replaced by the Manufacturing industry index in 1971, that was changed to a special series of production price index in 1972. *Cost Guarantee Committee Report*, 1976, 17.

21 Cost Guarantee Committee Report, 1976, 12.
22 Shipyard committee report 1977, 19.
23 Christian Landtman in *Wärtsilä* personnel magazine 5/77; Tankmar Horn in *Wärtsilä* personnel magazine 6/77; See also discussion on Finnish icebreaker exports in HS 3.11.1976; HS 17.9.1976.
24 Interview of Tankmar Horn in *Wärtsilä* personnel magazine 2/75; Interview of Christian Landtman in *Wärtsilä* personnel magazine 1/73.
25 For the public debate, see HS 3.11.1976; TS 30.11.1976; HS 12.6.1976.
26 Government proposal HE 479/62, VP 1979; KTM to the Cost Guarantee Committee 3.2.1975; VTL on Cost Guarantees, 2.12.1976, MTA.
27 *Cost Guarantee Committee Report*, 1976, 1–2; 25.
28 *Cost Guarantee Committee Report*, 1976, 20–21.
29 *Cost Guarantee Committee Report*, 1976, 29; VTL on Cost Guarantee System, 2.12.1976, MTA; Amendment of Export Guarantee Act, SäädK 1106/1983.
30 Herranen, *Valtion raha vauhditti*, 2009, 95–96.
31 Herranen, *Valtion raha vauhditti*, 2009, 95–96.
32 Kaukiainen, *Ulos Maailmaan!* 2008, 412–415; 419–420; 426; Ojala & Kaukiainen, "Finnish Shipping – A Nordic Exception?" 2012, 130.
33 Bertel Långhjelm, 'Kauppalaivaston uusiminen, rahoitusongelma,' *Navigator* 1/1956, 30–35.
34 Act of Supporting Exports of Shipbuilding and Metal Manufacturing, SäädK 445/1956.
35 Landtman, *Minnen från mina år vid Wärtsilä*, 2011, 52.
36 Herranen, *Valtion raha vauhditti*, 2009, 65; Uola, *Meidän isä on töissä telakalla*, 1996, 173–174; Dahl, "Länsikauppakin meille sentään jotakin merkitsee," 2016, 76; Landtman, *Minnen från mina år with Wärtsilä*, 2011, 8.
37 Kaukiainen, *Ulos Maailmaan!* 2008, 438.
38 Laivaryhmän mietintö [Ship Working Group Report], Kauppa- ja teollisuusministeriön työryhmä ja toimikuntaraportteja, Ucc:12, 1977, NA.
39 Kaukiainen, *Ulos maailmaan!*, 2008, 466–468; Kuisma, *Kylmä sota kuuma öljy*, 1997, 388–389; 392–393; 485–487; 489. On the tax relief policy for shipping: *Act of Tax Reliefs to Seafaring*, SäädK 554/1953; SäädK 229/1966; SäädK 853/1970; SäädK 433/1981.
40 *Ship Working Group Report*, 1977.
41 *Ship Working Group Report*, 1977, 9, 14.
42 *Ship Working Group Report*, 1977, 15, 32.
43 In 1977, Bank of Finland covered 30% of the KTR credit, the bank of the shipyard provided 25%, and the bank of the ship buyers 35%. *Ship Working Group Report*, 1977, 17–18.
44 *Ship Working Group Report*, 1977, 24.
45 Kaukiainen, *Ulos maailmaan!*, 2008, 464.
46 Ojala & Kaukiainen, "Finnish Shipping – A Nordic Exception?" 2012, 130.
47 PM KTM/Rekola on state subsidies for shipyards 20.4.1978, EAB1 telakkaavustukset, KTM, NA.
48 The relative importance of passenger ships was emphasised because they were expensive investments and thus absorbed resources from other kinds of tonnage. Yrjö Kaukiainen has evaluated that *Finlandia* (1981) cost as much as three ro-ro vessels. Kaukiainen, *Ulos maailmaan!* 2008, 464.
49 KTM on state subsidies for shipyards, 20.4.1978, EAB1, KTM, NA.
50 Id & Peter, *Specialisation and Innovations*, 2017, 126–127.
51 Horn to KTM on domestic ferry construction to secure employment at Turku shipyard 31.3.1978, EAB1, KTM, NA.
52 Shipbuilding reviews in *Navigator* 1982–1989.

53  Ministerial Committee for Monetary Policy meeting, proposal for subsidising Wärtsilä-SF-Line project, 1.3.1978; Attached memorandum KTM 27.21987, EAB1, KTM, NA.
54  KTM on state aid to get contracts, 7.9.1978; A. E.Vehmas, Etelä-Suomen Laiva to KTM 16.10.1978, EAB1 KTM, NA.
55  KTM summary on shipyard subsidies 13.5.1980, EAB1, KTM, NA.
56  *Navigator* 1/80; "Varustamoiden ja telakoiden elinkeinopoliittiset tavoitteet," *Navigator* 2/1980.
57  Originally, Finska Ångfartygs Aktiebolaget, literally translated as Finnish Steamship Company. In 1976, the company changed its name to EFFOA according to the pronunciation of its former Swedish abbreviation FÅA. In 1982, Svea was already absorbed by Johnson line.
58  Ministry of Finance meetings with Wärtsilä 1.12; Meeting with EFFOA 2.12, 3.12.1982; *Ship Order Working Group Report 1983*, Laivatilaustyöryhmä, VM, NA.
59  Meeting between Hagelstam and Österberg 12.1.1983, Laivatilaustyöryhmä, VM, NA.
60  Metal Union (Metallityöväen liitto Liittotoimikunta) 29.10.1982, STTY pöytäkirjat 2, ELKA.
61  Sulo Penttilä to STTY 22.10.1982, STTY Pöytäkirjat 2, ELKA.
62  Sulo Penttilä to Minister Jermu Laine 1.11.1982; Tapio Forsgren to Laine 19.11.1982, STTY pöytäkirjat 2, ELKA.
63  VM 59/10-27/82 nominating a working group, 22.11.1982, STTY pöytäkirjat 2, ELKA. The critical question of the government's responsibility for bringing the contract to Finland was also raised in the Parliament, see KK 329 and KK 330, 1982 vp.
64  Implemented in Finland: SopS 18-19/1980; Säädk 387/1980.
65  *Ship Order Committee Report*, 1983, 5–9.
66  Meeting between Hagelstam and Österberg 12.1.1983, Laivatilaustyöryhmä, VM, NA.
67  Meeting with Wärtsilä 1.12; Meeting with EFFOA 2.12 and 3.12.1982, Laivatilaustyöryhmä, VM, NA.
68  *Ship Order Committee Report*, 1983, 13, 15.
69  Hagelstam to Laine on the present situation in ferry order 11.1.1983, Laivatilaustyöryhmä, VM, NA.
70  Hagelstam to Laine on the present situation in ferry order 11.1.1983, Laivatilaustyöryhmä, VM, NA.
71  In mid-December, the working group had commented to the press that the report was almost finished, only lacking a grammar check, "Silja päättänee uusista lautoista vuodenvaihteessa," HS 18.12.1982. In January 1983, the publication of the results was repeatedly delayed: "Viking tilaamassa Japanista kahta matkustajalauttaa," HS 7.1.1983. On the delay of the working group report, see also "Vaitelias työryhmä jättää Silja-raporttinsa tiistaina," HS 8.1.1983; "Silja-raportti lykkääntyy helmikuuhun," HS 12.1.1983.
72  Meeting between Hagelstam and Österberg 12.1.1983, Laivatilaustyöryhmä, VM, NA.
73  Id & Peter, *Specialisation and Innovations*, 2017, 137.
74  Calculations on subsidies in ship financing 18.10.1983, PM 3/1983 Shipyard committee 13[?].10.1983, RR/JS 327, UPMA.
75  Id & Peter, *Specialisation and Innovations*, 2017, 138.
76  PM Reijo Ranta, calculations on subsidies in ship financing 18.10.1983, Sere 327, UPMA.
77  Shipyard Committee's meeting, 11.11.1983, Sere 327, UPMA.
78  Shipyard Committee's meeting, 23.11.1983, Sere 327, UPMA.

79 Shipyard Committee's interim report 8.3.1984; Shipyard Committee's meeting 2.12.1983, Sere 327, UPMA.
80 Act on Interest Subsidy Loans for Domestic Purchases of Ships SäädK 1093/85; Telegram from UM/KPO to OECD Embassies on shipbuilding 13.10.1987, Telakkateollisuus 1986–1987, 51.4, UMA; Herranen, *Valtion raha vauhditti*, 2009, 156; 241.
81 On European integration and Finnish foreign trade, see Aunesluoma, *Vapaakaupan tiellä*, 2011; Paavonen, *Vapaakauppaintegraation kausi*, 2008; Jensen-Eriksen, *Läpimurto*, 2007.
82 Commission report to the Council and the European Parliament on the Implementation 1987–1988 of the Sixth Council Directive on Aid to Shipbuilding, 1989, Telakkateollisuus 37.51, UMA.
83 Todd, *Industrial Dislocation*, 1991, 72–73.
84 Underlining with a pencil at Finnish Ministry of Foreign Affairs. Commission report to the Council and the European Parliament on the Implementation 1987–1988 of the Sixth Council Directive on Aid to Shipbuilding, 1989, Telakkateollisuus 37.51, UMA.
85 WM memorandum 24.8.1987, Telakkateollisuus 1986–1987, 51.4, UMA.
86 WM memorandum 24.8.1987, Telakkateollisuus 1986–1987, 51.4, UMA.
87 Blomqvist to Sutherland on shipbuilding industry 1986–1987, 29.9.1987, 51.4, UMA; KPO 966 on shipyard subsidies 26.11.1987, Telakkateollisuus 1986–1987, 51.4, UMA.
88 "Pääministeri Sorsa Hampurissa. Telakkasubventiot esille EC:ssä," *Navigator* 10/1986.
89 For instance, Finnish shipyard industry association had received information on state subsidies in Spain and Germany from Cuban negotiators. Discussion with Minister E. Rantala and director of Export Credit Ltd. E. Asp on ship credits in Cuba 21.-26.1.1979, STTY 1, ELKA.
90 KPO 573 on Chantiers D'Atlantiqua/WM 27.8.1985, Telakkateollisuus 1982–1985, 51.4, UMA.
91 KPO 573 on Chantiers D'Atlantiqua/WM 27.8.1985, Telakkateollisuus 1982–1985, 51.4, UMA; Telegram from Oslo to Helsinki 5.11.1987; PM KTM on domestic ship purchases in international competition 10.9.1987; WM on Silja NB 1990-project 6.9.1987, Telakkateollisuus 1986–1987, 51.4, UMA.
92 "MS Amorella Turusta Tukholmaan poikkeaa edukseen," *Navigator* 11/88.
93 KPO 1027 on state aid for shipyards, 11.12.1987; KPO 966 on state aid for shipyards, 26.11.1987, Telakkateollisuus 1986–1987, 51.4, UMA.
94 KPO 1027 on SF-line ferry and public subsidies 11.12.1987, Telakkateollisuus 1986–1987, 51.4, UMA.
95 According to the terms of Domestic Ship Financing (Kotimaisen alusrahoitusehdot, "KAR"), shipping companies could get credit with 6% interest rate, payback time being ten years plus 3.5 years grace period. Agenda for government meeting 24.9.1987; Proposal of amending the Act (HE 1093/1985) on interest subsidy loans for domestic purchases of ships; Government decision of principle and a proposal for the Parliament. Telakkateollisuus 1986–1987, 51.4, UMA; *Telakkatukityöryhmän muistio* [Committee report of the working group for shipyard subsidy] 27:1989, 7.
96 KPO 966 on state aid for shipyards, 26.11.1987, Telakkateollisuus 1986–1987, 51.4, UMA.
97 An undated draft for amending the Act (1093/1985) on interest subsidy loans for domestic purchases of ships; KPO to OECD Embassy 13.10.1987; KPO on Silja project and domestic ship orders, 9.9.1987, KTM to Ministerial Committee of Economic Policy on Finnish action regarding to shipyard subsidies 16.9.1987; Blomqvist to Sutherland 29.9.1987, Telakkateollisuus 1986–1987, 51.4, UMA.

200 National competitiveness and international economy


98  Telegram EEC 0469 on Finnish-EC shipbuilding discussion 22.3.1989; Telegram EEC B012 on Finnish-EC shipbuilding industry, 7.2.1989; Meeting about the Finnish state subsidy initiative, 2.3.1989; KPO 953 on governmental aid for shipbuilding, 28.10.1988, EY-Suomi 1.1.1988–31.10.1988, 37.51, UMA.

99  Telegram EEC 1716/1988 on state-aid for shipyards, EY-Suomi 1.1.1988–31.10.1988, 37.51, UMA.

100  Finland-EC discussion in Brussels 29.1.1988; Telegram EEC 0469 on Finnish-EC shipbuilding discussion; 22.3.1989: Telegram EEC B012 on Finland-EC shipbuilding discussion 7.2.1989; Meeting 2.3.1989, Telakkateollisuus 1989–1994, 37.51, UMA.

101  Telegram EEC 1083 on shipbuilding discussions in Brussels 12.7.1989, EC-Finland 1.4.-.31.12.1989, 37.51, UMA.

102  Telegram EEC 0469, on Finnish-EC shipbuilding discussions 22.3.1989; KPO 73 on shipbuilding state aid, Finnish-EC discussion in Brussels 29.1.1988, 1.2.1988, KPO 249 on French view of shipbuilding subsidies, 21.3.1988, EY-Suomi 1.1.1988–31.10.1988, 37.51, UMA.

103  Italics by the author. Telegram 1212 on Sorsa's visit and discussion with De Clerq in Brussels 15.12.1988, EY-Suomi 1.4.1989–31.12.1989, 37.51, UMA.

104  Telegram EECB019 on Finnish-EC shipbuilding discussion in European Commission 8.9.1988, EY-Suomi 1.1.-31.10.1988, 37.51, UMA.

105  KPO 500 on EC-South Korea shipbuilding discussion in Tokyo 13.10.1988, EY-Suomi 1.1.1988–31.10.1988, 37.51, UMA.

106  KPO 875 on shipbuilding discussion with Salvatore Salerno in Helsinki 30.9. and 1.10.1988; KPO on the Tiffany project and state aid, 21.11.1988; Finnish Embassy in Soul SEO-109 on EC/Korea and EC/Japan shipbuilding discussion in Tokyo 10.10.1988–11.10.1988; KPO 953 on shipbuilding subsidies, 28.10.1988; KPO 500 on EC/Korea and EC/Japan shipbuilding discussion in Tokyo 10.10.1988–11.10.1988; EY-Suomi 1.1.1988–31.10.1988, 37.51, UMA.

107  The state-owned oil company Neste bought a tanker from South Korea. Of private companies, even Hollming Shipping of the Hollming corporate group, that also owned shipyards, bought chemical tankers from Belgium. KTM on market situation of the Finnish shipbuilding industry, 13.10.1990, Telakkateollisuus 1990–1994, 37.51; Non-paper titled as Finland-EC; Agreement on aid to shipbuilding, 2.10.1989, EY/EU Telakkateollisuus 1989–1994, 37.51, UMA.

108  WM marketing strategy 17.6.1988, WM strategy folder, personal collection Matti Törmä, STX-Turku; KTM on situation in the shipyard industry 23.11.1989, appendix in Working Group for Shipyard Subsidy report VM 27/1989, 7.

109  KPO 1029 on state-aid for shipbuilding, 20.10.1989, EY-Suomi 1.4.1989–31.12.1989, 37.51, UMA.

110  KPO 1044 on trade politics and shipbuilding subsidies, 31.10.1989, EY-Suomi 1.4.1989–31.12.1989, 37.51, UMA.

111  Max Jakobsson on EFTA-EC partnership, Confederation of Finnish industries 13.4.1989, Koivisto 37, NA.

112  KPO 1626 memorandum 17.5.1990; KPO on Finnish-EC correspondence on state aid for shipbuilding, 11.6.1990; KPO 931 on Finnish-EC shipbuilding consultations in Brussels 15.10.1990, 22.10.1990, Telakkateollisuus 1990–1994, 37.51, UMA.

113  Aunesluoma, Vapaakaupan tiellä, 2011, 405–409; 458–463.

114  Laurila, Finnish-Soviet Clearing Trade and Payment System, 1995, 58.

115  Kiander, 1990-luvun talouskiriisi, 2001; Fellman, "Growth and Investment: Finnish Capitalism, 1850s-2005," 2008, 139–217.

116  SäädK 1265/1993; SäädK 1258/1996; SäädK 1060/1999. In 2001, 50% of Finnish ships had the highest ice class (1A Super) and 30% were in the second highest

class (1A). Ojala & Kaukiainen, "Finnish Shipping – A Nordic Exception?" 2012, 136–137.

117 In 1994–1996, the ice class deductions were also applied to ships purchased from abroad. After 1996, the ships needed to be bought from the EU countries. SäädK 1265/1993; SäädK 1258/1996.

118 Kemppi & Tervonen, *Merenkulkuelinkeinon tuet ja taloudelliset vaikutukset*, 1999.

119 Telegram EEC7105 on EC shipbuilding 1991–1994, 17.11.1994, 37.51, UMA.

120 *OECD Observer* 192:1995.

121 *OECD Observer* 192:1995; KPO 575 on Finnish-EC shipbuilding consultations in Turku 22.6.1993–23.6.1993, 7.7.1993; EU shipbuilding meeting in Wismar, 19.10.1994–21.10.1994, EC Telakkateollisuus 1991–1994, 37.51, UMA.

122 Wilhelm Kurth, "Agreement on Shipbuilding," *OECD Observer* 192/1995, 46.

123 Wilhelm Kurth, "Agreement on Shipbuilding," *OECD Observer* 192/1995, 44–46.

124 Parliamentary Committee for Economic Policy, statement TaVL 7/1995 vp.

125 Telegram EEC 1152, instructions to COREPER II meeting, 14.12.1994, EC Telakkateollisuus 1991–1994, 37.51, UMA.

126 OECD Shipbuilding Agreement. http://www.oecd.org/sti/ind/shipbuilding agreement-overview.htm. Retrieved 17.10.2016; *Kauppapolitiikka* 4/1994; Okko et al., *Telakkatuki ja tarjouskilpailut*, 1997.

127 Council Regulation (EC) No 1540/98 of 29.6.1998 establishing new rules on aid to shipbuilding, *Official Journal of European Communities*, 18.07.1998, L202/1-10.

128 Klaus Salkola, "Lama syvenee", *Navigator* 1/89.

# 8 Conclusions

Two ships were moored to the ship dock in Helsinki in 1988, the nuclear icebreaker *Vaygach* and the cruise ship *Fantasy*. The former was preparing for service among the Arctic ice along the Soviet Northern Coast, the latter was going to take off westwards under the Caribbean sun. One of the ships was ordered by a state organisation in a socialist country and the other was bought by a private-owned company in the leader of capitalist world; one had been paid through the bilateral clearing trade and payment system and the other had been financed by commercial banks and state export credit organisations. The nuclear icebreaker had been on the agenda of multiple intergovernmental discussions as the flagship of the Finnish–Soviet scientific-technical cooperation, the large cruise ship had been an object of Finland's negotiations with the EC for shipbuilding policy. *Vaygach* remained the last profitable order from the Soviet Union, *Fantasy's* construction process went through the biggest bankruptcy in the Finnish shipbuilding history.

Both the icebreaker and the passenger ship represented the technical know-how, organisational specialisation, and customer relations that the shipyard had developed in the Cold War era. Both of the ships materialised the industrial heritage on which the Finnish shipbuilding today has been built.

The primary objective of this book was to explore the connection between the Finnish shipbuilding and the Cold War: Was the industrialisation in Finland contingent rather than just collateral result of the polarised world order? The overarching conclusion of this study is that the history of the Finnish post-war shipbuilding was, indeed, *a Cold War History of Industrialisation*. It cannot be told without Finland's geopolitical location between the East and the West and its corollaries to the state-level decision-making, institutional business environment, and industrial strategies.

This is not to claim that everything in the Finnish shipbuilding, which took place during the Cold War, was a direct result of the prolonged confrontation between socialism and capitalism. The governmental policies and business decisions were often shaped yet seldom dictated by the geopolitics. While arguing that the Cold War—and even more, the end of the Cold War—shaped industrial transformation in Finland, we also have to delve into the limits of that framework of explanation.

The broad and diverse historiography of the Cold War technology and business has two overarching research interests. First, the politicisation of the fields of techno-science that contributed to the military and ideological competition, and the effects of this politicisation process in technological development. Second, the dynamics of the state–industry interaction that shaped the performance, goals, and institutional environment of the companies which had strategic importance. The scholarship originates from the studies of the expansive military-industrial clusters and strategic Big Science projects in the United States and other large military powers. Their enormous influence in the past and the present all over the world well justifies why these topics still are in the centre of attention.

The dominant position of large countries, strategic industries, and English-language archival sources alone, nevertheless, compels us to reappraise the concepts, narrative structures, and explanations we use when we assess the Cold War impact on a small country and civilian industry.

What the history of the Finnish shipbuilding industry has in common with the better-known Cold War technology histories is that the geopolitical context did politicise the technology and industry in Finland. The Cold War embedded technologies in the meanings that rooted from the polarised world order. The shared national goals in the peaceful relationship with the Soviet Union, industrialisation, and social stability also facilitated the close interaction between the state and industry in questions related to the foreign trade and industrial policy. Yet, the Cold War from the small country's perspective was a different framework of explanation than the one established in superpowers. The Finnish shipbuilding history provided lenses that emphasised transnational cooperation over international competition, and national welfare alongside national security.

The Cold War Finland was located in the precarious zone of neutrality, where it could not even dream of being a military power. Finland was in between the East and West but not exactly in the middle of these two centres of power. The weight of the superpowers was inversely proportional to their distance from Finland. Finland advocated democratic capitalism and was thus inclined to lean towards the West, but the Soviet Union was close by and loomed large. The geopolitical context restricted the room to manoeuvre in foreign relations and domestic affairs, but simultaneously created a unique set of economic possibilities for the export-oriented industry.

The Cold War did not start Finnish shipbuilding, but the industrial expansion early in the Cold War was fuelled by the Soviet interests in using it to create economic dependencies. Simultaneously, the Western embargo decreased the alternatives of the Soviet ship buyers and made Finnish shipyards the best political and technological compromise for certain types of ships. The Finnish side recognised the risks of economic warfare but also the potential positive effects of economic interaction that demonstrated to the Soviet Union the benefits of the capitalist, sovereign, yet friendly, Finland.

While the expansion of the Finnish shipbuilding industry started as a result of the Soviet dominance over Finland during the war reparations, the Finnish governments, trade negotiators, and companies had agency in shaping the relationship to prevent the total political and economic dependency on the Soviet Union. The relationship between the Soviet Union and Finland, the nuclear power and a small country, was truly asymmetric, but the economic relations created mutual interdependencies that increased Finnish leverage to enact its own goals.

Another prime example of the Cold War effect in the Finnish shipbuilding industry was the dualistic foreign trade policy. The Finnish shipyards adapted to the polarised world order by adjusting their financing arrangements, business practices, and production structures in a way that counterbalanced each other. The co-existence of the three different markets—Western, Eastern, and domestic—provided the Finnish shipyards with advantages in political and technical negotiations. Different markets provided a counter-cyclical effect that smoothed out some of the market fluctuation and facilitated technological diversification and specialisation by increasing volume of special purpose vessels.

The Cold War remained cold in Europe, but it was a war. National security was a priority that dominated political decision-making. Through the Finnish shipbuilding history, though, the Cold War concerns over national security got diverse and nuanced meanings. In the small country, no organisation, no politician, was big enough to be interested only in the national security. In diplomatic interaction, foreign trade policy, and domestic industrial policy the national security was closely interwoven with questions of national welfare.

That coupling of security and welfare gave the Finnish shipbuilding political gravity. Shipyards were big employers whose performance had a direct impact on social stability and the lure of communism in the 1950s. The political corollaries of the shipyard employment justified the Cost Guarantee System in the 1960s, and the first direct state-aid schemes in the 1970s.

In the 1980s, the political focus turned from the maximal employment to the international competitiveness. The coupling of the Finnish–Soviet relations and shipyard employment was replaced by the coupling of industrial competitiveness in the integrating Europe and its contribution to the domestic welfare.

The shipbuilding industry was of course not the only industrial branch with national importance in Finland, but its role in the Finnish–Soviet relations, domestic employment, and export trade made it an appropriate political instrument for many purposes. Big, impressive, and expensive ships provided tools for the Finnish politicians to promote Finland as a modern industrial country; in the Finnish–Soviet and Finnish–American relations, certain exceptional vessels became objects that shaped Finland's position within the zone of neutrality; in the Finnish–EC relations, the passenger cruise ships provided a platform to negotiate Finland's part in the European integration.

The Finnish shipbuilding engineers had a predominantly apolitical identity, but they acquired intimate familiarity with the political meanings of big ships and shipbuilding in the Cold War context. That helped them to employ arguments of the Finnish–Soviet peaceful coexistence and social stability to advance their projects or to lobby for beneficial state regulation.

Finnish businessmen got often well along with the Soviets. Protracted negotiations could mean weeks or even months in Moscow, where the business meetings were enriched by various recreational activities and long dinners with complimentary drinks. But no one could possibly blame the leaders of the Finnish big business for sympathy for communist ideology. Instead of the friendship between Finland and the Soviet Union as such, they were interested in the business opportunities the friendly relations provided.

The shipbuilders understood the peculiarities of the Soviet shipbuilding market. The market was not determined by demand and supply, but the orders came from the state planning system. The central planning organisation was a bureaucratic machine, but it had human faces at the highest level of the hierarchy. The profit-driven companies learned how to negotiate with the centrally planned economy, how to provide solutions for its needs, and how to accommodate Soviet interests in security and prestige.

To improve their competitive position in the socialist market, the Finnish companies engaged in scientific-technical and industrial cooperation that from a contemporary perspective appears occasionally curious but had certain rationality in the historical context. What started as a corporate brand-building, had concrete technical contribution to the expertise and experience of the Finnish Arctic maritime cluster.

The Cold War was not a static context. Finnish shipbuilding first underwent a sea change from a small-scale domestic producer into an internationally notable shipbuilder in terms of volume and technical specialisation and then downscaled its production capacity at the end of the period. Yet, there was more than just the industrial change that comes under scrutiny here: it was also the change of the political and economic environment we need to pay attention to.

The Cold War circumstances stabilised a certain international order in Europe. The degree of political stability particularly in the Soviet relations was critical for Finland, which tried to negotiate its position between East and West. Simultaneously and separated from the Cold War framework, other processes such as technological competition, economic deregulation, globalisation of production chains, and European integration processes pushed the shipbuilding industry to change in order to survive. The constant tension between the aspiration for political stabilisation and the economic necessity to transform became one distinguishing characteristic of the Finnish Cold War shipbuilding.

A central element that provided the Finnish shipbuilding industry with a relative degree of stability in the European comparisons was the bilateral trade institutions with the Soviet Union. The clearing trade and payment system addressed the shortage of convertible currencies and external financing, and the future-oriented trade agreements provided the shipyards with predictability and possibility to create counter-cyclical effects by scheduling Western and Soviet orders.

In the Finnish foreign trade administration, the real and alleged benefits of bilateral trade to the Finnish shipbuilding became the most important reason to invest intellectual and monetary resources in the maintenance of the clearing trade and payment system. These bilateral institutions of trade and payments, which were originally neither a political choice nor a symbol of the political relationship, eventually became both. The clearing trade system did not secure the continuation, profitability, or stability of the Finnish–Soviet ship trade. Those benefits resulted from the political preferences, managerial practices, and environmental conditions. However, the fact that the industrial and political actors believed in these qualities made a difference. It translated the bilateral institutions into a promise of successful continuance of the Finnish–Soviet privileged ship trade in the future.

In the mid-1970s, the Finnish shipyards seemed to remain unaffected by the global shipyard crisis when the logic of the bilateral trade turned the rising oil prices into profits through the increased volume of Soviet orders. In its apogee, the Finnish shipbuilding industry appeared as profitable and stable; it gathered momentum from specialised practices and institutions, and enjoyed political support in foreign trade and domestic policy.

The end of the special trajectory of the Finnish Cold War shipbuilding was not a sudden event but a disintegration process that took place during the long 1980s, from the late 1970s to the early 1990s. The Soviet trade and the diversified production structure protected Finland against the first hit of the European shipyard crisis, but could not isolate the Finnish shipyards from other external jolts, the Soviet economic reformations, and the global price competition. The Finnish shipbuilding industry was forced to rationalise when the profitability and volumes of the Soviet orders declined at the same time when the price and subsidy competition in the Western market intensified.

This end process re-politicised some aspects in the Finnish Cold War shipbuilding that had established as ordinary, such as the prepayments in the Soviet trade and the no-state-aid policy in the Western trade. Interestingly, the more difficult the Soviet trade became, the more the shipyards and trade administration underlined the special role of Finnish shipbuilding in the Soviet market. The disparity between the experience and expectations grew larger towards the end of the Cold War.

Finlandisation as a systematic practice in Finland to avoid critical discussion about the Soviet Union made the reality look fuzzy. Even though everyone knew that the rhetoric of the Finnish–Soviet special friendship and future-oriented business relations was merely rhetoric, no one knew exactly where the line between the reality and the rhetoric was located. Even though the shipbuilding companies recognised the need to change at the turn of the 1980s, no one knew the schedule or the strategy on how to change. Finlandisation and institutional rigidities created a dense fog that covered the future perspectives and made the companies slow to determine a new course.

The history did not end at the end of the Cold War. The concrete building berths, the supply chains, and the technical expertise of the maritime cluster are still expressions of the past industrialisation.

A *Cold War History of Industrialisation* is not a comprehensive account of the Finnish shipbuilding industry. It has merely illuminated the Cold War industrialisation process from certain perspectives. But I hope it opens avenues for further research: a critical re-evaluation of the intermingling of geopolitics, economy, and technology in the Cold War and its legacy in the post-Cold War world.

# Bibliography

**Archival sources**

Aalto-yliopiston arkisto [Aalto University Archive], Espoo, Finland
    TKK Hallintokollegion pöytäkirjat [Administrative council of Helsinki University of Technology]
    Laivanrakennuksen/koneosaston osastokokoukset [Department of Mechanical Engineering]
Elinkeinoelämän Keskusarkisto [Central Archives for Finnish Business Records], ELKA, Mikkeli, Finland
    Collection of Laivateollisuus, LATE
    Collection of Suomen telakkateollisuusyhdistys [Finnish Shipyard Association], STTY
    Collection of Valmet
    Collection of Wärtsilä
    Collection of Wärtsilä Marine (WM)
Foreign Relation of the United States Series, FRUS
    Available: https://history.state.gov/historicaldocuments
Helsingin kaupungin arkisto [Helsinki City Archive] HCA, Helsinki, Finland
    Kaupunginvaltuuston pöytäkirjat [Records of Helsinki City Council]
    Kaupungin hallituksen pöytäkirjat [Records of the Helsinki City Board]
    Kaupunginjohtajien arkisto [Collections of the Mayors]
Library of Congress, Washington D.C., US
    ADSD Oral history collections
    Hearings
    Reports and studies
Liikenneviraston arkisto [Finnish Transport Agency's Archive] LVA, Helsinki, Finland
    Laivatoimisto [Ship office]
    Liikennetoimisto [Traffic office]
Meriteollisuus Ry:n arkisto [Archives of Finnish Maritime Industries] MTA, Helsinki, Finland
MIT Archive, Cambridge, MA, US
    Department of Ocean Engineering
    Ira Dyer Papers
    MIT Reports to President
National Archive, Foreign Office, London, UK
    Folder 371/176260

National Archive, NARA, Washington D.C., US
  USCG collection
National Security Archive, NSA, Washington D.C., US
  Electronic collections. http://nsarchive.gwu.edu.
Porvarillisen työn arkisto [Archives of the Organisations of the Finnish National
  Coalition Party], PTA, Espoo, Finland
President Gerald Ford Archive, GFA, Ann Arbor, MI, US
  Byron M. Cavaney Files 1973–1977
  Mark Austad, US Ambassador in Finland
  National Security Council NSC, Europe, Canada, and Ocean Affair
  Congressional Relations Office Max L. Friedersdorf
  Office of Editorial Staff, Charles McCall Director of the Research Office
  White House Central Files
  WHCF Foreign Affairs FO 2 Diplomatic Consular Relations
STX Turku Shipyard
  Collections
Suomen kansalliskirjasto, digitaaliset aineistot [National Library of Finland, digital
  collections]
  Presidentti Urho Kekkosen julkaistu tuotanto [Published writings of President
    Urho Kekkonen]
Suomen kansallisarkisto [National Archives of Finland], NA, Helsinki, Finland
  Atomienergianeuvottelukunta [Atom Energy Negotiation Board]
  Kauppa- ja teollisuusministeriö [Ministry of Trade and Industry], KTM
  Presidentti Mauno Koiviston kokoelma [Collection of President Mauno Koivisto]
  Valtionvarainministeriö [Ministry of Finance], VM
Suomen kansallisarkiston Turun toimipiste [National Archives of Finland in Turku],
  NA(T), Turku, Finland
  Ab Crichton-Vulcan Oy
Suomen Pankin arkisto [Bank of Finland Archive], SPA, Helsinki, Finland
  Idänkaupan osasto [Eastern Trade Department]
Tekniikan Museo [Museum of Technology] Helsinki, Finland
  Collection of Valmet Shipyard
Ulkoministeriön arkisto [Archive of the Finnish Ministry of Foreign Affairs],
  Helsinki, Finland
  TT-komitean pöytäkirjat [Records of Finnish-Soviet Scientific-technical coop-
    eration committee]
  Atomienergianeuvottelukunta [Atom Energy Committee]
  EY-EU Teollisuus [EC industry], signum 37.51
  Jäänmurtajat [Icebreakers] signum 83M
  Teollisuus-Suomi/Telakkateollisuus [Finnish Shipbuilding Industry], 1982–1987
  Ulkomaankauppa/NL [Foreign trade, USSR], signum 42.2
  Ulkomaankauppa ja ulkomaankauppapolitiikka, NL [Foreign Trade and Foreign
    Trade Policy, USSR] signum 58 B1
  Arktiset Alueet [Arctic Areas], signums 1300 & 1360
UPM Archive, UPMA, Valkeakoski, Finland
  Collection of Rauma-Repola
  Collection of Jouko Sere

Urho Kekkosen arkisto, UKA, [Archives of the President Urho Kekkonen], Orimat-
tila, Finland
  Matkat [Travels]
  Salaiset [Classified]
  Vierailut [Visits]
  Politiikka [Politics]
  Vuosikirjat [Year Books]
  Henkilökohtaiset [Personal]
USCG Archive, Washington D.C., US
  Cutters
  Icebreaking
  Reports
USCG Museum, New London, US
  Archival Collections on Cutters
Weber State University, Steward Library, Ogden, UT, US
  Collection of Mark Austad
Wärtsilä yritysarkisto [Wärtsilä Corporation Archive]
  Oy Wärtsilä Ab.n vuosikertomukset [Wärtsilä Corporation Annual Financial Reports]
Wärtsilä Marinen konkurssipesän arkisto [Wärtsilä Marine Bankrupt Estate's
Archive] WMkp, Helsinki, Finland


**Oral history**

*Interviews conducted by the author*

Interview G. Wilkman 16.1.2014.
Interview C. Landtman 21.1.2014, and 9.9.2014 (with Aaro Sahari).
Interview M. Saarikangas 5.2.2014.
Interview H. Eskelinen and K. Ketola 26.3.2014 (with Aaro Sahari).
Interview P. Jumppanen 23.1.2014.
Interview M. Niini 17.4.2014.
Interview Kari Holopainen 9.11.2010.
Interview P. Häkkinen 19.2.2014.
Interview L. Fagernäs 20.10.2010.
Interview M. Törmä 19.2.2014.
Interview O. Urvas 14.5.2014.
Interview P. Varsta 3.5.2016.


*Other oral history sources*

Oral history collection of clearing trade, collected from the Academy of Finland Research Project at Center for Markets in Transition CEMAT in Helsinki
School of Business. Interviewers Piia Heliste, Inkeri Hivrensalo, Riitta Koso-
nen, Antti Leivonen, Tuomas Vaaramo, 2001–2004, stored in National Archive,
Finland.
Oral history seminars for actors of the Finnish Cold War foreign affairs, organized
by REIMAG project, University of Helsinki, 2015–2017.

## Parliamentary documents

### Säännöskokoelman sopimussarja (SopS) [Finnish international treaties]

Suomen Tasavallan ja Sosialististen Neuvostotasavaltain Liiton välinen kauppasopimus [Finnish-Soviet trade agreement], SopS 13/1948.

Sopimus ystävyydestä, yhteistoiminnasta ja keskinäisestä avunannosta Suomen Tasavallan ja Sosialististen Neuvostotasavaltain Liiton välillä, YYA [Agreement on friendship, cooperation and mutual assistance FCMA], SopS 17/1948.

Sopimus tieteellis-teknillisestä yhteistoiminnasta Suomen tasavallan ja Sosialististen Neuvostotasavaltain Liiton välillä tehdyn sopimuksen voimaansaattamisesta [Agreement on Finnish-Soviet scientific-technical cooperation], SopS 30/1955.

Asetus Sosialististen Neuvostotasavaltain Liiton kanssa tehdyn pysyvän hallitusten välisen taloudellisen yhteistyökomission muodostamista koskevan sopimuksen voimaansaattamisesta [Founding of the Finnish-Soviet intergovernmental economic commission], SopS 45/1967.

Sopimus taloudellisen, teknisen ja teollisen yhteistyön kehittämisestä [Agreement on the development of economic, technical and industrial cooperation between Finland and the Soviet Union], SopS 64/1971.

Pitkän ajanjakson ohjelma kaupallis-taloudellisen, teollisen ja tieteellis-teknisen yhteistyön kehittämiseksi ja syventämiseksi Suomen ja SNTLn välillä vuoteen 1990 [Long-Term Programme on the development and intensification of the economic-technical and scientific-technical cooperation between Finland and the USSR], SopS 54/1977.

Asetus tullitariffeja ja kauppaa koskevan yleissopimuksen 6, 16, ja 23 artiklan tulkinnasta ja soveltamisesta tehdyn sopimuksen voimaansaattamisesta [Agreement on interpretation and application of Articles VI, XVI and XXIII of the general agreement on tariffs and trade], SopS 18/1980.

Asetus tullitariffeja ja kauppaa koskevan yleissopimuksen 6 artiklan soveltamisesta tehdyn sopimuksen voimaansaattamisesta [Agreement on implementation of Article VI of the general agreement on tariffs and trade], SopS 19/1980.

Suomen Tasavallan ja Sosialististen Neuvostotasavaltojen Liiton välisen kaupallis-taloudellisen, teollisen ja tieteellis-teknisen yhteistyön kehittämistä ja syventämistä koskevaan vuoteen 1990 ulottuvaan pitkän ajanjakson ohjelmaan liittyvä pöytäkirja [Revisal of the Long-Term Programme between Finland and the USSR], SopS 10/1981.

Ulkoasiainministeriön ilmoitus Suomen Tasavallan ja Sosialististen Neuvostotasavaltojen Liiton välisen kaupallis-taloudellisen, teollisen ja tieteellis-teknisen yhteistyön kehittämistä ja syventämistä koskevaan vuoteen 1990 ulottuvaan pitkän ajanjakson ohjelmaan liittyvän pöytäkirjan allekirjoittamisesta [Revisal of the Long-Term Programme], SopS 19/1988.

Suomen tasavallan ja Venäjän federaation välinen sopimus suhteiden perusteista [Trade treaty between Finland and the Russian Federation], SopS 63/1992.

Suomen tasavallan hallituksen ja Venäjän federaation hallituksen välinen sopimus kaupasta ja taloudellisesta yhteistyöstä [Treaty between the governments of Finland and the Russian Federation], SopS 70/1992.

### Säädöskokoelma (Säädk) [collection of acts and decrees]

Laki metalli- ja laivanrakennusteollisuuden tuotteiden viennin turvaamisesta eräissä tapauksessa [Act of securing the export of metal manufacturing and shipbuilding products], SäädK 636/1950.

Laki merenkulun edistämiseksi myönnettävistä verohuojennuksista [An Act of tax reliefs to seafaring], SäädK 554/1953.

Laki laivanrakennus- ja muun metalliteollisuuden tuotannon ja viennin edistämisestä [Act of supporting exports of shipbuilding and metal manufacturing], SäädK 445/1956.

Vientitakuulaki [An Act of export guarantees], SäädK 479/1962.

Laki merenkulun edistämiseksi myönnettävistä verohuojennuksista [Act of tax reliefs to seafaring], SäädK 229/1966.

Laki merenkulun edistämiseksi myönnettävistä verohuojennuksista [Act of tax reliefs to seafaring], SäädK 853/1970.

Laki alushankintoihin myönnettävistä valtiontakauksista [Act of state guarantees to ship purchases], SäädK 573/1972.

Laki vientitakuulain muuttamisesta [Amendment of export guarantee act], SäädK 22/1974.

Laki laivanvarustustoiminnan verohuojennuksista [Act of tax reliefs to shipping], SäädK 4/1978.

Laki merenkulun verohuojennuksista [Act of tax reliefs to seafaring], SäädK 433/1981.

Laki vientitakuulain muuttamisesta [Amendment of export guarantee act], SäädK 1106/1983.

Laki kotimaassa tapahtuvaan aluksen hankintaan myönnettävistä korkotukilainoista [Act of subsidised loans to domestic ship purchases], SäädK 1093/1985.

Laki laivanvarustamotoimintaa harjoittaneille yrityksille myönnettävistö valtiontakauksista annetun lain muuttamisesta [Act of state guarantees to Finnish shipping companies], SäädK 1094/1985.

Laki erään konsernijärjestelyn verohuojennuksista [Act of tax arrangements related to an industrial reorganization], SäädK 907/1986.

Laki laivanrakennus ja laivanvarustamotoimintaa harjoittaville yrityksille myönnettävistä valtiontakauksisra annetun lain muuttamisesta [Amendment of the export guarantee act], SäädK/1989.

***Muut valtiopäiväasiakirjat (VP) [Other Parliamentary documents]***

Hallituksen esitykset [Government proposals submitted to the Parliament], HE.

Kirjalliset kysymykset [written questions submitted by a Member of Parliament to a Minister and Minister's replies], KK.

Täysistuntopöytäkirjat [Records of plenary sessions], PTK.

Valtiontilintarkastajain kertomukset [Parliamentary auditors' reports].

**Court decisions**

Korkeimman oikeuden ratkaisut [Decisions of the Supreme Court], KKO.

**Committee reports and unpublished studies**

Katariina Koivumaa & Timo Valtonen, *Idänkaupan suurvallasta rivijäseneksi. Tutkimus Suomen ja Neuvostoliiton välisten kauppasuhteiden ympäristöstä* [From a Eastern trade superpower to a normal member. A study of the environment of the Finnish-Soviet trade] (Helsinki: Ulkopoliittinen instituutti, 1991), KTM Tutkimukset ja julkaisut, jotka eivät ole vapaakappalekirjastoissa [unpublished studies], Ucha:98, 1991, NA.

Korjaustelakkatyöryhmän raportti [Committee report of shipdocs for repairs], KTM työryhmä- ja toimikuntaraportteja, Ucc:29, 1988, NA.

K-takuukomitean mietintö 28:1976 [Cost-Guarantee Committee report]. Helsinki: Kauppa- ja teollisuusministeriön komitearaportit, 1976.

Laivaryhmän mietintö [Ship working group report], Kauppa- ja teollisuusministeriön työryhmä ja toimikuntaraportteja, Ucc:12, 1977, NA.

Laivatilaustyöryhmän muistio [Ship order Committee report 1983], Unpublished committee report, Valtionvarainministeriö 1:1983, NA.

Merenkulun toimintaedellytykset, tukipolitiikka ja sopeutustoimet. Taloudelliset ja talouspoliittiset katsaukset [Working group on the operating environment, subsidy policy and adjustment measures of maritime transport] 22:2012. Helsinki: Valtion-varainministeriö, 2012.

Merenkulun kehittämistyöryhmä 1988 [Working group for seafaring 1988]. Unpublished, KTM työryhmä- ja toimikuntaraportteja, UCC:29, 1988, NA.

Monitoimimurtajien hankinta ja kaupallinen toiminta, tarkastuskertomus, 43/2003 [Auditors' report of the procurement and use of multipurpose icebreakers]. Helsinki: Valtiontalouden tarkastusvirasto, 2003.

Raportti talousneuvostolle Suomen teollisen pohjan vahvistamisesta 1992 [Report about the development of the Finnish economic foundation], unpublished, Kauppa-ja teollisuusministeriön neuvottelukuntaraportteja 1989–1994, Uce: 12, NA.

Suomen teollisuuden kehitysmahdollisuuksia, komiteamietintö 25:1979 [Finnish in-dustry's developmental potentia, Committee report of industrial advisor board]. Helsinki: Kauppa- ja teollisuusministeriö 1979.

Telakkatoimikunnan mietintö, komiteamietintö 69:1977 [Shipyard Committee report, Ministry of Trade and Industry Committee reports]. Helsinki: Kauppa- ja teollisuusministeriö 1977.

Telakkatoimikunta 84, komiteamietintö 53:1984 [Shipyard committee 84 report]. Helsinki: Kauppa- ja teollisuusministeriö 1984.

Telakkateollisuustyöryhmä 1988 [Shipbuilding industry committee report 1988], unpublished, KTM työryhmä ja toimikuntaraportteja 1989: UCC:30, NA.

Telakkatukityöryhmän muistio 27:1989 [Committee report of the working group for shipyard subsidy]. Helsinki: Valtionvarainministeri, 1989.

Teollisuusneuvottelukunnan mietintö teollistumisen edellytyksistä ja toimenpiteistä sen edistämiseksi 4:1959 [Industrial advisory board Committee report about the preconditions and measures needed for advancing industrialisation]. Helsinki: Valtioneuvosto, 1959.

Teollisuusneuvottelukunnan linjauksia teollisuuden elvyttämiseksi ja rakenteen uudistamiseksi 1991 [Industrial advisory board report about the restructuring and rejuvenation of industry], unpublished, Kauppa- ja teollisuusministeriön neuvot-telukuntaraportteja 1989–1994, Uce: 12, NA.

TTT-koordinointityöryhmän muistio 1989 [Committee report of working group for industrial, technological and scientific cooperation]. Helsinki: Kauppa- ja teollisuusministeriö 1988.

Tutkimus Suomen laivanrakennusteollisuuden kansainvälisestä kilpailukyvystä [A study of the competitiveness of the Finnish shipbuilding industry]. Helsinki: SITRA, 1970.

Ulkomaalaisomistustyöryhmän muistio, Ulkomaisen sijoitustoiminnan säätely 1989 [Committee report of regulations of foreign investments 1989] unpublished, KTM työryhmä ja toimikuntaraportteja 1989: UCC:30, NA.

Vientiluottotoimikunnan mietintö, komiteamietintö 32:1976 [Committee of export credits report]. Helsinki: Kauppa- ja teollisuusministeriö 1976.
Vientitakuutoimikunnan mietintö, komiteamietintö 7:1962 [Committee of export guarantees report]. Helsinki, Kauppa- ja teollisuusministeriö 1962.

## Statistical collections, databases, and standards

Association of West European shipbuilders and ship repairers, Annual reports, AWES.
Lloyd's Register of Shipping, Shipbuilding returns 1952–1990, LRS.
Suomen Metalliteollisuusyhdistys, Metalliteollisuuden vuosikirjat 1964–2014 [Annual reports of Finnish metal manufacturing].
Central Statistical Office of Finland, Suomen virallinen tilasto 1900–1995 [Official Statistics of Finland], SVT.
Suomen kauppalaivastotietokanta [Finnish Mercantile Marine Database]. http://kauppalaiva.nba.fi/.
Toimialaluokitus määritelmineen 1988 [Standard industrial classification]. Helsinki: Central Statistical Office of Finland, 1988.
International Standard Industrial Classification of All Economic Activities. New York: United Nations, 1968.
Tullin ulkomaankauppatilastot [Foreign trade statistics of the Finnish Custom].

## Newspapers and magazines

*Aftonbladet*
*Arctic Passion*
*Chicago TribuneFinancial Times*
*Helsingin Sanomat (HS)*
*Ingeniøren*
*Kauppalehti*
*Navigator*
*OECD Observer*
*Official Journal of European Communities*
*Scandinavian Shipping Gazette*
*Suomen Kuvalehti (SK)*
*Suomenmaa*
*Talouselämä*
*Teknisk Tidskrift*
*Teknisk Ukeblad*
*Teknillinen Aikakauslehti*
*The Guardian*
*The New York Times*
*Turun Sanomat*
*Ulkomatala*
*Washington Post*
*Wärtsilä – Personnel magazine*

## Memoirs and diaries

Blomberg, Jaakko. *Vakauden kaipuu: Kylmän sodan loppu ja Suomi.* Helsinki: WSOY, 2011.

Derjabin, Juri. *Omalla nimellä. Reunamerkintöjä Juri Komissarovin kirjoihin ja omaan elämään.* Helsinki: Otava, 1997.

Fjodorov, Vladimir. *NKP:n Suomen osastolla 1954–1989.* Helsinki: Otava, 2001.

Haapavaara, Heikki & Martin Saarikangas. *Iso-Masa, laivanrakentaja.* Helsinki: Ajatus 2002.

Holopainen, Kari. *Orpo piru. Muistumia neuvostokaupasta ja vähän muustakin.* Helsinki: Opus Liberum, 2007.

J.K. *Paasikiven päiväkirjat 1944–1956 II*, edited by Yrjö Blomsted & Matti Klinge. Porvoo: WSOY, 1986.

Karjalainen, Ahti & Jukka Tarkka. *Presidentin Ministeri: Ahti Karjalaisen ura Urho Kekkosen Suomessa.* Helsinki: Otava, 1989.

Koivisto, Mauno. *Kaksi kautta I. Muistikuvia ja merkintöjä 1982–1994.* Helsinki: Kirjayhtymä, 1994.

Koivisto, Mauno. *Kaksi Kautta: II, Historian Tekijät.* Helsinki: Kirjayhtymä, 1995.

Koulumies, Jyrki. *Kohtalona Kostamus. Risto Kangas-Ikkalan muistelmat.* Helsinki: Siltala, 2012.

Laine, Pekka. *Minusta tuli musta-Pekka.* Tampere: Mediapinta, 2014.

Landtman, Christian. *Minnen från mina år vid Wärtsilä.* Helsinki: Self-published, 2011.

Lundelin, Viljo. *Laivanrakentajana vuosina 1945–1988.* Uusikaupunki: Uudenkaupungin sanomat, 1998.

Piskulov, Juri. *Näin teimme idänkauppaa.* Jyväskylä: Gummerrus, 2009.

*Urho Kekkosen päiväkirjat 1*, 1958–1962, edited by Juhani Suomi. Otava: Helsinki, 2001.

Tarkka, Jukka. "Suomettujan tunnustuksia." In *"Entäs kun tulee se yhdestoista?" Suomettumisen uusi historia*, edited by Johan Bäckman, 660–673. Helsinki: WSOY, 2001.

## Literature

Abbate, Janet. *Inventing the Internet.* Cambridge: MIT Press, 2000.

Adams, Gordon. *The Politics of Defence Contracting: The Iron Triangle.* New York; Transaction Books, 1982.

Aho, Mikko. "Creators of Ships and Welfare – Shipbuilders' Experiences in the 1960s–1980s." In *From shipyards to the Seven Seas. On Finnish Shipbuilding Industry*, edited by Sari Mäenpää, 140–165. Turku: Forum Marinum, 2018.

Alasuutari, Pertti. "Suunnittelutaloudesta kilpailutalouteen. Miten muutos oli ideologisesti mahdollinen?" *Yhteiskuntapolitiikka* 69:1 (2004): 3–16.

Alasuutari, Pertti. *Toinen tasavalta. Suomi 1946–1994.* Tampere: Vastapaino, 1996.

Alho, Kari, Osmo Forssell, Juhani Huttunen, Markku Kotilainen, Ilkka Luukkonen, Olli-Tapio Mattila, Jorma Moilanen, & Pentti Vartija. *Neuvostoliiton kauppa Suomen kansantaloudessa.* Helsinki: ETLA, 1986.

Andersen, Håkon With. "Producing Producers: Shippers, Shipyards and the Cooperative Infrastructure of the Norwegian Maritime Complex since 1850." In *World of Possibilities. Flexibility and Mass Production in Western Industrialisation*, edited by Charles F. Sabel & Jonathan Zeitlin, 461–500. Cambridge University Press, 1997.

Androsova, Tatjana: "Economic Interests in Soviet-Finnish Relations." In *The Flexible Frontier: Change and Continuity in Finnish-Russian Relations*, edited by Maria Lähteenmäki, 127–144. Helsinki: Aleksanteri Institute, 2007.

Androsova, Tatjana. "Economic Interest in Soviet Post-war Policy on Finland." In *Reassessing Cold War Europe*, edited by Sari Autio-Sarasmo and Katalin Miklóssy, 33–48. London: Routledge, 2011.

Androsova, Tatjana. "Kauppapolitiikka Suomen ja Neuvostoliiton suhteissa vuoden 1944 jälkeen." *Historiallinen aikakauskirja* 100:2 (2002): 152–158.

Asner, Glen R. "The Linear Model, the U.S Department of Defense, and the Golden Age of Industrial Research." In *The Science-Industry Nexus: History, Policy, Implications*, edited by Karl Grandin, Nina Wormbs, & Sven Widmalm, 3–30. Sagamore Beach: Science History Publications, 2004.

Aunesluoma, Juhana. *Vapaakaupan tiellä: Suomen kauppa- ja integraatiopolitiikka maailmansodista EU-aikaan.* Helsinki: SKS, 2011.

Autio-Sarasmo, Sari. "Knowledge through the Iron Curtain: Soviet Scientific-Technical Cooperation with Finland and West Germany." In *Reassessing Cold War Europe*, edited by Sari Autio-Sarasmo & Katalin Miklóssy, 66–82. London: Routledge, 2011.

Autio-Sarasmo, Sari. "Soviet Economic Modernisation and Transferring Technologies from the West." In *Modernisation in Russia since 1900*, edited by Markku Kangaspuro & Jeremy Smith, 105–107. Helsinki: SKS, 2006.

Autio-Sarasmo, Sari. "Technological Modernisation in the Soviet Union and Post-Soviet Russia: Practices and Continuities." *Europe-Asia Studies* 68:1 (2016): 79–96.

Autio-Sarasmo, Sari. "Transferring Western Knowledge to a Centrally Planned Economy: Finland and the Scientific-Technical Cooperation with the Soviet Union." In *Planning in Cold War Europe. Competition, Cooperation, Circulations (1950s-1870s)*, edited by Michel Christian, Sandrine Kott, & Ondrej Matejka, 143–164. Berlin: De Gruyter Oldenbourg, 2018.

Autio-Sarasmo, Sari & Katalin Miklóssy. "The Cold War from a New Perspective." Introduction to *Reassessing Cold War Europe*, edited by Sari Autio Sarasmo & Katalin Miklóssy, 1–15. London: Routledge, 2010.

Barr, William & Edward A. Wilson. "The Shipping Crisis in the Soviet Eastern Arctic at the Close of the 1983 Navigation Season." *Arctic* 38:1 (1985): 1–17.

Bergesen, Helge, Arild Moe, & Willy Østreng. *In Search of Oil and Security. Soviet Interests in the Barents Sea.* Lysaker: Fridtjof Nansen Institute, 1986.

Bergholm, Tapio. *Sopimusyhteiskunnan synty II. Hajaannuksesta tulopolitiikkaan Suomen Ammattiyhdistysten Keskusliitto 1956–1969.* Helsinki: SAK, 2007.

Berndtson, Erkki. "Finlandization: Paradoxes of External and Internal Dynamics." *Government and Opposition* 26:1 (1991): 21–33.

Björklund, Nils. *Valmet - asetehtaiden muuntuminen kansainväliseksi suuryhtiöksi.* Jyväskylä: Gummerrus, 1990.

Blomkvist, Pär & Arne Kaijser. "Introduktion – De osynliga systemen." In *Den konstruerade världen – Tekniska system i historiskt perspektiv*, edited by Pär Blomkvist & Arne Kaijser, 7–17. Stockholm: Brutus Östlings Bokförlag Symposion, 1998.

Bruno, Lars & Stig Tenold. "The Basis for South Korea's Ascent in the Shipbuilding Industry, 1970–1990." *The Mariner's Mirror* 97:3 (2011): 201–217.

Bukharin, Oleg. "Russia's Nuclear Icebreaker Fleet." *Science and Global Security* 14.1 (2006): 25–31.

Callon, Michel. "Techno-economic Networks and Irreversibility." *The Sociological Review* 38:S1 (1990): 132–161.

Capasso, Arturo, Carmen Gallucci & Matteo Rossi. "Standing the Test of Time. Does Firm Performance Improve with Age? An Analysis of the Wine Industry." *Business History* 57:7 (2015): 1037–1053.

Chandler, Alfred. *Scale and Scope: The Dynamics of Industrial Competition.* Cambridge: Harvard Business School 1990.

Cho, Sung & Michael Porter. "Changing Global Industry Leadership: The Case of Shipbuilding." In *Competition in Global Industries*, edited by Michael Porter, 541–567. Cambridge: Harvard Business Press, 1986.

Christensen, René Schrøder. "Skibsbygning og værftsanlæg – utviklingen af et tankskibsværft." In *Et stålskibsvært* ved Odende Kanal, edited by Jens Toftgaard, 323–363. Odense: Syydansk Universitetsforlag, 2016.

Coen, Ross. *Breaking Ice for Arctic Oil: The Epic Voyage of the SS Manhattan through the Northwest Passage*. Fairbanks: University of Alaska Press, 2012.

Davies, Peter. *Japanese Shipping and Shipbuilding in the Twentieth Century: The Writings of Peter N. Davies*. Kent: Global Oriental, 2009.

Dahl, Niklas. *"Länsikauppakin meille sentään jotakin merkitsee." Johann Nykopp Suomen Washingtoning –lähettiläänä 1951–1958*. Master's thesis, University of Turku, 2016.

Edwards, Paul & Gabrielle Hecht. "History and the Technopolitics of Identity: The Case of Apartheid South Africa." *Journal of Southern African Studies* 36:3 (2010): 619–639.

Eerola, Ville. *Kun rauta kelluu. Välähdyksiä suomalaisen meriteollisuuden vuosisadasta*. Helsinki: Meriteollisuus Ry, 2017.

*Entangled Geographies: Empire and Technopolitics in the Global Cold War*, edited by Gabrielle Hecht. Cambridge: MIT Press, 2011.

Eyres, David & George Bruce. *Ship Construction*. Oxford: Elsevier, 2012.

Fellman, Susanna. "Growth and Investment: Finnish Capitalism, 1850–2005." In *Creating Nordic Capitalism: The Development of a Competitive Periphery*, edited by Susanna Fellman, Martin Iversen, Hans Sjögren, and Lars Thue, 139–217. Palgrave Macmillan, 2008.

Fellman, Susanna. "Kilpailupolitiikka koordinoidussa markkinataloudessa. Kartelli- ja kilpailulainsäädäntö Suomessa 1958–1988 institutionaalistaloushistoriallisesta näkökulmasta." *Kansantaloudellinen Aikakauskirja* 106 (2010): 141–161.

Fellman, Susanna. "Suomen sotakorvaukset ja metalliteollisuus." In *Historiaa tutkimaan*, edited by Jorma O. Tiainen, Ilkka Nummela, & Jorma Tiainen, 317–331. Jyväskylä: Atena, 1996.

Ferreiro, Larrie D. *Bridging the Seas: The Rise of Naval Architecture in the Industrial Age, 1800–2000*. Cambridge: MIT Press, 2020.

*Finnish-Soviet Economic Relations*, edited by Kari Möttölä, O.N. Bykov, & I.S. Korolev. London: Macmillan Press, 1983.

Forsberg, Tuomas & Matti Pesu. "The 'Finlandisation' of Finland: The Ideal Type, the Historical Model, and the Lessons Learnt." *Diplomacy & Statecraft* 27:3 (2016): 473–495.

Forsén, Björn, Annette Forsén, & Seppo Sarelius. *Saksan ja Suomen salainen sukellusveneyhteistyö*. Porvoo: WSOY, 1999.

Fridlund, Mats. "De nationalistiska systemen: konstruktion av teknik och svenskhet kring sekelskiftet 1900," In *Den konstruerade världen – Tekniska system i historiskt perspektiv*, edited by Pär Blomkvist & Arne Kaijser, 77–103. Stockholm: Brutus Östlings Bokförlag Symposion, 1998.

Fritzsche, Peter. *A Nation of Fliers: German Aviation and the Popular Imagination*. Cambridge: Harvard University Press, 1992.

Fukasaku, Yukiko. *Technology and Industrial Growth in Pre-war Japan: The Mitsubishi-Nagasaki Shipyard 1884–1934*. London: Routledge, 2005.

Gaddis, John Lewis. *We Now Know: Rethinking Cold War History*. Oxford University Press, 1997.

Gagliardone, Iginio. "A Country in Order": Technopolitics, Nation Building, and the Development of ICT in Ethiopia." *Information Technologies & International Development* 10:1 (2014): 3–19.

Galison, Peter. "The Many Faces of Big Science." *Introduction to Big Science. The Growth of Large-Scale Research*, edited by Peter Galison & Bruce Hevly, 1–17. Stanford: Stanford University Press, 1992.

Gavin, Francis J. *Nuclear Statecraft: History and Strategy in America's Atomic Age.* Ithaca: Cornell University Press, 2012.

Gärdebo, Johan. "Environing Technology: Swedish Satellite Remote Sensing in the Making of Environment 1969–2001." PhD diss., KTH Royal Institute of Technology, 2019.

Gilley, Bruce. "Not so Dire Straits: How the Finlandisation of Taiwan Benefits US Security." *Foreign Affairs* 89 (2010): 44–60.

Gorbačev, Û.N. *Sotrudničestvo SSSR I Finlândii V Oblasti Sudostroeniâ. Suomalais-neuvostoliittolainen yhteistyö laivanrakennuksen alalla.* Leningrad: Sudostroenie, 1990.

Gustafson, Thane. *Crisis amid Plenty: The Politics of Soviet Energy under Brezhnev and Gorbachev.* Princeton, NJ: Princeton University Press, 2014.

Haavikko, Paavo. *Wärtsilä 1834–1984: Wärtsilä-yhtiön ja siihen liitettyjen yritysten kehitysvaiheita kansainvälistyväksi monialayritykseksi.* Helsinki: Wärtsilä, 1984.

Hanhimäki, Jussi. "Henry Kissinger: Vision or Status Quo?" In *Visions of the End of the Cold War in Europe, 1945–1990*, edited by Frederic Bozo, Marie-Pierre Rey, N. Piers Ludlow, and Bernd Rother, 193–203. New York: Berghahn Books, 2012.

Hanhimäki, Jussi. "Non-aligned to What? European Neutrality and the Cold War." In *Neutrality and Neutralism in the Global Cold War. Between or within the Blocs?* edited by Sandra Bott, Jussi Hanhimaki, Janick Schaufelbuehl, & Marco Wyss, 31–46. London: Routledge, 2016.

Hanhimäki, Jussi. "Self-Restraint as Containment: United States' Economic Policy, Finland, and the Soviet Union, 1945–1953." *The International History Review* 17:2 (1995): 287–305.

Hanson, Philip. *The Rise and Fall of the Soviet Economy: An Economic History of the USSR 1945–1991*, first ed. 2003. London: Routledge, 2014.

Hanson, Philip. "The Soviet Union's Acquisition of Western Technology after Stalin: Some Thoughts of People and Connections." In *Reassessing Cold War Europe*, edited by Sari Autio Sarasmo & Katalin Miklóssy, 16–32. London: Routledge, 2010.

Haraguchi, Takeshi & Kazuya Sakurada, "The Lower Labour Market and the Development of the Post-war Japanese Shipbuilding Industry." In *Shipbuilding and Ship Repair Workers around the World: Case Studies 1950–2010*, edited byRaquel Varela, Hugh Murphy, & Marcel van der Linden, 591–614. Amsterdam: Amsterdam University Press, 2017.

Harki, Ilmari. *Sotakorvausten aika.* Jyväskylä: Gummerrus, 1971.

Häikiö, Martti. *Nokia oyj:n historia: Sturm und Drang. Suurkaupoilla eurooppalaiseksi elektroniikkayritykseksi 1983–1991.* Helsinki: Edita, 2001.

Häikiö, Martti. *Nokia Oyj:n historia. 1. Fuusio. Yhdistymisten kautta suomalaiseksi monialayritykseksi 1865–1982.* Helsinki: Edita, 2001.

Hecht, Gabrielle. *The Radiance of France: Nuclear Power and National Identity after World War II.* Cambridge: MIT Press, 1998.

Hecht, Gabrielle & Paul N. Edwards. *The Technopolitics of Cold War: Towards a Trans-regional Perspective.* Washington, D.C.: American Historical Association, 2007.

Heikkinen, Sakari. *Paper for the World: The Finnish Paper Mill's Association - Finnpap 1918–1996.* Helsinki: Otava, 2000.

Heikkinen, Sakari. "Sotakorvaukset ja Suomen kansantalous." In *Suomen sotakorvaukset,* edited by Hannu Rautkallio, 91–115. Helsinki: Paasilinna, 2014.

Heikkinen, Sakari & Heikki Tiihonen. *Valtiovarainministeriön historia: 3. Hyvinvoinnin turvaaja: 1966–2009.* Helsinki: Edita, 2010.

Helgesson, Claes-Fredrik. *Making a Natural Monopoly. The Configuration of a Techno-Economic Order in Swedish Telecommunications.* Diss., Stockholm School of Economics, Stockholm, 1999.

Hentilä, Seppo. "Living Next Door to the Bear: How did Finland Survive the Cold War?" *Historiallinen aikakauskirja* 2 (1998): 129–136.

Herranen, Timo. *Valtion raha vauhditti: Suomen erityisrahoituksen historia.* Helsinki: Edita, 2009.

Hirsh, Richard & Benjamin Sovacool. "Technological Systems and Momentum Change: American Electric Utilities, Restructuring, and Distributed Generation." *The Journal of Technology Studies* 32:2 (2006): 72–85.

Hirvensalo, Inkari. *Suomen ja SNTL:n välinen clearing-maksujärjestelmä.* Helsinki: Suomen Pankki, 1979.

Hjerppe, Riitta. "Finland's Foreign Trade and Trade Policy in the 20th Century." *Scandinavian Journal of History* 18:1 (1993): 57–76.

Hjerppe, Riitta & Jukka Jalava. "Economic Growth and Structural Change: A Century and a Half of Catching up." In *The Road to Prosperity: An Economic History of Finland,* edited by Jari Ojala, Jari Eloranta, & Jukka Jalava, 33–64. Helsinki: SKS, 2006.

Holopainen, Kari. "Suomen ja Neuvostoliiton välisen kaupan toimintaperiaatteet ja kaupan kehitys." *Kansantaloudellinen aikakauskirja* 3 (1981): 306–325.

Honkapohja, Seppo, E.A. Koskela, Willi Leibfritz & Roope Uusitalo. *Economic Prosperity Recaptured. The Finnish Path from Crisis to Rapid Growth.* Cambridge: MIT Press, 2009.

Horn, Tankmar. "Varustamoelinkeino ja telakkateollisuus – kaksi elinkeinoa, yhteiset edut." In *Kauppatienä meri. Suomen varustamoyhdistys 1932–1982,* edited by Heikki Päivike, 62–71. Helsinki: Suomen varustamoyhdistys, 1982.

Högselius, Per. "Lost in Translation? Science, Technology and the State since the 1970s." In *Science for Welfare and Warfare: Technology and State Initiative in Cold War Sweden,* edited by Per Lundin, Niklas Stenlås, & Johan Gribbe, 251–274. Sagamore Beach: Science History Publications, 2010.

Hughes, Thomas. *Networks of Power: Electrification in Western Society, 1880–1930.* Baltimore, MA: Johns Hopkins University, 1983.

Hughes, Thomas. "Regional Technological Style." In *Technology and Its Impact on Society: Symposium* No. 1, 1977, 211–234, Stockholm, 1979.

Hughes, Thomas. *Rescuing Prometheus: Four Monumental Projects That Changed the World.* New York: Pantheon, 1998.

Hughes, Thomas. "The Seamless Web: Technology, Science, etcetera, etcetera." *Social Studies of Science* 16:2 (1986): 281–292.

Hughes, Thomas. "The Dynamics of Technological Change: Salients, Critical Problems and Industrial Revolutions." In *Technology and Enterprise in a Historical Perspective,* edited by Giovanni Dosi, Renato Giannetti, & Pierangelo Maria Toninelli, 97–118. Oxford University Press, 1992.

Hughes, Thomas. "The Evolution of Large Technological Systems." In *The Social Construction of Technological Systems: New Directions in the Sociology and History of*

Technology, edited by Wieber Bijker; Thomas Hughes, & Trevor Pinch, first ed., 1987, 45–76. Cambridge: MIT Press, 2012.

Hughes, Thomas. "Technological momentum." In Technology and Society. Building Our Sociotechnical Future, edited by Deborah Johnson & Jameson Wetmore, 141–150. Cambridge: MIT press, 2009.

Hukkinen, Juhana. "Suomen vientimenestys Neuvostoliiton markkinoilla." Kansantaloudellinen aikakauskirja 3 (1990): 268–284.

Id, Kalle & Bruce Peter. Innovation and Specialisation. The Story of Shipbuilding in Finland. Nautilus Forlag: Copenhagen, 2017.

Ihamuotila, Jaakko. "Cooperation from the Company Point of View." In Finnish-Soviet Economic Relations, edited by Kari Möttölä, O.N. Bykov, & I.S. Korolev. London: Macmillan Press, 1983.

Inboden, Will. "Is Finland Rejecting 'Finlandization'." Foreign Policy (December 2014).

Inozemtsev, N.N. "Introduction." In Finnish-Soviet Economic Relations, edited by Kari Möttölä, N. Bykov, & I.S. Korolev, XIX–XXI. London: Macmillan Press, 1983.

Jakobson, Max. Finland in the New Europe. Washington, D.C.: CSIS, 1998.

Jensen-Eriksen, Niklas. "A Potentially Crucial Advantage." Revue économique 64: 6 (2013): 1085–1104.

Jensen-Eriksen, Niklas. "Business, Economic Nationalism and Finnish Foreign Trade during the 19th and 20th Centuries." Revue Française d'Histoire Économique-The French Economic History Review 3 (2015): 40–57.

Jensen-Eriksen, Niklas. "CoCom and Neutrality: Western Export Control Policies, Finland and the Cold War, 1949–58." In Reassessing Cold War Europe, edited by Sari Autio Sarasmo & Katalin Miklóssy, 49–65. London: Routledge: London, 2010.

Jensen-Eriksen, Niklas. "Industrial Diplomacy and Economic Integration: The Origins of All-European Paper Cartels, 1959—72." Journal of Contemporary History 46:1 (2011): 179–202.

Jensen-Eriksen, Niklas. Läpimurto: Metsäteollisuus kasvun, integraation ja kylmän sodan Euroopassa 1950–1973. Helsinki: SKS, 2007.

Jensen-Eriksen, Niklas. "Lost at Sea: Finnish Government, Shipping Companies and the United Nations Embargo against China during the 1950s." Scandinavian Journal of History 38:5 (2013): 568–589.

Jensen-Eriksen, Niklas. "The First Wave of the Soviet Oil Offensive: The Anglo-American Alliance and the Flow of 'Red Oil' to Finland during the 1950s." Business History 49:3 (2007): 348–366.

Jensen-Eriksen, Niklas. "Telakkateollisuus ja kylmä sota." In Suomen sotakorvaukset, edited by Hannu Rautkallio, 212–247. Helsinki: Paasilinna, 2014.

Jensen-Eriksen, Niklas. "The Northern Front in the Technological Cold War: Finland and East-West Trade in the 1970s and 1980s." Journal of Cold War Studies 21:4 (2019): 150–174.

Jensen-Eriksen, Niklas & Jari Ojala. "Tackling Market Failure or Building a Cartel? Creation of an Investment Regulation System in Finnish Forest Industries." Enterprise & Society 16:3 (2015): 521–555.

Johansen, Hans Chr. "International søfart mellen verdenskrisen og 1960'ernes højkonjunktur." In Et stålskibsvært ved Odende Kanal, edited by Jens Toftgaard, 267–291. Odense: Syydansk Universitetsforlag, 2016.

Johnman, Lewis & Hugh Murphy. British Shipbuilding and the State since 1918: A Political Economy of Decline. University of Exeter Press, 2002.

Josephson, Paul. Red Atom: Russia's Nuclear Power Program from Stalin to Today. University of Pittsburgh Press, 2005.

Josephson, Paul. *The Conquest of the Russian Arctic.* Cambridge: Harvard University Press 2014.

Judt, Tony. *Postwar: A History of Europe Since 1945.* London: Vintage Books, 2010.

Jussila, Osmo, Seppo Hentilä, & Jukka Nevakivi. *From Grand Duchy to a Modern State: A Political History of Finland since 1809.* London: C. Hurst & Co. Publishers, 1999.

Juntunen, Tapio. "Helsinki Syndrome: The Parachronistic Renaissance of Finlandization in International Politics." *New Perspectives: Interdisciplinary Journal of Central & East European Politics & International Relations* 25:1 (2017): 55–83.

Kaataja, Sampsa. "Expert Groups Closing the Divide. Estonian-Finnish Computing Cooperation since the 1960s." In *Beyond the Divide. Entangle Histories of The Cold War Europe,* edited by Simo Mikkonen & Pia Koivunen, 101–120. New York: Berghahn Books, 2015.

Kallinen, Tauno. "Suomen ja itäryhmän maiden välinen metalliteollisuustuotteiden ulkomaankauppa 1954–1962." In *Metalliteollisuus Suomen kansantaloudessa,* 223–242. Helsinki: Taloudellinen tutkimuskeskus, 1963.

Kallioinen, Mika, Jarkko Keskinen, Liisa Lähteenmäki, Tapani Paavonen, & Kari Teräs. "Kilpailun voittokulku: Kartelleista ja säännöstelystä globaaliin markkinatalouteen." In *Valta Suomessa,* edited by Petteri Pietikäinen, 56–78. Helsinki: Gaudeamus, 2010.

Kansikas, Suvi. "Balancing between Moscow and Brussels: Finland's Integration Policy Towards the EC and Its Political Constraints." In *Northern Europe in the Cold War, 1965–1990. East-West Interactions of Trade, Culture and Security,* edited by Poul Villaume, Ann-Marie Ekengren, & Rasmus Mariager, 81–103. Turku: Kikimora Publications, 2016.

Kansikas, Suvi. "Dismantling the Soviet Security System. Soviet–Finnish Negotiations on Ending Their Friendship Agreement, 1989–91." *The International History Review* 42:1 (2017): 1–22.

Kansikas, Suvi. "Room to Maneoevre? National Interests and Coalition-Building in The CMEA, 1969–74." In *Reassessing Cold War Europe,* edited by Sari Autio Sarasmo & Katalin Miklóssy, 193–209. Routledge: London, 2010.

Kansikas, Suvi. *Socialist Countries Face the European Community: Soviet-bloc Controversies over East-West Trade.* Frankfurt am Main: Peter Lang GmbH, 2014.

Kaukiainen, Yrjö. "Coal and Canvas: Aspects of the Competition between Steam and Sail, c. 1870–1914." In *Sail and Steam, Selected Maritime Writings of Yrjö Kaukiainen,* edited by Lars Scholl & Merja-Liisa Hinkkanen. SG John's: International Maritime Economic History Association, 2004.

Karlsson, Tobias. "From Boom to Bust. Kockums, Malmö (Sweden), 1950–1986." In *Shipbuilding and Ship Repair Workers around the World: Case Studies 1950–2010,* edited by Varela, Raquel, Hugh Murphy, & Marcel van der Linden, 143–164. Amsterdam University Press, 2017.

Kaukiainen, Yrjö. "Modernization of Finnish Coastal Shipping and Railway Competition c. 1830–1913." In *Sail and Steam, Selected Maritime Writings of Yrjö Kaukiainen,* edited by Lars U. Scholl & Merja-Liisa Hinkkanen, 79–90. St. John's: International Maritime Economic History Association, 2004.

Kaukiainen, Yrjö. "The Transition from Sail to Steam in Finnish Shipping, 1850–1914." *Scandinavian Economic History Review* 28:2 (1980): 161–184.

Kaukiainen, Yrjö. *The History of Finnish Shipping.* London: Routledge, 1993.

Kaukiainen, Yrjö. "Tons and Tonnages: Ship Measurement and Shipping Statistics, c. 1870–1980." *International Journal of Maritime History* 7:1 (1995): 29–56.

Kaukiainen, Yrjö. *Ulos Maailmaan! Suomalaisen merenkulun historia.* Helsinki: SKS, 2008.

Kaukiainen, Yrjö & Pirkko Leino-Kaukiainen. *Navigare necesse: Merenkulkulaitos 1917–1992.* Helsinki: Merenkulkuhallitus, 1992.

*Kauppa ja kansojen etu. Neuvostoliiton ja Suomen kauppasuhteiden juhlakirja.* Jyväskylä: Gummerrus, 1987.

Kähönen, Aappo. "Veteen piirretty viiva. Neuvostoliiton ja Suomen suhteet esimerkkinä kylmästä sodasta." *Historiallinen aikakauskirja* 100:2 (2002): 159–166.

Kähönen, Aappo. *The Soviet Union, Finland and the Cold War: The Finnish Card in Soviet Foreign Policy, 1956–1959.* Helsinki: SKS, 2006.

Kekkonen, Urho. *Onko maallamme malttia vaurastua,* second ed. Helsinki: Otava, 1952.

Kemppi, Heikki & Juha Tervonen. *Merenkulkuelinkeinon tuet ja taloudelliset vaikutukset.* Liikenneministeriön julkaisuja 17. Helsinki: Ministry of Transportation, 1999.

Keränen, Seppo. *Moskovan Tiellä: Urho Kekkonen Ja Neuvostoliitto 1945–1980.* Helsinki: Otava, 1990.

Keskinen, Tuomas. *Idänkauppa: 1944–1987.* Helsinki: Kauppalehti, 1987.

Kettunen, Pauli. *Globalisaatio ja kansallinen Me: Kansallisen katseen historiallinen kritiikki.* Tampere: Vastapaino, 2008.

Kettunen, Pauli. *Historia petollisena liittolaisena. Näkökulmia työväen, työelämän ja hyvinvointivaltion historiaan.* Helsinki: Työväen historian ja perinteen tutkimuksen seura, 2015.

Kettunen, Pauli. "The Transnational Construction of National Challenges: The Ambiguous Nordic Model of Welfare And Competitiveness." In *Beyond Welfare State Models: Transnational Historical Perspectives on Social Policy,* edited by Pauli Kettunen & Klaus Petersen, 16–40. Cheltenham: Edward Elgar Publishing, 2011.

Kiander, Jaakko. *1990-luvun talouskriisi. Suomen Akatemian tutkimusohjelma: Laman opetukset. Suomen 1990-luvun kriisin syyt ja seuraukset.* Helsinki: Valtion taloudellinen tutkimuskeskus VATT, 2001.

Kivilahti, Terhi & Jouko Rautava. "New Framework for Trade between Finland and the Soviet Union." *Bank of Finland Bulletin* 12 (1990): 6–10.

Klinge, Matti. "Ecce Finnia Tridentem! - Tässä Suomi valtikkasi!" In *"Entäs kun tulee se yhdestoista?" Suomettumisen uusi histori,* edited by Johan Bäckman, 23–56. Helsinki: WSOY, 2001.

Kochetkova, Elena. *The Soviet Forestry Industry in the 1950s and 1960s: A Project of Modernisation and Technology Transfer from Finland.* Diss., University of Helsinki, 2017.

Kohvakka, Mikko. "Science, Technology and Changing Power Relations: The Negotiation Process of the Agreement on Finnish-Soviet Scientific-Technical Cooperation, 1955." *Scandinavian Journal of History* 36:3 (2011): 349–370.

Koivumaa, Katariina & Timo Valtonen. *Suomen Neuvostoliiton kauppa ja muuttuva ympäristö.* Helsinki: Ulkopoliittinen instituutti & Neuvostoliittoinstituutti, 1990.

Korhonen, Vesa, Seija Lainela & Paula Lähdesmäki. *Neuvostotalous muutoksessa.* Helsinki: Suomen Pankki, 1990.

Kuisma, Markku. "Government Action, Cartels, and National Corporations-the Development Strategy of a Small Peripheral Nation during the Period of Crisis and Economic Disintegration in Europe (Finland 1918–1938)." *Scandinavian Economic History Review* 41:3 (1993): 242–268.

Kuisma, Markku. *Kylmä sota kuuma öljy. Neste, Suomi ja kaksi Eurooppaa.* WSOY: Porvoo, 1997.

Kuisma, Markku. *Kahlittu raha, kansallinen kapitalismi. Kansallis-Osake-Pankki 1940–1995.* Helsinki: SKS, 2004.

Kuorelahti, Elina. "Boom, Depression and Cartelisation: Swedish and Finnish Timber Export Industry 1918–1921." *Scandinavian Economic History Review* 63:1 (2015): 45–68.

Kuusikko, Kirsi. "Yksityisoikeudellinen ja julkisoikeudellinen luottamuksensuoja – eräitä Wärtsilä Meriteollisuus –tapauksen herättämiä mietteitä." *Defensor Legis* 6 (1999): 1027–1044.

Kuusterä, Antti & Juha Tarkka. *Suomen Pankki 200 vuotta II. Parlamentin pankki.* Helsinki: Otava, 2012.

Lainela, Seija. "Neuvostoliiton ulkomaankauppajärjestelmän uudistus ja sen vaikutukset clearing-kauppaan." In *Neuvostotalous muutoksessa*, edited by Vesa Korhonen, Seija Lainela, & Paula Lähdemäki. Helsinki: Bank of Finland, 1990.

Landtman, Christian. *The Development and Future of Operation in Ice and of Icebreaking Research.* Paper presented at the seventh International Conference on Port and Ocean Engineering under Arctic Conditions in Helsinki April 5–7, 1983.

Landtman, Christian. "Technische Gesichtspunkte über modern grosse Eisbrecher." *Jarbuch der Schiffbautechnischen Gesellschaft* 55. Berlin: Springer-Verlag, 1961.

Laquer, Walter. "Europe: The Specter of Finlandisation." *Commentary* 64 (1977): 37–41.

Laurila, Juhani. *Finnish-Soviet Clearing Trade and Payment System: History and Lessons.* Helsinki: Bank of Finland, 1995.

Leslie, Stuart. *The Cold War and American Science: The Military-Industrial-Academic Complex at MIT and Stanford.* New York: Columbia University Press, 1993.

Linnamo, Jussi & Tauno Kallinen. "Itäryhmän maiden metalliteollisuustuotanto ja metalliteollisuustuotteiden ulkomaankauppa." In *Metalliteollisuus Suomen kansantaloudessa*, 205–222. Helsinki: Taloudellinen tutkimuskeskus, 1963.

Lorenz, Edward. *Economic Decline in Britain. The Shipbuilding Industry, 1890–1970.* Oxford: Clarendon Press, 1991.

Lundin, Per & Niklas Stenlås. "Technology, State Initiative and National Myths in Cold War Sweden: An Introduction." In *Science for Welfare and Warfare: Technology and State Initiative in Cold War Sweden*, edited by Per Lundin, Niklas Stenlås, & Johan Gribbe, 1–33. Science History Publications: Sagamore Beach 2010.

Majander, Mikko. *Paasikivi, Kekkonen ja avaruuskoira.* Helsinki: Siltala, 2010.

Majander, Mikko. "The Limits of Sovereignty: Finland and the Question of the Marshall Plan in 1947." *Scandinavian Journal of History* 19:4 (1994): 309–326.

Majchrzak, Sarah Graber. "The Gdansk Shipyard. Production Regime and Workers' Conflict in the 1970s and 1980s in the People's Republic of Poland." In *Shipbuilding and Ship Repair Workers around the World: Case Studies 1950–2010*, edited by Raquel Varela, Hugh Murphy, & Marcel van der Linden, 365–396. Amsterdam University Press, 2017.

Malinen, Pasi. *Ostaa, Myy, vaihtaa ja valmistaa - Tapaustutkimus telakkateollisuudesta, telakan ja telakkatoimittajan välisestä vaihdannasta.* Turku School of Economics and Business Administration, 1998.

Malinen, Pasi. "Telakkatoimittaja ja telakka. Suhde eri ajanjaksoina." In *Tuotantotavan muutos Suomen laivarakennuksessa*, edited by Heikki Leimu & Juha Pusila, 126–165. Turku School of Economics and Business Administration, 1995.

Malone, Paul. "Finlandization as a Method of Living Next Door to Russia." *International Perspectives: The Canadians Journal on World Affairs* 10/7 (1981): 20–23.

Matala, Saara. "Idänkauppa oli varmaa mutta sitten se loppui." *Historiallinen Aikakauskirja* 2 (2012): 188–203.

Matala, Saara & Aaro Sahari. "Small Nation, Big Ships Winter Navigation and Technological Nationalism in a Peripheral Country, 1878–1978." *History and Technology* 33:2 (2017): 220–248.

Mattson, Esa. *Suomen idänkauppaneuvottelut 1950–1965. Telakkateollisuuden idänvienti, ulkomaankauppahallinto ja valtionhallinto.* Master's thesis, University of Helsinki, 1998.

Maude, George. "The Further Shores of Finlandisation." *Cooperation and Conflict* 17:1 (1982): 3–16.

McGovern, Tom. "Why do Successful Companies Fail? A Case Study of the Decline of Dunlop." *Business History* 49:6 (2007): 886–907.

MacKenzie, Donald. *Inventing Accuracy: A Historical Sociology of Nuclear Missile Guidance.* Cambridge: MIT Press, 1990.

McLauchlan, Gregory & Gregory Hooks. "Last of the Dinosaurs? Big Weapons, Big Science, and the American State from Hiroshima to the End of the Cold War." *The Sociological Quarterly* 36:4 (1995): 749–776.

McKenzie, Francine. "GATT and the Cold War: Accession Debates, Institutional Development, and the Western Alliance, 1947–1959." *Journal of Cold War Studies* 10:3 (2008): 78–109.

Meronen, Mikko. "Shipbuilding and Engineering Workshops in Turku 1800–1880." In *From Shipyards to the Seven Seas. On Finnish shipbuilding industry*, edited by Sari Mäenpää, 28–73. Turku: Forum Marinum, 2018.

*Metalliteollisuus Suomen kansantaloudessa.* Helsinki: Taloudellinen tutkimuskeskus, 1963.

Michelsen, Karl-Erik. *Viides sääty: insinöörit suomalaisessa yhteiskunnassa.* Helsinki: Suomen historiallinen seura, 1999.

Michelsen, Karl-Erik & Tuomo Särkikoski. *Suomalainen Ydinvoimalaitos.* Helsinki: Edita, 2005.

Michelsen, Karl-Erik. "Sotakorvaukset: Suuren teollisen projektin anatomia." In *Suomen sotakorvaukset*, edited by Hannu Rautkallio, 188–211. Helsinki: Paasilinna, 2014.

Mikkonen, Simo & Pia Koivunen. "Beyond the Divide." Introduction to *Beyond the Divide: Entangled Histories of Cold War Europe*, edited by Simo Mikkonen & Pia Koivunen, 1–19. New York: Berghahn, 2015.

Mitrunen, Matti. "Essays on the Political Economy of Development." PhD diss., Department of Economics, Stockholm University, 2019.

Moilanen, Teppo. "Uusi junankuljetusmetoodi" Valtionrautateiden ensimmäiseen sähköveturihankintaan johtaneista teknillisistä ja poliittisista tekijöistä." *Tekniikan Waiheita* 34:1 (2014): 43–62.

Murphy, Hugh. "Labour in the British Shipbuilding and Ship Repairing Industries in the Twentieth Century." In *Shipbuilding and Ship Repair Workers around the World: Case Studies 1950–2010*, edited by Varela, Raquel, Hugh Murphy, & Marcel van der Linden, 47–116. Amsterdam University Press, 2017.

Myllylä, Martti. "Konepajat ennen itsenäisyyden aikaa." In *Navis Fennica 3*, edited by Erkki Riimala, 20–35. Porvoo: WSOY, 1994.

Myllylä, Martti. "Venäjän laivatilaukset." In *Navis Fennica 3*, edited by Erkki Riimala, 36–54. Porvoo: WSOY, 1994.

Myllyntaus, Timo. "Design in Building an Industrial Identity: The Breakthrough of Finnish Design in the 1950s and 1960s." *Icon* 16 (2010): 201–225.

Napolitano, Maria Rosaria, Vittoria Marino, & Jari Ojala. "In Search of an Integrated Framework of Business Longevity." *Business History* 57:7 (2015): 955–969.

Nelson, Paul Henry. *Soviet-Finnish Relations: Finlandization or fraternization?* Master's thesis, Naval Postgraduate School, Monterey, California, 1980.

Nevakivi, Jukka. *Miten Kekkonen pääsi valtaan ja Suomi suomettui.* Helsinki: Otava, 1996.

Niemelä, Jukka. "Miksi telakoilla ei enää lakkoilla vanhaan malliin?" In *Tieteen boheemi - Boheemin tiede*, edited by Anne Kovalainen & Jarmo Ikonen. Turku School of Economics and Business administration, 1994.

Niemelä, Jukka. "Työelämän suhteet ja työn uudelleenorganisointi Masa-Yardsissa." In *Näkökulmia Suomen telakoiden toimintatapojen muutoksiin*, edited by Heikki Leimu, Matti Nallikari, & Jukka Niemelä. Turku University, 1992.

Ojala, Jari. "Työn tuottavuus merenkulussa 1710–2010." In *Työ, talous ja yliopisto: Jaakko Pehkonen 50 vuotta*, edited by Kari Heimonen & Hannu Tervo, 170–179. Jyväskylän yliopiston kauppakorkeakoulu, 2010.

Ojala, Jari & Petri Karonen. "Business: Rooted in Social Capital over the Centuries." In *Roads to Prosperity: An Economic History of Finland*, edited by Jari Ojala, Jari Eloranta, & Jukka Jalava, 93–126. Helsinki: SKS, 2006.

Ojala, Jari & Yrjö Kaukiainen. "Finnish Shipping - A Nordic Exception?" In *Global Shipping in Small Nations. Nordic Experiences after 1960*, edited by Stig Tenold, Martin Jes Iversen, & Even Lange, 129–155. New York: Palgrave Macmillan, 2012.

Okko, Paavo, Pasi Malinen, Jouko Toivonen, & Nygrén Patrik. *Telakkatuki ja tarjouskilpailut.* Ministry of Trade and Industry Studies and Reports 3. Helsinki: KTM 1997.

Oksanen, Heikki. "Euro ja Suomi politiikan ja talousoppien valossa." *Kansantaloudellinen aikakauskirja* 113:2 (2017): 183–205.

Olesen, Thomas Roslyng. *Da værfterne lukkede: Transformationen af den danske værftsindustri 1975–2015.* Odense: Syddansk Universitetsforlag, 2016.

Olsson, Kent. "Big Business in Sweden: The Golden Age of the Great Swedish Shipyards, 1945–1974." *Scandinavian Economic History Review* 43:3 (1995): 310–338.

Olsson, Lars. "Offshore som livboj. Varvkrisen och försöken till omorientering, 1974–1985." In *Den konstruerade världen: Tekniska system i historiskt perspektiv*, edited by Pär Blomkvist & Arne Kaijser, 205–229. Stockholm: Brutus Östlings Bokförlag Symposion, 1998.

Olsson, Lars. "Skall vi bygga atomfartyg? Svenks varvindustri och frågan om atomdrift till sjöss, 1955–65." *Varv, Årsskrift för Varvhistoriska Föreningen i Göteborg* (1997): 4–29.

Olsson, Lars. *Technology Carriers. The Role of Engineers in the Expanding Shipbuilding System.* Diss., Chalmers University of Technology, Gothenburg, 2000.

Oreskes, Naomi. "Science in the Origins of the Cold War." In *Science and Technology in the Global Cold War*, edited by Naomi Oreskes & John Krige, 11–29. Cambridge: MIT Press, 2014.

*Osakeyhtiö Hietalahden sulkutelakka ja konepaja, aikaisemmin Helsingfors Skeppsdocka, 1965–1935.* Helsinki: Tilgmannin kirjapaino, 1935.

Outinen, Sami. *Sosiaalidemokraattien tie talouden ohjailusta markkinareaktioiden ennakointiin. Työllisyys sosiaalidemokraattien politiikassa Suomessa 1975–1998.* Helsinki: Into kustannus, 2015.

Paavonen, Tapani. "Special Arrangements for the Soviet Trade in Finland's Integration Solutions - A Consequence of Finland's International Position or Pursuit Of Profit?" In *East-West Trade and the Cold War*, edited by Jari Eloranta & Jari Ojala, 153–165. University of Jyväskylä, 2005.

Paavonen, Tapani. *Vapaakauppaintegraation Kausi: Suomen Suhde Länsi-Euroopan Integraatioon FINN-EFTAsta EC-vapaakauppaan.* Helsinki: SKS, 2008.

Paju, Petri. *Ilmarisen Suomi" ja sen tekijät. Matematiikkakonekomitea ja tietokoneen rakentaminen kansallisena kysymyksenä 1950-luvulla.* Diss., University of Turku, 2008.

Pääkkönen, Tuukka. *Turun Pernon telakan lakkokulttuuri-lakot, niiden väitetyt syyt ja toimintaperiaatteet vuosina 1976–1984.* Master's thesis, Turku University, 2016.

Perez, Carlota. *Technological Revolutions and Financial Capital: The Dynamics of Bubbles and Golden Ages.* Cheltenham: Edward Elgar, 2002.

Peterssen, Phillip A. "Scandinavia and the "Finlandisation" of Soviet Security." *Proceedings of the Academy of Political Science* 38:1 (1991): 60–70.

Pinch, Trevor J. & Wiebe Bijker. "The Social Construction of Facts and Artifacts." In *Technology and Society. Building our Sosiotechnical Future,* edited by Deborah Johnson & Jameson Wetmore, 107–140. Cambridge: MIT Press, 2009.

Poulsen, René Taudal & Henrik Sornn-Friese. "Downfall Delayed: Danish Shipbuilding and Industrial Dislocation." *Business History* 53:4 (2011): 557–582.

Pusila, Juha. "Telakat paikallisilla työmarkkinoilla." In *Tuotantotavan muutos Suomen laivarakennuksessa,* edited by Heikki Leimu & Juha Pusila, 29–75. Turku School of Economics and Business Administration, Series Discussion and Working Papers 4:1995.

Quester, George H. "Finlandisation as a Problem or an Opportunity?" *The Annals of the American Academy of Political and Social Science* 512:1 (1990): 33–45.

Rainio-Niemi, Johanna. "A Nordic Paradox of Openness and Consensus? The Case of Finland." In *The Paradox of Openness: Transparency and Participation in Nordic Cultures of Consensus,* edited by Norbert Gèotz & Carl Marklund, 27–49. Leiden: Brill, 2014.

Rainio-Niemi, Johanna. "Cold War Neutrality in Europe. Lessons to be Learned?" In *Engaged Neutrality. An Evolved Approach to the Cold War,* edited by Heinz Gärtner, 15–36. Lanham: Rowman and Littlefield, 2017.

Rainio-Niemi, Johanna. *The Ideological Cold War: The Politics of Neutrality in Austria and Finland.* New York: Routledge, 2014.

Ranki, Risto. *Haltia vai haltija? Harri Holkerin hallituksen talouspoliittinen ministerivaliokunta.* Helsinki: Edita, 2000.

Rantanen, Paavo. "The Development of the System of Bilateral Agreements between Finland and the Soviet Union." In *Finnish-Soviet Economic Relations,* edited by Kari Möttölä, O.N. Bykov, & I.S. Korolev. London: Macmillan Press, 1983.

Rentola, Kimmo. *Niin kylmää että polttaa: Kommunistit, Kekkonen ja Kreml 1947–1958.* Helsinki: Otava, 1997.

Rentola, Kimmo. "From Half-Adversary to Half-Ally: Finland in Soviet Policy, 1953–58." *Cold War History* 1:1 (2000): 75–102.

Rentola, Kimmo. "Great Britain and the Soviet Threat in Finland, 1944–1951." *Scandinavian Journal of History* 37:2 (2012): 171–184.

Reynolds, David. "Science, Technology, and the Cold War." In *The Cambridge History of the Cold War,* edited by Melvyn Leffler & Odd Arne Westad, 378–399. Cambridge University Press, 2010.

Ristilehto, Seppo. *Liiketoimintashokki. Tapaustutkimus laivanrakennus ja autoteollisuusalan yritysten kriisiratkaisuista ja ohjaustoimenpiteistä.* Diss., Turku School of Economy and Business Administration, 2004.

Riviezzo, Angelo, Mika Skippari, & Antonella Garofano. "Who Wants to Live Forever: Exploring 30 Years of Research on Business Longevity." *Business History* 57:7 (2015): 970–987.

Sahari, Aaro. "Saving the Finnish Shipbuilding Industry. Allan Staffans and Actors within the Finnish Maritime Industry from War to The Economic Boom 1916–1946." In *From Shipyards to the Seven Seas. On Finnish Shipbuilding Industry*, edited by Sari Mäenpää, 108–137. Turku: Forum Marinum, 2018.

Sahari, Aaro. *Valtio ja suurteollisuuden synty. Laivanrakennusteollisuuden kehittyminen teknopoliittissa järjestelmissä Suomessa 1918–1954*. Diss., University of Helsinki, 2018.

Salminen, Ari. *Tapaustutkimus talouden, politiikan ja hallinnon keskinäisistä kytkennöistä: Suomen idänkaupan suuryritykset*. University of Helsinki, 1983.

Salminen, Ari. *Ulkomaankaupan erityisesti idänkaupan päätöksenteko valtion keskushallinnossa: Julkishallinnollinen tutkimus ulkomaankaupan päätöksentekojärjestelmästä ja organisaatiosta poliittisen demokratian ja parlamentarismin toteutumisen kannalta*. University of Tampere, 1978.

Schmid, Sonja. "Defining (Scientific) Direction: Soviet Nuclear Physics and Reactor Engineering." In *Science and Technology in the Global Cold War*, edited by Naomi Oreskes & John Krige, 317–342. Cambridge: MIT Press, 2014.

Schmid, Sonja. "Nuclear Colonisation? Soviet Technopolitics in the Second World." In *Entangled Geographies: Empire and Technopolitics in the Global Cold War*, edited by Gabrielle Hecht, 125–154. Cambridge: MIT Press, 2011.

*Science for Welfare and Warfare: Technology and State Initiative in Cold War Sweden*, edited by Per Lundin, Niklas Stenlås, & Johan Gribbe. Sagamore Beach: Science History Publications, 2010.

Seppänen, Esa. *Idänkaupan isäntä*. Helsinki-kirjat, 2011.

*Shipbuilding and Ship Repair Workers around the World: Case Studies 1950–2010*, edited by Raquel Varela, Hugh Murphy, & Marcel van der Linden. Amsterdam University Press, 2017.

Siddiqi, Asif. "Fighting Each Other: The N-1, Soviet Big Science, and the Cold War at Home." In *Science and Technology in the Global Cold War*, edited by Naomi Oreskes & John Krige, 189–226. Cambridge: MIT Press, 2014.

Siltala, Sakari. *Puu-Valion nousu ja uho: Murtuva yhteistyökapitalismi ja osuusaate 1982–2004*. Diss., University of Helsinki, 2013.

Sipilä, Petri. "Laivasarjoista erikoisaluksiin." In *Navis Fennica: Suomen Merenkulun Historia. Part 3 "Telakat, Satamat Ja Valtion Alukset"*, edited by Erkki Riimala, 67–95. Helsinki: WSOY, 1994.

Sipilä, Petri. "Sotakorvausalukset ja uudistuvat telakat." In *Navis Fennica: Suomen merenkulun historia. Part 3, Telakat, satamat ja valtion alukset*, edited Erkki Riimala, 62–66. Helsinki: WSOY, 1994.

Slaven, Anthony. *British Shipbuilding 1500–2010. A history*. Lancaster: Crucible Books, 2013.

Schmid, Sonja. "Defining (Scientific) Direction: Soviet Nuclear Physics and Reactor Engineering." in *Science and Technology in the Global Cold War*, edited by Naomi Oreskes & John Krige, 317–342. Cambridge: MIT Press, 2014.

Soikkanen, Timo. *Presidentin ministeriö: Ulkoasiainhallinto ja ulkopolitiikan hoito Kekkosen kaudella. Uudistumisen, ristiriitojen ja menestyksen vuodet 1970–81*. Helsinki: Otava, 2008.

Starck, Christian. *Foreign and Domestic Shocks and Fluctuations in the Finnish Economy, 1960–1988*. Helsinki: Bank of Finland, 1990.

Stopford, Martin. *Maritime Economics*, third ed. New York: Routledge, 2009.

Stråth, Bo. *The Politics of De-industrialization. The Contraction of the West European Shipbuilding Industry*. London: Croom Helm, 1987.

Summerton, Jane. "Stora tekniska system – en introduktion till forskningsfältet." In *Den konstruerade världen – Tekniska system i historiskt perspektiv*, edited by Pär Blomkvist & Arne Kajser, 19–44. Stockholm: Brutus Östlings Bokförlag, 1998.

*Suomi-SNTL: Tieteellis-teknisen ja taloudellisen yhteistyön vuorovaikutus. Raportti Suomen ja Neuvostoliiton välisen yhteistyön metodologiaa koskevasta tutkimuksesta osat I-III.* Helsinki: Valtion painatuskeskus, 1980.

Suomi, Juhani. *Epävarmuuden vuodet. Mauno Koiviston aika 1984–86.* Helsinki: Otava, 2006.

Suomi, Juhani. *Urho Kekkonen: 1950–1956, Kuningastie.* Helsinki: Otava, 1990.Sutela, Pekka. "Finnish Trade with USSR: Why Was It Different?" *BOFIT Online* 7 (2005).

Sutela, Pekka. "The Folklore of Finland's Eastern Trade." *Europe-Asia Studies* 59:1 (2007): 137–162.

Sutela, Pekka. *Trading with the Soviet Union: The Finnish Experience 1944–1991.* Helsinki: Kikimora Publication, 2014.

Sörensen, Pekka. "Hans Von Rettig, Shipyards and the Collaborating Shipping Companies 1925–1960." *From Shipyards to the Seven Seas. On Finnish Shipbuilding Industry*, Sari Mäenpää, 74–109. Turku: Forum Marinum, 2018.

*Technology and East-West Trade, Congress of the United States, Office of Technology Assessment*, NTIS order #PB83-234955, 1979.

Tenold, Stig. "Norway's Interwar Tanker Expansion – A Reappraisal." *Scandinavian Economic History Review* 55:3 (2007): 244–261.

Tenold, Stig. "Saving a Sector–But which One? The Norwegian Guarantee Institute for Ships and Drilling Vessels Ltd." *International Journal of Maritime History* 13:1 (2001): 39–62.

Teräs, Kari. "From War Reparations to Luxury Cruise Liners. Production Changes and Labour Relations at the Turku Shipyard (Finland) between 1950 and 2010." In *Shipbuilding and Ship Repair Workers around the World: Case Studies 1950–2010*, edited byRaquel Varela, Hugh Murphy, & Marcel van der Linden, 193–219. Amsterdam: Amsterdam University Press, 2017.

Tiihonen, Seppo. *The Ministry of Finance. Two Hundred Years of State-Building, Nation-Building & Crisis Management in Finland.* Helsinki: SKS, 2012.

Todd, Daniel. *Industrial Dislocation: The Case of Global Shipbuilding.* New York: Routledge, 1991.

Tuominen, Maija. *Valmet-Wärtsilä -fuusio ja telakkateollisuuden työvoiman vähennykset Turussa vuosina 1986–1987: Esimerkki rakennemuutoksesta ja sen hallinnasta.* Helsinki: Ministry of Labour, 1988.

*Tuotantotavan muutos Suomen laivarakennuksessa*, edited by Heikki Leimu & Juha Pusila. Series Discussion and Working Papers 4. Turku School of Economics and Business Administration, 1995.

Uola, Mikko. *Hollming 1945–2000: Sotakorvausveistämöstä monialakonserniksi.* Rauma: Hollming, 2001.

Uola, Mikko. *"Meidän isä on töissä telakalla." Rauma-Repolan laivanrakennus 1945–1991.* Helsinki: Otava, 1996.

van der Linden, Mercel, Hugh Murphy, & Raquel Varela. "Introduction." In *Shipbuilding and Ship Repair Workers around the World: Case Studies 1950–2010*, edited byRaquel Varela, Hugh Murphy, & Marcel van der Linden, 15–46. Amsterdam: Amsterdam University Press, 2017.

van Rooij, Arjan. "Sisyphus in Business: Success, Failure and the Different Types of Failure." *Business History* 57:2 (2015): 203–223.

Vesikansa, Jyrki. "Tankmar Horn (1924–2018)". Kansallisbiografia (digital database: https://kansallisbiografia.fi). Helsinki: SKS, 2014.

Vesikansa, Jyrki. "Olavi Mattila (1918–2013)". *Kansallisbiografia* (digital database: https://kansallisbiografia.fi). Helsinki: SKS, 2013.

Vihavainen, Timo. *Kansakunta rähmällään: suomettumisen lyhyt historia.* Helsinki: Otava, 1991.

Viita, Pentti. *Kapitalismin ja sosialismin puristuksessa. Suomen ja Neuvostoliiton taloussuhteet 1944–1991.* Helsinki: BSV Kirja, 2006.

von Knorring, Nils. *Aurajoen veistämöt ja telakat.* Espoo: Schildts Förlags Ab, 1995.

Wahlqvist, Sirpa. *Sydämellä rakennetut seililaivat. Sotakorvauskuunareiden rakentaminen ja rakentajat F.W. Hollming Oy:n telakalla Raumalla 1945–1952.* Diss., Turku University 2011.

Westad, Odd Arne. "The Cold War and the International History of the Twentieth century." In *The Cambridge History of the Cold War,* edited by M.P. Leffler & O.A. Westad, 1–19. Cambridge: Cambridge University Press, 2010.

Westad, Odd Arne. *The Cold War: A World History.* London: Allen Lane, 2017.

Weinberger, Hans. "The Neutrality Flagpole: Swedish Neutrality Policy and Technological Alliances, 1945–1970." In *Technologies of Power: Essays in Honor of Thomas Parke Hughes and Agatha Chipley Hughes,* edited by Michael Thad Allen & Gabrielle Hecht, 253–293. Cambridge: MIT-Press, 2001.

Wolfe, Audra. *Competing with the Soviets: Science, Technology, and the State in Cold War America.* Baltimore, MA: JHU Press, 2012.

Wuokko, Maiju. "Layers of Disunity: The Presidential Politics of Finnish Business, 1981–1982." *Scandinavian Journal of History* 38:5 (2013): 612–635.

Wuokko, Maiju. *Markkinatalouden etujoukot. Elinkeinoelämän valtuuskunta, Teollisuuden keskusliitto ja like-elämän poliittinen toiminta 1970–1980-lukujen Suomessa.* Diss., University of Helsinki, 2016.

Zilliacus, Benedict. *Wilhelm Wahlforss: Benedict Zilliacus kertoo Wärtsilän voimamiehestä.* Helsinki: Wärtsilä, 1984.

# Index

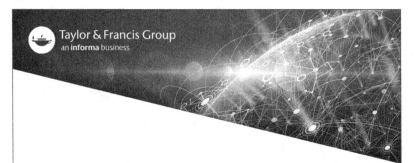

Printed in the United States
by Baker & Taylor Publisher Services